PENGUIN REFERENCE
Penguin Pocket Kings and Queens

David Crystal was born in 1941 and spent the early years of his life in Holyhead, North Wales. He went to St Mary's College, Liverpool, and University College, London, where he read English and obtained his Ph.D. in 1966. He was a lecturer in linguistics at the universities of Bangor and Reading, becoming Professor of Linguistics at the University of Wales, Bangor. He is editor of *The Penguin Encyclopedia* and related publications, the former editor of the Cambridge family of general encyclopedias, compiler of several dictionaries, and author of publications on the theory and practice of reference works. He is co-founder of a company which manages a large reference database and which is developing systems for improving document classification and internet search. A past president of the Society of Indexers, in 2001 his book *Words on Words* (co-authored with Hilary Crystal) was awarded the Wheatley Medal for an outstanding index. In 1995 he was awarded the OBE for services to the English language.

THE PENGUIN POCKET KINGS AND QUEENS

Edited by David Crystal

PENGUIN BOOKS

PENGUIN BOOKS

Published by the Penguin Group
Penguin Books Ltd, 80 Strand, London WC2R 0RL, England
Penguin Group (USA) Inc., 375 Hudson Street, New York, New York 10014, USA
Penguin Group (Canada), 90 Eglinton Avenue East, Suite 700, Toronto, Ontario, Canada M4P 2Y3
(a division of Pearson Penguin Canada Inc.)
Penguin Ireland, 25 St Stephen's Green, Dublin 2, Ireland (a division of Penguin Books Ltd)
Penguin Group (Australia), 250 Camberwell Road, Camberwell, Victoria 3124, Australia
(a division of Pearson Australia Group Pty Ltd)
Penguin Books India Pvt Ltd, 11 Community Centre, Panchsheel Park, New Delhi – 110 017, India
Penguin Group (NZ), cnr Airborne and Rosedale Roads, Albany, Auckland 1310, New Zealand
(a division of Pearson New Zealand Ltd)
Penguin Books (South Africa) (Pty) Ltd, 24 Sturdee Avenue, Rosebank, Johannesburg 2196, South Africa

Penguin Books Ltd, Registered Offices: 80 Strand, London WC2R 0RL, England

www.penguin.com

First published 2006
1

Copyright © Crystal Reference Systems Ltd, 2006
All rights reserved

The moral right of the author has been asserted

Set in ITC Stone Sans and ITC Stone Serif
Typeset by Data Standards Ltd, Frome, Somerset
Printed in England by Clays Ltd, St Ives plc

ISBN-13: 978-0-141-02716-6
ISBN-10: 0-141-02716-9

Contents

Acknowledgements   vi

Preface   vii

Part One: Monarchs of the British Isles   1

British Monarchs   3

British Royal Family Tree   128

Ready Reference   136

    Rulers of England and Great Britain   137

    Rulers of Scotland (to 1603)   139

    High Kingship of Ireland   140

    British Order of Succession   141

Part Two: Monarchs of the World   143

World Monarchs   145

Ready Reference   287

    Royal Rulers   288

Acknowledgements

Crystal Reference

GENERAL EDITOR
David Crystal

DEVELOPMENT EDITOR
Ann Rowlands

EDITORIAL ASSISTANTS
Peter Preston
Todd Warden-Owen

EDITORIAL MANAGER
Hilary Crystal

DATABASE MANAGEMENT
Tony McNicholl

TECHNOLOGY DEVELOPMENT
Philip Johnstone
Dan Wade

CRYSTAL REFERENCE
ADMINISTRATION
Ian Saunders
Rob Phillips

Penguin Books

COMMISSIONING EDITOR
Georgina Laycock

EDITORIAL MANAGERS
Jodie Greenwood
Ellie Smith

PRODUCTION
Kristen Harrison

TEXT DESIGN
Richard Marston

TYPESETTING
Data Standards Ltd

Preface

This book provides information on the monarchs of the world.

Part One presents those who have ruled in the British Isles – in England, Scotland, Wales, and Ireland. The entries, you will see, vary greatly in size. In the early centuries, especially in Ireland, the facts are extremely sparse, often amounting to little more than names, dates, and battles. As we approach modern times, the problem is the reverse – the need to provide succinct accounts of people about whom huge amounts have been written.

The coverage does not restrict itself to monarchs, but includes queen consorts, regents, guardians, and protectors, as well as the most famous pretenders to the throne. In the case of the present Queen, the chief members of the royal family are also included.

Part Two presents a selection of monarchs from other countries. The focus is on Europe, and on those countries which have had most interaction with Britain – friendly or otherwise, through marriages and wars – over the centuries. The royal rulers of France and Spain loom large, but special attention is also paid to the stadtholders of The Netherlands and other local rulers in the days before the modern states were formed.

Acknowledging the international perspective of this section, I have included some of the most famous monarchs from other parts of the world, such as Egypt, China, and Japan. In a short book, of course, I have had to be highly selective. However, there is a comprehensive guide to the monarchs of these countries in the Ready Reference section beginning on p. 287.

Additionally, the book contains around a hundred panels which present a wide range of items of related interest. They provide summary information about royal dynasties as well as an account of associated political and social notions and the main British royal residences. Celebratory events associated with Queen Elizabeth II, notably her coronation and jubilee year (2002) are also summarized, and at the end of Part One there is a British royal family tree.

David Crystal

Part One:
Monarchs of the
British Isles

British Monarchs

Adelaide, Queen (1792–1849) Queen consort of King William IV of Great Britain, the eldest daughter of George, Duke of Saxe-Coburg-Meiningen. In 1818 she married William, Duke of Clarence, who succeeded his brother, George IV, to the throne as William IV (1830–7). Their two children, both daughters, died in infancy.

Áed (c.560–98) High King of Ireland (586–98), the son of Ainmire, and member of the House of Cenél Conaill (Northern Uí Néill). He gave Dál Riada independence from Ireland at the Convention of Druim Ceat. He was slain in battle at Bealach Dun Bolg by Bran Dubh, King of Leinster. (*see panel* p. 140, High Kingship of Ireland)

Áed Allán (c.710–43) High King of Ireland (734–43), the son of Fergal, and member of the House of Cenél nEógain (Northern Uí Néill). He was slain in the Battle of Magh Seirigh by Domnall Midi. (*see panel* p. 140, High Kingship of Ireland)

Áed Findliath (c.840–79) High King of Ireland (862/3–79), the son of Niall Caille, and member of the House of Cenél nEógain (Northern Uí Néill). He fought the Danes in several battles, not always with success. (*see panel* p. 140, High Kingship of Ireland)

Áed Oirdnide (c.770–819) High King of Ireland (797–819), the son of Niall Frossach, and member of the House of Cenél nEógain (Northern Uí Néill). During his reign, I Coluim Cille was

ACT OF SETTLEMENT

The Act of Settlement is an important British statute of 1701 which determined the succession of the English throne after the death of Queen Anne and her heirs, if any. It excluded the Catholic Stuarts from the succession, which was to pass to the Protestant Electress Sophia of Hanover, descendant through the female line of James I. Future monarchs were to be communicant members of the Church of England, and were not permitted to leave the country without the consent of parliament. The House of Hanover, which ruled Britain 1714–1901, owed its claim to this Act.

ACTS OF UNION

The Acts of Union joined England in legislative union with Scotland (1707) and Ireland (1800). The 1707 Act brought 45 Scottish MPs to join the new House of Commons of Great Britain, and 16 peers became members of the House of Lords. The Scottish legal system remained separate. The 1800 Act created the United Kingdom of Great Britain and Ireland, which came into effect in 1801, and lasted until 1922. This was brought about after the collapse of the Irish rebellion (1798) in order to increase British security in the French wars. The Irish parliament was abolished; 100 Irish MPs were added to the UK House of Commons, and 32 peers to the Lords. The Churches of England and Ireland were united.

plundered by Norsemen in 797 and 801. He was slain in the Battle of Da Fearta by Maolcanaigh. (*see panel* p. 140, High Kingship of Ireland)

Áed Slaine (c.575–604) High King of Ireland (598–604), the son of Diarmait I, and member of the House of Síl nÁedo Sláine (Southern Uí Néill). He ruled jointly with Colmán Rímid. (*see panel* p. 140, High Kingship of Ireland)

Áed Uaridnach (c.580–612) High King of Ireland (604–12), the son of Domnall Ilchelgach, and member of the House of Cenél nEógain (Northern Uí Néill). He was slain in the Battle of da Fhearta. (*see panel* p. 140, High Kingship of Ireland)

Aedh *see* **Aodh**

Æthelbert *see* **Ethelbert**

Æthelflaed *see* **Ethelflaed**

Ailill Molt (c.440–82) High King of Ireland (463/6–82), the son of Dathi. He was slain in the Battle of Ocha by Lugaid. (*see panel* p. 140, High Kingship of Ireland)

Ainmire (c.540–69) High King of Ireland (566–9), the son of Sedna, and member of the House of Cenél Conaill (Northern Uí Néill). He was slain by Fearghus, the son of Nellin. (*see panel* p. 140, High Kingship of Ireland)

Albert, Prince, in full **Francis Albert Augustus Charles Emmanuel, Prince of Saxe-Coburg-Gotha** (1819–61) Prince consort to Queen Victoria, born at Schloss Rosenau, near Coburg, Germany, the younger son of the Duke of Saxe-Coburg-Gotha and Louisa, daughter of the Duke of Saxe-Coburg-Altenburg. He studied in Brussels and Bonn, and in 1840 married his first cousin, Queen Victoria – a marriage that became a lifelong love match. Ministerial distrust and public misgivings because of his German connections limited his political influence, although his counsel was usually judicious and far-sighted. He took a keen interest in industry, technology, and the arts, and presided over the Royal Commission that raised support for the Great Exhibition of 1851, whose profits enabled the building of museum sites in South Kensington and the Royal Albert Hall (1871). He died of typhoid in 1861, occasioning a long period of seclusion by his widow. The Albert Memorial in Kensington Gardens was erected to his memory in 1871.

Alexander I, also known as **Alasdair mac Maíl Coluim** (c.1077–1124) King of Scots (1107–24), the fifth son of Malcolm Canmore and Queen Margaret. In 1107 he succeeded his brother, Edgar, but only to that part of the kingdom north of the Forth. Sovereignty of Lothian and Cumbria passed to his younger brother David. He married Sibilla, an illegitimate daughter of Henry I of England. A pious churchman, he founded several bishoprics and abbeys, but his championing the independence of the Scottish Church involved him in quarrels with the English metropolitan sees. He was also a fierce warrior, ruthlessly killing any descendants of Lulach in his northern dominion. In 1114, he led troops to support Henry I in his campaign to subjugate Wales.

Alexander II (1198–1249) King of Scots (1214–49), born in Haddington, East Lothian, Scotland, who succeeded his father, William I, in 1214. He allied with the disaffected English barons and made an incursion as far south as Dover. The accession of Henry III of England allowed a rapprochement, cemented by his marriage in 1221 to Henry's sister, Joan, and the frontier question was settled by the Treaty of York (1237). Joan's death without children in 1238, and Alexander's marriage to Marie de Coucy, the daughter of a Picardy nobleman, then strained relations with England. His reign is notable for the vigorous assertion of royal authority in the western Highlands and the south-west during the years of peace with England.

Alexander III (1241–86) King of Scots (1249–86), the son of Alexander II. In 1251 he married **Margaret** (1240–75), the eldest daughter of Henry III of England. He completed the consolidation of the western part of the kingdom by annexing the Hebrides and the Isle of Man, after defeating Haakon IV of Norway at Largs in 1263. He ended the centuries-old rivalry between the royal houses of Scotland and Norway, and the period between 1266 and the death of Queen Margaret in 1275 has often been seen as a golden age for Scotland.

Alexandra, Queen (1844–1925) Queen consort of King Edward VII of Great Britain, the eldest daughter of King Christian IX of Denmark (reigned 1863–1906). She married Edward in 1863 when he was Prince of Wales, and became known for her charity work; in 1902 she founded the Imperial (now

Royal) Military Nursing Service, and in 1912 instituted the annual Alexandra Rose Day in aid of hospitals.

Alfred, known as **Alfred the Great** (849–99) King of Wessex (871–99), born in Wantage, Oxfordshire, England, the fifth son of King Ethelwulf. When he came to the throne, the Danes had already conquered much of Northumbria, parts of Mercia, and East Anglia, and threatened to subdue Wessex itself. He inflicted on them their first major reverse at the Battle of Edington, Wiltshire (878), and began to win back Danish-occupied territory by capturing the former Mercian town of London (886). He stole the military initiative from the Danes by reorganizing his forces into a standing army, building a navy, and establishing a network of burhs (fortified centres). These developments were complemented by his revival of religion and learning, a programme designed to win God's support for victory over the pagan Danes and to consolidate loyalty to himself as a Christian king. He personally translated several edifying Latin works into English. He forged close ties with other English peoples not under Danish rule, and provided his successors with the means to reconquer the area under Danish rule and secure the unity of England. The famous story of his being scolded by a peasant woman for letting her cakes burn has no contemporary authority, and is first recorded in the 11th century.

Andrew (Albert Christian Edward),

Duke of York (1960–) British prince, the second son of Queen Elizabeth II. He studied at Gordonstoun School, Moray, Scotland, and Lakefield College, Ontario, Canada, then trained at the Royal Naval College, Dartmouth, where he was commissioned as a helicopter pilot. He saw service in the Falklands War (1982). In 1986 he married **Sarah (Margaret) Ferguson** (1959–), and was made Duke of York. They have two children, **Princess Beatrice Elizabeth Mary** (1988–) and **Princess Eugenie Victoria Helena** (1990–). The couple separated in 1992, and divorced in 1996. He left the navy in 2001, and took up a role as ambassador for British Trade International.

Anne (1665–1714) Queen of Great Britain and Ireland (1702–14), born in London, the second daughter of James II (then Duke of York) and his first wife, Anne Hyde. In 1672 her father became a Catholic, but Anne was brought up as a staunch Protestant. In 1683 she married Prince George of Denmark (1653–1708), bearing him 17 children. Probably only six were born alive and only one survived infancy – William, Duke of Gloucester, who died in 1700 at the age of 12. For much of her life she was greatly influenced by her close friend and confidante, Sarah Churchill, the future Duchess of Marlborough. In 1688, when her father James II was overthrown, she supported the accession of her sister Mary and her brother-in-law William, and in 1701, after the death of her own son, signed the Act of Settlement designating the Hanoverian descendants of James I as her successors. Her reign saw the union of the parliaments of Scotland and England (1707), and the War of the Spanish Succession (1701–13). She finally broke with the Marlboroughs in 1710–11, when Sarah was supplanted by a new favourite, Sarah's cousin, Mrs Abigail Masham, and the Whigs were replaced by a Tory administration. She was the last Stuart monarch.

Anne (Elizabeth Alice Louise), Princess (1950–) British Princess Royal, the only daughter of Queen Elizabeth II and Prince Philip, born in London. In 1973 she married Lieutenant (later Captain) Mark Phillips of the Queen's Dragoon Guards, but they were divorced in 1992; their children are: **Peter Mark Andrew** (1977–) and **Zara Anne Elizabeth** (1981–). She married **Timothy Laurence** (1955–) in 1992. An accomplished horsewoman, she has ridden in the British Equestrian Team, and was European cross-country champion (1972). She is a keen supporter of charities and overseas relief work; as president of Save the Children Fund she has travelled widely, promoting its activities. Since 1988 she has been a member of the International Olympic Committee and is president of the British Olympic Association. Her daughter, Zara Phillips, won the European Eventing Championship in 2005.

Anne of Bohemia (1366–94) Queen consort of England, the first wife of Richard II. The daughter of Emperor Charles IV (reigned 1355–78). She

married Richard in 1382 and died childless. It is probably through her entourage that the writings of John Wycliffe were introduced into Bohemia and gained prominence through the work of John Huss.

Anne of Cleves (1515–57) German princess and queen consort of England, the fourth wife of Henry VIII, the daughter of John, Duke of Cleves, a noted champion of Protestantism in Germany. She was selected for purely political reasons after the death of Jane Seymour, and in 1540 was married to Henry, who found her appearance disappointing. The marriage was annulled by parliament six months later.

Anne of Denmark (1574–1619) Danish princess, and queen consort of Scotland and England. The daughter of King Frederik II of Denmark (reigned 1559–88), in 1589 she married James VI of Scotland, the future James I of England. She was a lavish patron of the arts and architecture, and appeared in dramatic roles in court masques by Ben Jonson.

Aodh, also known as **Aedh** (c.840–78) King of Scots (877–8). Shortly after succeeding his brother Constantine I, he was murdered at Strathallan by Giric (Gregory the Great), who had conspired with Aedh's nephew Eochaid. Both Giric and Eochaid ruled jointly following Aedh's death. He did marry, and one son ruled later as Constantine II of Scotland (900–43), while another son, Donald mac Aed, became King of Strathclyde in 908.

Athelstan or **Æthelstan** (c.895–939) Anglo-Saxon king, the grandson of Alfred the Great, and the son of Edward the Elder, whom he succeeded as King of Wessex and Mercia in 924. A warrior king of outstanding ability, he extended his rule over parts of Cornwall and Wales, and kept Norse-held Northumbria under control. In 937 he defeated a confederation of Scots, Welsh, and Vikings from Ireland in a major battle (Brunanburgh), and his fame spread far afield. At home, he improved the laws, built monasteries, and promoted commerce.

Báetáin I (c.545–72) High King of Ireland (569–72), the son of Muirchertach and member of the House of Cenél nEógain (Northern Uí Néill). He ruled jointly with Eochaid, but they were both slain by Cronin, chief of Cianachta Glinne Gemhin. (*see panel* p. 140, High Kingship of Ireland)

Báetáin II (c.545–86) High King of Ireland (572–86), the son of Ninnid macDaui, and member of the House of Cenél Conaill (Northern Uí Néill). He was slain in battle at Leim An Eich. (*see panel* p. 140, High Kingship of Ireland)

Beaton or **Bethune, David** (1494–1546) Scottish statesman and Roman Catholic clergyman, born in Balfour, Fife, Scotland. He studied at the universities of St Andrews, Glasgow, and Paris, and was at the French court (1519) as Scottish 'resident' and twice later as ambassador to negotiate James V's marriages. In 1525 he took his seat in the Scots Parliament as Abbot of Arbroath and was appointed Privy Seal. Made a cardinal in 1538, he became Archbishop of St Andrews. On James's death, he produced a forged will, appointing himself and three others regents of the kingdom during the minority of Mary, Queen of Scots. The nobility, however, elected the Protestant Earl of Arran regent. Beaton was arrested, but soon regained favour and was made chancellor (1543). He was assassinated by a band of conspirators in his castle of St Andrews.

Bedford, John of Lancaster, Duke of (1389–1435) English prince, the third son of Henry IV. In 1414 his brother, Henry V, created him Duke of

BALMORAL CASTLE
Balmoral Castle is a castle and estate of 9700 ha/24 000 acres located on Upper Deeside, Aberdeenshire, Scotland. It is used by the British royal family as a holiday home. Prince Albert purchased the original 15th-c castle and grounds for Queen Victoria in 1852, but it was felt to be too small, so a new castle was designed and built nearby, completed in 1856. The grounds, gardens, and ballroom are open to the public between April and July.

Bedford, and during the war with France he was appointed Lieutenant of the Kingdom. After Henry's death (1422), Bedford became Guardian of England, and Regent of France during the minority of his nephew, Henry VI. He defeated the French in several battles, but in 1428 failed to capture Orléans. In 1431 he had Joan of Arc burned at the stake in Rouen, and crowned Henry VI King of France in Paris; but in 1435 a treaty was negotiated between Charles VII and the Duke of Burgundy, which ruined English interests in France. He died at Rouen, and was buried in the cathedral there.

Bladud A legendary king of Britain, who discovered the hot spring at Bath and founded the city. One story is that he was a leper who found that the mud cured him.

Blathmac (c.630–c.666) High King of Ireland (656/8–65/6), the son of Áed Slaine, and member of the House of Síl nÁedo Sláine (Southern Uí Néill). He ruled jointly with his brother Diarmait II. They both died of the plague. (*see panel* p. 140, High Kingship of Ireland)

Bloody Mary *see* **Mary I**

Boleyn, Anne, also spelled **Bullen** (c.1507–36) English queen consort, the second wife of **Henry VIII** from 1533–6. Daughter of Sir Thomas Boleyn by Elizabeth Howard, she secretly married Henry (January 1533), and was soon declared his legal wife (May); but within three months his passion for her had cooled. It was not revived by

the birth (September 1533) of a princess (later Elizabeth I), still less by that of a stillborn son (January 1536). She was arrested and brought to the Tower, charged with treason, and beheaded (19 May). Henry married Jane Seymour 11 days later.

Bolingbroke *see* **Henry IV**

Boru *see* **Brian**

Boudicca, also known as **Boadicea** (1st-c) British Celtic warrior-queen, wife of **Prasutagus**, king of the Iceni, a tribe inhabiting what is now Norfolk and Suffolk. On her husband's death (60), the Romans seized her territory and treated the inhabitants brutally. She gathered a large army, destroyed the Roman colony of Camulodunum (Colchester), Londinium (London), and Verulamium (St Albans), putting to death as many as 70 000 Romans and Romano-Britons. Defeated in battle by Suetonius Paulinus, she took poison.

Brian, known as **Brian Bóruma** or **Boroimhe** or **Boru** ('Brian of the Tribute') (c.930–1014) King of Ireland (1002–14), born in what is now County Clare, and son of the Gaelic King Cennétig of Munster. In 976 he became chief of Dál Cais, and allied with the rival clan of the Eoghanists, led them to victory over the Vikings of Limerick. The Eoghanists, envious of the power of Dál Cais, formed an alliance with the Vikings and murdered Brian's brother Mahoun. Brian declared war on the Eoghanists and their Viking allies, defeated them, and by 984 had made himself King of Leinster. After further campaigns in all parts of the country, his rule was acknowledged over the whole of Ireland. In 1014, Maelmurra of Leinster joined forces with Sitric, the Viking King of Dublin, and raised an army against Brian. The two forces met at Clontarf, and though Brian was killed, his army triumphed, and the Vikings' rule in Ireland was ended.

Bruce, Robert (1274–1329) King of Scots (1306–29) as Robert I, and hero of the Scottish War of Independence. As Earl of Carrick, in 1296 he swore fealty to Edward I of England, but soon joined the Scottish revolt under Wallace. In 1306 he quarrelled with John Comyn, his political rival, stabbing him to death; then assembled his vassals and was crowned king at Scone. He was forced to flee to Ireland, but returned in 1307 and defeated the English at Loudoun Hill. After Edward's death (1307), the English were forced from the country, and all the great castles were recovered except Berwick and Stirling. In 1312 the Hebrides were ceded to him by the King of Norway. Raids on the north of England led to the Battle of Bannockburn (1314), when the English were routed. Sporadic war with England continued until the Treaty of Northampton (1328), which recognized the independence of Scotland, and Bruce's right to the throne. He was recognized by the pope as King of Scotland (1323), and died of leprosy six years later. He was succeeded by David II, the son of his second wife.

BUCKINGHAM PALACE

Buckingham Palace is the London residence of the British sovereign, and the administrative headquarters of the monarchy. George III bought Buckingham House in 1761 for his wife Queen Charlotte to use as a family home near to St James's Palace. It was reconstructed in the 1820s by George IV. The escalating costs of the project led to the dismissal of the architect, John Nash, on the king's death in 1830. Edward Blore was appointed to complete the work, but the palace remained unused until Queen Victoria's accession in 1837. The famous east façade was refaced in Portland Stone by Sir Aston Webb in 1913. The gates, railings, and forecourt, where the Changing of the Guard takes place, were added two years earlier. Some of its 600 rooms were opened to the public for the first time in summer 1993. Over 50 000 people visit the Palace each year, many at investitures and the royal garden parties.

Cadwallon, also spelled **Caedwalla** or **Cadwalader** (?–634) Pagan king of Gwynedd, NW Wales (from c.625). With Penda, the Mercian king, he invaded the Christian Kingdom of Northumbria in 633 and slew King Edwin (Eadwine) at the Battle of Heathfield (Hatfield Chase), near Doncaster. He ravaged the kingdom, according to the Venerable Bede, but was himself defeated and killed by King Oswald at the Battle of Heavenfield near Hexham.

Canmore, Malcolm *see* **Malcolm III**

Canute or **Cnut**, sometimes known as **the Great** (c.995–1035) King of England (from 1016), Denmark (from 1019), and Norway (from 1028), the younger son of Sweyn Forkbeard. He first campaigned in England in 1013, and after his brother Harald's death (1019) became King of Denmark. He successively challenged Ethelred the Unready and his successor Edmund Ironside for the English throne. He defeated Edmund in 1016 at the Battle of Ashingdon (possibly Ashdon, Essex), secured Mercia and Northumbria, and became King of all England after Edmund's death. In 1017 he married **Emma of Normandy**, the widow of Ethelred. He ruled England according to the accepted traditions of English kingship, and maintained the peace throughout his reign. A story is told by the 12th-century historian, Henry of Huntingdon, that Canute rebuked his flatterers by showing that even he, as king, could not stop the incoming tide – nor, by implication, the might of God.

Caractacus, Caratacus, or **Caradoc** (1st-c) A chief of the Catuvellauni, the son of Cunobelinus. He mounted a gallant but unsuccessful guerrilla operation in Wales against the Romans in the years following the Claudian conquest (43). Betrayed by the Brigantian queen, Cartimandua, he was taken to Rome (51), where he was exhibited in triumph, and pardoned by Claudius.

Carausius, Marcus Aurelius (c.245–93) Army officer, born in Menapia (modern Belgium). He set himself up in Britain as emperor (c.287), and ruled there until his murder by one of his officers, Allectus. Originally a Batavian pilot, he was put in command of the Roman fleet in the Channel to ward off pirates.

Caroline of Ansbach, Wilhelmina (1683–1737) Queen consort of George II of Great Britain, born in Ansbach, Germany, the daughter of a German prince. She exercised a strong influence over her husband, and was a leading supporter of his chief minister, Robert Walpole.

Caroline of Brunswick, Amelia Elizabeth (1768–1821) Queen consort of George IV of Great Britain, born in Brunswick, Germany, the daughter of George III's sister, Augusta. She married the Prince of Wales in 1795, but the marriage was disagreeable to him, and although she bore him a daughter, **Princess Charlotte**, they lived apart. When George became king (1820), she was offered an annuity to renounce the title of queen and live abroad; when she refused, the king persuaded the government to introduce a Divorce Bill. Although this failed, she was not allowed into Westminster Abbey at the coronation (1821).

Cartimandua (1st-c) Pro-Roman queen of the Brigantes, the British Celtic tribe that inhabited what is today the north of England. She protected the northern borders of the Roman province of Britain after the conquest (43), until her overthrow by her husband, the anti-Roman Venutius, in 68–9.

Catherine of Aragón (1485–1536) Queen consort of England, the first wife of Henry VIII (1509–33), born in Alcalá de Henares, Spain, the fourth daughter of Ferdinand and Isabella of Spain. She was first married in 1501 to Arthur (1486–1502), the son of Henry VII, and following his early death was betrothed to her brother-in-law Henry, then a boy of 11. She married him in 1509, and bore him five children, but only the Princess Mary survived. In 1527 Henry began a procedure for annulment of the marriage, which was refused by Pope Clement VII. Henry then proceeded on his own; a court presided over by Thomas Cranmer pronounced his marriage to Catherine invalid (1533), thereby breaking with the pope, and starting the English Reformation. Catherine then retired to lead an austere religious life until her death.

Catherine of Valois (1401–37) Queen consort of England, the wife of Henry V, and the youngest daughter of Charles VI ('the Foolish') of France. After a stormy courtship, when England and France went to war over Henry's dowry demands, she married Henry at Troyes in 1420. In 1421 she gave birth to a son, the future Henry VI. After Henry's death in France in 1422, she secretly married **Owen Tudor**, a Welsh squire, despite parliamentary opposition; their eldest son, Edmund, Earl of Richmond, was the father of Henry VII.

Cellach (c.620–c.658) High King of Ireland (642/3–56/8), the son of Máel Cobo, and member of the House of Cenél Conaill (Northern Uí Néill). He was joint ruler with his brother Conall Cáel. He was slain in battle at Brugh Mic An Og. (*see panel* p. 140, High Kingship of Ireland)

Cennfáelad (c.645–75) High King of Ireland (671–5), the son of Blathmac, and member of the House of Síl nÁedo Sláine (Southern Uí Néill). He was slain by Finsnechta Fledach in the

Battle of Aircealtair at Tigh ua Maine. (*see panel* p. 140, High Kingship of Ireland)

Cerdic (fl. 5th–6th-c) Legendary Saxon leader who was said to have invaded Britain, landing in Hampshire with his son **Cynric** in 495. He is recorded as the founder of the royal dynasty of what became the most powerful Anglo-Saxon kingdom, Wessex.

Charles I (1600–49) King of Britain and Ireland (1625–49), born in Dunfermline, Fife, Scotland, the second son of **James I**. He failed in his bid to marry the infanta Maria of Spain (1623), marrying instead the French princess, **Henrietta Maria**, and thus disturbing the nation, for the marriage articles permitted her the free exercise of the Catholic religion. Three parliaments were summoned and dissolved in the first four years of his reign; then for 11 years he ruled without one, using instead judges and prerogative courts. He warred with France (1627–9), and in 1630 made peace with Spain, but his continuing need for money led to unpopular economic policies. His attempt to anglicize the Scottish Church brought active resistance (1639), and he then called a parliament (1640). In 1642, having alienated much of the realm, he entered into the Civil War, which saw the annihilation of his cause at Naseby (14 June 1645), and his surrender to the Scots at Newark (1646). After many negotiations, during which his attempts at duplicity exasperated opponents, and a second Civil War

(1646–8), he came to trial at Westminster, where his dignified refusal to plead was interpreted as a confession of guilt. He was beheaded at Whitehall (30 January 1649).

Charles II (1630–85) King of Britain and Ireland (1660–85), born in London, the son of Charles I. As Prince of Wales, he sided with his father in the Civil War, and was then forced into exile. On his father's execution (1649), he assumed the title of king, and was crowned at Scone, Scotland (1651). Leading poorly organized forces into England, he met disastrous defeat at Worcester (1651). The next nine years were spent in exile until an impoverished England, in dread of a revival of military despotism, summoned him back as king (1660). In 1662 he married the Portuguese princess, **Catherine of Braganza**. It was a childless marriage, though Charles was the father of many illegitimate children. His war with Holland (1665–7) was unpopular, and led to the dismissal of his adviser, Lord Clarendon (1667), who was replaced by a group of ministers (the Cabal). He negotiated skilfully between conflicting political and religious pressures, including the trumped-up 'Popish Plot', and refused to deny the succession of his brother James. For the last four years of his life, he ruled without parliament.

Charles (Philip Arthur George), Prince of Wales (1948–) Eldest son of Queen Elizabeth II and Prince Philip, Duke of Edinburgh, and heir apparent to the throne, born at Buckingham

Palace, London. Duke of Cornwall as the eldest son of the monarch, he was given the title of Prince of Wales in 1958, and invested at Caernarfon (1969). He studied at Cheam and Gordonstoun, and entered Trinity College, Cambridge, in 1967. He served in the RAF and Royal Navy (1971–6), and in 1981 married **Lady Diana Frances**, younger daughter of the 8th Earl Spencer. They had two sons: **Prince William Arthur Philip Louis** (1982–) and **Prince Henry Charles Albert David** (1984–). The couple separated in 1992, and divorced in 1996. During this period he was, along with Princess Diana, the focus of continual media interest, attracting unprecedented attention from biographers. Diana was killed in a car crash in 1997. The announcement of his marriage to longtime partner, divorcée Camilla Parker Bowles, in April 2005, was accompanied by legal controversy. The civil ceremony took place in Windsor Guildhall followed by a service of dedication at Windsor Castle. Charles is noted for his views on conservation and community architecture. Among his many charitable works is the Prince's Trust which he founded in 1976 to provide training opportunities for young people.

Charlotte (Augusta), Princess
(1796–1817) Princess of Great Britain and Ireland, the only daughter of George IV and Caroline of Brunswick, who separated immediately after her birth. The heir to the British throne, she was brought up in strict seclusion. In 1816 she married Prince Leopold of Saxe-Coburg (later to be King Leopold I of the Belgians), but died in child-birth the following year.

Charlotte Sophia of Mecklenburg-Strelitz (1744–1818) Queen consort of Great Britain and Ireland, the wife of George III. She married George shortly after his accession to the throne, in 1761, and bore him 15 children. Their eldest son was the future George IV, born in 1762.

Cináed (c.700–28) High King of Ireland (724–8), the son of Irgalach, and member of the House of Síl nÁedo Sláine (Southern Uí Néill). He was slain in the Battle of Druim Corcrain by Flaithbertach. (*see panel* p. 140, High Kingship of Ireland)

Clare, Richard de, or **Richard Strongbow**, 2nd Earl of Pembroke and Strigul (?–1176) Anglo-Norman nobleman. With the permission of Henry II he helped the dethroned Irish king, Dermot MacMurrough, in 1167, in his bid to reclaim Leinster and Wexford from Rory O'Connor, King of Connaught. Strongbow captured Waterford in 1170, married Eva, the eldest daughter of MacMurrough and, having subdued much of eastern Ireland, was confirmed by Henry II as King of Leinster, assuring by his marriage and his military conquests Anglo-Norman domination of Ireland. Strongbow fought for Henry in Normandy (1173) and was rewarded by the restoration of Waterford, Wexford, and Dublin, marching into Munster in 1174. He continued fighting the Irish until his death in 1176.

CIVIL LIST
The civil list is a payment made since 1760 from public funds for the maintenance of the senior members of the royal family (except the Prince of Wales, who derives his income from the revenues of the Duchy of Cornwall). It covers the salaries of the household staff, travel, entertaining, and public engagements at home and abroad. A sum payable from the Treasury is fixed by Act of Parliament at the beginning of each reign; in exchange, the new sovereign surrenders to the Exchequer the revenues from the Crown Estates. During the reign of Queen Elizabeth II, the original sum has had to be reviewed upwards several times because of inflation. For 1991–2000 the annual sum was fixed at £10 420 000, of which £7 900 000 was intended for the Queen; for the decade to 2011, the annual sum is fixed at £8.9 million. In 1992 it was decided that only the Queen, the Queen Mother, and the Duke of Edinburgh would receive payments from the civil list. In that year the income from the Crown Estates was £113 693 000. The Queen has paid tax since 1993.

Clarence, William, Duke of *see* **William IV**

Cnut *see* **Canute**

Colin, also known as **Culen** and **Cuilén mac Illuilb** (c.922–71) King of Scotland (967–71), son of King Indulf, and the third cousin of both Duff (Dubh), the previous king, and his successor Kenneth II. He attempted to violate the tanistry system (in which an heir to the throne is nominated by the king) and take the throne from Duff by force, but was defeated at Drum Crup. When Duff was murdered in 967, probably by Colin's men, he laid claim to the throne and began a reign marked by chaos. He was assas-

sinated in Lothian in 971 by Riderch, King of Strathclyde, in an act of revenge for Colin's seizure of Riderch's daughter and the murder of his brother during a campaign to re-assert control over Strathclyde. He became the fourth king of Scotland to be murdered in succession. His son Constantine succeeded to the throne three reigns later in 995.

Colmán Rímid (c.575–604) High King of Ireland (598–604), the son of Báetáin II, and member of the House of Cenél nEógain (Northern Uí Néill). He ruled jointly with Áed Slaine. (*see panel p. 140, High Kingship of Ireland*)

Conall Cáel (c.620–54) High King of

COAT OF ARMS

The Royal Coat of Arms is borne only by the Sovereign. Used in many ways in connection with the administration and government of the country, the arms can be found on coins, buildings, medals, and the products and vehicles of Royal Warrant holders. The Coat of Arms carries a shield, quartered, showing the emblems of different parts of the United Kingdom. The three lions of England are in the first and fourth quarters, the lion of Scotland in the second, and the harp of Ireland in the third. On the arms of the Prince of Wales, the arms of the ancient Principality of Wales additionally appear in the centre. A garter, symbolizing the Order of the Garter, surrounds the shield and bears the legend *Honi soit qui mal y pense* ('Evil to him who evil thinks'). The shield is supported by the English lion and Scottish unicorn with the royal crown above. The motto of the Sovereign, *Dieu et mon droit* ('God and my right'), appears below.

The Scottish version of the Royal Coat of Arms shows the lion of Scotland in the first and fourth quarters, the three lions of England in the second and the harp of Ireland in the third. The mottoes read *In defence* and *No one will attack me with impunity*.

Ireland (642/3–54), the son of Máel Cobo, and member of the House of Cenél Conaill (Northern Uí Néill). He was joint ruler with his brother Cellach. He was slain by Diarmait II. (*see panel* p. 140, High Kingship of Ireland)

COMMONWEALTH

The Commonwealth was an English republican regime, established in 1649 after the execution of Charles I, and lasting until the Instrument of Government created a Protectorate in 1653. It failed to achieve political settlement at home, but its armies pacified Scotland and Ireland. The Navigation Acts (1650, 1651) and war with the Dutch (1652–4) fostered overseas trade and colonies. It should not be confused with the modern Commonwealth of Nations.

COMPETITORS FOR THE CROWN OF SCOTLAND

In 1290, following the death of Margaret I, Scotland had no obvious heir to the throne, and the country was ruled by four Guardians. Fearing civil war, William Fraser, Bishop of St Andrews called upon Edward I of England to adjudicate between thirteen claimants, commonly called Competitors.

The Competitors for the Crown of Scotland were:

- Eric II, King of Norway
- Floris V, Count of Holland
- John Comyn, Lord of Badenoch
- John de Balliol
- John de Hastings, 2nd Baron Hastings
- Nicholas de Soules
- Patrick de Dunbar, 7th Earl of Dunbar
- Patrick Galithly
- Robert de Brus, Earl of Annandale
- Robert de Pinkeney
- Roger de Mandeville
- William de Ros, 2nd Baron de Ros
- William de Vesci, Baron de Vesci

Edward I used the situation to his advantage, insisting that the King of Scotland should be subservient to the King of England. Nine of the claimants agreed to Edward's proposals, and were then reduced to three: John de Balliol, Robert de Brus [Bruce], and John de Hastings, all of whom were descendants of the three daughters of David, Earl of Huntingdon. After further deliberation, Edward I awarded the crown to John Balliol, the descendant of the Earl's eldest daughter, and the senior legitimate heir by primogeniture. Robert Bruce's claim was equally valid in law because, although descended from the second daughter, he was a generation nearer David I. In 1296, Balliol renounced his fealty to England, whereupon Edward immediately marched north and Balliol was forced to surrender himself and his kingdom to Edward. However, in 1306 the crown was assumed by a grandson of Robert de Brus, who became King Robert I.

CORONATION ROBES

The **Coronation Dress** of Queen Elizabeth II was commissioned in 1952 and designed by Norman Hartnell. It replaced the crimson surcoat and purple surcoat that would have been worn under the Parliamentary Robe and the Purple Robe of State. The dress is made of white satin with short sleeves, a fitted bodice, and a full skirt flaring out. The neckline is cut square over the shoulders curving into a gentle heart shape in the centre. There are three embroidered, jewel-encrusted bands running like garlands horizontally across the skirt. These bands are repeated round the hem of the skirt, and form a border for the bodice and sleeves. The embroidery depicts the emblems of the United Kingdom and the Commonwealth. There are Tudor roses (England), thistles (Scotland), shamrock (Ireland), leeks (Wales), lotus (India and Ceylon), protea (South Africa), wattle flower (Australia), wheat cotton and jute (Pakistan), maple leaf (Canada), and fern (New Zealand).

On her way to her coronation the Queen wore the dress with the George IV State Diadem, the diamond necklace made for Queen Victoria, and the matching diamond drop earrings.

The **Parliamentary Robe**, also called the Robe of State, was worn on entry into the Abbey with the Coronation Dress. It was made for the Queen in 1953 and consists of an ermine cape, decorated all over with small black Canadian ermine tails, and a long crimson velvet train. It is now used for the state Opening of Parliament.

Conchobar (c.795–833) High King of Ireland (819–33), the son of Donnchad Midi, and member of the House of Clann Cholmáin (Southern Uí Néill). (*see panel* p. 140, High Kingship of Ireland)

Congal Cennmagair (c.680–710) High King of Ireland (704–10), the son of Fearghus, and member of the House of Cenél Conaill (Northern Uí Néill). (*see panel* p. 140, High Kingship of Ireland)

Congalach Cnogba (c.920–56) High King of Ireland (944–56), the son of Mael Mithig, and member of the House of Sil nÁedo Sláine (Southern Uí Néill). His grandfather was Kenneth MacAlpin, King of the Scots (c.841–58).

The **Pallium Regale**, also called the *Imperial Mantle* or *Robe Royal of Cloth-of-gold*, is a mantle decorated with silver coronets, fleurs-de-lis, purple and green thistles, green shamrocks, green leaves, and with imperial eagles in silver in the four corners. It is shaped like a cope, but with four corners instead of a rounded hemline.

The **Royal Stole** is a richly and heavily embroidered cloth-of-gold scarf, with gold and silver thread and set with jewels. It has a square panel at either end, each with a red St George's Cross on a silver background. On a background of floral emblems of the Commonwealth are the emblems of the four Evangelists. There are also St Edward's crowns, imperial eagles, and the dove of the Holy Ghost, as well as the flags of St Patrick, St Andrew, and St George. The present royal stole was newly made for the Queen in 1953, and presented by some of the Commonwealth countries.

The **Colobium Sindonis** resembles a surplice, and is the first robe to be put on.

The **Supertunica** is also called the *Gold Surcoat*. This is the second robe put on. It is a long coat of cloth-of-gold, reaching to the ankles, and lined with rose-coloured silk, with wide flowing sleeves, and fastened by a girdle or cincture. It is woven with a design of green palm trees between pink roses, green shamrock, and purple thistle.

The **Purple Robe of State** is also called the *Robe of Estate* or *Imperial Robe*. This is worn at the end of the coronation service in place of the crimson parliamentary robe, and with the Imperial State Crown.

In 944, he defeated the Norse army at Muine Brogain, but was killed in an ambush at Tigh-Gighrainn. (*see panel* p. 140, High Kingship of Ireland)

Connaught, Prince Arthur, Duke of (1850–1942) British prince and soldier, born in London, the third son of Queen Victoria. After training at the Royal Military Academy, Woolwich,

he served in Canada, Gibraltar, Egypt, and India (1869–90). Thereafter he was commander-in-chief in Ireland (1900–4) and in the Mediterranean (1907–9), and Governor-General of Canada (1911–16). He was created Duke of Connaught and Strathearn in 1874. In 1879 he married **Princess Louise Margaret of Prussia** (1860–1917). Of their children, **Margaret** (1882–1920) married the future King Gustav VI Adolf of Sweden in 1905.

Constantine I, also known as **Causantín mac Cináeda** (836–77) King of Scots and King of the Picts (863–77), succeeding his uncle Donald I of Scotland. A warrior king, he spent much of his reign fighting the Vikings or expanding his kingdom. In 864, he defeated the Norsemen led by Olaf the White from Dublin. A later force led by Thorsten the Red was also successfully defeated. In 872, he assassinated his brother-in-law Arthgal (King of Strathclyde), and the southern regions of what is now Scotland became part of his own Alba. His bribing of rivals kept the peace for a time until his defeat at the hands of a Norse raiding party known as the Black Strangers from Dublin. He was killed in battle against the Vikings in 877, and was succeeded by his brother Aedh. His son Donald became King Donald II of Scotland following the joint reign of Kings Eochaid and Giric.

Constantine II, also known as **Causantín mac Áeda** (c.874–952) King of Scotland (900–43), son of King Aedh and first cousin of the previous king, Donald II. During his reign, the Vikings laid waste to much of the kingdom (particularly Dunkeld and parts of Alba) until they were driven from Scotland following their decisive defeat at Scone in 904. He restructured the Christian Church in Scotland, including a Synod at Scone in 906, and introduced a system of earls (*mormaers*) to help defend the kingdom. Thereafter, his main concern

was Saxon Northumbria, where the Vikings had resettled under Ragnall. His victories over Ragnall at the Battles of Corbridge in 914 and 918 led to a cessation of hostilities with the Norse. In the 930s, Constantine married his daughter to Olaf III Guthfrithsson, the Norse king of Dublin, in order to create a more stable relationship with the Vikings. However, this did not help to check the advance of the English. In 934 King Athelstan of England invaded Scotland and took Constantine's son as a hostage, which led to the battle at Brunanburgh in 937 where Constantine was defeated and his eldest son Cellach was killed. He abdicated in 943 in favour of his cousin Malcolm I, and entered a Culdee monastery in St Andrews, Fife, where he became abbot and died in 952. His surviving son Indulf succeeded Malcolm on the throne.

Constantine III, also known as **Causantín mac Cuilén** (c.970–97) King of Scotland (995–7), son of King Colin, third cousin once removed of the previous king, Kenneth II, and fourth cousin of his successor Kenneth III. It is probable that he succeeded to the throne through the failing tanistry system (in which an heir to the throne is nominated by the king) by killing Kenneth II. He died at Rathinveramon, probably at the hands of Kenneth III, and his place of burial is not known today. He was the fifth king of Scotland to be murdered in succession.

Cornwall, Duchess of, formerly

Camilla (Rosemary) Parker Bowles, née **Shand** (1947–) Consort of Charles, Prince of Wales, the eldest son of Elizabeth II of the United Kingdom. The daughter of Bruce and Rosalind Shand, she grew up in Sussex and was educated at the Queen's Gate School in London before attending finishing school in Switzerland and France. She first met Prince Charles in 1970 and they became close friends. In 1973 she married cavalry officer Andrew Parker Bowles (divorced 1995); they have two children. Following Charles's divorce from Princess Diana (1996), Camilla became Charles's constant companion. The couple were married in April 2005 at a civil ceremony in Windsor Guildhall, followed by a service of dedication in St George's Chapel at Windsor Castle.

Cromwell, Oliver (1599–1658) Oliver Cromwell was born in Huntingdon, Cambridgeshire, to a strongly Protestant family. He was the younger son of Henry Cromwell of Hinchinbrook, who became a member of one of Queen Elizabeth's parliaments, and his wife, Elizabeth Steward, the daughter of Sir Thomas Steward of Ely. His first cousin was the great parliamentarian, John Hampden. Cromwell's education was strongly Calvinist and anti-Catholic. He went to study at Cambridge, but left there at 18 to take care of his mother after his father's death. He then briefly studied law at Lincoln's Inn. In 1620 he married Elizabeth Bourchier, the daughter of a prosperous London merchant, with whom he had four daughters and five sons.

Cromwell sat as MP for Huntingdon in the stormy parliament of 1628–9, during which he became a convinced critic of King Charles I. After the dissolution of parliament by the king, he farmed on his small estate at Huntingdon, then at St Ives and later at Ely, where he had been left property by an uncle (1638). He sat for Cambridge during the Short Parliament of 1640, and during the Long Parliament was a vehement supporter of Puritanism.

When war broke out (1642) between the king's forces and the parliamentarians, he fought for the latter at Edgehill. He formed his unconquerable Ironsides force, combining rigid discipline with strict morality, and it

CROWN ESTATE

The Crown Estate includes all property belonging by heredity to the British sovereign, comprising over 120 000 ha/300 000 acres in England, Scotland, and Wales. Over half of Britain's foreshore is included, together with the sea bed within territorial waters. Revenue from the Crown Estate is made over to the government at the beginning of each reign.

was his cavalry that secured the victory at Marston Moor (1644). He also led the New Model Army to decisive success at Naseby (1645) under Fairfax. Then he marched on London to coerce the Presbyterians in parliament, and was probably responsible for abducting the king from Holmby (1647). He failed to persuade Charles I to accept constitutional limitations, and the king fled from captivity at Hampton Court Palace to the Isle of Wight to negotiate with the Scots his return to the throne. The Royalists took up arms again, and the second Civil War broke out. Cromwell quelled the Welsh insurrection in support of Charles I, and defeated the invading army of Hamilton. He then brought the king to trial, and was one of the signatories of his death warrant (1649).

After Charles' execution, the monarchy was abolished and the Commonwealth established, with Cromwell as chairman of the Council of State. As army commander and Lord-Lieutenant of Ireland, he ruthlessly concluded the ongoing fighting there by storming Drogheda and Wexford and massacring their garrisons (1649). In 1650 he turned his attention to Scotland, where Charles II had been acclaimed king, finally

CROWN JEWELS

The crown jewels comprise the regalia and jewellery belonging to a sovereign. The English crown jewels have been displayed at various sites in the Tower of London for 300 years, since 1967 in the Jewel House. After the abolition of the monarchy in 1649, much of the regalia was sold or broken up, with the exception of the gold anointing spoon (12th-c) and eagle-headed ampulla (14th-c). Most of the crown jewels date from the Restoration (1660). They include St Edward's Crown, used in most coronations since that of Charles II; the Imperial State Crown; the gold spurs made for Charles II's coronation; the armills (gold-enamelled bracelets); the King's Orb; the King's Sceptre with the Cross (since 1909 containing the Star of Africa, the largest cut diamond in the world at 530 carats); the King's Sceptre with the Dove; the jewelled Sword of State and four other ceremonial swords; the Imperial Crown of India; and Queen Elizabeth the Queen Mother's crown, which is set with the Koh-i-Noor (Persian 'mountain of light') diamond. The Scottish crown jewels (or 'Honours of Scotland') are located in Edinburgh Castle.

subduing the Scots at Dunbar (1650) and Worcester (1651). The latter battle effectively ended the Civil War, and united the three kingdoms of England, Scotland, and Ireland.

In 1653 he dissolved the Rump of the Long Parliament and, after the failure of his Puritan Convention (Barebones Parliament), established a Protectorate (1653). He refused the offer of the crown in 1657. At home he reorganized the national Church and established Puritanism, but permitted religious toleration: he readmitted Jews into Britain, allowed private use of the Book of Common Prayer, and did not make things much worse for the English Catholics than they had been before; the fiery zeal of his youth gave way to a more tolerant pragmatism. He also provided judicial administration in Scotland (which prospered under his rule), and gave Ireland parliamentary representation. Under him the Commonwealth became the head and champion of Protestant Europe. In his foreign policy he ended the war with Portugal (1653) and Holland (1654); made treaties with France against Spain (1655, 1657); defeated the Spanish at the Battle of the Dunes (1658), and took Dunkirk.

Cromwell died in London, and was buried in the tomb of the kings at Westminster Abbey. After the Restoration in 1660 he was convicted

CROWN PROCEEDINGS ACT

The Crown Proceedings Act (1947) permits ordinary civil actions against the crown. It had been possible before this date for someone to take certain proceedings against the crown by personal petition (*petition of right*), as in breach-of-contract cases. The significance of the 1947 Act is that it permitted action in tort (delict, in Scotland) in respect of conduct by crown servants. The crown had enjoyed a special status by virtue of the doctrine that the monarch could do no wrong. The extension of the activities of the state in the 20th century necessitated a revision of this immunity. *Crown Privilege*, now known as *public interest immunity*, which is the right of the crown to withhold documents on certain grounds (such as national security), is still claimed in some cases. However, the monarch remains personally immune from civil or criminal liability. Not all of the Act applies to Scotland, Scots law having traditionally viewed remedies against the crown differently. The analogous act in the USA is the Federal Tort Claims Act (1946).

of treason; his body was disinterred and hung from the gallows at Tyburn. He was succeeded by his son Richard, who was forced into exile in France in 1659.

Cromwell, Richard (1626–1712) English statesman, the third son of Oliver Cromwell. He served in the parliamentary army, sat in parliament (1654, 1656), and was a member of the Council of State (1657). In 1658 he succeeded his father as Lord Protector (his two elder brothers having died); but he soon fell out with parliament, which he dissolved in 1659. He recalled the Rump Parliament of 1653, but found the task of ruling beyond him, and was forced to abdicate in 1659. After the Restoration (1660) he lived in France and Geneva, under the alias 'John Clarke', but returned to England in 1680, and spent the rest of his life in Cheshunt, Hertfordshire.

Cuilean *see* **Colin**

Culen *see* **Colin**

Cymbeline, also known as **Cunobelinus** (?–c.43) Pro-Roman king of the Catuvellauni, who from his capital at Camulodunum (Colchester) ruled most of south-eastern Britain. Shakespeare's character was based on Holinshed's half-historical Cunobelinus.

Dafydd ap Gruffydd (?–1283) Prince of Gwynedd in North Wales, the brother of Llywelyn ap Gruffydd. He opposed his brother's accession, but eventually supported him in his battles with the English. He succeeded his brother in 1282, but was betrayed and executed the following year – the last native prince of Wales.

David I (c.1085–1153) King of Scots (1124–53), the youngest son of Malcolm Canmore and Queen (later St) Margaret. Educated at the court of Henry I of England, he became Earl of Huntingdon through his marriage to **Maud de Senlis** (c.1113). Once king, he emphasized his independence, systematically strengthened royal power, and firmly secured the foundations of the mediaeval Kingdom of Scotland. He supported the Church, endowing abbeys such as Melrose and Kelso. In 1136, as a nominal supporter of the claims of his niece, Empress Matilda, to the English crown, he embarked on wars of territorial conquest against Stephen. He was defeated in 1138 at the Battle of the Standard, near Northallerton, but from 1141 occupied the whole of northern England to the Ribble and the Tees.

David II (1324–71) King of Scots (1329–71), the only surviving son of Robert Bruce, born in Dunfermline, Fife, Scotland. He became king at the age of five. In 1334, after the victory of Edward III of England at Halidon Hill (1333), he fled to France. He returned in 1341, and later invaded England, but was defeated and captured at Neville's Cross (1346), and was kept prisoner for 11 years. The Treaty of Berwick (1357) restored him to the throne, provided that he made an English prince his heir, and after his death he was succeeded by his sister's son, Robert II.

Diana, Princess of Wales, formerly **Lady Diana (Frances) Spencer** (1961–97) Former wife of Charles, Prince of Wales, and younger daughter of the 8th Earl Spencer, born at Sandringham, Norfolk. She was educated in Norfolk, and at West Heath School, Sevenoaks, Kent. She became Lady Diana Spencer when her father succeeded to the earldom in 1975, and worked as a kindergarten teacher in Pimlico before marrying the Prince of Wales to great popular acclaim in 1981. They had two sons, **Prince William (Arthur Philip Louis)** (1982–) and **Prince Henry (Charles Albert David)** (1984–), known as **Prince Harry**. Seriously interested in social concerns, she became a popular public figure in her own right, and was honorary president of many charities, particularly those caring for the homeless, deprived and sick children, and people suffering from AIDS.

DECLARATION OF RIGHTS

The Declaration of Rights is an English statute which ended the brief interregnum after James II quit the throne in December 1688, establishing William III and Mary II as joint monarchs. One of the fundamental instruments of constitutional law, the Bill effectively ensured that monarchs must operate with the consent of parliament, and must not suspend or dispense with laws passed by that body. It also stated that no Roman Catholic could ever be sovereign of Britain. It was supplemented in 1701 by the Act of Settlement.

Through her visit to Angola, she raised public awareness of the Red Cross campaign for a world ban on landmines. The royal couple were legally separated in 1992, and divorced in 1996. She continued to travel and work with a range of good causes, both in Britain and abroad, while receiving unprecedented worldwide media attention, with newspapers competing to report on her family situation and on her (real or imaginary) personal relationships; and it was while trying to escape the pursuit of paparazzi in Paris that she died in a car accident in August 1997. Thousands of people flocked to London for her funeral, which took place amid an unprecedented level of public mourning. A memorial exhibition chronicling her life, which opened in 1998, closed in 2004 due to declining numbers of visitors. A British inquest into her death was opened in 2004.

Diarmait I (c.520–c.565) High King of Ireland (544–64/5), the son of Fergus Ceirrbheoil. During his reign, Tara was abandoned, having been the seat of Irish high kings for centuries. He was slain at Rath Beag by Aedh Dubh. After Diarmait, each Ard Rí (High King) dwelt in his own ancestral territory. (*see panel p. 140, High Kingship of Ireland*)

DEFENDER OF THE FAITH (Latin *fidei defensor*)

The title of Defender of the Faith was conferred on Henry VIII of England by Pope Leo X as a reward for the king's written opposition to the teachings of Martin Luther. After the Reformation, the title was confirmed by parliament, and is still used by British sovereigns. The initials *F.D.* appeared on British coinage from the reign of George I.

Diarmait II (c.630–c.666) High King of Ireland (656/8–65/6), the son of Áed Slaine, and member of the House of Síl nÁedo Sláine (Southern Uí Néill). He ruled jointly with his brother Blathmac. They both died of the plague. (*see panel* p. 140, High Kingship of Ireland)

Domnall (c.600–c.643) High King of Ireland (628–42/3), the son of Áed, and member of the House of Cenél Conaill (Northern Uí Néill). He defeated Congal, King of the Dal Riada and Ulster, ending the control of the kings of Dal Riada over Irish lands. (*see panel* p. 140, High Kingship of Ireland)

Domnall Ilchelgach (c.540–66) High King of Ireland (564/5–6), the son of Muirchertach, member of the House of Cenél nEógain (Northern Uí Néill), and joint ruler with his brother Forggus. They died of the plague on the same day. (*see panel* p. 140, High Kingship of Ireland)

Domnall mac Lochlainn (c.1060–1121) High King of Ireland (1119–21), the son of Ardgal, and member of the House of Cenél nEógain (Northern Uí Néill). His life-long conflict with Muirchertach ua Briain remained undecided at the close of their lives. (*see panel* p. 140, High Kingship of Ireland)

Domnall Midi (c.720–63) High King of Ireland (743–63), the son of Murchadh, and first member of the House of Clann Cholmáin (Southern Uí Néill). (*see panel* p. 140, High Kingship of Ireland)

Domnall ua Néill (c.935–80) High King of Ireland (956–80), the son of Muirchertach of the Leather Cloaks, and member of the House of Cenél nEógain (Northern Uí Néill). During his reign, a severe famine took place in 963. (*see panel* p. 140, High Kingship of Ireland)

Donald I, also known as **Donald MacAlpin** (c.812–63) King of Scots (c.858–63), younger brother of Alpin II of Dal Riada. He succeeded his brother Kenneth I and established the laws of Aed (or Aedh), including the custom of tanistry, whereby an heir to the throne is nominated by the king. He died unmarried and without issue.

Donald II, also known as **Domnall mac Causantín** (c.862–900) King of Scotland (889–900), son of King Constantine I and first cousin of the previous king, Eochaid, and of his successor Constantine II. Donald expelled Eochaid following the death of his co-ruler Giric and took the throne as an act of revenge for Giric's murder of Donald's uncle, Aedh, in 878. He extended Scotland by including the Kingdom of Strathclyde to create the Kingdom of Alba, thus being recognized in the Annals of Ulster as 'ri Alban' as opposed to 'rex Pixtorum'. His reign was marked by renewed raids by the Vikings, who conquered large areas of northern Scotland through the leadership of Sigurd the Mighty from his base on Orkney. Donald was also involved in efforts to reduce the Highland robber tribes. He was succeeded by his cousin Constantine II, and his son Malcolm later became King Malcolm I of Scotland.

Donald III, also known as **Domnall mac Donnchada** or **Domnall Bán** or **Donaldbane** (c.1033–99) King of Scotland (1093–4 and 1094–7), son of Duncan I, brother of the previous king Malcolm III, and uncle of his first successor Duncan II. He became *mormaer* (provincial ruler) of Gowry (1060) and succeeded his brother Malcolm, claiming the throne on the outdated basis of tanistry (in which an heir to the throne is nominated by the king). In 1094, he was deposed by Malcolm's son, Duncan II, with the support of William II (Rufus) of England. Following Duncan's death later that year, Donald regained the throne, sharing his rule with his nephew Edmund (Donald in Scotia, Edmund in Lothian and Strathclyde). They were deposed by Malcolm's son Edgar in 1097, again with the assistance of English troops. Donald died, imprisoned at Rescobie, Angus, in 1099.

Donaldbane *see* **Donald III**

Donnchad Donn (c.895–944) High King of Ireland (919–44), the son of Flann Sinna, and member of the House of Clann Cholmáin (Southern Uí Néill). (*see panel* p. 140, High Kingship of Ireland)

Donnchad Midi (c.745–97) High King of Ireland (770–97), the son of Domnall Midi, and member of the House of Clann Cholmáin (Southern Uí Néill). He devastated Munster in 770 and is thought to have died at the Battle of Drumree in Meath. (*see panel* p. 140, High Kingship of Ireland)

Dubh *see* **Duff**

Dudley, Lord Guildford (?–1554) The fourth son of the Lord Protector John Dudley, Earl of Warwick, and briefly husband of **Lady Jane Grey**. His father married him to the unwilling Jane Grey in 1553 as Edward VI lay dying, and then proclaimed her queen. After the accession of Mary I (Edward's sister), Dudley and his wife were imprisoned and beheaded on Tower Hill.

DUCHY OF CORNWALL

The oldest of English duchies, instituted by Edward III in 1337 to provide support for his eldest son, Edward, the Black Prince. Since 1503 the eldest son of the sovereign has inherited the dukedom; it consists of lands (totalling c.52 000 ha/130 000 acres) in Cornwall, Devon, Somerset, and south London, including the Oval cricket ground. The present Prince of Wales pays one quarter of the revenue into the Treasury.

DUCHY OF LANCASTER

A duchy created in 1267 from estates originally given by Henry III to his son Edmund in 1265. It was attached to the Crown in 1399 when the last Duke of Lancaster became Henry IV. The duchy lands consist of some 21 000 ha/52 000 acres of farmland and moorland, mostly in Yorkshire; the revenue is paid direct into the monarch's private allowance (the Privy Purse), so the duchy functions as a department of state. It is controlled by the Chancellor of the Duchy of Lancaster, a political appointment generally held by a member of the cabinet.

Duff, also known as **Dub(h) mac Maíl Coluim** (c.930–67) King of Scotland (962–7), son of Malcolm I, succeeding to the throne after Indulf was killed. Cuilean, the son of Indulf, challenged him for the throne, contrary to the established order of tanistry law (in which an heir to the throne is nominated by the king), but was defeated at Drum Crup (probably Crief) in a battle that saw the deaths of Doncha, the Abbot of Dunkeld, and Dubdou, the *mormaer* (provincial ruler) of Atholl. Duff became very ill and the kingdom fell into lawlessness, but he recovered, pursuing and executing the ringleaders throughout Moray and Ross. In a revenge attack in 967, Duff was assassinated at Forres castle and his body concealed in a stream-bed near the bridge of Kinloss. The murderers were executed, and Duff was re-buried on Iona. One of his sons became King Kenneth III of Scotland.

Duncan I, also known as **Donnchad mac Crínáin** (1001–40) King of Scotland (1034–40), grandson of King Malcolm II. He came to the throne having previously ruled as Rex Cumbrorum in the Kingdom of Strathclyde, and is said to be the first example of direct-line accession of the Scottish throne as opposed to the previous tanistry system (in which an heir to the throne is nominated by the king). In 1039, he marched south and besieged Durham, but was forced to retreat with heavy losses. He then tried to seize Moray, but was twice defeated by Thorfinn, the Earl of Orkney's son. An unpopular king, he had become embroiled in a feud with Macbeth over claims to the throne. The latter joined forces with Thorfinn, and Duncan was slain in battle by Macbeth near Elgin, Moray in 1040. Two of his sons also became kings, as Malcolm III 'Canmore' and Donald III (Donaldbane).

Duncan II, also known as **Donnchad mac Maíl Coluim** (c.1060–94) King of Scotland (1094), eldest son of Malcolm III by his first wife Ingibjorg, and grandson of Duncan I. He spent fifteen years as a hostage in England before being released by William II in 1087. With English help, he deposed his uncle, Donald III, but was killed by the *mormaer* (provincial ruler) of the Mearns after only six months' rule, and Donald was restored to the throne.

Eadgar *see* **Edgar**

Eadred *see* **Edred**

Eadwig *see* **Edwy**

Ecgberht/Ecgbryht *see* **Egbert**

Edgar, also known as **Etgair mac Maíl Coluim** (1074–1107) King of Scotland (1097–1107), fourth son of Malcolm III, brother of Duncan II, and brother of his successor Alexander I. His mother was Margaret 'Atheling', granddaughter of Edmund II and niece of Edward the Confessor. On the death of his father he took refuge in England, but William II of England recognized him as the rightful King of Scotland and sent an army to help Edgar seize the throne from his uncle, Donald III. In 1100, his sister Matilda (Maud) married Henry I of England. His affinity with England and the ceding of the Western Isles to the King of Norway led to him being called 'Edgar the Peaceable'. He died unmarried and without issue.

Edgar or **Eadgar** (943–75) King of all England (from 959), the younger son of Edmund I (reigned 939–46). He was chosen as King of Mercia and Northumbria when his brother Eadwig (?–959) was deposed there in 957, and King of all England after the death of Eadwig, who still controlled Wessex and Kent. He encouraged the English monastic revival as a means of enhancing his prestige and power. In c.973 he introduced a uniform currency based on new silver pennies, whose design was subsequently altered every few years by periodic recoinages.

Edinburgh, Prince Philip, Duke of (1921–) The husband of Queen Elizabeth II of the United Kingdom, the son of Prince Andrew of Greece and Princess Alice of Battenberg, born in Corfu, Greece. He studied at Cheam, Gordonstoun, and Dartmouth, and entered the Royal Navy in 1939 as Lieutenant Philip Mountbatten. He became a naturalized British subject in 1947, when he was married to the **Princess Elizabeth** (20 November). Seriously interested in science and the technology of industry, as well as in youth adventure training, he is also a keen sportsman, yachtsman, qualified airman, and conservationist. In 1956 he began the Duke of Edinburgh Award scheme to foster the leisure activities of young people.

Edmund, also known as **Etmond mac Maíl Coluim** (c.1071–c.1100) King of Scotland (1094–7), son of Malcolm III 'Canmore' and St Margaret 'the Exile'. He shared rule with his uncle Donald

III, Edmund reigning in Lothian and Strathclyde, and Donald in Scotia. They were deposed by Edmund's brother Edgar in 1097 with help from William II 'Rufus' of England. Donald was imprisoned until his death in 1099, but Edmund was pardoned and spent the rest of his life as a monk in Montacute Abbey in Somerset, England.

Edmund I (921–46) King of the English (939–46), the half-brother of Athelstan. On Edmund's accession, Scandinavian forces from Northumbria, reinforced by levies from Ireland, quickly overran the east midlands. He re-established his control over the southern part of the area under Danish rule (942) and Northumbria (944) and, until his murder by an exile, ruled a reunited England.

Edmund II, known as **Edmund Ironside** (c.980–1016) King of the English for a few months in 1016, the son of Ethelred II (the Unready). He was chosen king by Londoners on his father's death (April 1016), while Canute was elected at Southampton by the Witan. Edmund hastily levied an army, defeated Canute, and attempted to raise the siege of London, but was routed at Ashingdon, or possibly Ashdon, Essex (October 1016). He agreed to a partition of the country, but died a few weeks later, leaving Canute as sole ruler.

Edmund, St, originally **Edmund Rich**, known as **St Edmund the Martyr** (c.841–70) King of East Anglia,

the adopted heir of Offa of Mercia. He fought against the Danish invasion at Hoxne in Suffolk (870), and was defeated. Tradition claims that he was taken captive, and when he refused to abjure his Christian faith he was shot to death with arrows by the pagan Danes. A miracle cult quickly sprang up, and in 903 his remains were moved from Hoxne to Bury St Edmunds. His feast day is 20 November.

Edred, also known as **Eadred** (c.923–55) King of the English (946–55), fourth son of the West Saxon king, Edward the Elder, half brother of King Athelstan and King Edmund I (the Magnificent). Upon his succession after the murder of Edmund, he received oaths of allegiance from the Northumbrians, but they soon proclaimed Eric Bloodaxe, the son of the Norwegian ruler Harald I Fairhair, as their king. In spite of Edred's ravaging of Northumbria in 948 and its subsequent submission to him, they installed another Norse king (Olaf Sihtricson) as their ruler until his overthrow in 952, when Eric Bloodaxe replaced him until his expulsion and death in 954. Northumbria resumed its allegiance to Edred and fell permanently under English rule, bringing to an end the last independent Scandinavian kingdom in England. A strongly religious man, Edred was a friend of Dunstan, abbot of Glastonbury (later Archbishop of Canterbury), and supported the monastic revival by appointing St Aethelwold to the Abbacy of Abingdon. In latter years and in very poor health, Edred placed his affairs in the hands of Dunstan, who allowed the Danes of England to live under their own laws. Edred brought up Edmund's sons, Edwy and Edgar, as his heirs, and they both became king in turn. He died unmarried and was succeeded by his nephew, King Edwy.

Edward I (1239–1307) King of England (1272–1307), the elder son of Henry III and Eleanor of Provence, born in London. He married **Eleanor of Castile** (1254) and later **Margaret of France**, the sister of Philip IV (1299). In the Barons' War (1263–7), he at first supported Simon de Montfort, but rejoined his father, and defeated de Montfort at Evesham (1265). He then won renown as a crusader to the Holy Land in the Eighth Crusade (1270–2), and did not return to England until 1274, two years after his father's death. In two devastating campaigns (1276–7, 1282–3) he annexed north and west Wales, and ensured the permanence of his conquests by building magnificent castles. He re-asserted English claims to the overlordship of Scotland when the line of succession failed, and decided in favour of John Balliol (c.1250–1315) as king (1292). But Edward's insistence on full rights of suzerainty provoked the Scottish magnates to force Balliol to repudiate Edward and ally with France (1295), thus beginning the Scottish Wars of Independence. Despite prolonged campaigning and victories such as Falkirk (1298), he could not subdue Scotland as he had done Wales. He died while leading his army against Robert Bruce.

Edward II (1284–1327) King of England (1307–27), the fourth son of Edward I and Eleanor of Castile, born in Caernarfon, Gwynedd, Wales. In 1301 he was created Prince of Wales, the first English heir apparent to bear that title, and in 1308 married **Isabella**, the daughter of Philip IV of France. Throughout his reign, Edward mismanaged the barons, who sought to rid the country of royal favourites (such as **Piers de Gaveston**) and restore their rightful place in government. The Ordinances of 1311 restricted the royal prerogative in matters such as appointments to the king's household. Edward was humiliated by reverses in Scotland, where he was decisively defeated by Robert Bruce in the Battle of Bannockburn (1314). The Ordinances were formally annulled (1322), but the king's new favourites, the Despensers, were acquisitive and unpopular, and earned the particular enmity of Queen Isabella. With her lover, Roger Mortimer Earl of March (c.1287–1330), she toppled the Despensers (1326) and imprisoned Edward in Kenilworth Castle. He renounced the throne in favour of his eldest son (1327), who succeeded as Edward III, and was then murdered in Berkeley Castle, near Gloucester.

Edward III, known as **Edward of Windsor** (1312–77) King of England (1327–77), born in Windsor, England, the elder son of Edward II and Isabella of France. He married Philippa of Hainault in 1328, and their eldest child Edward, later called the Black Prince, was born in 1330. By banishing Queen

Isabella from court, and executing her lover, Roger Mortimer Earl of March (c.1287–1330), he assumed full control of the government (1330), and began to restore the monarchy's authority and prestige. He supported the attempts of Edward Balliol (c.1283–1364) to wrest the Scots throne from David II, and his victory at Halidon Hill (1333) forced David to seek refuge in France until 1341. In 1337, after Philip VI had declared Guyenne forfeit, he revived his hereditary claim to the French crown through Isabella, the daughter of Philip IV, thus beginning the Hundred Years War. Renowned for his valour and military skill, he destroyed the French navy at the Battle of Sluys (1340), and won another major victory at Crécy (1346). David II was captured two months later at the Battle of Neville's Cross, near Durham, and remained a prisoner until 1357.

Edward IV (1442–83) King of England (1461–70, 1471–83), the eldest son of Richard, Duke of York, born in Rouen, France. His father claimed the throne as the lineal descendant of Edward III's third and fifth sons (respectively Lionel, Duke of Clarence, and Edmund, Duke of York), against the Lancastrian King Henry VI (the lineal descendant of Edward III's fourth son, John of Gaunt). Richard was killed at the Battle of Wakefield (1460), but Edward entered London in 1461, was recognized as king on Henry VI's deposition, and with the support of his cousin, Richard Neville, Earl of Warwick, decisively defeated the Lancastrians at Towton. He threw off

his dependence on Warwick, and secretly married **Elizabeth Woodville** (1464). Warwick forced him into exile in Holland (October 1470), and Henry VI regained the throne. Edward returned to England (March 1471), was restored to kingship (11 April), then defeated and killed Warwick at the Battle of Barnet (14 April), and destroyed the remaining Lancastrian forces at Tewkesbury (4 May). Henry VI was murdered soon afterwards, and Edward remained secure for the rest of his reign.

Edward V (1470–83) King of England (April–June 1483), born in London, the son of Edward IV and Elizabeth Woodville. Shortly after his accession, he and his younger brother, Richard, Duke of York, were imprisoned in the Tower by their uncle Richard, Duke of Gloucester, who usurped the throne as Richard III. The two princes were never heard of again, and were most probably murdered (August 1483) on their uncle's orders. In 1674 a wooden chest containing the bones of two children was discovered in the Tower, and these were interred in Westminster Abbey as their presumed remains.

Edward VI (1537–53) King of England (1547–53), born in London, the son of Henry VIII by his third queen, Jane Seymour. During his reign, power was first in the hands of his uncle, the Duke of Somerset, and after his execution in 1552, of John Dudley, Duke of Northumberland. Edward became a devout Protestant, and under the Protectors the English Reformation flourished. He died of tuberculosis in London, having agreed to the succession of Lady Jane Grey (overthrown after nine days by Mary I).

Edward VII (1841–1910) King of the United Kingdom (1901–10), born in London, the eldest son of Queen Victoria. Educated privately, and at Edinburgh, Oxford, and Cambridge, in 1863 he married **Alexandra**, the eldest daughter of Christian IX of Denmark. They had three sons and three daughters: **Albert Victor** (1864–92), Duke of Clarence; **George** (1865–1936); **Louise** (1867–1931), Princess Royal; **Victoria** (1868–1935); **Maud** (1869–1938), who married Haaken VII of Norway; and **Alexander** (born and died 1871). As Prince of Wales, his behaviour led him into several social scandals, and the queen excluded him from affairs of state. As king, he carried out several visits to Continental capitals which strove to allay international animosities.

Edward VIII (1894–1972) King of the United Kingdom (January–December 1936), born in Richmond, Greater London, the eldest son of George V. He studied at Osborne, Dartmouth, and Oxford, joined the navy and (in World War I) the army, travelled much, and achieved considerable popularity. He succeeded his father in 1936, but abdicated (11 December) in the face of opposition to his proposed marriage to **Wallis Simpson**, an American who had been twice divorced. He was then given the title of Duke of Windsor, and the marriage

took place in France in 1937. They lived in Paris, apart from a period in the Bahamas (1940–5), where Edward was governor. He died in Paris and was buried at Windsor Castle. In recent years claims have been made that he was a Nazi sympathizer.

Edward (Antony Richard Louis), Prince (1964–) Prince of the United Kingdom, the third son of Queen Elizabeth II. He studied at Gordonstoun School, Scotland, then spent several months as a house tutor in New Zealand at Wanganui School. After graduating from Cambridge with a degree in history, he joined the Royal Marines in 1986, but left the following year and began a career in the theatre, beginning as a production assistant with Andrew Lloyd Webber's Really Useful Theatre Company. In 1993 he formed his own company, Ardent Productions. He was made Earl of Wessex and Viscount Severn in honour of his marriage to Sophie Rhys-Jones (1965–), known as Countess of Wessex, in 1999. Their daughter, Louise Alice Elizabeth Mary Mountbatten-Windsor, Lady Louise Windsor, was born in 2003.

Edward the Black Prince (1330–76) Prince of England, born in Woodstock, Oxfordshire, England, the eldest son of Edward III. He was created Earl of Chester (1333), Duke of Cornwall (1337), and Prince of Wales (1343). In 1346, though still a boy, he fought at Crécy, and is said to have won his popular title (first cited in a 16th-c work) from his black armour. He won several victories in the

Hundred Years War, including Poitiers (1356). He had two sons: **Edward** (1356–70) and **Richard**, the future Richard II. In 1362 he was created Prince of Aquitaine, and lived there until a revolt forced him to return to England (1371). A great soldier, he was a failure as an administrator.

Edward the Confessor, St (c.1003–66) King of England (1042–66), the elder son of Ethelred the Unready and Emma of Normandy, and the last Anglo-Saxon king before the Conquest. After living in exile in Normandy, he joined the household of his half-brother Hardicanute in 1041, then succeeded him on the throne. He married **Edith**, the only daughter of the powerful Earl Godwinson of Wessex in 1045. Until 1052 he maintained his position against the Godwin family by building up Norman favourites, and in 1051 very probably recognized Duke William of Normandy (later William I) as his heir. But the Godwins regained their ascendancy, and on his deathbed in London, Edward (who remained childless) named Harold Godwinson (Harold II) to succeed. The Norman Conquest followed soon after. Edward's reputation for holiness began in his lifetime, and he rebuilt Westminster Abbey in the Romanesque style. His cult grew in popularity, and he was canonized in 1161; his feast day is 13 October.

Edward the Elder (c.870–924) King of Wessex (from 899), the elder son of Alfred the Great. He built on his father's successes and established

himself as the strongest ruler in Britain. By one of the most decisive military campaigns of the whole Anglo-Saxon period, he conquered and annexed to Wessex the southern part of the area under Danish rule (910–18). He also assumed control of Mercia (918). Although he exercised no direct power in the north, all the chief rulers beyond the River Humber, including the King of the Scots, formally recognized his overlordship in 920.

Edward the Martyr, St (c.963–78) King of England (975–8). During his reign there was a reaction against the policies in support of monasticism espoused by his father, Edgar. He was murdered by supporters of his step-mother, Elfrida, and canonized in 1001; his feast day is 18 March.

Edwin, St (584–633) King of Northumbria from 616, brought up in North Wales. Under him, Northumbria became united. He pushed his power west as far as Anglesey and Man, obtained the overlordship of East Anglia, and (by a victory over the West Saxons) that of all England, save Kent. He was con-verted to Christianity, and baptized with his nobles in 627. He fell in battle with the Mercians and Welsh at Hatfield Chase, and was afterwards canonized; his feast day is 12 October.

Edwy, also known as **Eadwig** (c.941–59) King of the English (955–7) and ruler of Wessex and Kent (957–9), son of Edmund I, succeeding his uncle Edred at the age of 13. Conflicts within his court and the Church led to the exile of Dunstan, although the latter's monastic revival was not impeded. In 957, Mercia and Northumbria shifted their allegiance to proclaim his brother Edgar as their king. Edwy's defeat at Gloucester led to the kingdom being divided, and for the next two years Edwy controlled only the region south of the Thames. His marriage to Aelgifu was ended by Archbishop Odo of Canterbury in 958 on the grounds of their being too closely akin. He ruled more wisely in his later years, and made gifts to the Church until his early death.

Egbert, in Anglo-Saxon **Ecgberht** or **Ecgbryht** (?–839) King of Wessex (802–39). After his victory in 825 over the Mercians at Ellendun (now Wroughton) in Wiltshire, the areas of Essex, Kent, Surrey, and Sussex submitted to him. In 828 he was recognized as overlord of England, but his conquest of Mercia itself (829) was soon reversed. He extended his control over Cornwall, defeating an alliance between the Vikings and Britons at Hingston Down (838). These successes gave him mastery over southern England from Kent to Land's End, and established Wessex as the strongest Anglo-Saxon kingdom.

Eleanor of Aquitaine (c.1122–1204) Queen consort of Louis VII of France (1137–52) and, after the annulment of this marriage (on the ostensible plea of consanguinity), of Henry Duke of Normandy and Count of Anjou. When he became the Angevin king, Henry II of England (1154–89), the lands they claimed stretched from Scotland to the Mediterranean. She was imprisoned (1174–89) for supporting the rebellion of her sons against the king, two of whom became kings as Richard I (in 1189) and John (1199).

Eleanor of Castile (1246–90) Queen consort of Edward I of England (1254–90), the daughter of Ferdinand (or Fernando) III. She bore her husband 13 children, accompanied Edward to the Crusades (1270–3), and is said to have saved his life by sucking the poison from a wound. She died at Hadby, Nottinghamshire, and the *Eleanor Crosses* at Northampton, Geddington, and Waltham Cross are the survivors of the twelve erected by Edward at the halting places of her cortège. The last stopping place was Charing Cross, London, where a replica now stands. She was buried at Westminster Abbey.

Eleanor of Provence (1223–91) Queen consort of Henry III of England (1236–72), the daughter of Raymond Berengar IV, Count of Provence. In the Barons' War of 1264 she raised an army of mercenaries in France to support her husband, but her invasion fleet was wrecked. After the accession of her son, Edward I, in 1272 she retired to a convent.

Elizabeth I, known as **the Virgin Queen** and later **Good Queen Bess** (1533–1603) Queen of England and Ireland (1558–1603), Elizabeth was born at Greenwich Palace, the daughter of Henry VIII and his second wife Anne Boleyn, who was later beheaded.

When her father married his third wife, Jane Seymour, in 1536, Elizabeth and her elder half-sister Mary Tudor (the future Mary I) were declared illegitimate by parliament in favour of Jane Seymour's son, the future Edward VI. Elizabeth's childhood was precarious – she suffered her mother's execution, and her father's dislike – but she was well educated and, unlike her sister, was brought up in the Protestant faith. During the reign of Edward VI (1547–53) when she was 16, Thomas Seymour, Lord High Admiral of England, plotted to marry her and overthrow the government, but Elizabeth evaded his advances and he was subsequently executed for treason. During the reign of Mary I (1553–8), her identification with Protestantism aroused the suspicions of her Catholic sister, and she was imprisoned in the Tower of London.

Her accession to the throne in 1558 on Mary's death was greeted with general approval, in the hope of religious tolerance after the persecutions of the preceding reigns. Under the able guidance of Sir William Cecil (later Lord Burghley) as secretary of state, Mary's Catholic legislation was repealed, and the Church of England fully established (1559–63). Cecil also gave support to the Reformation in Scotland, where Mary, Queen of Scots, had returned in 1561 to face conflict with the Calvinist reformers led by John Knox.

Imprisoned and forced to abdicate in 1567, Mary, Queen of Scots, escaped to England, where she was placed in confinement and soon became a focus for Catholic resistance to Elizabeth. In 1570 the papal bull, *Regnans in excelsis*, pronounced Elizabeth's excommunication and absolved her Catholic subjects from allegiance to her. Government retribution against English Catholics, at first restrained, became more repressive in the 1580s. Several plots against the queen were exposed, and the connivance of Mary in yet another plot in 1586 (the Babington conspiracy) led to her execution at Fotheringay Castle in 1587. The harsher policy against Roman Catholics, England's support for the Dutch rebellion against Spain, and the licensed piracy of such men as John Hawkyns and Francis Drake against Spanish possessions in the New World, all combined to provoke an attempted Spanish invasion in 1588. The Great Armada launched by Philip II of Spain reached the English Channel, only to be dispersed by storms and English harassment, and limped back to Spain after suffering considerable losses.

For the remainder of her reign, Elizabeth continued her policy of strengthening Protestant allies and dividing her enemies. She allowed marriage negotiations with various foreign suitors, but with no real intention of getting married or of settling the line of succession. With the death of Mary, Queen of Scots, she was content to know that the heir apparent, James VI of Scotland, was a Protestant. She indulged in romances with such court favourites as Robert Dudley, Earl of Leicester, and later with Robert Devereux, Earl of Essex, until his rebelliousness led to his execution in 1601.

Elizabeth's fiscal policies caused growing resentment, with escalating taxation to meet the costs of foreign military expeditions. Famine in the 1590s brought severe economic depression and social unrest, only partly alleviated by the Poor Law of 1597, which charged parishes with providing for the needy. England's vaunted sea-power stimulated voyages of discovery, with Drake circumnavigating the known world in 1577, and Sir Walter Raleigh mounting a number of expeditions to the North American coast in the 1580s. But England's only real Elizabethan colony was Ireland, where opportunities for English settlers to enrich themselves at the expense of the native Irish were now exploited more ruthlessly than ever before, and provoked a serious rebellion under Hugh O'Neill, Earl of Tyrone, in 1597.

At Elizabeth's death in March 1603, the Tudor dynasty came to an end, and the throne passed peacefully to the Stuart king, James VI of Scotland as James I of England. Her long reign had coincided with the emergence of England as a world power and the flowering of the English Renaissance. The legend of the 'Virgin Queen', assiduously promoted by the queen herself and her court poets and playwrights, outlived her to play a crucial part in shaping the English national consciousness.

Elizabeth II (1926–) Queen of the United Kingdom (1952–) and head of the Commonwealth, born in London, the daughter of George VI. Formerly Princess Elizabeth Alexandra Mary, she was proclaimed queen on 6 February 1952, and crowned on 2 June 1953. Her husband was created Duke of Edinburgh on the eve of their wedding (20 November 1947), and styled Prince Philip in 1957. They have three sons, **Charles Philip Arthur George** (14 November 1948), **Andrew Albert Christian Edward** (19 February 1960), and **Edward Anthony Richard Louis** (10 March 1964), and a daughter **Anne Elizabeth Alice Louise** (15 August 1950). Elizabeth's long and mainly peaceful reign has been marked by vast changes in her people's lives, in her country's power, how Britain is viewed abroad, and how the monarchy is regarded and portrayed. When Elizabeth became queen, post-war Britain still had a substantial empire, dominions, and dependencies, most of which achieved independence in the 1950s–1960s. Her reign has seen a revolution in social behaviour and attitudes, and increased prosperity. The 1990s in particular were a problematic period for the royal family. The Windsor Castle fire and the divorces of Prince Charles from Diana, Princess of Wales, and of Prince Andrew from Sarah, Duchess of York, were followed by Diana's death in a car crash in Paris in 1997. This particular tragedy brought to a head the debate about the monarchy's role and continued formality. Overall, however, Elizabeth II has provided the nation's main symbol of continuity, and her many visits to Commonwealth and other countries have won her wide respect.

Elizabeth (Queen Mother), originally

Lady Elizabeth Bowes-Lyon
(1900–2002) Queen-consort of Great Britain, born in St Paul's Walden Bury, Hertfordshire. Her father became 14th Earl of Strathmore in 1904. Much of her childhood was spent at Glamis Castle in Scotland, where she helped the nursing staff in World War 1. In 1920 she met the **Duke of York**, the second son of George V; they were married in April 1923. **Princess Elizabeth** (later Queen Elizabeth II) was born in 1926 and **Princess Margaret** in 1930. She was a strong support to her husband, during the period of Edward VIII's abdication in 1936, and after her husband came to the throne as King George VI, she scored striking personal success in royal visits to Paris (1938) and to Canada and the USA (1939). She was with the king when Buckingham Palace was bombed in 1940, travelling with him to visit heavily damaged towns throughout the war. After George VI's death (1952), the Queen Mother continued to undertake public duties, flying thousands of miles each year and becoming a widely loved figure. In 1978 she became Lord Warden of the Cinque Ports, the first woman to hold the office. Even after her 100th birthday, which prompted a nation-wide celebration, she continued to attend public events. Her death generated a wave of popular emotion, with 200 000 people queuing many hours to walk past her coffin in Westminster Hall. A million lined the route of her funeral, and the nation marked her death with a level of ceremony not seen in the UK for half a century.

Elizabeth (of York) *see* **Henry VII**

Eochaid, also known as **Eocha** or **Eochaidh** (fl.872–89) King of Scotland (878–89), jointly with Giric. He was the nephew of the previous king Aedh, first cousin of his successor Donald II, and son of Run Macarthagail, King of Strathclyde. Eochaid was not eligible to take the throne of Scotland using the tanistry system (in which an heir to the throne is nominated by the king), because he was descended from the daughter of the royal line. In order to become king, he joined forces with Giric (his first cousin once removed) to take the throne by force. It has been suggested that Eochaid then employed the services of his first cousin Donald, with whom he thought he was on better terms, to remove Giric. However, as soon as Donald did take the throne in 889, he forced Eochaid into exile. Eochaid was the first to give freedom to the Scottish Church, which had been constrained due to the rules and regulations of the Picts.

Eochaid (c.545–72) High King of Ireland (569–72), the son of Domnall Ilchelgach and member of the House of Cenél nEógain (Northern Uí Néill). He ruled jointly with Báetáin I, but they were both slain by Cronin, chief of Cianachta Glinne Gemhin. (*see panel* p. 140, High Kingship of Ireland)

Ethelbald or **Æthelbald** (c.834–60) King of Wessex (856–60), eldest son of King Ethelwulf (Æthelwulf) of Wessex. Together, they led the West Saxons to victory against the Danes at Aclea in

851, Ethelbald subsequently depriving his father of Wessex in 856. On his father's death, he married his stepmother Judith, daughter of Charles the Bald, King of the Franks, although the marriage was annulled on the grounds of consanguinity.

Ethelbert or **Æthelbert** (c.552–616) King of Kent (c.560–616), the first English king to adopt Christianity. During his long reign, Kent achieved hegemony over England south of the Humber. He received with kindness the Christian mission from Rome led by St Augustine, which landed in Thanet in 596, and allowed them to settle at Canterbury, and he himself was baptized with his court. He was also responsible for the first written code of English laws.

Ethelbert or **Æthelbert** (c.835–65) King of Wessex (860–5), son of King Æthelwulf of Wessex. He succeeded to the sub-kingdom of Kent during his father's lifetime, and Surrey, Sussex, and Essex upon his death. He reunited them with Wessex when he succeeded his brother Ethelbald (Æthelbald) in 860, his younger brothers Ethelred (Æthelred) and Alfred renouncing their claim. His reign was marked by serious attacks by the Danes, who destroyed Winchester in 860, and by raids led by Ragnar Lodbrok on Kent and Northumbria. He died without issue in 865.

Ethelflaed or **Æthelflaed** (?–918) Anglo-Saxon ruler of Mercia, the daughter of Alfred the Great. She married **Ethelred**, the ealdorman of Mercia (c.888), and fought alongside him to repel the Danish invaders, their battle culminating in a decisive victory near Tettenhall in 911. After Ethelred's death in that year, she was recognized as 'Lady of the Mercians'. She built fortified strongholds throughout Mercia, and led counterattacks on the Danes.

Ethelred I, also spelled **Æthelred** (c.830–71) King of Wessex (865–71), the elder brother of Alfred the Great. During his reign, the Danes launched their main invasion of England and established their kingdom (866). He died soon after his victory over the invaders at Ashdown, in the former county of Berkshire.

Ethelred II, known as **Ethelred the Unready**, also spelled **Æthelred** (c.968–1016) King of England (978–1016), the son of Edgar. He was aged about 10 when the murder of his half-brother, Edward the Martyr, placed him on the throne. In 1002 he confirmed an alliance with Normandy by marrying as his second wife Duke Richard's daughter **Emma** – the first dynastic link between the two countries. Renewed attacks by the Vikings on England began as raids in the 980s, and in 1013 Sweyn Forkbeard secured mastery over the whole country, forcing Ethelred into exile in Normandy. After Sweyn's death (1014), he returned to oppose Canute, but the unity of English resistance was broken when his son, Edmund Ironside, rebelled. He died in London. 'Unready' is a mistranslation of *Unraed*, not recorded as his nickname until after the Norman Conquest; it means 'ill-advised' and is a pun on his given name, Ethelred (literally, 'good counsel').

Ethelwulf, also spelled **Æthelwulf** (d.858) Anglo-Saxon King of England (839–56), the son of the West Saxon king, Egbert. In 835 the Danes had begun large-scale raids on the English coast, and in 851 he fought a victorious battle against the Danish army at Aclea in Surrey. He married his daughter to the Mercian king, Burgred, in 853. In 856 he was deposed by rivals on his return from Rome but continued to rule Kent until his death. Four of his sons became kings of Wessex, including Alfred the Great (reigned 871–99).

consent, and finally broken off in 1803.

Fergal (c.685–722) High King of Ireland (710–22), the son of Maelduin, and member of the House of Cenél nEógain (Northern Uí Néill). He was slain in the battle of Almhain by Dunchadh. (*see panel* p. 140 High Kingship of Ireland)

Finsnechta Fledach (c.650–95) High King of Ireland (675–95), the son of Donnchad, and member of the House of Síl nÁedo Sláine (Southern Uí Néill). He was slain by Áed at Grellach Dollaig. (*see panel* p. 140, High Kingship of Ireland)

Fitzherbert, Mrs Maria Anne, *née* **Smythe** (1756–1837) Wife of George IV, probably born in Brambridge, Hampshire, England. A Roman Catholic widow, she secretly married **George** (then Prince of Wales) in 1785. This marriage, contracted without the king's consent, was invalid under the Royal Marriages Act of 1772; the prince afterwards denied that there had been a marriage at all. On his marriage to Princess Caroline of Brunswick in 1795 the connection was interrupted, resumed with the pope's

Flaithbertach (c.700–65) High King of Ireland (728–34), the son of Loingsech, and member of the House of Cenél Conaill (Northern Uí Néill). He died at Ard Macha having resigned his kingdom for a monastic life. (*see panel* p. 140, High Kingship of Ireland)

Flann Sinna (c.855–916) High King of Ireland (879–916), the son of Máel Sechnaill I, and member of the House of Clann Cholmáin (Southern Uí Néill). He died of the plague. (*see panel* p. 140, High Kingship of Ireland)

Fogartach (c.700–24) High King of Ireland (722–4), the son of Niall, and member of the House of Síl nÁedo Sláine (Southern Uí Néill). He was slain by Cináed at the battle of Delgean. (*see panel* p. 140, High Kingship of Ireland)

Forggus (c.540–66) High King of Ireland (564/5–6), the son of Muirchertach, member of the House of Cenél nEógain (Northern Uí Néill), and joint ruler with his brother Domnall Ilchelgach. They died of the plague on the same day. (*see panel* p. 140, High Kingship of Ireland)

Frederick (Augustus), Duke of York (1763–1827) Second son of King George III of Britain. A soldier by profession, he was unsuccessful both in the field in The Netherlands (1793–99) and as British commander-in-chief (1798–1809), and earned the description of the 'grand old Duke of York' in

FASHION

The British royal family has, throughout history, had great power over fashion trends. This was demonstrated by the Prince Regent (later George IV), Queen Victoria, and more recently by Queen Elizabeth and Princess Diana.

The Queen's designers and dressmakers have included Sir Norman Hartnell, famous for creating the young Princess Elizabeth's wedding and coronation gowns, and Sir (Edwin) Hardy Amies, known for his tailored suits for women.

Diana, Princess of Wales, favoured the designs of Catherine Walker, Christina Stambolian, Paul Costelloe, and Victor Edelstein; her bridal gown, however, was made by the Emanuels. In 1997 Princess Diana placed many of her dresses up for auction, raising $3.5 million for charitable causes.

In May 2002, as part of the Queen's Jubilee celebrations, the wedding dresses of the last five queens of England were on display at Kensington Palace. It was the first time the dresses had been seen in one place. The exhibition ran for a year, alongside the permanent Royal Ceremonial Dress Collection. The dresses included Queen Victoria's ivory silk gown from her marriage to Prince Albert in 1840; the gowns of Queen Alexandra in 1863, and Queen Mary in 1893; Queen Elizabeth the Queen Mother's straight-line dress worn for her marriage to Albert, Duke of York in 1923; and Queen Elizabeth II's Norman Hartnell gown, worn for her marriage to Lieutenant Philip Mountbatten in 1947, in ivory silk with its interwoven flower design in crusted pearl and crystal embroidery.

Madame Tussaud's wax museum in London had an exhibit showing Diana, Princess of Wales, Sarah Ferguson, Duchess of York, and Sophie Rhys-Jones, Countess of Wessex. They were each wearing replicas of their bridal gowns. The original gowns were designed by the Emanuels, Lindka Cierach, and Samantha Shaw, respectively. The Princess of Wales' original wedding dress is kept on display at her family home. It was a silk taffeta dress with a 25ft train; the veil was held in place by the Spencer family tiara; and the bouquet was of gardenias, lilies of the valley, white freesias, golden roses, white orchids, and stephanotis.

the nursery rhyme. However, his painstaking reform of the army proved of lasting benefit, especially to Wellington. He founded the Duke of York's School in London, and is commemorated by the Duke of York's column in Waterloo Place, London.

FROGMORE HOUSE

Frogmore House is set within Home Park, in the grounds of Windsor Castle, situated on the River Thames at Windsor. The estates came into royal ownership during the reign of Henry VIII. The house was originally built between 1680 and 1684 and modernized at the end of the 18th century by architect James Wyatt. In 1792 George III bought Frogmore for Queen Charlotte, who used it as a country retreat. The house contains many examples of the artwork of earlier members of the royal family. In the gardens stands the mausoleum where Queen Victoria and her husband Prince Albert were buried. The interiors of Frogmore House were fully restored in 1991. Today, the house is no longer a royal residence, but the house and gardens are sometimes used by the royal family for official purposes. The house, gardens, and mausoleum are open to the public on a limited number of days each year.

George I (1660–1727) King of Great Britain and Ireland (1714–27), born in Osnabrück, Germany, the great-grandson of James I of England, and proclaimed king on the death of Queen Anne. Elector of Hanover since 1698, he had commanded the imperial forces in the Marlborough wars. He divorced his wife and cousin, the Princess Dorothea of Zell, imprisoning her in the castle of Ahlde, where she died (1726). He took relatively little part in the government of the country. His affections remained with Hanover, and he lived there as much as possible.

George II (1683–1760) King of Great Britain and Ireland (1727–60), and Elector of Hanover, born at Herrenhausen, Hanover, Germany, the son of George I. In 1705 he married Caroline of Ansbach (1683–1737). Though he involved himself more in the government of the country than his father had, the policy pursued during the first half of the reign was that of Sir Robert Walpole. In the War of the Austrian Succession, he was present at the Battle of Dettingen (1743), the last occasion on which a British sovereign commanded an army in the field. His reign also saw the crushing of Jacobite hopes at the Battle of Culloden (1746), the foundation of British India after the Battle of Plassey (1757), the beginning of the Seven Years War, and the capture of Quebec (1759).

George III (1738–1820) King of Great Britain and Ireland (1760–1820), Elector (1760–1815) and King (from 1815) of Hanover, born in London, the eldest son of Frederick Louis, Prince of Wales (1707–51). His father predeceased him and his grandfather, George II, whom he thus succeeded. Eager to govern as well as reign, he caused considerable friction. With Lord North he shared in the blame for the loss of the American colonies, and popular feeling ran high against him for a time in the 1770s. In 1783 he called Pitt (the Younger) to office,

---

GARDEN PARTIES
Royal garden parties are held in June/July by the Queen – three in the grounds of Buckingham Palace, and the other at the Palace of Holyroodhouse, Edinburgh. Up to 10 000 people are invited to each event, to which formal or national dress must be worn.

which brought an end to the supremacy of the old Whig families. In 1810 he suffered a recurrence of a mental derangement, most likely caused by the inherited disease porphyria, and the Prince of Wales was made regent. DNA research in 2004 on a sample of his hair concluded that his condition was probably made more acute due to the application of arsenic powder as a skin cosmetic and wig dressing.

George IV (1762–1830) King of Great Britain and Hanover (1820–30), born in London, the eldest son of George III. He became prince regent in 1810, because of his father's insanity. Rebelling against a strict upbringing, he went through a marriage ceremony with Mrs Fitzherbert, a Roman Catholic, which was not recognized in English law. The marriage was later declared invalid, and in 1795 he married Princess Caroline of Brunswick, whom he tried to divorce when he was king. Her death in 1821 ended a scandal in which the people sympathized with the queen. His reign saw the passage of the Catholic Emancipation Act. He was a leader of taste, fashion, and the arts, and gave his name to the 'Regency' period, now synonymous with elegance and style.

George V (1865–1936) King of the United Kingdom (1910–36), born in London, the second son of Edward VII. He served in the navy, travelled in many parts of the empire, and was created Prince of Wales in 1901. He married Mary of Teck in 1893. His reign saw the Union of South Africa (1910), World War 1, the Irish Free State settlement (1922), and the General Strike (1926).

George VI (1895–1952) King of the United Kingdom (1936–52), born at Sandringham, Norfolk, the second son of George V. He studied at Dartmouth Naval College and Trinity College, Cambridge, and served in the Grand Fleet at the Battle of Jutland (1916). In 1920 he was created Duke of York, and married Lady Elizabeth Bowes-Lyon in 1923. They had two children: Princess Elizabeth (later Queen Elizabeth II) and Princess Margaret. An outstand-

GENTLEMEN AT ARMS

The Honourable Corps of Gentlemen at Arms are non-combatant troops in attendance upon the sovereign. They provide an escort at coronations, state openings of parliament, receptions, royal garden parties, and during state visits; because of their close proximity to the sovereign, they are known as 'the nearest guard'. Originated as the 'Gentlemen Spears' by Henry VIII in 1509, today the 27 members are chosen from officers in either the Army or the Royal Marines who have received decorations.

ing tennis player, he played at Wimbledon in the All-England Championships in 1926. He ascended the throne in 1936 on the abdication of his elder brother, Edward VIII. During World War 2 he set a personal example coping with wartime restrictions, continued to reside in bomb-damaged Buckingham Palace, visited all theatres of war and delivered many broadcasts, for which he overcame a speech impediment. In 1947 he toured South Africa and substituted the title of Head of the Commonwealth for that of Emperor of India, when that subcontinent was granted independence by the Labour government. Unnoticed by the public, his health was rapidly declining, yet he persevered with his duties, his last great public occasion being the opening of the Festival of Britain in 1951.

Giric, also known as **Gregory the Great** (fl.878–89) King of Scotland (878–89), jointly with Eochaid. He claimed joint rulership by murdering his first cousin Aedh, although as son of Aedh's uncle, Donald I, he had an arguable claim to the throne, whilst Eochaid did not, being descended through the female line. In 889, Giric was killed in battle at Dundurn, Perthshire by Donald, son of King Constantine I.

Glendower, Owen, Welsh **Owain Glyndwr** or **Owain ap Gruffudd** (c.1354–c.1416) Welsh chief, born in Powys, Wales. He claimed descent from Bleddyn ap Cynfyn and from Llewelyn. He studied law at Westminster, and became esquire to the Earl of Arundel. In 1400 he rebelled against Henry IV, proclaimed himself Prince of Wales, established an independent Welsh parliament, made plans for a university in Wales, and joined the coalition with Harry Percy (Hotspur) (1364–1403), who was defeated at the Battle of Shrewsbury (1403). Aided by the French and Bretons, he captured Harlech and Cardiff (1404), concluded an alliance with France (1405), and summoned a Welsh parliament in the same year. He continued to fight for Welsh independence until his death. His end is unknown.

Gloucester, Prince Henry, Duke of (1900–74) Prince of the United

---

'GOD SAVE THE KING/QUEEN'

The British national anthem was written anonymously in the 18th century. First sung at the Drury Lane theatre in 1745, it is the oldest of all national anthems, and the music has often been used for those of other countries: it is still used for the national anthem of Liechtenstein. In the USA, the melody is used in a popular patriotic song, 'America', or 'My Country 'Tis of Thee'.

Kingdom, the third son of George V. Educated privately and at Eton, he became a captain in the 10th Hussars and was created duke in 1928. In 1935 he married **Lady Alice Montagu-Douglas-Scott** (1901–), and they had two children: William (1941–72) and Richard, who succeeded him. He served as Governor-General of Australia (1945–7).

Gloucester, Prince Richard, Duke of *see* **Richard III**

Gloucester, Richard (Alexander Walter George), Duke of (1944–) British prince, the younger son of Henry, Duke of Gloucester (the third son of George V). In 1972 he married **Birgitte van Deurs** (1946–); they have one son, **Alexander, Earl of Ulster** (1974–), and two daughters, **Lady Davina Windsor** (1977–) and **Lady Rose Windsor** (1980–).

Glyndwr, Owen *see* **Glendower, Owen**

Gorboduc A legendary king of Britain, first heard about in Geoffrey of Monmouth's *History*. He was the subject of an early Elizabethan tragedy in Senecan style, written by Norton and Sackville (1561).

Grey, Lady Jane (1537–54) Queen of England for nine days in 1553, born in Bradgate, Leicestershire, the eldest daughter of Henry Grey, Marquess of Dorset, and great-granddaughter of Henry VII. In 1553 the Duke of Northumberland, foreseeing the death of Edward VI, aimed to secure the succession by marrying Jane (against her wish) to his fourth son, Lord Guildford Dudley. Three days after Edward's death she was named as his successor (9 July), but was forced to abdicate in favour of Mary, who had popular support. She was imprisoned, and beheaded on Tower Green.

Gruffudd ap Llywelyn (1007–63) King of the Welsh (1039–63), grandson of Maredudd ab Owain, King of Deheubarth and the son of Llywelyn ap Seisyllt, ruler of Gwynedd. He was King of all Wales from 1055 to 1063 and the only Welsh ruler to unite the ancient kingdoms of the whole of Wales. He reclaimed territory east of Offa's Dyke from English settlers, establishing his court at Rhuddlan, and in 1039 he became ruler of Deheubarth after driving Hywel ap Edwin from his kingdom. By 1055, having taken Gwent and Morgannwg, he claimed sovereignty over the whole of Wales and when Aelfgar, son of the earl of Mercia, fell from favour he found Gruffydd ap Llywelyn a valuable ally. Their defeat of English forces in Herefordshire led Harold, Earl of Wessex (later King Harold I) to invade Wales and arrange a settlement. In 1058, the conflict between Aelfgar (now Earl of Mercia) and Harold was renewed, forcing Harold to strengthen the border defences. In the second of two surprise attacks by Harold on Rhuddlan in 1063, Gruffudd was driven into central Wales, where he was killed by fellow Welshmen who disagreed with his alliance with the Mercian dynasty. His death left Wales weak and fragmented only a few years before the Norman invasion.

GOLDEN JUBILEE

Several projects commemorated Queen Elizabeth II's 50 years on the throne in 2002

Golden Jubilee Coin A £5 coin was issued in January 2002, its design similar to coins commemorating the Coronation and the Silver Jubilee. It carries the legend: ELIZABETH·II·DEI·GRA· REGINA FID·DEF /·AMOR·POPULI·PRÆSIDIUM·REG ('the love of the people is the queen's protection'). The obverse shows the Queen on horseback facing to the left; the reverse shows the Queen in profile facing to the right.

Golden Jubilee Emblem The emblem comprises a gold crown on a purple background, with 2002 in white lettering around the band of the crown. In lettering around the crown in a full circle is written: THE·QUEEN'S·GOLDEN·JUBILEE.

Golden Jubilee Medal A circular gold medal was instituted on 15 February 2002; its ribbon is blue with narrow red edge stripes and a white-edged narrow red middle stripe. It was awarded to members of the armed forces and emergency services who had completed at least five years' service by 7 February 2002. The obverse shows Queen Elizabeth II facing right wearing the high Imperial State Crown. The legend reads: ELIZABETH·II·DEI· GRATIA·REGINA·FID·DEF· ('Elizabeth II, thanks be to God, queen, defender of the faith'). The reverse shows St Edward's Crown at the top, with a shield bearing the royal coat of arms below and the dates of reign 1952 to the left and 2002 to the right.

Guardians of Scotland Nobles who administered the Scottish affairs of state during the interregnums of the 13th century.

First Interregnum (1290–2)

  – William Fraser, Bishop of St Andrews
  – Duncan Macduff, 8th Earl of Fife
  – Alexander Comyn, Earl of Buchan
  – Robert Wishart, Bishop of Glasgow
  – James Stewart, 5th High Steward of Scotland
  – John Comyn, Lord of Badenoch

Second Interregnum (1296–1306)

  – Andrew de Moray (1297)
  – Sir William Wallace (1297–8)

'Royal Treasures: A Golden Jubilee Celebration' In 1962 a new gallery at Buckingham Palace was opened to display items from the Royal Collection – the first time that parts of the Palace had been opened to the general public. The new Queen's Gallery re-opened in May 2002 for the Golden Jubilee celebrations, occupying the space of the palace's private chapel. This inaugural exhibition contained over 450 works selected from across the entire Royal Collection. Taken from eight royal residences and over five centuries, the exhibition included painting, drawings, watercolours, furniture, sculpture, ceramics, silver, gold, arms, jewellery, miniatures, books, and manuscripts.

Drawings by Leonardo da Vinci The Royal Collection holds an important group of drawings by the Renaissance master Leonardo da Vinci. Usually housed in the Royal Library, Windsor Castle, ten of these drawings were put together as a travelling exhibition to be shown at museums and galleries in the UK as part of the Golden Jubilee celebrations.

The Queen's Christmas Cards An exhibition of enlarged photographs was displayed in the Ballroom at Sandringham House in Norfolk. It consisted of family photographs used for the greeting cards sent by the Queen and the Duke of Edinburgh to friends and employees over the years since the accession.

Another exhibition of photographs was on display at Windsor Castle, consisting of photographs, both amateur and professional, taken over the Queen's reign – a record of official visits through-

---

– Robert the Bruce, Earl of Carrick (1298–1300)
– John Comyn (1298–1301, 1302–4)
– William Lamberton, Bishop of St Andrews (1299–1301)
– Sir Ingram de Umfraville (1300–1)
– John de Soules (1301–4)

Guthorm or **Guthrum** (?–890) Danish King of East Anglia, and opponent of King Alfred the Great. He led a major Viking invasion of Anglo-Saxon England in 871 (the 'Great Summer Army'), seized East Anglia, and conquered Northumbria and Mercia. He attacked Wessex early in 878 and drove Alfred into hiding in

out the UK and abroad as well as family portraits. Portraits by such well-known photographers as Lord Snowdon, Patrick Lichfield, and Cecil Beaton were among the exhibits.

Visits to foreign and Commonwealth countries by the Queen and the Duke of Edinburgh

New Zealand 22–27 February Visits to Christchurch, Wellington, and Auckland. The Queen and the Duke of Edinburgh previously visited New Zealand in 1953–4, 1963, 1970, 1981, 1986, 1988, 1992, and 2000.

Australia 27 February–3 March In South Australia they visited Adelaide. The Queen also visited the Barossa Valley, while the Duke of Edinburgh visited Ceduna and Port Lincoln. In Queensland they visited Brisbane and Cairns, and the Duke of Edinburgh visited Roma.

On Saturday 2 March the Queen opened the Commonwealth Heads of Government Meeting (CHOGM) at Coolum, near Brisbane. The Queen and the Duke of Edinburgh previously visited Australia in 1954, 1963, 1970, 1973, 1974, 1977, 1980, 1981, 1982, 1986, 1988, 1992, and 2000.

Jamaica 5–7 March The Queen and the Duke of Edinburgh visited Jamaica previously in 1953, 1966, 1975, 1983, and 1994.

Canada 4–15 October Visits to Nunavut, British Columbia, Manitoba, Ontario, New Brunswick and the National Capital Region. The Queen and the Duke of Edinburgh previously visited Canada in 1997.

Somerset. By May of that year Alfred had recovered sufficiently to defeat the Danes at the crucial Battle of Edington in Wiltshire. In the ensuing treaty, Guthorm agreed to leave Wessex and accept baptism as a Christian, and he and his army settled down peacefully in East Anglia.

Gwyn or **Gwynne, Nell**, popular name of **Eleanor Gwyn** (c.1650–87) Mistress of Charles II, possibly born in London. Of humble parentage, she lived precariously as an orange girl before going on the boards at Drury Lane, where she quickly established herself as a comedienne. She had at least one son by the king – Charles

Beauclerk, Duke of St Albans – and
James Beauclerk is often held to have
been a second.

GREAT SEAL

The Great Seal of the Realm is the chief seal of the British Crown. In today's constitutional monarchy the seal remains an important symbol of the sovereign's role as Head of State. A new Great Seal matrix is engraved at the beginning of each reign on the order of the sovereign. The Queen has had two Great Seals during her reign. The first was designed by Gilbert Ledward and came into service in 1953. The second was designed by sculptor James Butler and came into service in 2001. It is held by the Lord High Chancellor, and the process of sealing takes place in the office of the Clerk of the Crown in Chancery, at the House of Lords. The matrix is used to create seals for a range of documents requiring royal approval, such as letters patent, royal proclamations, commissions, some writs, and documents which confer power to sign and ratify treaties. The colour of the seal denotes the type of document.

Hardicanute, also spelled **Harthacnut** (c.1018–42) King of Denmark (1035–42), and the last Danish King of England (1040–2), the only son of Canute and Emma of Normandy. Canute had intended that Hardicanute should succeed him in both Denmark and England simultaneously, but he was unable to secure his English inheritance until his step-brother, Harold I, died in 1040. Hardicanute's death without children led to the restoration of the Old English royal line in the person of Edward the Confessor, the only surviving son of Emma and Ethelred the Unready.

Harold I, nickname **Harold Harefoot** (c.1016–40) King of England (1037–40), illegitimate son of Canute and Ælfgifu of Northampton. Canute had intended that Hardicanute, his only son by Emma of Normandy, should succeed him in both Denmark and England. But in view of Hardicanute's absence in Denmark, Harold was accepted in England, first as regent (1035–6), and from 1037 as king.

Harold II (c.1022–66) Last Anglo-Saxon King of England (1066), the second son of Earl Godwin. By 1045 he was Earl of East Anglia, and in 1053 succeeded to his father's earldom of Wessex, becoming the right hand of Edward the Confessor. After Edward's death (January 1066), Harold, his nominee, was crowned as king. He defeated his brother Tostig and Harold Hardrada, King of Norway, at Stamford Bridge (September 1066), but Duke William of Normandy then invaded England, and defeated him near Hastings (14 October 1066), where he died, shot through the eye with an arrow.

Hengist and **Horsa** (5th-c) Brothers,

HAMPTON COURT
Hampton Court is a royal residence situated by the River Thames. It was built by Cardinal Wolsey, who occupied it until 1529. Thereafter it became the favourite residence of British monarchs for over two centuries. Queen Victoria declared it open to the public in 1851, and its gardens and maze are a major tourist attraction.

leaders of the first Anglo-Saxon settlers in Britain, said by Bede to have been invited over by Vortigern, the British king, to fight the Picts in about 450. According to the *Anglo-Saxon Chronicle*, Horsa was killed in 455, and Hengist ruled in Kent until his death in 488.

Henrietta Anne, Duchess of Orléans (1644–70) Youngest daughter of Charles I of Great Britain and Henrietta Maria, and sister of Charles II, born in Exeter, Devon, while the English Civil Wars were still at their height. Brought up by her mother in France, she married Louis XIV's homosexual brother Philippe, but was also rumoured to have been for a time the mistress of the French king himself. She played an important part in the negotiations of the Secret Treaty of Dover (1670) between Charles and Louis. There were strong rumours that her subsequent death was caused by poison, although it was more probably a case of a ruptured appendix.

Henrietta Maria (1609–69) Queen consort of Charles I of England, born in Paris, France, the youngest child of Henry IV of France. She married Charles in 1625, but her French attendants and Roman Catholic beliefs made her unpopular. In 1642, under the threat of impeachment, she fled to Holland and raised funds for the Royalist cause. A year later she landed at Bridlington, and met Charles near Edgehill. At Exeter she gave birth to Henrietta Anne, and a fortnight later she was compelled to flee to France (1644). She paid two visits to England after the Restoration (1660–1, 1662–5), and spent her last years in France.

Henry I (1068–1135) King of England (1100–35) and Duke of Normandy (1106–35), the youngest son of William the Conqueror. Under Henry, the Norman empire attained the height of its power. He conquered Normandy from his brother, Robert Curthose, at the Battle of Tinchebrai (1106), maintained his position on the European mainland, and exercised varying degrees of authority over the King of Scots, the Welsh princes, the Duke of Brittany, and the Counts of Flanders, Boulogne, and Ponthieu. His government of England and Normandy became increasingly centralized and interventionist, with the overriding aim of financing warfare and alliances, and consolidating the unity of the two countries as a single cross-Channel state. His only legitimate son, **William Adelin**, was drowned in 1120, and in 1127 he nominated his daughter Empress **Matilda**, widow of Emperor Henry V of Germany, as his heir for both England and Normandy. But Matilda and her second husband, Geoffrey of Anjou, proved unacceptable to the king's leading subjects. After Henry's death at Lyons-la-Forêt, near Rouen, the crown was seized by Stephen, son of his sister, Adela.

Henry II (1133–89) King of England (1154–89), born in Le Mans, France, the son of Empress Matilda, Henry I's daughter and acknowledged heir, by her second husband, Geoffrey of Anjou. Already established as Duke of

HOUSE OF HANOVER

The first king of the House of Hanover, George I, was the great-grandson of James I, and his only Protestant descendant. However, he arrived in Britain without his wife, whom he had imprisoned for adultery some years before, and with two strikingly unattractive mistresses, christened by irreverent London society the Maypole and the Elephant.

The Hanoverian kings were notable for constantly quarrelling with their sons. George II was never on good terms with his father, whom he succeeded in 1727, nor with his eldest son, Frederick, Prince of Wales. The Prince of Wales, however, died in 1751, leaving his 22-year-old son to succeed his grandfather as George III.

In 1771, George III's brother, the Duke of Cumberland, married a commoner. George disapproved strongly, and was even more disturbed to discover afterwards that his other brother, the Duke of Gloucester, had been secretly married for six years to a lady of similar background. His solution was the Royal Marriages Act of 1772, which prevented British descendants of George II from marrying without the sovereign's consent. Unfortunately, this measure had unexpected effects. The Prince of Wales, later George IV, a true Hanoverian who was in constant conflict with

Normandy (1150) and Count of Anjou (1151), and as Duke of Aquitaine by marriage to Eleanor of Aquitaine (1152), he invaded England in 1153, and was recognized as the lawful successor of the usurper, Stephen. He founded the Angevin or Plantagenet dynasty of English kings, and ruled England as part of a wider Angevin empire. He restored and transformed English governance after the disorders of Stephen's reign. His efforts to restrict clerical independence caused conflict with his former Chancellor Thomas Becket, Archbishop of Canterbury, which was ended only with Becket's murder (1170). He led a major expedition to Ireland (1171), which resulted in its annexation. The most serious challenge to his power came in 1173–4, when his son, the young Henry, encouraged by Eleanor, rebelled in alliance with Louis VII of France, William I of Scotland, and Count Philip of Flanders. All parts of the king's dominions were threatened, but his enemies were defeated. In 1189 he faced futher disloyalty from his

his father, contracted an illegal marriage to the Catholic Mrs Fitzherbert in 1785. He was later coerced into repudiating this marriage, and marrying Caroline of Brunswick for the sake of the succession, but they disliked one another intensely and produced only one child, the Princess Charlotte. The Duke of Sussex, George III's sixth son, also ignored the Royal Marriages Act, and had two morganatic wives, but most of the royal dukes simply remained unmarried and kept mistresses instead. The Duke of Clarence, in particular, had ten illegitimate children with a well-known actress, Mrs Jordan.

In 1817, however, Princess Charlotte died giving birth to a stillborn son. Not one of George III's seven surviving sons now had an heir, and only one, the Duke of Cumberland, had a wife of child-bearing age. Consequently, three of the others hurriedly married the following year, the Duke of Clarence giving up Mrs Jordan to do so. He duly succeeded his brother in 1830 as William IV, but still had no legitimate children, so when he died, it was the daughter of the Duke of Kent, Princess Victoria, who came to the throne.

The throne of Hanover was subject to Salic Law, and could not be inherited by a woman. On the death of William IV, it therefore passed to the Duke of Cumberland and later to his son. The kingdom disappeared when Germany was unified in 1866.

family when his sons, John and Richard, allied with Philip II of France, who overran Maine and Touraine. Henry agreed a peace which recognized Richard as his sole heir for the Angevin empire, and he died shortly afterwards.

Henry III (1207–72) King of England (1216–72), the elder son and successor, at the age of nine, of John. He declared an end to his minority in 1227, and in 1232 stripped the justiciar, Hubert de Burgh, of power. His arbitrary assertion of royal rights conflicted with the principles of Magna Carta, and antagonized many nobles. Although he failed to recover Poitou (Aquitaine) in 1242, he accepted for his son Edmund the Kingdom of Sicily (1254), then occupied by the Hohenstaufens. This forced him to seek the support of the barons who, under the leadership of the king's brother-in-law, Simon de Montfort, imposed far-reaching reforms by the Provisions of Oxford (1258), which gave them a definite say in government. When Henry sought to restore royal power, the barons rebelled and captured the king at Lewes (1264), but were defeated at Evesham (1265). The Dictum of Kenilworth (1266), though favourable to Henry, urged him to observe Magna Carta. Organized resistance ended in 1267, and the rest of the reign was stable. He was succeeded by his elder son, Edward I.

Henry IV, originally **Henry Bolingbroke** (1366–1413) King of England (1399–1413), the first king of the House of Lancaster, the son of John of Gaunt. He was surnamed Bolingbroke from his birthplace in Lincolnshire. In 1397 he supported Richard II against the Duke of Gloucester, and was created Duke of Hereford, but was banished in 1398. After landing at Ravenspur, Yorkshire, Henry induced Richard, now deserted, to abdicate in his favour. During his reign, rebellion and lawlessness were rife, and he was constantly hampered by lack of money. Under Owen Glendower the Welsh maintained their independence, and Henry's attack on Scotland in 1400 ended in his defeat. Henry Percy (Hotspur) and his house then joined with the Scots and the Welsh against him, but they were defeated at Shrewsbury (1403). He was a chronic invalid in his later years.

Henry V (1387–1422) King of England (1413–22), born in Monmouth, Wales, the eldest son of Henry IV. He fought against Glendower and the Welsh rebels (1402–8), and became Constable of Dover (1409) and Captain of Calais (1410). To this time belong the exaggerated stories of his wild youth. The main effort of his reign was his claim, through his great-grandfather Edward III, to the French crown. In 1415 he invaded France, and won the Battle of Agincourt against great odds. By 1419 Normandy was again under English control, and in 1420 was concluded the 'perpetual peace' of Troyes, under which Henry was recognized as heir to the French throne and Regent of France, and married Charles VI's daughter, Catherine of Valois.

Henry VI (1421–71) King of England (1422–61, 1470–1), born in Windsor, the only child of Henry V and Catherine of Valois. During Henry's minority, his uncle John, Duke of Bedford, was Regent of France, and another uncle, Humphrey, Duke of Gloucester, was Lord Protector of England. Henry was crowned King of France in Paris in 1431, two years after his coronation in England. But once the Burgundians had made a separate peace with Charles VII (1435), Henry V's French conquests were progressively eroded, and by 1453 the English retained only Calais. Henry had few kingly qualities, and from 1453 suffered from periodic bouts of insanity. Richard, Duke of York, seized power as Lord Protector in 1454, and defeated the king's army at St Albans in 1455, the first battle of the Wars of the Roses. Fighting resumed in 1459, and although York himself was killed at Wakefield (1460), his heir was proclaimed king as Edward IV after Henry's deposition (1461). In 1464 Henry returned from exile in Scotland to lead the Lancastrian cause, but was captured and imprisoned (1465–70). Richard Neville, Earl of Warwick, restored him to the throne (October 1470), his nominal rule ending when Edward IV returned to London (April 1471). After the Yorkist victory at Tewkesbury (May 1471), where his only son was killed, Henry was murdered in the Tower.

Henry VII (1457–1509) King of England (1485–1509), born at Pembroke Castle, Pembrokeshire, Wales. Henry's claim to the English throne was traced back tenuously through his father, Edmund Tudor, the younger son of Catherine of France and of her clerk to the wardrobe, the Welshman Owen Tudor. Through his mother, Margaret Beaufort, Henry claimed descent from Edward III's son, John of Gaunt, and Katherine Swynford. Known as Duke of Richmond before his accession, he was the founder of the Tudor dynasty. After the Lancastrian defeat at Tewkesbury (1471), Henry was taken to Brittany, where several Yorkist attempts on his life and liberty were frustrated. In 1485 he landed unopposed at Milford Haven, and defeated Richard III at Bosworth. As king, his policy was to restore peace and prosperity to the country, and this was helped by his marriage of reconciliation with Elizabeth of York, daughter of Edward IV. He was also noted for the efficiency of his financial and administrative policies. He firmly dealt with Yorkist plots, such as that led by Perkin Warbeck. Peace was concluded with France, and the marriage of his heir, Prince Arthur, to Catherine of

Aragón cemented an alliance with Spain. He was succeeded by his son, Henry VIII.

Henry VIII (1491–1547) King of England (1509–47), born in Greenwich, Greater London, the second son of Henry VII. Soon after his accession he married **Catherine of Aragón**, his brother Arthur's widow. As a member of the Holy League, he invaded France (1512), winning the Battle of Spurs (1513); and while abroad, the Scots were defeated at Flodden. In 1521 he published a book on the Sacraments refuting Luther, receiving from the pope the title 'Defender of the Faith'. From 1527 he determined to divorce Catherine, whose children, except for Mary, had died in infancy. He tried to put pressure on the pope by humbling the clergy, and in defiance of the Roman Catholic Church was privately married to **Anne Boleyn** (1533). In 1534 it was enacted that his marriage to Catherine was invalid, and that the king was the Supreme Head of the English Church. The policy of Dissolution of the Monasteries then began. In 1536 Catherine died, and Anne Boleyn was executed on the grounds of infidelity. Henry then married **Jane Seymour**, who died leaving a son, afterwards Edward VI. In 1540 **Anne of Cleves** became his fourth wife, in the hope of attaching the Protestant interest of Germany; but dislike of her appearance caused him to divorce her speedily. He then married **Catherine Howard** (1540), who two years later was executed on grounds of infidelity (1542). In 1543 his last marriage was to **Catherine Parr**, who survived him. His later years saw ineffectual and expensive wars with France and Scotland, but a powerful English navy was created.

Henry, Prince of Wales (1594–1612) Eldest son of James I (of England) and Anne of Denmark. Notable for the strict morality of his way of life, in marked contrast to his father, and known to support a vigorously Protestant and anti-Spanish foreign policy, he became the focus for the hopes of those at court with Puritan sympathies. His death, loudly rumoured to be a result of poison, brought nationwide regret, while the hopes of forward Protestants centred increasingly upon Henry's sister, Elizabeth, and her husband, Frederick V of the Palatinate.

HOLYROODHOUSE

The Palace of Holyroodhouse is the official residence in Scotland of the reigning monarch, situated at the end of the Royal Mile in Edinburgh. It is said to have been founded as an Augustinian monastery by King David in 1128. Its name derives from a vision in which the king saw a cross, or 'rood', belonging to his mother St Margaret between the antlers of an attacking stag. The palace was first built in the early 16th century and expanded by successive kings. Mary, Queen of Scots, spent much of her life there. It was substantially reconstructed under Charles II in the 1670s by the architect Sir William Bruce (d.1710). After a period of neglect by British monarchs, Queen Victoria reintroduced the custom of staying at the palace, and a new programme of renovation took place. Today, the palace is used for state ceremonies and official receptions.

HORSE GUARDS

The Royal Horse Guards is an elite regiment of the British Army, first raised in 1661; its nickname is 'the Blues'. Amalgamated in 1969 with the Royal Dragoon Guards, 'the Blues and Royals' form, with the Life Guards, the British Sovereign's *Household Cavalry*.

HOUSEHOLD

The *royal household* is the collective term for those departments which serve members of the royal family in matters of day-to-day administration. In mediaeval times no distinction existed between the sovereign's ministers and personal servants; a survival of this earlier fusion of posts is to be found today in the titles of government Whips, such as Treasurer of the Household and Comptroller of the Household.

Howard, Catherine (?–1542) Fifth wife of Henry VIII, a granddaughter of the 2nd Duke of Norfolk. She was married to the king in the same month as he divorced Anne of Cleves (July 1540). However, after Henry learned of Catherine's alleged pre-marital affairs (1541), she was arrested for treason and beheaded, together with her cousin Lady Jane Rochford, in the Tower of London. All persons supposed privy to her conduct, as well as several relatives and servants, were imprisoned and suffered the forfeiture of their property and possessions.

Hywel Dda, also known as **Hywel ap Cadell ap Rhodri** or **Hywel the Good** (890–950) King of the Welsh, grandson of Rhodri Mawr. He became king of Seisyllwg and Brycheiniog c.900 and added Dyfed c.904, creating the kingdom of Deheubarth. In 942 he also became ruler of Gwynedd and Powys, thus having control over most of Wales with the exception of Glamorgan. He kept peace with the English, earning a reputation as a diplomat more than a warrior. He created Wales' first formal legal system, and the codification of the law at Whitland, Pembrokeshire in 940 won him the epithet 'Hywel the Good'. Hywel's law, *Cyfraith Hywel*, was noted for its common sense, mercy, and respect for women and children. The Law of Hywel was modified over the centuries, eventually being displaced by English law following the conquest of Wales by Edward I, although some aspects of it remained in use until at least the 15th century.

Indulf or **Indulph**, also known as **Indulb mac Causantín** (c.904–62) King of Scotland (954–62), son of King Constantine II, second cousin of the previous king Malcolm I, and second cousin first removed of his successor Duff (Dubh). In a decisive battle over Edwin of Deira, he recaptured the fortress of Dun Eden (now Edinburgh) after his father Constantine II had abandoned the Lothian in his flight before Athelstan. Like his father before him, Indulf had intended to abdicate and become a monk. He is said to have been killed by invading Vikings in 962 at the Battle of the Bauds in Findochty, Banffshire. It is unclear whether at the time he was still king or if he had already abdicated. His son, Cuilean (Colin), later became king in 966.

Isabella of Angoulême (?–1246) Queen consort of England, the wife of King John, whom she married in 1200. In 1214 she was imprisoned by John at Gloucester, and after his death in 1216 returned to France, where she married a former lover, the Comte de la Marche, in 1220. Isabella was the mother of Henry III. Her daughter by John, **Isabella** (1214–41), married Emperor Frederick II.

Isabella of France (1292–1358) Queen consort of England, the wife of Edward II, and daughter of Philip IV of France. She married Edward in 1308 at Boulogne, but then became the mistress of Roger Mortimer, Earl of March, with whom she overthrew and murdered the king (1327). Her son, Edward III, had Mortimer executed in 1330, and Isabella was sent into retirement, eventually to join an order of nuns.

IONA

Iona is a remote island off Mull, western Scotland, the site of a monastery established in AD 563 by the Irish missionary St Columba and 12 companions to convert the inhabitants of northern Britain to Christianity. The monastery flourished until the onset of Viking attacks (c.800), then declined until c.1200, when a Benedictine abbey was founded on the site. Iona was the burial ground of the kings of Dal Riada and the early kings of Scotland, notably Kenneth I, Malcolm I, Duncan I, Donald III, and Macbeth.

James I (of England) (1566–1625) The first Stuart King of England (1603–25), also King of Scotland (1567–1625) as James VI, born in Edinburgh, the son of Mary, Queen of Scots, and Henry, Lord Darnley. On his mother's forced abdication, he was proclaimed king, and brought up by several regents. When he began to govern for himself, he ruled through his favourites, which caused a rebellion and a period of imprisonment. In 1589 he married **Anne of Denmark**. Hating Puritanism, he managed in 1600 to establish bishops in Scotland. On Elizabeth's death, he ascended the English throne as great-grandson of James IV's English wife, Margaret Tudor. At first well received, his favouritism again brought him unpopularity.

James I (of Scotland) (1394–1437) King of Scots (1424–37; in name only from 1406), born in Dunfermline, Fife, Scotland, the second son of Robert III. After his elder brother David was murdered at Falkland (1402), allegedly by his uncle, the Duke of Albany, James was sent for safety to France,

but was captured by the English, and remained a prisoner for 18 years. Albany meanwhile ruled Scotland as governor until his death in 1420, when his son, Murdoch, assumed the regency, and the country rapidly fell into disorder. Once released (1424), James dealt ruthlessly with potential rivals to his authority, executing Murdoch and his family. He brought state finance under his direct control and curtailed the power of the nobles. He improved the administration of justice for the common people, raising his popularity, but he was assassinated by a small group of dissidents led by Sir Robert Stewart. James was the first of many Stewart kings to act as a patron of the arts, and almost certainly wrote the tender, passionate collection of poems, *The Kingis Quair* ('The King's Quire' or book), c.1423–4.

James II (of England) (1633–1701) King of England and Ireland (1685–8), also of Scotland, as James VII, born in London, the second son of Charles I. Nine months before his father's execution, he escaped to Holland. At the Restoration (1660) he was made Lord High Admiral of England, and commanded the fleet in the Dutch Wars; but after becoming a convert to Catholicism he was forced to resign his post. The national ferment occasioned by the Popish Plot (1678) became so formidable that he had to retire to the European mainland, and several unsuccessful attempts were made to exclude him from the succession. During his reign his actions in favour of Catholicism raised general indignation, and William, Prince of

Orange, his son-in-law and nephew, was formally asked by leading clerics and landowners to invade (1688). Deserted by ministers and troops, James escaped to France, where he was warmly received by Louis XIV. He made an ineffectual attempt to regain his throne in Ireland, which ended in the Battle of the Boyne (1690), and remained at St Germain until his death.

James II (of Scotland) (1430–60) King of Scots (1437–60), the son of James I. He was six years old at his father's murder, and three rival families vied for power until James was able to assume control after his marriage to **Mary of Gueldres** (1449). He confiscated the estates of the Livingstone family, then quarrelled with William, Earl of Douglas, killed him in a brawl (1450), and confiscated the Douglas estates (1453). A growing stability in domestic politics was made ineffective by his involvement in the English struggles between the houses of York and Lancaster. In 1460 he marched for England with a powerful army, and laid siege to Roxburgh Castle, which had been held by the English for over a century, but was killed by the bursting of a cannon.

James III (1452–88) King of Scots (1460–88), the son of James II. Too young to rule when his father died, the country once again was ruled by assorted persons who wanted power for themselves. James himself began to govern from 1469, but was a weak monarch, and was unable to restore strong central government. A break-

down of relations with England brought war in 1480, and the threat of English invasion resulted in a calculated political demonstration by his nobles, who hanged unpopular royal favourites at Lauder Bridge in 1482. The rebellion which brought about his downfall and death at Sauchieburn resulted from a further crisis of confidence in the king. The eldest of his sons, James, who had appeared with the rebels in the field, succeeded as James IV.

James IV (1473–1513) King of Scots (1488–1513), the eldest son of James III. He became active in government at his accession, at the age of 15, and gradually exerted his authority over the nobility. In 1503 he married Margaret Tudor, the elder daughter of Henry VII – an alliance which led ultimately to the union of the crowns. However, he adhered to the French alliance when Henry VIII joined the League against France, and was induced to invade England by the French. He was defeated and killed, along with the flower of his nobility, at the Battle of Flodden, Northumberland.

James V (1512–42) King of Scots (1513–42), the son of James IV. An infant at his father's death, he grew up amid the struggle between the pro-French and pro-English factions in his country. In 1536 he visited France, marrying **Magdeleine**, the daughter of Francis I (1537), and after her death, **Mary of Guise** (1538). War with England followed from the French alliance (1542), and after attempting to invade England he was routed at Solway Moss. He retired to Falkland Palace, Fife, where he died soon after the birth of his daughter Mary (later, Mary, Queen of Scots).

Joan of Navarre, also known as **Joanna of Navarre** (c.1370–1437) Queen consort of Henry IV of England, and stepmother of Henry V. She married first the Duke of Brittany (1386), by whom she had eight children; after his death (1399), she married Henry IV (1402), leaving her older children in Brittany. After Henry's death in 1413, her situation became difficult, because Brittany, ruled by her eldest son John, was hostile to England. She was falsely accused of witchcraft, and imprisoned for three years.

John, also known as **John Lackland** (1167–1216) King of England (1199–1216), the youngest son of Henry II, born in Oxford, Oxfordshire, and one of the least popular monarchs in English history. He tried to seize the crown during Richard I's captivity in Germany (1193–4), but was forgiven and nominated successor by Richard, who thus set aside the rights of Arthur, the son of John's elder brother Geoffrey. Arthur's claims were supported by Philip II of France, and, after Arthur was murdered on John's orders (1203), Philip marched against him with superior forces, conquering all but a portion of Aquitaine (1204–5). In 1206 John refused to receive Stephen Langton as Archbishop of Canterbury, and in 1208 his kingdom was placed under papal interdict. He was then excommunicated (1209), and finally conceded (1213). His oppressive government, and failure to recover Normandy, provoked baronial opposition, which led to demands for

JUBILEE BRIDGE 2002

A new pedestrian bridge across the River Thames was opened in 2002 to coincide with the Queen's Golden Jubilee celebrations. It links Cannon Street railway station to the north and Bankside to the south. Its length is 240m/787ft. It is the first covered bridge across the Thames since the building of the original London Bridge in 1176. The original Cannon Street station and bridge were built in 1865–6 for South East Railways. The Alexandra Bridge was built in 1870, and the up-stream side was opened to the public as a footbridge, on payment of a toll, between 1872 and 1877. The Jubilee Bridge is fixed to the supports of the original Alexandra Bridge, and is equipped with observation towers and accessed by elevators.

JUBILEE FACTOIDS

The Queen had made 14 visits to Australia, 20 visits to Canada, 6 visits to Jamaica, and 10 visits to New Zealand during her reign, by the end of 2002.

During their visit to New Zealand and Australia in 1970, the Queen and the Duke of Edinburgh took the first 'Royal Walkabout'.

The Queen began her first Commonwealth tour on 24 November 1953.

The 1953 FA Cup Final was the first football match attended by the Queen.

During her reign to 2002 the Queen launched 17 ships.

By the end of 2002 the Queen had opened Parliament 48 times.

The Queen's wedding ring was made from Welsh gold.

During her reign to 2002 the Queen had attended 31 Royal Variety performances.

During the Queen's reign there have been six Archbishops of Canterbury: Geoffrey Fisher, Michael Ramsey, Donald Coggan, Robert Runcie, George Carey, and Rowan Williams.

The Queen made her first Christmas Broadcast, live from New Zealand, in 1953.

During her reign to 2002 the Queen owned more than 30 corgis.

The Queen's first corgi, Susan, was an 18th birthday present in 1944.

In 2002 the Queen had four corgis: Pharos, Swift, Emma, and Linnet.

A dachshund named Pipkin belonging to Princess Margaret and one of Her Majesty's corgis mated, creating a new breed of dog known as the 'dorgi'.

There have been eight dorgis: Tinker, Pickles, Chipper, Piper, Harris, Brandy, Cider, and Berry.

During her reign to 2002 the Queen sent almost 100,000 birthday telegrams to centenarians.

During her reign to 2002 the Queen sent more than 280,000 telegrams to couples celebrating anniversaries.

During her reign to 2002 the Queen personally held 459 Investitures.

During her reign to 2002 the Queen gave 88 State banquets.

In 1972, to mark the Queen's silver wedding anniversary, the President of Cameroon gave Her Majesty a 7-year-old bull elephant called 'Jumbo'.

During her reign to 2002 the Queen made 251 official overseas visits to 128 different countries.

During her reign to 2002 the Queen had given weekly audiences to ten Prime Ministers: Winston Churchill, Sir Anthony Eden, Harold Macmillan, Sir Alec Douglas-Home, Harold Wilson, Edward Heath, James Callaghan, Margaret Thatcher, John Major, and Tony Blair.

During her reign to 2002 the Queen sat for over 120 portraits.

Queen Elizabeth II is the fortieth British monarch since William the Conqueror.

Queen Elizabeth II is one of only five British monarchs to celebrate a Golden Jubilee; the others were Henry III, Edward III, George III, and Victoria.

The Queen's Jubilee coincided with the 50th anniversary of Agatha Christie's play, *The Mousetrap*, and the centenary of Marmite.

constitutional reform. The barons met the king at Runnymede, and forced him to grant the Great Charter (Magna Carta) (June 1215), the basis of the English constitution. His repudiation of the Charter precipitated the first Barons' War (1215–17).

John of Gaunt (1340–99) Duke of Lancaster, born in Ghent, Belgium, the fourth son of Edward III, and ancestor of Henry IV, V, VI, and VII. In 1359 he married his cousin, **Blanche of Lancaster**, and was created duke in 1362. After her death (1369), he married **Constance**, the daughter of Pedro (Peter) the Cruel of Castile, and assumed the title of King of Castile, though he failed by his expeditions to oust his rival, Henry of Trastámara. In England he became highly influential as a peacemaker during the troubled reign of Richard II. He was made Duke of Aquitaine by Richard (1390), and sent on several embassies to France. On his second wife's death (1394) he married his mistress, **Catherine Swynford**, by whom he had three sons; from the eldest descended Henry VII.

John de Balliol, also known as **John Balliol** (c.1250–1313) King of Scotland (1292–6), born in Barnard Castle, northern England. He was the son of John, 5th Baron de Balliol and his wife Devorgilla, daughter of Alan, Lord of Galloway. He was one of 13 'competitors' for the Scottish crown, following the death of Margaret, 'Maid of Norway', in 1290. Edward I of England became final arbiter, and arrived in Scotland together with a large army to make Scotland a feudal dependency of England. Finding Balliol amenable to swearing fealty, Edward declared him the rightful king, and took his oath of loyalty. In 1294, Edward ordered Scotland to supply soldiers for his war with France, but a council of ecclesiastics and noblemen made a defensive alliance with Philip IV of France against England. This Treaty marked the beginning of the 'Auld Alliance' between Scotland and France which was to last for nearly 300 years. In April 1296, Balliol renounced his fealty to Edward I, who immediately marched north, thus commencing the Wars of Scottish Independence. He defeated the Scots at the Battle of Dunbar in East Lothian and captured the castles of Roxburgh, Edinburgh, and Stirling. In July 1296 at Brechin Castle, Balliol was forced to surrender himself and his kingdom to Edward. Edward marched north as far as Elgin before turning south to Scone, to carry off the Stone of Destiny upon which the Scottish kings were crowned. It was taken to Westminster Abbey, where it remained for the next 700 years before being returned to Scotland in 1996. Balliol was held prisoner in the Tower of London, but in 1299 he was allowed to go to France, where he lived in exile until his death.

He struggled throughout his reign to defeat Sigurd, Earl of Orkney, who held Caithness and parts of northern Scotland, but without any lasting success. In 973 he paid homage to King Edgar of England in return for recognition that the Scots now held Lothian, which they had seized from the Angles. He broke his promise (c.994) to keep the peace, invaded England, was defeated, and lost Lothian again. He was challenged by Colin's son Constantine, who killed him in a blood feud at Fettercairn, Kincardineshire in 995, and was elected king in his place. His son became King Malcolm II.

Kenneth I, known as **Kenneth MacAlpin** (c.810–858) King of the Scots of Dal Riada (from 841), King of the Picts (from c.843), and the son of Alpin. He combined the territories of both peoples in a united kingdom of Alba (Scotland N of the Forth–Clyde line). He moved his religious centre to Dunkeld, where he transferred the remains of St Columba from the Isle of Iona. He is thought to have died of a tumour at Forteviot, and was buried on the Isle of Iona. He was succeeded by his brother Donald I.

Kenneth II, also known as **Cináed mac Maíl Coluim** (c.932–95) King of Scotland (971–95), son of Malcolm I and younger brother of Duff (Dubh) who had ruled before Colin (Cuilean). He is said to have killed Colin's brother Olaf shortly after coming to the throne to prevent him becoming a rival for the kingship, and he became sole king when he killed another brother Amlaíb in 977. Early in his reign, he ravaged the British kingdom, but lost much of his force on the River Cornag. He also attacked Eadulf, earl of the northern half of Northumbria.

Kenneth III, also known as **Cináed mac Duib** (c.950–1005) King of Scotland (997–1005), son of King Duff (Dubh), fourth cousin of the previous king, Constantine III, and first cousin of his successor Malcolm II. Kenneth was killed in battle in March 1005 at Monzievaird, Perthshire, by his kinsman Malcolm, who abolished the tanistry system (in which an heir to the throne is nominated by the king), killing all of Kenneth's male descendants. His granddaughter Gruoch was mother to one king, Lulach, and wife of another, Macbeth.

Kent, Edward (George Nicholas Paul Patrick), Duke of (1935–) British prince, the eldest son of **George, Duke of Kent**. He was commissioned in the army in 1955, and in 1961 married **Katharine Worsley** (1933–). He retired from the army in 1976. They have three children: **George Philip Nicholas Windsor, the Earl of St**

KENSINGTON AND CHELSEA

Kensington and Chelsea is a borough of Greater London, north of the River Thames. It was granted the designation 'Royal Borough' by Edward VII in 1901. It contains Kensington Palace, Kensington Gardens, and Nottingham House, the birthplace of Queen Victoria.

KENSINGTON PALACE

A royal residence in the London borough of Kensington and Chelsea, containing the London apartments of several members of the royal family. William III purchased the building in 1689, and commissioned Christopher Wren to improve it. It remained the home of successive sovereigns until the late 18th century. Parts of the palace are open to the public, including the Royal Ceremonial Dress Collection.

Andrews (1962–), **Helen Marina Lucy, Lady Helen Windsor** (1964–), and **Nicholas Charles Edward Jonathan, Lord Nicholas Windsor** (1970–). George, Earl of St Andrews, married **Sylvana Tomaselli** (1957–) and they have one son, **Edward, Lord Downpatrick** (1988–), and two daughters, **Marina Charlotte Windsor** (1992–) and **Amelia Windsor** (1995–). Lady Helen Windsor married Timothy Taylor to become Lady Helen Taylor; they have two sons, **Columbus George Donald Taylor** (1994–) and **Cassius Edward Taylor** (1996–), and two daughters, **Eloise** (2003–) and **Estella** (2004–).

Kent, George Edward Alexander Edmund, Duke of (1902–42) Son of King George V and Queen Mary. Educated at Dartmouth Naval College, he served in the foreign office and inspected factories for the home office, the first member of the British royal family to work in the civil service. In 1934 he was created duke, and married **Princess Marina of Greece and Denmark** (1906–68). He was killed on active service, as chief welfare officer of RAF Home Command, when his Sunderland flying-boat crashed in Scotland.

Kent, Prince Michael of (1942–) British prince, the younger brother of Edward, Duke of Kent. He married in 1978 **Baroness Marie-Christine Von Reibniz**, and their children are **Frederick Michael George David**

Louis, Lord Frederick Windsor
(1979–) and **Gabriella Marina
Alexandra Ophelia, Lady Gabriella
(Ella) Windsor** (1981–).

Knut, Sveinsson *see* **Canute**

Ll

Lackland, John *see* **John**

Laeghaire *see* **Lóegaire**

Lionheart, Richard the *see* **Richard I**

Llywelyn ap Gruffydd (?–1282) Prince of Gwynedd in North Wales, the son of Gruffydd ap Llywelyn and grandson of Llywelyn ap Iorwerth. In 1246 he succeeded his uncle Dafydd ap Llywelyn as ruler of Wales, in association with his brother, Owain the Red. He attempted, but ultimately failed, to enlist the support of the pope against the English crown. In 1256, having overthrown Owain, he launched a campaign to win the allegiance of other Welsh princes and by 1263 controlled much of Wales. In 1258 he proclaimed himself Prince of Wales, and was recognized by the Treaty of Shrewsbury in 1265, by which he agreed to hold the principality of Wales subject to the crown of England. When Edward I succeeded to the English throne in 1272, he was invaded and forced to submit by the Treaty of Conwy in 1277. In 1282 he rebelled against Edward, but was killed in battle near Builth, and with him Wales lost her political independence.

Llywelyn ap Iorwerth, known as **Llywelyn Fawr** ('Llywelyn the Great') (?–1240) Prince of Gwynedd in North Wales, the grandson of Owain Gwynedd. He seized power in 1194 from his uncle, Dafydd I, and soon had most of northern Wales under his control. In 1205 he married Joan, the illegitimate daughter of King John of England. Though doing homage to John's successor, Henry III, in 1218, he gained recognition of Welsh rights in the Magna Carta (1215) and extended his rule over most of Wales, but by 1223 he had to withdraw to the north. Llywelyn's generous patronage of the bardic tradition brought a flowering of Welsh literature and letters. He was a generous supporter of the Church and a zealous fighter for national unity. He was succeeded by his son, Dafydd II.

Lóegaire, also known as **Laeghaire** (c.420–c.463) High King of Ireland (c.454/6–c.463), the son of Niall Noígiallach, and the first Christian king. During his reign, Pope Celestinus I sent Palladius to propagate the faith in Ireland. The Irish port town of Dún Laoghaire in Co Dublin derives its name from him. (*see* panel p. 140, High Kingship of Ireland)

Loingsech (c.670–704) High King of Ireland (695–704), the son of Aenghus, and member of the House of Cenél Conaill (Northern Uí Néill).

HOUSES OF LANCASTER AND YORK

The House of Lancaster was descended from John of Gaunt, Duke of Lancaster, the third son of Edward III. John's son, Henry IV, usurped the throne from his cousin, Richard II, in 1399. Richard was childless, despite two marriages, but Henry was legally only fourth in line to the throne. Richard's designated successors were Roger Mortimer, Earl of March – the grandson of Edward III's second son, Lionel of Antwerp – and his brother and son, both called Edmund. They remained the alternative claimants to the throne throughout the reigns of Henry IV and his son, Henry V, until Edmund, Earl of March, died without heirs in 1425. However, in 1406, Edmund's sister Anne had married Richard, Earl of Cambridge, another grandson of Edward III. Thus the Earl of March's claim to the throne passed to the House of York in the person of Anne's son, Richard, who became the 3rd Duke of York on the death of his uncle at Agincourt in 1415. Richard was the first member of his family to give himself the surname Plantagenet.

Also descended from Edward III were the Beauforts: the children of John of Gaunt and his long-term mistress, Catherine Swynford. On their eventual marriage in 1396, the Beauforts were declared legitimate for all purposes except that of succession to the throne. John Beaufort, Earl of Somerset, was wealthy and influential, and his standing was enhanced when his daughter Joan became Queen of Scotland in 1424. Somerset's niece, Cicely Neville, the youngest daughter of the Earl of Westmoreland, married Richard, Duke of York in c.1437, and thereafter the House of York was descended from three of Edward III's sons.

On Henry V's untimely death in 1422, the throne passed to his only child, the infant Henry VI. Although the new king had several uncles, by 1447 they were all dead. The frail and sickly Henry was the only remaining male descended legitimately from

During his reign, plague and famine ravaged Ireland for three years. He was slain by Ceallach in the Battle of Corann. (*see panel* p. 140, High Kingship of Ireland)

Lud According to Geoffrey of

John of Gaunt. The Duke of York and his four vigorous sons were his undisputed heirs.

Despite the birth of a son, Edward, in 1453, things generally went badly for Henry. The French war, prosecuted with such success by his father and uncles, ended disastrously a few months before Edward's birth, with the loss of all the English possessions in France except Calais. Moreover, the king then suffered a complete physical and mental collapse. During his periods of incapacity, the Duke of York was twice appointed protector of the realm, but this merely served to arouse the hostility of the aggressive queen, Margaret of Anjou. In October 1460, York finally asserted his right to the crown, but was killed shortly afterwards at the Battle of Wakefield.

The Wars of the Roses, of which this was the beginning, were so called because the badge of the House of York was a white rose, and the badge of the House of Lancaster a red one. The Yorkists were immediately successful, the new Duke of York seizing the throne in March 1461 to become Edward IV, with the help of the powerful Richard Neville, Earl of Warwick, known to history as Warwick the Kingmaker. Edward's position was not secure, however, even though he succeeded in capturing Henry in 1465, and the queen and the Prince of Wales sought asylum in France. He lost the support of his brother George, Duke of Clarence, and alienated the Earl of Warwick, who then came to terms with Queen Margaret and her patron, Louis XI of France. Warwick, having recently married his elder daughter to the Duke of Clarence, then completed his dynastic aims by marrying his younger daughter to the Prince of Wales. An invasion in 1470 restored Henry VI, and Edward fled to Burgundy.

Edward was a resolute man, however. With the help of the Duke of Burgundy, he returned to England with an army in 1471, defeating and killing Warwick at Barnet, and then defeating and

Monmouth, a legendary king of Britain who first walled the principal city, from that time called Kaerlud after him, and eventually London. He is buried near Ludgate, which preserves his name.

Lugaid (c.460–507) High King of

capturing the queen at the battle of Tewkesbury – at which the Prince of Wales was killed, along with the last two male Beauforts. With the mysterious death of Henry in the Tower on the day Edward returned to London, the royal House of Lancaster was extinct, and Edward's hold on the throne was secure. The wealth and influence of Warwick the Kingmaker was further tied to the House of York by the marriage of the king's brother, Richard, Duke of Gloucester, to the young widow of the Prince of Wales in 1472. The last of the rebels, the unreliable Duke of Clarence, although reconciled with the king for a time, was executed in 1478.

On Edward's death in 1483, however, the apparent stability of the country dissolved almost overnight. The Duke of Gloucester imprisoned the new king, Edward V, and his brother Richard, Duke of York (immortalized in legend as the Princes in the Tower) and probably had them murdered shortly afterwards. Gloucester then usurped the throne as Richard III, declaring that Edward IV and his sons were illegitimate (a complete fabrication). The Wars of the Roses resumed, and in 1485 there was an invasion from France in the name of the House of Lancaster, headed by Henry Tudor, Duke of Richmond. His claim to the throne was tenuous in the extreme – his mother, Margaret Beaufort, was the daughter and the heiress of John, Duke of Somerset, but this family had always been excluded from the succession. However, as Henry's invasion was successful (Richard III being killed in August 1485 at Bosworth Field) the crown passed to the House of Tudor by right of conquest, and Richmond became Henry VII. To strengthen his position, he then assimilated the rights to the throne of the House of York (which were much better than his own) by marrying Edward IV's eldest daughter, Elizabeth.

The last male Plantagenet, Clarence's son Edward, Earl of Salisbury and Warwick, was beheaded on Tower Hill in 1499.

Ireland (c.482–507), the son of Lóegaire (Laeghaire). During his reign, the throne of Dal Riada was moved to Scotland. (*see panel* p. 140, High Kingship of Ireland)

Lulach, also known as **Lulach mac**

Gilla Comgain (c.1030–58) King of Scotland (1057–8), son of Gruoch (Lady Macbeth) by her first husband, Gillacomgan, *mormaer* (provincial ruler) of Moray, and the first Scottish king to be crowned at Scone. He was recognized as king for eight months, but was killed and succeeded by Malcolm Canmore. His death marked the passing of the purely Celtic kings of Scotland.

LORD CHAMBERLAIN

The Lord Chamberlain is the chief official of the royal household, overseeing all aspects of its management, and bearing responsibility for matters ranging from the care of works of art to the appointment of royal tradesmen. The office should be distinguished from the **Lord Great Chamberlain**, whose duties are largely ceremonial; in particular, at coronations, he presents the sovereign to the people.

Macbeth (c.1005–57) King of Scots (1040–57). The *mormaer* (provincial ruler) of Moray (c.1031), he became king (1040) after slaying Duncan I in battle near Elgin, and in 1050 went on a pilgrimage to Rome. He was defeated and killed by Duncan's son, Malcolm Canmore, at Lumphanan, Aberdeenshire, and was the last Scottish king to be buried on Iona. Macbeth represented the northern Scots who were opposed to the ties with the Saxons, advocated by Duncan. Shakespeare's version of events comes from the accounts of Holinshed and Boece.

MacMurrough, Dermot, also known as **Diarmaid Mac Murchada** (c.1110–71) King of Wexford and Leinster, Ireland (1126), who asserted his rule over neighbouring Waterford and Ossory in the 1130s. He ravaged the country with great cruelty, and abducted Dervorgill, wife of the Lord of Breifne (1152). In 1166 he was defeated by a combined force of chieftains. His enemy Tiernan O'Rourke formed an allegiance with the high king Rory O'Connor and the Dublin Normans to drive MacMurrough into exile in France. MacMurrough offered to become vassal to the English king, Henry II, in return for his assistance in the restoration of his kingship in Ireland. MacMurrough subsequently sought aid from Henry's Anglo-Norman vassals in England, such as Richard de Clare, Earl of Pembroke (Strongbow), recapturing Wexford in 1167. Richard de Clare in turn stormed Waterford and Dublin (1170) and was granted Wexford, Waterford and Dublin, proclaiming himself King of Leinster. He married Eva, eldest daughter of MacMurrough (1170), assuring Anglo-Norman domination of Ireland.

Máel Cobo (c.590–615) High King of Ireland (612–15), the son of Áed, and member of the House of Cenél Conaill (Northern Uí Néill). He was slain by Suibne Menn in the Battle of Sliabh Toadh. (*see panel* p. 140, High Kingship of Ireland)

Máel Sechnaill I (c.825–62) High King of Ireland (846–62), the son of Mael Ruanaid, and member of the House of Clann Cholmáin (Southern Uí Néill). He became king following his capture of the Dane Thorgest, chief of the Lochlonnaigh, at Skryne in Meath. He had numerous military successes against the Viking invaders, causing them to abandon several of their conquests. (*see panel* p. 140, High Kingship of Ireland)

Máel Sechnaill II (c.960–1022) High King of Ireland (980–1002, 1014–22), the son of Domnall ua Néill, and member of the House of Clann Cholmáin (Southern Uí Néill). He abdicated in 1002 in favour of Brian Boru, who was a more effective warrior against the Viking invaders, though he remained a military leader. He was restored to the throne in 1014 after the reign of Brian. (*see panel* p. 140, High Kingship of Ireland)

Malcolm I, also known as **Máel Coluim mac Domnaill** (c.900–54) King of Scotland (943–54), son of Donald II and successor to Constantine II, who abdicated in 943 to enter a monastery. In 945, he formed an alliance with Edmund I of England, receiving Cumbria on condition that he would defend the county and support England in the event of attack by the Vikings. This alliance remained after the death of both kings. Edmund's successor Edred enlisted Malcolm's aid against Anlaf, King of Northumberland, and in defence against Norse raids, but Malcolm sent raids to England, reuniting the northern counties with his kingdom. Returning from his crusade in 954, he found unrest in his own northerly regions. He put down an insurrection of men from Moray led by Cellach, whom he killed, but later that year he was slain at Ulurn or

MAGNA CARTA

The Magna Carta (Latin 'Great Charter') was imposed by rebellious barons on King John of England in June 1215 at Runnymede, designed to prohibit arbitrary royal acts by declaring a body of defined law and custom which the king must respect in dealing with all his free subjects. Of its 63 clauses, many of which concerned John's misuse of his financial and judicial powers, the most famous are clause 39 – 'No freeman shall be taken or imprisoned except by the lawful judgment of his equals or by the law of the land' – and clause 40 – 'To no one will we sell, to no one will we deny or delay right or justice'. The principle that kings should rule justly was of long standing, but in Magna Carta the first systematic attempt was made to distinguish between kingship and tyranny. While failing to resolve all the problems raised by the nature of the English crown's relations with the community, it endured as a symbol of the sovereignty of the rule of law, and was of fundamental importance to the constitutional development of England and other countries whose legal and governmental systems were modelled on English conventions.

Auldearn in Moray in revenge for the death of their chief. His sons Duff and Kenneth were later to succeed to the Scots throne.

Malcolm II, also known as **Máel Coluim mac Cináeda** (c.954–1034) King of Scotland (1005–34), son of Kenneth II, and first cousin to his predecessor Kenneth III. He was the last to be elected by the method of tanistry (in which an heir to the throne is nominated by the king) and the last king of the House of Alpin. He was defeated by Northumbrian forces at Durham in 1006, but when the English became preoccupied with Danish raids in 1018, he marched south, defeated the Anglo-Saxons at Carham, and regained Lothian. In 1031, King Canute invaded Scotland and forced Malcolm to pay homage, though it appears that his kingdom, including Lothian, was otherwise unaffected. He made an alliance with King Owen the Bald of Strathclyde, whilst the marriage of his daughter to the Norse Earl of Orkney, Sigurd the Stout, extended his influence northwards. His attempt to claim Strathclyde after Owen's death led to dissent and to Malcolm's death in 1034 at Glamis. His grandson Duncan succeeded to the throne as the first king of the House of Atholl.

Malcolm III, also known as **Malcolm Canmore** or **Máel Coluim mac Donnchada** (c.1031–93) King of Scotland (1058–93), eldest son of King Duncan I. He returned from exile in 1054, and conquered southern Scotland; but he did not become king until he had defeated and killed Macbeth (1057), who had killed his father in 1040, and disposed of Macbeth's stepson, Lulach (1058). He married Ingibjorg, widow of Thorfinn, Earl of Orkney, beginning the process of welding the northern islands into Scotland. He married as his second wife the English Princess Margaret (later St Margaret), sister of Edgar the Ætheling. She promoted the Roman Catholic Church in Scotland throughout Malcolm's reign. Unable to read, Malcolm substituted Saxon for Gaelic as the court language. Determined to counter foreign influence, he invaded England five times, but after three defeats he was obliged to swear subservience to William I under the Treaty of Abernethy in 1072. In 1093, he and Edward (his eldest son by Margaret) were killed in battle at Alnwick, Northumberland. Four of his sons became kings of Scotland (Duncan II, Edgar, Alexander I, and David I), whilst a fifth (Edmund) ruled as co-ruler of Scotland with his uncle Donald III. He was succeeded by his brother Donald.

Malcolm IV, also known as **Máel Coluim mac Eanric** (c.1141–65) King of Scotland (1153–65), eldest son of Henry, Earl of Huntingdon, and grandson of King David I. He met Henry II of England at Chester in 1157, where they ratified the Treaty of Chester by which Malcolm surrendered Cumberland and Westmorland in exchange for the Earldom of Huntingdon. In 1159, he went with Henry to the French wars, and was present at the siege of Toulouse. When he returned, six of his Earls, who disapproved of Malcolm's involvement in English affairs, besieged him in Perth Castle. Intervention by the clergy brought reconciliation, but Malcolm's homage to Henry in 1163 led to further rebellion. He died unmarried, without issue, and was the last Scottish monarch to have a Scottish name. He later became known as 'Malcolm the Maiden' because of a long-standing belief that his life had been strictly chaste.

Margaret, also known as **Margaret, Maid of Norway** (1283–90) Queen of Scotland (1286–90), born in Tønsberg, Norway. She was the daughter of Eric II of Norway and granddaughter of Alexander III. With no obvious heir following the death of Alexander III, she ascended to the throne at the age of three under a regency of six nobles appointed by the Scottish Parliament. Under the Treaty of Birgham in 1290, she was betrothed to Prince Edward, eldest son of Edward I of England. She set sail from Norway, but was taken ill and died soon after landing at Orkney. Her body was taken back to Norway, where she was buried beside her mother in Christ's Kirk at Bergen. In the two years that followed, Scotland was left with 13 claimants to the throne.

Margaret (of Scotland), St
(c.1046–93) Scottish queen, born in Hungary. She moved to England, but after the Norman Conquest fled to Scotland with her younger brother, Edgar the Ætheling. She married the Scottish king, Malcolm Canmore, and did much to civilize the realm, and to assimilate the old Celtic Church to the rest of Christendom. She was canonized in 1250; her feast day is 16 November or 19 June.

Margaret (Rose), Princess
(1930–2002) British princess, born at Glamis Castle, Angus, Scotland, the second daughter of George VI and sister of Elizabeth II. In 1955, when she was third in succession to the throne, she denied rumours of her possible marriage to **Group-Captain Peter Townsend** (a divorcé), amid a great deal of publicity and concern that a constitutional crisis could be precipitated by such a marriage. In 1960 she married **Antony Armstrong-Jones** (divorced, 1978), who was created Viscount Linley and Earl of Snowdon in 1961. The former title devolved upon their son, **David Albert Charles** (1961–), who married Serena Alleyne Stanhope in 1993; their children are **Charles Armstrong-Jones** (1999–) and **Margarita Armstrong-Jones** (2002–). Their daughter is **Sarah Frances Elizabeth** (1964–), who married Daniel Chatto in 1994; their children are **Samuel Chatto** (1996–) and **Arthur Chatto** (1999–).

Margaret of Anjou (1430–82) Queen consort of England, probably born in Pont-à-Mousson, France. The daughter of René of Anjou, she was married to Henry VI of England in 1445. Owing to his mental weakness she was in effect sovereign, and the war of 1449, in which Normandy was lost, was laid by the English to her charge. In the Wars of the Roses, after a brave struggle of nearly 20 years, she was finally defeated at Tewkesbury (1471), and imprisoned for four years in the Tower, until ransomed by Louis XI. She then retired to France, where she died in poverty.

Margaret Tudor (1489–1541) Queen of Scotland, born in London, the eldest daughter of Henry VII. She became the wife of James IV of Scotland (1503), and the mother of James V, for whom she acted as regent. After James IV's death in 1513 she married twice again, to the Earl of Angus (1514), and Lord Methven (1527). She was much involved in the political intrigues between the pro-French and pro-English factions in Scotland. Her great-grandson was James VI of Scotland and I of England.

Marshal, William, 1st Earl of Pembroke (and Strigul) (c.1146–1219) Knight, and regent of England (1216–19), a nephew of the Earl of Salisbury. He won a military reputation fighting the French, supported Henry II against Richard I, and went on a crusade to the Holy Land. Pardoned by Richard, he was made an earl, appointed a justiciar, and shared the marshalcy of England with his brother, **John**, until the latter's death gave him full office. He saw further fighting in Normandy (1196–9), supported the new king (John) but spent the years 1207–12 in Ireland, returning to become the king's chief adviser. After John's death in 1216, he was appointed regent for the nine-year-old Henry III, and as such concluded a peace treaty with the French.

Mary I, Tudor (1516–58) Queen of England and Ireland (1553–8), born in Greenwich, Greater London, the daughter of Henry VIII by his first wife, Catherine of Aragón. She was a devout Catholic, and during the reign of Edward, her half brother, she lived in retirement, refusing to conform to the new religion. Despite Northumberland's conspiracy to prevent her succession on Edward's death (1553), she relied on the support of the country, entered London, and ousted Lady Jane Grey. Thereafter she proceeded cautiously, repealing anti-Catholic legislation and reviving Catholic practices, but her intention was to restore papal supremacy with the assistance of Cardinal Pole, and to cement a Catholic union with Philip II of Spain. These aspirations provoked Wyatt's rebellion, followed by the execution of Jane Grey and the imprisonment of Mary's half-sister, Elizabeth, on suspicion of complicity. Mary's unpopular marriage to Philip (1554) was followed by the repeal of the antipapal laws of Henry VIII, the restoration of ecclesiastical courts and the laws against heresy (1555), and the burning at the stake of some 300 Protestants. This earned her the name of 'Bloody Mary' in Protestant hagiography, though her direct responsibility is unlikely. The persecutions of her reign were no more severe than many on the European continent, but were unprecedented in England.

Mary II (1662–94) Queen of Britain and Ireland from 1689, born in St James's Palace, London, the daughter of the Duke of York (later James II) and his first wife, **Anne Hyde** (1638–71). She was married in 1677 to her first cousin, William, Stadtholder of the United Netherlands, who in November 1688 landed in Torbay with an Anglo-Dutch army in response to an invitation from seven Whig peers hostile to the arbitrary rule of James II. When James fled to France, she came to London from Holland and was proclaimed queen, sharing the throne with her husband, who became William III. Both sovereigns accepted the constitutional revolution implicit in the Declaration of Rights. She was content to leave executive authority with William (except when he was abroad or campaigning in Ireland), but she was largely responsible for raising the moral standard of court life, and enjoyed a popularity which her husband never attained. She died of smallpox, and left no children.

Mary, Queen of Scots (1542–87) Mary was the daughter and only child of James V of Scotland by his second wife, a Frenchwoman called Mary of Guise. While James lay on his death-bed at Falkland, Mary was born at Linlithgow Palace, West Lothian, Scotland. She became queen upon his death when she was a week old, and Henry VIII attempted to betrothe her to his son, Prince Edward of England, in order to establish control of her and Scotland. The betrothal was annulled by the Scottish parliament, precipitating war with England. After the Scots' defeat at Pinkie (1547) she was sent by her mother to France. There she was brought up at the glittering French court of Henry II, where she

excelled at hunting and dancing, and was carefully educated in the manner of a Frenchwoman. She married the Dauphin (1558), later Francis II, but was widowed at 18 (1560), and became the dowager Queen of France with her own estates and a substantial income.

Her presence was increasingly called for in Scotland, where the death of her mother (1560) had left the country in a highly fluid and dangerous political state. Effective power was in the hands of the Protestant Lords of the Congregation, who had held an illegal parliament to implement the Reformation and ban the authority of the pope. Mary therefore returned to Scotland in 1561. A Protestant riot threatened the first mass held in her private chapel at Holyrood, and a religious standstill was imposed, which in effect banned the mass to all but the queen and her household.

Ambitious for the English throne, in 1565 she married her cousin, Henry Stuart, Lord Darnley, a grandson of Margaret Tudor. However, disgusted by his debauchery, she soon became alienated from him. The vicious murder, in her presence, of Rizzio, her Italian secretary, by Darnley and a group of Protestant nobles (March 1566), confirmed her insecurity. The birth of a son (June 1566), the future James VI, failed to reconcile her to Darnley. While ill with smallpox, Darnley was mysteriously killed in an explosion at Kirk o' Field (1567). The chief suspect was the Earl of Bothwell, who underwent a mock trial and was acquitted. Mary's involvement is unclear, but shortly afterwards she was carried off by Bothwell, who had divorced the wife he had only recently married. Mary publicly pardoned his seizure of her person, created him Duke of Orkney, and three months after her husband's death married the man most people regarded as his murderer.

This fatal step united her nobles in arms against her. Her army melted away without striking a blow on the field of Carberry, and nothing was left to her but surrender to the confederate lords. She was constrained at Loch Leven by a minority of the most radical of the Protestant nobles under Morton, and made to sign an act of abdication in favour of her son who, five days afterwards, was crowned as James VI. After escaping, she raised an army, but was defeated again by the confederate lords at Langside (1568). Placing herself under the protection of Queen Elizabeth, she found herself instead in an English prison. She would remain Elizabeth's prisoner for the rest of her life.

The presence of Mary in England was a constant source of unease to Elizabeth and her advisers. She had a claim to the English throne through Darnley, and a large Catholic minority naturally looked to Mary as the likely restorer of the old faith. Yet her position as guest or prisoner was always ambiguous. Plot followed plot in England, though after that of Ridolfi (1571), few if any posed any real threat. The last, by Anthony Babington in 1586, was known to Walsingham's agents from the outset. Letters from Mary seemingly approving Elizabeth's death passed along a postal route which went via Walsingham, who opened them himself. Mainly on the evidence of copies of these letters, Mary was brought to trial in 1586. Early in 1587 Elizabeth signed her death warrant, and she was executed at Fotheringay Castle. Buried at Peterborough, in 1612 her body was moved to Henry VII's chapel at Westminster, where it still lies.

Mary's beauty and personal accomplishments have never been disputed. She spoke or read in six languages, sang well, played various musical instruments, and had a library which included the largest collection of Italian and French poetry in Scotland. The portrayals of her after 1571 largely fall into one of two types: Catholic martyr or papist plotter, making all the more difficult a proper assessment of Mary as Queen of Scots.

Mary of Modena, *née* **Maria Beatrice d'Este** (1658–1718) Queen consort of Britain and Ireland (1685–88), the second wife of James II. The only daughter of Alfonso IV, Duke of Modena, she married James in 1673 when he was Duke of York. They lost five daughters and a son in infancy, but in 1688 she gave birth to James Francis Edward Stuart (the future 'Old Pretender'). When William of Orange (the future William III) landed in England later that year, she escaped to France with her infant son, to be joined there later by her deposed husband. She spent the rest of her life at St Germain.

Mary of Teck, in full **Victoria Mary Augusta Louise Olga Pauline Claudine Agnes** (1867–1953) Queen consort of Great Britain, the wife of George V, born in Kensington Palace, London, the only daughter of Francis, Duke of Teck, and Princess Mary Adelaide of Cambridge, a granddaughter of George III. In 1891 she accepted a marriage proposal from the Duke of Clarence, who within six weeks died from pneumonia. She then married his brother, the Duke of York, in 1893. After his accession (as George V) in 1910, she accompanied him to Delhi as Empress of India for the historically unique Coronation Durbar of December 1911. Although by nature stiff and reserved, she was more sympathetic to changing habits than her husband, whom she helped to mould into a 'people's king'. After the abdication of her eldest son, Edward VIII, she once again strengthened the popular appeal of the monarchy throughout the reign of her second son, George VI, whom she survived by 13 months.

Mary Tudor (1495/6–1533) Royal princess, the daughter of Henry VII. She was betrothed to Archduke Charles of Austria in 1507, but when her brother, Henry VIII, succeeded to the throne he renounced the match, and arranged her marriage with Louis XII of France (1514). Following Louis' death (1515), Mary secretly married Charles Brandon, Duke of Suffolk, with whom she had been in love for several years. One of their daughters became the mother of Lady Jane Grey, who was titular Queen of England for nine days (1553).

Matilda of Flanders (c.1031–83) Queen consort of William I of England, born in Flanders, France. She married William in 1050 in Normandy, and during his absences in England the Duchy of Normandy was under her regency, with the aid of their son, Robert Curthose. The embroidery of the Bayeux Tapestry was once wrongly attributed to her.

Moray, James Stuart, Earl of (1531–70) Regent of Scotland (1567–70), the illegitimate son of James V of Scotland by a daughter of the Earl of Mar, and half-brother of Mary, Queen

MAUNDY THURSDAY

Maundy Thursday is the Thursday before Easter, so called from Latin *mandatum*, 'commandment', the first word of the anthem traditionally sung on that day. In memory of Christ's washing his disciples' feet (*John* 13.4–10), it was once the custom for monarchs to wash the feet of poor people on Maundy Thursday. Special money (*Maundy money*) is given by the sovereign to the same number of elderly poor people as there are years in the sovereign's age.

MUSIC AT THE CORONATION

The following music was played at the Coronation of Her Majesty
Queen Elizabeth II in 1953.

- 'Trumpet Tune' ~ Henry Purcell
- 'I Was Glad' (anthem for chorus and organ) ~ Charles H. H.
  Parry
- 'Behold, O God Our Defender' (for chorus) ~ Herbert Howells
- 'Let My Prayer Come Up' ~ William H Harris
- Coronation Anthem No.1 'Zadok the Priest' (for chorus and
  orchestra) ~ George Frederic Handel
- 'Be Strong and of Good Courage' (confortare) ~ George Dyson
- 'Rejoice in the Lord Always' (for chorus) ~ Anonymous
- 'Thou Wilt Keep Him in Perfect Peace' (for chorus and organ)
  ~ Samuel Sebastian Wesley
- 'All People That on Earth Do Dwell' ~ Ralph Vaughan
  Williams
- Communion Service in G: Sanctus Sanctus ~ Ralph Vaughan
  Williams
- 'O Taste and See', Psalm 34 (motet for chorus and organ ad lib)
  ~ Ralph Vaughan Williams
- 'Gloria in Excelsis' ~ Charles Villiers Stanford
- Coronation Te Deum (for chorus and orchestra) ~ William
  Walton
- Fanfare ~ Anonymous
- 'God Save the Queen', British National Anthem ~ arr. Gordon
  Jacob
- 'Orb and Sceptre', Coronation march (for orchestra) ~ William
  Walton
- 'Crown Imperial', Coronation march (for orchestra) ~ William
  Walton
- Fanfares ~ Sir Ernest Bullock
- Nicene Creed (Mass in G minor) ~ Ralph Vaughan Williams
- 'O Lord, Our Governor' ~ Healy Willan
- 'Threefold Amen' ~ Orlando Gibbons
- 'Veni, Creator Spiritus' ~ arr. Sir Ernest Bullock

of Scots. He acted as Mary's chief adviser (1560), but supported the Protestant John Knox and opposed Mary's marriage to Darnley. After an attempted coup, he was outlawed and took refuge in England (1565). Pardoned the following year, he became regent for Mary's baby son, James VI, when she abdicated (1567), and defeated her army at Langside (1568). His Protestant and pro-English policies alienated some Scots nobles, and he was killed at Linlithgow by one of Mary's supporters.

Morton, James Douglas, 4th Earl of (c.1516–81) Regent of Scotland (1572–8) for James VI. Although a Protestant, he was made Lord High Chancellor by Mary Stuart (1563); yet he was involved in the murders of Rizzio (1566) and Darnley (1567), and played an important part in the overthrow of the queen. He joined the hostile noble confederacy, leading its forces at Carberry Hill and Langside, and succeeded the Earl of Mar as regent. However, his high-handed treatment of the nobles and Presbyterian clergy caused his downfall (1581). He was arraigned for his part in Darnley's murder, and executed at Edinburgh.

Muirchertach (c.480–c.536) High King of Ireland (507–34/6), the son of Muireadhach, and member of the House of Cenél nEógain (Northern Uí Néill). He married Duinseach, daughter of Duach Teangabha, King of Connacht. (*see panel* p. 140, High Kingship of Ireland)

Muirchertach mac Lochlainn (c.1110–66) High King of Ireland (1156–66), the son of Niall, and member of the House of Cenél nEógain (Northern Uí Néill). (*see panel* p. 140, High Kingship of Ireland)

Muirchertach ua Briain (c.1060–1121) King of Munster (1083–1121), High King of Ireland (1086–1119), and the son of Toirrdelbach ua Briain. After resigning his kingdom through ill-health, it was taken unlawfully by Diarmaid, but Muirchertach took him prisoner and assumed his kingdom again. His lifelong conflict with Domnall mac Lochlainn remained undecided at the close of their lives. (*see panel* p. 140, High Kingship of Ireland)

Niall Caille (c.810–46) High King of Ireland (833–46), the son of Áed Oirdnide, and member of the House of Cenél nEógain (Northern Uí Néill). It was during his reign that the Norse took and fortified Dublin. (*see panel* p. 140, High Kingship of Ireland)

Niall Frossach, known as **Niall of the Showers** (c.740–78) High King of Ireland (763–70), the son of Fearghal, and member of the House of Cenél nEógain (Northern Uí Néill). After reigning seven years, he retired to a monastery in Scotland and is thought to have died while on pilgrimage at I Coluim Cille. One of several stories explaining his byname refers to three showers (of silver, honey, and wheat) said to have fallen in different places in Ireland after praying for relief from a famine. (*see panel* p. 140, High Kingship of Ireland)

Niall Glúndub (c.895–919) High King of Ireland (916–19), the son of Áed Findliath, and member of the House of Cenél nEógain (Northern Uí Néill). His grandfather was Kenneth MacAlpin, King of the Scots (841–58). He had many successful battles with the Danes but was slain by them, along with many nobles from the northern part of Ireland, in the Battle of Athcliath (Dublin). (*see panel* p. 140, High Kingship of Ireland)

Niall Noígiallach, Niall of the Nine Hostages (fl.5th-c) King of Tara (?–453?), the son of Eochaidh Muighmheadhoin, and usually recognized as the first High King of Ireland. He led an expedition into Alba to protect Irish settlers from Pictish oppression. He crushed and obtained allegiance from the Picts, raided Britain, and with Saxon support was instrumental in forcing the withdrawal of Roman forces from Britain. His name referred to his taking of hostages from nine kingdoms (Munster, Leinster, Connacht, Ulster, Meath, Dal Riada, Caledonia, Strathclyde and Northumbria). (*see panel* p. 140, High Kingship of Ireland)

HOUSE OF NORMANDY

The Norman kings were descended from the Viking leader Hrolfr – Rollo, in French – who acquired the lands of Normandy in 911. William I was a sixth-generation descendant of Rollo. Such succession laws as existed in the 11th century laid down that the lands a man inherited from his father should be passed on to his eldest son, while property he had obtained in other ways could be left as he wished. Accordingly, on William's death, the Duchy of Normandy was inherited by the eldest son, Robert Curthose, and the throne of England by his favourite son, William II. Henry I had theoretically no right to the throne at all (having been excluded from the succession in 1089), but secured election by the barons as soon as he heard of William II's death, taking advantage of the fact that Robert Curthose was absent on a Crusade at the time. He then seized Normandy from Robert in 1106. Henry's marriage strengthened his claim to the throne: his wife, the daughter of St Margaret, was the niece of Edgar the Ætheling, the legitimate Saxon heir of Edward the Confessor. In 1120, the heir to the throne, William, died in a shipwreck, precipitating a succession crisis. Henry recognized as heir his only surviving legitimate child, the Empress Matilda. In 1128, her first husband having died, she married Geoffrey Plantagenet, the 14-year-old son of the Count of Anjou. However, in the last year of his life, Henry quarrelled with Matilda and Geoffrey, causing those barons who were loyal to him to oppose Matilda as heir. When Henry died in 1135, this situation helped his nephew Stephen to seize the throne, causing a civil war. The war continued inconclusively until Stephen's heir Eustace died in 1153. His second son, William, had never expected to be king, and a settlement was arranged in which Stephen was to retain the throne during his lifetime, while recognizing Matilda's son, Henry, as his heir (as Henry II). Thus, when Stephen died the following year, the throne passed to the House of Plantagenet.

O'Connor, Rory or **Roderick (Ruaidhrí ua Conchobair)** (c.1116–98) The last High King of Ireland (1166–86) and King of Connaught (1156–86). The son of Toirrdelbach ua Conchobair (1088–1156), he vanquished the land of Teffia, but suffered reverses at Athlone and Ardee (1159). Taking advantage of the weakness of the north, he went to Dublin and was inaugurated High King of all Ireland (1166). He made an annual endowment of 10 cows for teaching poor scholars. He called two important assemblies in 1167 and 1168 to adopt laws and determine justice. His ascendancy was brief, however, for his rivalry with Dermot MacMurrough persuaded the latter to call Richard de Clare (Strongbow) and his Anglo-Norman forces to his aid (1171). They defeated O'Connor and routed Dublin; when Henry II reasserted his authority over his vassals in 1172, O'Connor and the remaining Irish chiefs were forced by the Treaty of Windsor (1175) to acknowledge Henry as king and accept the infiltration of the English into Ireland. O'Connor remained King of Connaught and nominal high king, but his power declined and he retired to a monastery before his death. (*see panel p. 140, High Kingship of Ireland*)

Odo (c.1036–97) Anglo-Norman clergyman, Bishop of Bayeux, and half-brother of William I. He fought at the Battle of Hastings (1066) and was created Earl of Kent. He played a conspicuous part under William in English history, and was regent during his absences in Normandy, but left England after rebelling against William II. He rebuilt Bayeux Cathedral, and may have commissioned the Bayeux Tapestry.

Offa (?–796) King of Mercia (757–96).

ORDER IN COUNCIL

An Order in Council is legislation made by the Monarch in Council allowed by Act of Parliament, but which does not need to be ratified by parliament. It is the main means through which the powers of the royal prerogative are exercised. In practice the decisions are taken by government ministers, not by the monarch.

He was the greatest Anglo-Saxon ruler in the 8th century, treated as an equal by Charlemagne. He asserted his authority over all the kingdoms south of the Humber, and regarded their rulers as subordinate provincial governors. He was responsible for constructing Offa's Dyke, stretching for 70 miles along the Welsh border, and established a new currency based on the silver penny which, with numerous changes of design, remained the standard coin of England for many centuries. His reign represents an important but flawed attempt to unify England, with the Mercian supremacy collapsing soon after his death.

Oswald, St (c.605–42) Anglo-Saxon King of Northumbria (633–41), the son of Ethelfrith of Bernicia. Having been converted at Iona, he established Christianity in Northumbria with St Aidan's help. He fell in battle with the pagan King Penda. His feast day is 5 August.

Owain Glyndwr, **Owen Glendower** *see* **Glendower, Owen**

Parr, Catherine (1512–48) Sixth wife of Henry VIII, the daughter of Sir Thomas Parr of Kendal. She married first Edward Borough, secondly Lord Latimer, and in 1543 became Queen of England by marrying Henry VIII. A learned, tolerant, and tactful woman, she persuaded Henry to restore the succession to his daughters, Mary I and Elizabeth, and showed her stepchildren much kindness. Very soon after Henry's death (1547) she married a former suitor, Lord Thomas Seymour of Sudeley, but died in childbirth the following year.

Penda (c.575–655) King of Mercia (c.632–55). He established mastery over the English Midlands, and was frequently at war with the kings of Northumbria. His forces defeated and killed Edwin at Hatfield in Yorkshire (633), and also Edwin's successor, Oswald, when he invaded Penda's territories (642); but Penda was himself slain in battle near Leeds while campaigning against Oswald's successor, Oswiu.

Philippa of Hainault (c.1314–1369) Queen consort of England, who married her second cousin Edward III at York in 1327. She brought Flemish weavers to England, encouraged coalmining, and made the French poet and historian Jean Froissart her secretary. She is said to have roused the English troops before the defeat of the Scots at the Battle of Neville's Cross in 1346, and to have interceded with Edward for mercy for the burgesses of Calais after the long siege in 1347. Queen's College, Oxford, founded by Philippa's chaplain in 1341, was named after her.

Phillips, Mark, Captain (1948–) Former husband of Princess Anne, and a noted horseman. He trained at Sandhurst Military Academy, and joined the Queen's Dragoon Guards in 1969. In 1973 he married Princess Anne (now the Princess Royal), but was divorced from her in 1992. He was a regular member of the British equestrian team (1970–6), and won many team events, including the gold medal at the Olympic Games in Munich in 1972.

HOUSE OF PLANTAGENET

The House of Plantagenet acquired its name from the family badge of Geoffrey, Count of Anjou – a sprig of broom (in Old French, 'plante genet'). Geoffrey married Matilda, the only surviving legitimate child of Henry I of England. Their son, Henry II, succeeded his mother's cousin, Stephen, as King of England in 1154. Besides his father's lands of Anjou, Poitou, and Maine, Henry had also acquired vast territories in south-west France on his marriage to Eleanor of Aquitaine. Becoming King of England made him the wealthiest ruler in Europe, but the heartland of his empire was in France, not in England, and he spent two-thirds of his reign there.

Henry's reign is most notable for the conquest of Ireland (1169–72), and for his part in the murder of Thomas à Becket, Archbishop of Canterbury. In 1164 Becket was exiled as a result of a quarrel with the king over the extent to which priests who committed crimes should be subject to royal justice. On his return to England in 1170, he was murdered in Canterbury Cathedral by four knights, who thought they were carrying out the king's wishes. This act of sacrilege provoked universal outrage, and Henry had to perform an elaborate act of penance, but Becket's death had no lasting effect on Henry's international status. More damage was done by his disagreements with his sons. Their insurrection was encouraged by Philip II of France, who hoped in this way to acquire some of the Plantagenet lands for himself. When Henry died, he had been defeated by a coalition of Philip and his own son Richard.

Richard I, the Lionheart, spent less than a year of his 10-year reign in England. In 1189–92 he was away on Crusade with King Philip. On his way home he was captured and handed over to the Holy Roman Emperor (Henry VI), who kept him in prison for over a year, during which time Philip, back in France, managed to overrun most of Normandy. Richard was released in 1194, and spent most of the next five years recovering his lost territories. He was killed by an arrow at the siege of Châlus-Chabrol in 1199, leaving no legitimate children.

King John initially inherited only part of Richard's domains, many barons in the French territories opting to support Prince Arthur, the son of John's elder brother, Geoffrey. John managed to oust Arthur, and probably had him murdered in 1203. However, John made enemies of many important French barons, and gave Philippe of France the opportunity to confiscate all his French territories, of which he was legally the feudal superior. John was unable to organize an effective defence, and Philippe overran almost all the Plantagenet lands in France.

In 1205 John fell out with Pope Innocent III over the election of the Archbishop of Canterbury. Although the quarrel was resolved in 1213, England was placed under an interdict, all church services being suspended during 1208–13, and John himself was excommunicated, which put him in a vulnerable position by denying him the support of the Church against rebels and invaders. In 1215 the discontented barons induced John to sign the Magna Carta, conceding sovereignty of the rule of law over the king's whim. John had no intention of implementing Magna Carta, however, and the barons finally invited King Louis VII of France to seize the throne. When John died in 1216, England was embroiled in civil war.

The Council of Regency which governed in the name of the new king, John's nine-year-old son, Henry III, soon ended the war. Henry failed to regain any of the Plantagenet lands in France, and by 1259 his only foreign possession was Gascony, which he held as a fief of the King of France. As his father had done, Henry came into conflict with his most powerful barons, who disliked Henry's preference for non-English favourites. The quarrel resulted in war in 1264. The barons, under Simon de Montfort, won the Battle of Lewes, but Simon was killed the following year at Evesham, and the rebellion fizzled out.

Edward I was on his way back from the Crusades when his father died, and did not return until 1274. He was a warlike king, who spent most of his life on campaigns. During 1276–84 he was mainly occupied in the conquest of Wales, which was finally achieved in 1283 after the death of the Prince of Wales, Llywelyn ap Gruffydd. Edward then turned his attention to Scotland, where a succession crisis had arisen following the death of Alexander III in 1286. Edward managed to put his protégé, John Balliol, on the Scottish throne (*see* Competitors for the Crown of Scotland, p. 19), but failed to be generally accepted as overlord of Scotland. His efforts in this direction, which earned him the nickname Hammer of the Scots, initiated a succession of Anglo-Scottish wars lasting for more than 200 years. Edward died during a campaign against the Scots in 1307.

Edward II was forced to abandon his father's unfinished war with Scotland after being defeated at Bannockburn in 1314. He was a stubborn man, who was determined not to give in to the attempts of the barons to limit his freedom of action, especially after the murder in 1312 of his favourite, Piers de Gaveston. Civil war was again the result, and eventually, with the connivance of his son, his wife, and her lover, Roger Mortimer, Edward was forced to abdicate in 1327. He was murdered shortly afterwards at Berkeley Castle.

Edward III was a much more tactful and pragmatic ruler than his father, and managed to secure the goodwill of both parliament and the nobility. This enabled him to concentrate on attempting to regain his family's lost lands in France, beginning the conflict known as the Hundred Years War. Edward had some successes, notably at Crécy (1346) and Poitiers (1356), and achieved most of his aims by the Treaty of Brétigny (1360), but later in his reign all his gains were reversed. In 1349 the Black Death reached England, interrupting war plans and killing about a third of the population. As the king lapsed gradually into senility towards the end of his reign, the later stages of the war were conducted by Edward, Prince of Wales, known from the colour of his armour as the Black Prince, but he died in 1376, leaving his 10-year-old only son, Richard, to succeed to his grandfather's throne.

Richard II gained a good deal of prestige at the beginning of his reign by his courageous handling of the Peasants' Revolt at the age of 14, but it was soon dissipated. Like many of the Plantagenets, he was obstinate and tyrannical, and his indulgence of his favourites and contemptuous treatment of those he disliked led to insurrection and humiliating defeat. He managed to recover his position temporarily, but had made so many enemies that his first cousin, Henry Bolingbroke, Duke of Lancaster (the son of Edward III's third son, John of Gaunt) was able to take advantage of his absence in Ireland in 1399 to seize the throne. Richard, who was childless, was imprisoned in Pontefract Castle and died there in suspicious circumstances the following year.

PRINCE OF WALES

In the UK, the title conferred (by custom, not law) on the sovereign's eldest son. Wales was ruled by a succession of independent princes from the 5th century; the first to be acknowledged by an English king was Llywelyn ap Gruffydd (r.1246–82) in 1267. Tradition holds that after the death of Llywelyn in battle (against the English) and the execution of his brother, Edward I presented his own infant son to the Welsh people at Caernarfon Castle as their prince. The title has been used since that time.

English and British Princes of Wales

- 1958– Charles Philip Arthur George, son of Elizabeth II
- 1910–36 Edward (Edward VIII)
- 1901–10 George (George V)
- 1841–1901 Albert Edward (Edward VII)
- 1762–1820 George (George IV)
- 1751–60 George (George III)
- 1729–51 Frederick Louis, son of George II
- 1714–27 George (George II)
- 1688 James Francis Edward Stewart 'the Old Pretender', son of James II (*styled, but never created*)
- 1638–60 Charles (Charles II) (*styled, but never created*)
- 1616–25 Charles (Charles I)
- 1610–12 Henry, son of James I
- 1504–9 Henry (Henry VIII)
- 1489–1504 Arthur, son of Henry VII
- 1471–83 Edward (Edward V)
- 1454–71 Edward of Westminster, son of Henry VI
- 1399–1413 Henry of Monmouth (Henry V)
- 1376–7 Richard (Richard II)
- 1343–76 Edward 'the Black Prince', son of Edward III
- 1301–7 Edward (Edward II of England)

PRINCESS ROYAL

The Princess Royal is a title sometimes bestowed on the eldest, or only, daughter of a sovereign. George V's daughter Mary was Princess Royal until her death in 1965, and the title was conferred by the Queen on Princess Anne in 1987.

PRIVY COUNCIL

The Privy Council is a body which advises the British monarch, appointed by the crown. In previous times, particularly the Tudor period, it was a highly influential group, and might be regarded as the precursor of the cabinet. Today its role is largely formal, enacting subordinate legislation (proclamations and Orders in Council). Its membership is over 300, but the quorum is three.

PROTECTORATE

The Protectorate was a regime established by the Instrument of Government, the work of army conservatives, England's only written constitution. The Lord Protectors, Oliver Cromwell (ruled 1653–8) and his son Richard (ruled 1658–9), issued ordinances and controlled the armed forces, subject to the advice of a Council of State and with Parliament as legislative partner. It failed to win support, and its collapse led to the Restoration.

QUEEN ELIZABETH II'S CORONATION MEDAL

The coronation medal is a circular silver medal instituted on 2 June 1953; it has a dark red ribbon with two narrow dark blue stripes in the centre and narrow white stripes at each edge. A total of 138,214 medals was made, awarded to members of the armed forces. The obverse shows Queen Elizabeth II facing right, in a high-collared ermine cloak, wearing the collar of the Garter and badge of the Bath; there is no legend. The reverse shows the Royal Cypher EIIR surmounted by a large crown. The legend around the edge reads: ·QUEEN·ELIZABETH·II·CROWNED·2nd·JUNE·1953.

Rhodri Mawr, also known as **Rhodri the Great** (820–78) King of the Welsh, son of Merfyn Frych, and the first king to unite most of Wales. He became King of Gwynedd in 844, of Powys in 855, and of Seisyllwg (including Ceredigion and Ystrad Tywi) in 872. He prevented the Danes and the English from settling his territories, showing that Wales could exist independently of English rule, and his victory over the Vikings in 856 won him the epithet Mawr. He and his son, Gwriad, died in battle in 878 against the English of Mercia.

Rhys ap Gruffudd, also known as **The Lord Rhys** (1132–97) King of the Welsh (1155–97), grandson of Rhys ap

Tewdwr. He was the last of the rulers of Deheubarth to establish a wide degree of power, particularly at the expense of the Norman marcher lords, some of whom left to join the Norman invasion of Ireland. He assisted Richard, Earl of Pembroke, to take the throne of Leinster, thereby upsetting Henry II, who wanted Ireland for himself. When Henry II became King of England in 1154, Rhys was persuaded to submit, losing most of the land he had previously gained when Ceredigion and Cantref Bychan were restored to their Norman lords. He failed to take Carmarthen in 1159, but victory at Llandovery in 1162 and other successes made Henry realize the need to have Rhys as an ally, and Henry appointed him the 'justiciar' of S Wales in 1171. In 1176 Rhys held a cultural event at Cardigan Castle, which is considered to be the first recorded example of an eisteddfod. His last years were clouded by disputes among his sons, which destroyed Deheubarth after his death.

Rich, Edmund *see* **Edmund, St**

Richard I, known as **Richard Coeur de Lion** or **Richard the Lionheart**

REGENT

The regent is a person appointed to act for the monarch if he/she is incapacitated, unavailable, or under 18. In the UK, it is customary for the next heir to the throne to be regent: from 1811 to 1820 the Prince of Wales (later George IV) acted as regent because of the supposed insanity of his father, George III.

RESTORATION

The Restoration refers to the return of Charles II to England (June 1660) at the request of the Convention Parliament, following the collapse of the Protectorate regime; but many royal prerogative powers and institutions were not restored. The bishops and the Church of England returned, but parliament took the lead in passing the Clarendon Code (1661–5) outlawing dissent from the Book of Common Prayer (1662). The severe religious controls stood in sharp contrast to a new ribaldry in public life and at court, where 'gallantry' was a euphemism for sexual intrigue. However, theatres, which had been banned by the Puritans, staged a revival with a new form of social comedy of manners characterized by glittering, cynical, licentious, and extravagant language and plot. Women's roles, until then played by boys, were taken by actresses, the most notable among them being Nell Gwynne of the King's Company of Players. A more opulent style of dress, interior decoration, furniture, and textiles became fashionable, caricatured by contemporary engravers such as William Hogarth.

(1157–99) King of England (1189–99), born in Oxford, Oxfordshire, the third son of Henry II and Eleanor of Aquitaine. Of his 10-year reign, he spent less than a year in England, devoting himself to crusading and defending the Angevin lands in France. Already recognized as an outstanding soldier, he took Messina (1190), Cyprus, and Acre (1191) during the Third Crusade, and advanced to within sight of Jerusalem. On the return journey, he was arrested in Vienna (1192), and remained a prisoner of the German Emperor Henry VI until he agreed to be ransomed (1194). The rest of his reign was occupied in warfare against Philip II of France, while the government of England was conducted by the justiciar, Hubert Walter. Richard was mortally wounded while besieging the castle of Châlus, Aquitaine.

Richard II (1367–1400) King of England (1377–99), born in Bordeaux, France, the younger son of Edward the Black Prince, who succeeded his grandfather, Edward III, at the age of 10. He displayed great bravery in confronting the rebels in London during the Peasants' Revolt (1381); but already parliament was concerned about his favourites, and the reign was dominated by the struggle between Richard's desire to act independently, and the magnates'

concern to curb his power. He quarrelled with his uncle, John of Gaunt,
and his main supporters were found
guilty of treason in the 'Merciless
Parliament' of 1388. After Richard had
declared an end to his minority (1389),
he built up a stronger following, and
during 1397–8 took his revenge by
having the Earl of Arundel executed,
the Duke of Gloucester murdered, and
several lords banished, the exiles
including Gaunt's son, Henry
Bolingbroke (later Henry IV). His final
act of oppression was to confiscate the
Lancastrian estates after Gaunt's death
(1399). Having failed to restrain the
king by constitutional means, the
magnates resolved to unseat him from
the throne. Bolingbroke invaded
England unopposed, and Richard was
deposed in his favour (September
1399). He died in Pontefract Castle,
Yorkshire, possibly of starvation.

Richard III (1452–85) King of England
(1483–5), born in Fotheringay Castle,
Northamptonshire, the youngest son
of Richard, Duke of York. He was
created Duke of Gloucester by his
brother, Edward IV, in 1461, accompanied him into exile (1470), and
played a key role in his restoration
(1471). Rewarded with part of the
Neville inheritance, he exercised vice-
regal powers in northern England, and
in 1482 recaptured Berwick-upon-
Tweed from the Scots. When Edward
died (1483) and was succeeded by his
underage son, Edward V, Richard
acted first as protector, but within
three months, he had overthrown the
Woodvilles (relations of Edward IV's
queen), seen to the execution of Lord

Hastings (c.1430–83), and had himself
proclaimed and crowned as the rightful king. Young Edward and his
brother were probably murdered in
the Tower on Richard's orders (though
not all historians agree). He tried to
stabilize his position, but failed to win
broad-based support. His rival, Henry
Tudor (later Henry VII), confronted
him in battle at Bosworth Field, and
Richard died fighting bravely against
heavy odds. Though ruthless, he was
not the absolute monster Tudor historians portrayed him to be, nor is
there proof he was a hunchback.

Richmond, Henry Tudor, Duke of
see **Henry VII**

Robert I *see* **Bruce, Robert**

Robert II (1316–90) King of Scots
(1371–90), the son of Walter, hereditary
steward of Scotland. He acted as sole
regent during the exile and captivity of
David II. On David's death, he became
king in right of his descent from his
maternal grandfather, Robert I, and
founded the Stuart royal dynasty.

Robert III (c.1337–1406) King of
Scotland (1390–1406), eldest son of
King Robert II. He was created Earl of
Carrick by his great-uncle King David
II in 1368. A horse's kick in 1388
disabled him, and his father considered him unfit to govern on his
behalf, preferring his brother Robert,
Earl of Fife, later Duke of Albany. He
did succeed to the throne upon his
father's death, changing his
baptismal name from John, owing to
its defeatist associations with John de

Balliol, but the real power remained in the hands of his brother. In 1399 the Scottish parliament condemned his misrule, and appointed his elder son David, Duke of Rothesay, to govern for him, but David was imprisoned by Albany and died in 1402. In 1406, fearing for the lives of himself and his son James, Robert sheltered at Rothesay Castle and arranged for James to be smuggled to France. However, James was captured by the English, whereupon Robert died, probably from grief. He was buried at Paisley, as he did not consider himself worthy enough to be buried at Scone, the traditional burial ground of the Scottish kings.

Robert, Duke of Normandy *see* **Henry I**

ROYAL ASSENT

The royal assent is a legal stage through which a bill has to pass in the UK before it becomes law. Because the legislature in the UK is the Monarch-in-Parliament, after a bill has passed through both Houses of Parliament, the monarch's assent is required in order that it may become law. This approval is a formality; it has never been withheld in modern times.

ROYAL COMMISSION

The Royal Commission is a body appointed by the sovereign on the prime minister's recommendation to investigate and report on the operation of laws which it is proposed to change. It may also deal with social, educational, or other matters about which the government wishes to make general, long-term policy decisions.

ROYAL PREROGATIVE

The royal prerogative refers to the set of powers, most of which are ill-defined, remaining within the preserve of the British monarch. These include the power to declare war, make treaties, appoint judges, pardon criminals and, most significantly, dissolve Parliament. In practice all these powers are taken on the advice of, and in effect made by, the prime minister and other government ministers.

ROYAL RESIDENCES

Royal residences are the palaces and houses used by the sovereign and the royal family. *Occupied Royal Residences* are those which are being held in trust for future generations. They enable the sovereign to fulfil the function of head of state, and are used for ceremonial and official occasions, as well as being a major visitor attraction (some 1.7 million visitors each year). *Private Estates* are those which the sovereign has inherited from earlier members of the royal family.

The Tower of London and the Palace of Westminster were the main residences of English monarchs from Edward the Confessor to Henry VIII. Henry then acquired the Palace of Whitehall; Inigo Jones' Banqueting Hall is the only part surviving today. Later residences include Hampton Court Palace, Greenwich Palace, St James's Palace, and Kensington Palace. George III acquired Buckingham House in 1762. It became the sovereign's official London residence during the reign of Queen Victoria.

Albert, Prince of (1844–1900) Second son of Queen Victoria, born at Windsor Castle, Windsor. He studied at Bonn and Edinburgh before entering the Royal Navy in 1858. In 1866 he was created Duke of Edinburgh, and in 1874 married the Russian **Grand Duchess Marie Alexandrovna** (1853–1920). In 1893 he succeeded his uncle as reigning Duke of Saxe-Coburg-Gotha.

Saxe-Coburg-Gotha, Alfred Ernest

Sechnussach (c.640–71) High King of Ireland (665/6–71), the son of

ST JAMES'S PALACE

St James's Palace is the senior palace of the British sovereign, and the home of several members of the royal family. Built mainly between 1531 and 1536 for Henry VIII, only parts of the original palace remain (notably the red-brick gatehouse and the chapel royal), and much of the building dates from the 18th century. It is the official residence of the sovereign, although the sovereign has lived at Buckingham Palace since Queen Victoria's accession (1837). This is why High Commissioners present letters to the Court of St James, and Ambassadors are still formally accredited to it.

The palace is used for ceremonial and official functions, and is not open to the public. After the death of a monarch, it is the place where the Accession Council meets. A new sovereign is announced by Garter King of Arms from the Proclamation Gallery overlooking Friary Court. The palace contains the offices of the Royal Collection Department, the Marshal of the Diplomatic Corps, the Central Chancery of the Orders of Knighthood, the Chapel Royal, the Gentlemen at Arms, the Yeomen of the Guard and the Queen's Watermen. It also contains Clarence House, the London home of the late Queen Elizabeth the Queen Mother.

Blathmac, and member of the House of Síl nÁedo Sláine (Southern Uí Néill). He was slain by Dubhduin, chief of Cinel Cairbre. (*see panel* p. 140, High Kingship of Ireland)

Seymour, Jane (c.1509–37) Third wife of Henry VIII, the mother of Edward VI, and the sister of Protector Somerset. She was a lady-in-waiting to Henry's first two wives, and married him 11 days after the execution of Anne Boleyn. She died soon after the birth of her son, later Edward VI.

Simnel, Lambert (c.1475–c.1535) Pretender to the throne, the son of a joiner. Exploited by Roger Simon, a priest from Oxford, because of his resemblance to Edward IV, he was coached to impersonate one of his sons imprisoned in the Tower. He was set up in Ireland in 1487 as, first, a son of Edward IV, and then as the Duke of Clarence's son, Edward, Earl of Warwick (1475–99). He had some success among Yorkist adherents, and was crowned at Dublin as Edward VI, but after landing in Lancashire with 2000 German mercenaries he was defeated at Stoke Field, Nottinghamshire. After imprisonment, he was supposedly employed in the royal kitchens.

Stephen (c.1090–1154) Last Norman king of England (1135–54), the son of Stephen-Henry, Count of Blois, and Adela, the daughter of William the Conqueror. He had sworn to accept Henry I's daughter, Empress Matilda, as queen, but seized the English crown and was recognized as Duke of Normandy on Henry's death in 1135. Though defeated and captured at the Battle of Lincoln (February 1141), he was released nine months later after

SANDRINGHAM HOUSE

Sandringham House is a royal residence in Norfolk which has been the private home of the royal family since 1862, when the Prince of Wales completed a purchase contemplated by his father Prince Albert. It became the home of the Prince of Wales after his marriage in 1863. The present queen and other members of the royal family regularly spend Christmas at Sandringham, and the tradition of the monarch's Christmas broadcasts began there in 1932. Both George V and George VI died at Sandringham.

Sandringham Estate is a commercial business managed privately on the sovereign's behalf, hosting country shows and other events throughout the year. The house, museum and grounds are open to visitors. Sandringham Country Park (250 ha/600 acres) has been open all year since 1968.

SAXE-COBURG-GOTHA

Saxe-Coburg-Gotha was the name of the British royal family, 1901–17. King Edward VII inherited it from his father, Prince Albert, the second son of the Duke of Saxe-Coburg-Gotha, who owned lands in central Germany. The obviously Germanic name was changed to Windsor during World War 1 as a means of asserting the 'Englishness' of royalty and playing down the extent of its German blood.

STONE OF SCONE, also known as the **Coronation Stone** or **Stone of Destiny**

The Stone of Scone is a rectangular block of sandstone used in the coronation of Scottish and English monarchs. For centuries, since the time of Kenneth I MacAlpin, the first King of Scots, Scottish monarchs were seated upon the stone during their coronation ceremonies at the now-ruined abbey in Scone, near Perth. Following John de Balliol's renunciation of his fealty in 1296, Edward I took the stone to England, where it was later placed under the Coronation Chair (St Edward's Chair) in Westminster Abbey as a symbol of the authority of English kings over Scotland. In 1328, as part of the Treaty of Northampton between Scotland and England, Edward III agreed to return the captured Stone to Scotland, but it was to remain in England for another six centuries.

On Christmas Day 1950, four Scottish students removed the Stone from Westminster Abbey and took it to Scotland. In the process, they dropped it and it broke into two pieces but it was repaired by Glasgow stonemason Robert Gray. Fearing that the stone would not be returned, the stone's custodians left it in the symbolic safe keeping of the Church at Arbroath Abbey until it was taken back to Westminster. On 15 November 1996, the British government finally returned it to Scotland, and it was transported to Edinburgh Castle, where it remains. Provision has been made to transport the stone to Westminster Abbey when it is required there for future coronation ceremonies.

SCONE

Scone is a village in Perth and Kinross District, Scotland, near the River Tay; it had a population of 6559 in 2001. Originally the capital of the Pictish kingdom and the centre of the early Celtic Church, it was the traditional site for the crowning of Scottish kings for over 800 years. Kenneth I MacAlpin was crowned the first King of the Scots upon the Stone of Scone on the Moot Hill in the 9th century. The last coronation held at Scone was that of Charles II as King of Scots in 1651. The Abbey Palace of Scone was the lodging of the kings before their coronation, and the town that grew up around the Palace was the seat of government. The Abbey of Scone and the Bishops' Palace were destroyed during the Reformation in 1559. The Gowries built a new palace in 1580, but after the Gowrie conspiracy, Sir David Murray was created Lord Scone and given the Lands and Palace of Scone as a reward for helping to save the life of King James VI. Today, Scone Palace is the family home of the Earls of Mansfield, who are the descendants of David Murray.

SILVER JUBILEE MEDAL

The silver jubilee medal is a circular silver medal instituted on 6 February 1977; it has a watered white ribbon, representing silver, with cardinal red edge stripes, a garter blue middle stripe, and a further (1mm) cardinal red stripe down the centre. Thirty thousand were awarded to members of the armed forces. The obverse shows Queen Elizabeth II facing right wearing the high Imperial State Crown; the legend reads: ELIZABETH·II·DEI·GRATIA·REGINA·FID·DEF· ('Thanks be to God, Queen, Defender of the Faith'). The reverse shows St Edward's Crown at the top, a wreath of silver-birch foliage and catkins around the edge, with the legend: THE/25TH/YEAR OF/THE REIGN OF QUEEN/ELIZABETH II/6 FEBRUARY/1977.

Matilda's supporters had been routed at Winchester. But Matilda strengthened her grip on the West Country; David I of Scotland annexed the northern English counties by 1141; and Matilda's husband, Count Geoffrey of Anjou, conquered Normandy by 1144–5. Stephen was also repeatedly challenged by baronial rebellions, and after 18 years of virtually continuous warfare, he was forced in 1153 to accept Matilda's son, the future Henry II, as his lawful successor. His reputation as the classic incompetent king of English mediaeval history is nevertheless undeserved. He was remarkably tenacious in seeking to uphold royal rights, and his war strategy was basically sound. His inability to defend the Norman empire was due largely to the sheer weight of his military burdens, especially the major offensives of the Scots in the north and the Angevins in the south.

Stephen-Henry, Count of Blois (1046–1102) The son of Theobald II, Count of Blois and Champagne, born in Blois, France. In 1081 he married Princess Adela of England, the daughter of William I of England and Matilda of Flanders. He served in the First Crusade (1095–9) and was killed in the Battle of Ascalon in Palestine (1102). One of their children became Stephen, King of England.

Stuart or **Stewart, Prince Charles Edward (Louis Philip Casimir)**, known as **the Young Pretender** and **Bonnie Prince Charlie** (1720–88) Claimant to the British crown, born in Rome, the son of James Francis Edward Stuart. Educated in Rome, he became the focus of Jacobite hopes. In 1744 he went to France to head the planned invasion of England, but after the defeat of the French fleet he was unable to leave for over a year. He landed with seven followers at Eriskay in the Hebrides (July 1745) and raised his father's standard at Glenfinnan. The clansmen flocked to him, Edinburgh surrendered, and he kept court at Holyrood. Victorious at Prestonpans, he invaded England, but turned back at Derby for lack of evident English support, and was routed by the Duke of Cumberland at Culloden Moor (1746). The rising was ruthlessly suppressed, and he was hunted for five months. With the help of Flora Macdonald and other islanders he crossed from Benbecula to Portree, disguised as her maid. He landed in Brittany, then lived in France and Italy, where (after his father's death in 1766) he assumed the title of Charles III of Great Britain.

Stuart or **Stewart, Prince James (Francis Edward)**, also known as **the Old Pretender** (1688–1766) Claimant to the British throne, born in London, the only son of James II of England and his second wife, Mary of Modena. As a baby he was conveyed to St Germain, and proclaimed successor on his father's death (1701). After failing to land in Scotland in 1708, he served with the French in the Low Countries. In 1715 he landed at Peterhead during the Jacobite rising, but left Scotland some weeks later. Thereafter he lived mainly in Rome, where he died.

HOUSE OF STUART

The Stuarts, or Stewarts, got their name from the founder of the house, Walter Fitzalan, High Steward of Scotland, who married Marjorie Bruce, the daughter of Robert I, in 1315. On the death of Marjorie's childless brother David II in 1371, their son Robert Stewart became King of Scots as Robert II. Robert was succeeded by his eldest son, John, who reigned as Robert III in order to avoid what was regarded as an unlucky name for a ruler, and he in turn was succeeded by his only surviving son, James I.

There were doubts about the legitimacy of Robert II's family by his first wife, to whom he was so closely related that their marriage, which took place after the birth of their children, required a papal dispensation. This meant that the son of Robert II's second wife, the Earl of Atholl, had a good claim to the throne, and in 1437 James I was murdered by members of Atholl's family. He was succeeded by his six-year-old son, James II.

For the next 130 years the Scottish kings succeeded to the throne as children, the oldest (at 15) being James IV. This led to prolonged regencies and perpetual instability. However, the bloodline of the Stewarts survived, son following father, until the death of James V in 1542 and the accession of his only surviving child, the infant Mary, Queen of Scots. She grew up at the French court as the prospective wife of the Dauphin. Mary always spelled her name 'Stuart', according to French custom, and this spelling was generally adopted by her descendants.

In 1561, Mary's husband having died, she returned to Scotland. In 1565 she married her cousin, Henry Stuart, Lord Darnley; their son was born in 1566 and Darnley was mysteriously murdered a few months later. Within a year Mary had to abdicate in favour of her young son, James VI. She escaped to England, but was imprisoned for many years by Elizabeth I and finally executed in 1587. James VI was descended on both sides from Henry VII, and was therefore Elizabeth's obvious successor. On her death, he ascended the throne of England as James I. James's son, Charles I, became king when his father died in 1625, but because of the Civil War, and the execution of Charles in 1649, his son, Charles II, did not become king until the restoration of the monarchy in 1660, following eleven years of republican rule under Oliver Cromwell.

Up to this point the Stuarts had never failed to produce heirs, but this now changed. Charles II had eighteen acknowledged bastards but no legitimate children, so on his death he was succeeded by his brother, James II. James had alienated public opinion by becoming a Catholic. As long as his second marriage was childless, and his heir was his Protestant daughter Mary, all was well, but when his wife finally produced a healthy son in 1688, James was deposed in favour of Mary II and her husband William III.

William and Mary were also childless. When William died in 1702, he was succeeded by Mary's sister, Anne, who despite having borne an estimated twelve children, had no heir either; the only one of her children to survive babyhood, William, Duke of Gloucester, died in 1700 at the age of 11. In order to exclude Anne's Catholic half-brother James from the throne, the Act of Settlement of 1701 settled the succession of Anne's closest Protestant relatives, the aging Electress Sophia of Hanover and her son George, who became the first king of the House of Hanover in 1714, as George I. His mother, although reputedly determined to outlive Anne and become Queen of England, had died eight weeks before, aged 83.

Despite two rebellions, in 1715 and 1745, the Stuart pretenders, James and his son Charles Edward (Bonnie Prince Charlie), never succeeded in regaining their throne. Charles Edward had no legitimate children, and the last of the Stuarts, his brother Henry, died in exile in France in 1807.

Suibne Menn (c.590–628) High King of Ireland (615–28), the son of Fiachna, and a member of the House of Cenél nEógain (Northern Uí Néill). He was slain by Congal Claen at Traigh Brena. (*see panel* p. 140, High Kingship of Ireland)

Sweyn or **Svein**, known as **Forkbeard** (?–1014) King of Denmark (c.985–1014) and England (1013–14), the son of Harold Bluetooth, and the father of Canute. He first attacked England in 994, and had broken the back of English resistance by 1012. During his final campaign in 1013, he established mastery over the whole country and was recognized as king, while Ethelred the Unready withdrew to exile in Normandy.

Ireland for over a decade. (*see panel* p. 140, High Kingship of Ireland)

Toirrdelbach ua Conchobair (1088–1156) King of Connacht (1106–56), High King of Ireland (1121–56), and the son of Ruaidri na Saide Bulde mac Aeda Gai. During his reign, he supported the monasteries, set up a mint, and built bridges across the River Shannon. (*see panel* p. 140, High Kingship of Ireland)

Tuathal Máelgarb (c.510–44) High King of Ireland (534/6–44), the son of Cormac Caech. He was slain at Greallach Eillte by Maelmor, the son of Airgeadan. (*see panel* p. 140, High Kingship of Ireland)

Toirrdelbach ua Briain (c.1040–86) King of Munster (1063–86), High King of Ireland (1072–86), the son of Teig O'Brien, and grandson of Brian Boroimhe. He held the sovereignty of the greater part of

TANISTRY

Tanistry is a system of succession found among various Celtic tribes, notably in Scotland and Ireland, by which the king or chief of a clan nominated an heir from within his male kinship group. The system contrasts with that of primogeniture, as found in England, whereby the eldest son automatically inherits. The usual rule for qualification was that a candidate had to be descended in the male line from a common ancestor (usually a great-grandfather or great-great-grandfather), and had to be seen as a superior, suitable, able, and willing claimant by the Council of Chiefs. This system of succession left the headship open to rival claims, and was a frequent source of strife both in families and between the clans. Tanistry in Scotland was abolished by a legal decision in the reign of James VI of Scotland, and the English land system was substituted. In Ireland, it remained fully in force among the main dynasties, as well as lesser lords and chieftains, until the early 17th century, and lingered, albeit in much reduced form, until as late as the 1840s.

TRANSPORT

- **The Royal Yacht *Britannia*** was launched by Queen
  Elizabeth II on 16 April 1953, and was commissioned for service
  on 7 January 1954. She was first used by the Queen and the
  Duke of Edinburgh when they embarked on 1 May 1954 at
  Tobruk for the final stage of their Commonwealth Tour. The
  Queen was last on board *Britannia* for an official visit on 9
  August 1997, when she travelled to Arran. De-commissioned
  in December 1997, *Britannia* had travelled more than a million
  miles on royal and official duties.
- **Royal Cars** The royal fleet includes five Rolls-Royces and three
  Daimlers in the royal maroon livery. A Rolls-Royce Phantom
  VI was presented to the Queen for her Silver Jubilee in 1978.
  For private use the Queen drives a Daimler Jaguar saloon and a
  Vauxhall estate. The Duke of Edinburgh has a Range Rover.
  The Bentley State Limousine was created to mark the Queen's
  Golden Jubilee in 2002. Special features include a rear door
  that allows the Queen to stand up straight before stepping
  down to the ground. The rear compartment seats two people
  and has two rear-facing occasional folding chairs for additional passengers. The livery is royal maroon and black with a
  red stripe along each side.
- **Royal Carriages** Most of the collection of historic carriages
  and coaches are still in use today for state ceremonial
  processions and other royal occasions. Among them are the

TARA

Tara is a prehistoric hillfort, 40 km/23 miles north-west of Dublin,
Ireland. It is the supposed site of St Patrick's conversion of
Lóegaire in the 5th century, and the traditional seat of the kings
of Ireland from pre-Christian times to the death of Máel Sechnaill
II of Meath in 1022. Archaeologically its earthworks are poorly
known, apart from the Mound of the Hostages, a megalithic
passage grave of the early 3rd millennium BC. In 2004, amid
much controversy, plans were announced for a motorway that
would pass within half a mile of the hillfort.

Gold State Coach (first used in 1762), the Scottish State Coach (built in 1830), the Irish State Coach (built in 1851 and restored in 1989), the Glass Coach (built in 1881), Queen Alexandra's State Coach, the State Landau (1920), and the Australian State Coach (1988, presented to the Queen by the Australian people to mark Australia's bicentenary). Cars and carriages are housed and maintained in the Royal Mews next to Buckingham Palace, directed by the Crown Equerry.

- **The Royal Train** consists of carriages drawn from a choice of eight purpose-built saloons. These are pulled by one of two Royal Class 47 diesel locomotives, Prince Henry or Prince William. The carriages are liveried in royal maroon with red and black coach lining and a grey roof. The carriages include the royal compartments, and sleeping, dining, and support cars. It also has modern office and communications facilities which allow work and meetings to take place. There has been a royal train since 1842 when a royal saloon, used by Queen Victoria, was part of a train pulled by the engine *Phlegethon*.

- **Royal Air Travel** is catered for by The Queen's Flight, who are amalgamated with No. 32 (Royal) Squadron based at RAF Northolt. Currently the aircraft used by the royal family are the four-engined BAe 146, the twin-engined Hawker S125 jet aircraft, and a Sikorsky S-76 helicopter. The helicopter is operated by the Royal Household from Blackbushe Aerodrome in Hampshire. It is liveried in the blue and red of the Brigade of Guards; the jets are liveried in red, white, and blue.

HOUSE OF TUDOR

The House of Tudor derived from the Welsh family of ap Tudor, which first appeared on the pages of history when Owen Tudor married Henry V's widow, Catherine de Valois, in about 1428. Their son Edmund moved further into the forefront of English politics by marrying the Lady Margaret Beaufort, only child and heiress of the Duke of Somerset, and being created Earl of Richmond. Their son Henry VII became King of England by defeating and killing Richard III at the Battle of Bosworth Field in 1485, and in the following year improved his tenuous claim to the throne by marrying Elizabeth of York, the eldest daughter of Edward IV.

In 1502 Henry's elder son and heir, Arthur, Prince of Wales, married Catherine, daughter of the first monarchs of united Spain, Ferdinand and Isabella. He died shortly afterwards. When Henry VIII, Henry VII's only surviving son, succeeded his father in 1509, he was persuaded to marry his brother's widow in order to keep her dowry and connections in the family. However, although Catherine had six children, only one, Mary, survived. In 1533, therefore, desperate to produce an heir and unable to persuade the pope to annul his marriage, Henry himself declared it invalid on the grounds that Catherine had been previously married to his brother, and so the later match was incestuous. He announced that he, and not the pope, was now the head of the Church of England, and married Anne Boleyn, his pregnant mistress. Unfortunately for him, Anne's child was another daughter, Elizabeth.

Henry's passion for Anne soon cooled. He had her executed for alleged adultery in 1536, and immediately married Jane Seymour, another of the court ladies. The following year, Jane produced an heir for Henry, later to become Edward VI, but died in childbirth. Despite three more marriages, Henry had no further children. Edward succeeded his father in 1547, but was never healthy, and died himself six years later at the age of 16.

The legitimacy of all Henry's children was in doubt. Supporters of the king were obliged to regard Mary as illegitimate, but few people believed it. If Mary was legitimate, Elizabeth was not. Consequently, on Edward's death it was feasible for the Duke of Northumberland, John Dudley, to declare that neither of Henry's daughters should succeed, and to put his daughter-in-law, the 16-year-old Lady Jane Grey, briefly on the throne. After nine days, however, she was deposed in favour of Mary I, and was later beheaded. Mary was unmarried and already 37. The following year she married King Philip of Spain, but the marriage was childless. When Mary died in 1558 she was succeeded unopposed by her half-sister, Elizabeth I.

Elizabeth made many gestures towards marrying, but in fact never did so. Her position on the throne was always questionable, because in Roman Catholic eyes the legitimate candidate was her cousin Mary, Queen of Scots, the granddaughter of Henry VIII's elder sister, Margaret. In 1569 Mary fled to England after being defeated in her attempts to regain her Scottish throne from her son James, and Elizabeth was thereafter able to keep her imprisoned and attempt to neutralize her influence. Mary continued to be a focus of plots against Elizabeth, and the queen was forced to have her executed in 1587. Nevertheless, on her deathbed, Elizabeth acknowledged Mary's son, James, as her heir (he was descended from Margaret Tudor through both his parents), and in 1603 he succeeded to the throne as James I, the first king of the House of Stuart.

TOWER OF LONDON

The Tower of London is a palace-fortress started by William I as a wooden fortification in 1067 and replaced by him with one in stone (c.1077–97). Successive Norman, Plantagenet, and Tudor monarchs added to it until Edward I completed the outer wall, extending to around 7 ha/18 acres. The keep or White Tower is one of the earliest fortifications on such a scale in western Europe, begun by William I in 1078. The Armour Collection, one of the world's greatest, was started by Henry VIII and increased by Charles II. From 1300 to 1810 the Tower housed the Royal Mint, and in 1303 the crown jewels were moved there for safe keeping. It is now a world heritage site.

From the 12th century to the 20th century the Tower served as a state prison. In 1101 Ralf Flamberd, Bishop of Durham, became the Tower's first prisoner. Among other notable prisoners to have been detained (and sometimes executed) there, were John II of France (1356), Richard II (1399), Henry VI (1464–71), Sir Thomas More (1535), Anne Boleyn (1536), Catherine Howard (1542), Archbishop Cranmer (1553–4), Lady Jane Grey and the future Queen Elizabeth I (both in 1554), Sir Walter Raleigh (1592, 1603–16), Robert Devereux, Earl of Essex (1601), Guy Fawkes (1605–6), and Samuel Pepys (1697). Many Scots were imprisoned in the Tower after the Jacobite defeat at Culloden (1745), among them Simon Fraser, Lord Lovat, who was the last man to be beheaded on Tower Hill. During World War 1 Sir Roger Casement was imprisoned in St Thomas' Tower, and 11 spies were hanged in the outer ward by the Martin Tower. In World War 2 Rudolf Hess was imprisoned in the Lieutenant's House for four days.

The ancient Ceremony of the Keys still takes place at the Tower every night, conducted by the Chief Yeoman Warden, the sentries, and the Tower guards.

her uncle Leopold, who remained a constant correspondent.

Companioned in girlhood almost exclusively by older people, she developed a precocious maturity and surprising firmness of will, which soon became apparent. Her closest confidant was the Whig prime minister, Lord Melbourne, a gallant and charming adviser, whose opinion the young queen sought over all matters. With the fall of Melbourne's government in 1839, Victoria invited Sir Robert Peel, the Conservative leader, to form a government, but she set aside the precedent which decreed dismissal of the current Whig ladies of the bedchamber. A political crisis ensued, whereupon Peel resigned, and the Melbourne administration, which she personally preferred, was prolonged for two years.

Next came the question of marriage, and Victoria fell in love with one of the candidates put forward by her advisers: her cousin Prince Albert of Saxe-Coburg and Gotha. They were married in 1840, both aged 20, and after initial pressure of public opinion against Victoria for marrying the 'pauper prince' from Germany, they settled into a harmonious and exemplary relationship. Albert's irreproachable sexual morality was almost unprecedented at court, and the Victorian age came to be synonymous with a great revival of public morality. The royal couple produced four sons and five daughters. Their first son, Edward, Prince of Wales, born in 1841, who was to become the future King Edward VII, infuriated his parents with his wayward behaviour.

Victoria, in full **Alexandrina Victoria** (1819–1901) Victoria, Queen of Great Britain (1837–1901), was born at Kensington Palace, London. She was the only child of George III's fourth son, Edward, Duke of Kent, and Victoria Maria Louisa of Saxe-Coburg, the sister of Leopold who later became King of the Belgians. The Prince Regent (later George IV) insisted she be named after Alexander I of Russia, her godfather, so she was christened Alexandrina Victoria. Her father died soon after her birth, and her mother, by then the Duchess of Kent, came under the influence of Sir John Conroy who, hoping to hold the power behind the throne in the event of the Duchess becoming regent, organized 'regal' tours promoting her.

Victoria reached the age of 18 before the death of her uncle, William IV, in 1837. She was crowned at Westminster in 1838, and her first acts were to exclude Conroy from the court and to distance herself from her mother. She speedily demonstrated a clear grasp of the constitutional principles in which she had been so painstakingly instructed in the many letters from

Having been strongly influenced by Albert, with whom she worked in closest harmony, after his death (1861) Victoria went into lengthy seclusion, neglecting many duties, which brought her unpopularity. However, with her recognition as Empress of India, under Disraeli's solicitous administration, and the celebratory golden (1887) and diamond (1897) jubilees, she again rose high in her subjects' favour, and greatly increased the prestige of the monarchy. Repeating the preference for Melbourne over Peel, she took a strong liking for Disraeli, and despised Gladstone. At various points in her long reign she exercised some influence over foreign affairs; and the marriages of her children had important diplomatic as well as dynastic implications in Europe.

She grieved for Albert to the end, having his clothes laid out on his bed each evening, his water bowl filled each morning, and sleeping beneath a huge photograph of him, taken when he was dead, which hung over her bed. Victoria died at Osborne, her retreat at Cowes, Isle of Wight. She was the longest-reigning English monarch, and was succeeded by her son as Edward VII.

Vortigern (fl.425–50) Semi-legendary British king who, according to Bede, recruited Germanic mercenaries led by Hengist and Horsa to help fight off the Picts after the final withdrawal of the Roman administration from Britain (409). Tradition has it that the revolt of these troops opened the way for the Germanic conquests and settlements in England.

Warbeck, Perkin (c.1474–99)
Pretender to the English throne, born
in Tournai, Belgium. In 1492 he was
persuaded by enemies of Henry VII to
impersonate Richard, Duke of York,
the younger of the two sons of Edward
IV who had been murdered in the
Tower of London (1483). With the
promise of support from many quarters in England, Ireland, Scotland, and
on the European mainland, he made
two unsuccessful attempts to invade
England (1495–6), and was captured at
Beaulieu during a third attempt (1497).
Imprisoned in the Tower, he was
executed after trying to escape.

**Warwick, John Dudley, Earl of,
Duke of Northumberland** (1502–53)
English soldier and statesman. He was
deputy governor of Calais, and served
under Edward Seymour, Duke of
Somerset, in his Scottish campaigns.
Created Earl of Warwick (1546), he was
appointed joint regent for Edward VI
and High Chamberlain of England
(1547). As virtual ruler of England, he
was created Duke of Northumberland
in 1551 and brought about the downfall and eventual execution of
Somerset (1550–2). He married his

WARRANTS

Royal warrants are granted to people or companies who have
regularly supplied goods or services for five consecutive years to
the monarch, his or her consort, the Queen Mother, or the Prince
of Wales. They are advised by the Lord Chamberlain, who is head
of the Royal Household and chairman of the Royal Household
Tradesmen's Warrants Committee. A business may hold warrants
from more than one member of the royal family, and a handful
of companies hold all four. Strict regulations govern the warrant,
which allows the tradesman or company to use the words 'By
Appointment' and the Royal Coat of Arms on products, premises,
and delivery vehicles. A royal warrant is initially granted for five
years, after which time it comes up for review. A warrant may be
cancelled at any time and is automatically reviewed if the grantee
dies, leaves the business, or if the business is sold or bankrupted.

WESSEX

Wessex was a kingdom of the Anglo-Saxon heptarchy (seven kingdoms), with its main centres at Winchester and Hamwic (Southampton). Under Alfred (871–99), Wessex – by then incorporating Kent and Sussex – was the only English kingdom to withstand the onslaughts of the Danes. Alfred's successors reconquered the Danelaw (the area under Danish rule), and had united all England under a single monarchy by 954. In the novels of Thomas Hardy, Wessex is used to mean the south-western counties of England, mainly Dorsetshire.

fourth son, Lord Guildford Dudley, to Lady Jane Grey, and proclaimed her queen on the death of Edward VI, but was executed for treason on the accession of Mary I.

William I (of England), known as **the Conquerer** (c.1028–87) Duke of Normandy (1035–87) and the first Norman King of England (1066–87), the illegitimate son of Duke Robert of Normandy. Edward the Confessor, who had been brought up in Normandy, most probably designated him as future King of England in 1051. When Harold Godwinson, despite an apparent oath to uphold William's claims, took the throne as Harold II, William invaded with the support of the papacy, defeated and killed Harold at the Battle of Hastings, and was crowned king on Christmas Day, 1066. The key to effective control was military conquest backed up by aris-tocratic colonization, so that by the time of the Domesday Book (1086),

WESTMINSTER ABBEY

Westminster Abbey is the collegiate church of St Peter in Westminster, London. There was probably a monastic settlement on this site from the 8th century. The first recorded abbey church, consecrated in 1065, was replaced from 1245 by the present building in early English Gothic style. The monastery was dissolved in 1540. Westminster Abbey has a special importance in English history, serving as a coronation church and national shrine, with many memorials to those who have shaped the country's history and culture.

WINDSOR CASTLE

Windsor Castle is the largest of England's castles, situated on the River Thames at Windsor. It was founded by William I and first used as a royal residence by Henry I. The process of converting Windsor from a fortress into a palace began in the 16th century. The castle stands on the edge of Windsor Great Park, formerly a royal hunting ground. The principal changes to the castle were made in the early 19th century, when George IV commissioned Sir Jeffry Wyatville as his architect; he built the machicolated walls and several towers, raised the massive Round Tower, giving the castle its outline, and remodelled the State Apartments, adding the Waterloo Chamber. This section was severely damaged by fire in 1992. Restoration work was completed in 1997 and the castle re-opened to the public at the end of that year.

WITAN or WITENAGEMOT

The council of the Anglo-Saxon kings, once regarded as the first English 'parliament'; its name in Old English means 'meeting of wise men'. It was not a popular or representative assembly imposing constitutional restraints on kingship, but in essence an informal advisory body of aldermen, thegns, and bishops, who gathered formally to discuss royal grants of land, church benefices, charters, aspects of taxation, defence, foreign policy, and law. It nevertheless upheld the convention that kings should take into account the views of powerful subjects. The succession of a king had usually to be acknowledged by the witan. The Norman monarchs in 1066 replaced the witan with the *curia regis*, or king's court.

the leaders of Anglo-Saxon society south of the Tees had been almost entirely replaced by a new ruling class of Normans, Bretons, and Flemings, who were closely tied to William by feudal bonds. He died near Paris in an accident on horseback, while defending Normandy's southern border.

William I (of Scotland), known as

HOUSE OF WINDSOR

At the beginning of World War 1, the royal house of Britain was officially the House of Saxe-Coburg-Gotha, as that was the family of George V's grandfather, Prince Albert. However, it was felt that in wartime the British royal family should not have a German name, and in 1917 King George V decreed that all his family would henceforth take the surname of Windsor.

On George V's death, his eldest son, Edward VIII, became king, but abdicated shortly afterwards in order to marry Wallis Warfield Simpson. As a 40-year-old twice-divorced commoner, she was not considered to be a suitable wife either for the king or for the head of the Church of England. The throne passed to Edward's brother, George VI, and on his death to Elizabeth II.

The Act of Succession of 1702 decrees that no person who is a Catholic or is married to a Catholic can succeed to the throne. Therefore, neither Prince Michael of Kent, nor the Earl of St Andrews, both of whom have married Catholics, appears in the line of succession (see p. 141), although their children, who are not Catholics, do. The line then passes on to the Earl of Harewood, and his sons and many grandchildren.

William the Lion (c.1142–1214) King of Scots (1165–1214), the brother and successor of Malcolm IV. In 1173–4 he invaded Northumberland during the rebellion against Henry II, but was captured at Alnwick, and by the Treaty of Falaise (1174) recognized Henry as the feudal superior of Scotland. Despite his difficulties with England, he made Scotland a much stronger kingdom. In 1189 Scottish independence was restored, and in 1192 Celestine III declared the Scottish Church free of all external authority save the pope's.

William II, known as **William Rufus** (c.1056–1100) King of England (1087–1100), the second surviving son of William the Conqueror. His main goal was the recovery of Normandy from his elder brother Robert Curthose. From 1096, when Robert relinquished the struggle and departed on the First Crusade, William ruled the duchy as *de facto* duke. He also led expeditions to Wales (1095, 1097), conquered Carlisle and the surrounding district (1092), and after the death of Malcolm III he exercised a controlling influence over Scottish affairs. Contemporaries condemned

A large peripheral royal family is a new phenomenon in Britain. Despite the fact that George III had seven surviving sons and six daughters, there are very few British descendants of George III apart from those listed in the family tree on pp. 128–35. Among them are: the Duke of Beaufort, who is descended from Queen Mary's niece, Lady Mary Cambridge; Captain Alexander Ramsay of Mar and his daughters, the grandson and the great-grand-children of Edward VII's second brother, Arthur, Duke of Connaught; the family of Lady May Abel-Smith, the grand-daughter of the youngest brother, Leopold, Duke of Albany; and the Mountbatten family, descendants of Prince Louis of Battenburg who, as First Lord of the Admiralty, changed his name at the same time and for the same reasons as George V. His wife, Victoria, was Queen Victoria's granddaughter, the daughter of Princess Alice. The family includes the Marquess of Milford Haven, his cousin Lady Mountbatten of Burma, and Prince Philip.

Many people are, of course, illegitimately descended from royalty. In particular, the maternal grandmother of Princess Louise's husband, the Duke of Fife, was Lady Elizabeth FitzClarence, one of the many illegitimate children of William IV.

his government of England as arbitrary and ruthless. He exploited his rights over the Church and the nobility beyond the limits of custom, and quarrelled with Anselm, Archbishop of Canterbury. His personal conduct outraged the moral standards of the time, for he was most probably a homosexual. He was killed by an arrow while hunting in the New Forest. It has been supposed that he was murdered on the orders of his younger brother, who succeeded him as Henry I, but his death was almost certainly accidental.

William III, known as **William of Orange** (1650–1702) Stadtholder of the United Provinces (1672–1702) and King of Great Britain (1689–1702), born in The Hague, The Netherlands, the son of William II of Orange by Mary, the eldest daughter of Charles I of England. Before he attained his majority, he was kept out of national politics by Johan de Witt, Raadpensionaris (Grand Pensionary) of the province of Holland. His later marriage (1677) to his cousin, **Mary** (1662–94), the daughter of James II by Anne Hyde, further increased his involvement in foreign politics. Once he reached 18 years of age, the States-General appointed him as commander for the duration of a single campaign, and he became stadtholder in 1672, initially only of Holland and Zeeland, but other provinces soon joined in appointing him. That year de Witt, who was William's principal antagonist, was executed following a plot. Afterwards William achieved military successes against Prussia and France, thus increasing his power. Invited to redress the grievances of the English against King James II, William landed at Torbay in 1688 with an English and Dutch army, and forced James to flee. William and Mary were proclaimed joint rulers early the following year. He defeated James's supporters at Killiecrankie (1689) and at the Boyne (1690), then concentrated on the War of the League of Augsburg against France (1689–97), in which he was finally successful. In later years, he had to withstand much parliamentary opposition to his proposals, and there were many assassination plots. His political ambitions were European in scale, and tended to conflict with the interests of The Netherlands. He died in London, childless, the crown passing to Mary's sister, Anne.

William IV, known as **the Sailor King** (1765–1837) King of Great Britain and Ireland, and King of Hanover (1830–7), born in London, the third son of George III, and before his accession known as **Duke of Clarence**. He entered the navy in 1779, saw service in the USA and the West Indies, became admiral in 1811, and Lord High Admiral in 1827–8. His

elder brother having died, he succeeded George IV in 1830. Widely believed to have Whig leanings at his accession, he developed Tory sympathies, and did much to obstruct the passing of the first Reform Act (1832). He was the last monarch to use prerogative powers to dismiss a ministry with a parliamentary majority when he sacked Melbourne in 1834 and invited the Tories to form a government. He was succeeded by his niece, Victoria.

Windsor, Duke of *see* **Edward VIII**

Windsor, Lady Louise *see* **Edward, Prince**

Windsor, (Bessie) Wallis, Duchess of, *née* **Warfield,** previous married names **Spencer** and **Simpson** (1896–1986) Wife of Edward VIII, born in Blue Ridge Summit, Pennsylvania, USA. An extrovert socialite, in 1916 she married **Lieutenant Earl Winfield Spencer** of the US Navy, but in 1927 the marriage was dissolved. The following year, in London, she married **Ernest Simpson**, an American-born Briton. Well-known in London society, she met Edward, the Prince of Wales, at a country-house party in 1931. In 1936, the year of his accession, she obtained a divorce in England, and the king subsequently made clear to Stanley Baldwin and his government his determination to marry her, even if it meant giving up the throne. They married in 1937 in France, but she was not accepted by the British royal family until the late 1960s. She and Edward lived in France and the

Bahamas; after Edward's death she lived virtually as a recluse, and was in ill health for many years before she died, in Paris. She was buried beside her husband at Windsor Castle.

Woodville, Elizabeth (1437–92) Queen consort of Edward IV of England. A widow, she married Edward IV in 1464, and was crowned in 1465. When Edward fled to Flanders in 1470, she sought sanctuary in Westminster. In 1483 her sons, Edward V and Richard, Duke of York, were murdered (the 'Princes in the Tower'). After the accession of Henry VII in 1485, her rights as dowager queen were restored, but in 1487 she was forced to retire to a convent, where she died. Her eldest daughter, **Elizabeth of York** (1465–1503), married Henry in 1486.

York, Richard, Duke of *see* **Edward V**

York, Richard, 3rd Duke of (1411–60) English nobleman, claimant to the English throne, and father of Edward IV, Richard III, and George, Duke of Clarence. He loyally served the weak-minded Henry VI in Ireland and France, and was appointed protector during his illnesses, but was always in conflict with the king's wife, Margaret of Anjou, and her Lancastrian forces. In 1460 he marched on Westminster and claimed the crown, was promised the succession and appointed protector again, but was killed in a rising by Lancastrian forces in Wakefield.

HOUSE OF YORK
see **HOUSES OF LANCASTER AND YORK**

British royal family tree

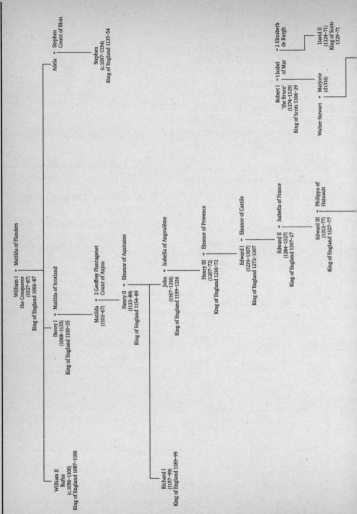

William I the Conqueror (1027–87) King of England 1066–87 = Matilda of Flanders

Adela = Stephen Count of Blois

Stephen (c.1097–1154) King of England 1135–54

William II Rufus (c.1056–1100) King of England 1087–1100

Henry I (1068–1135) King of England 1100–35 = Matilda of Scotland

Matilda (1102–67) = 2 Geoffrey Plantagenet Count of Anjou

Henry II (1133–89) King of England 1154–89 = Eleanor of Aquitaine

Richard I (1157–99) King of England 1189–99

John (1167–1216) King of England 1199–1216 = Isabella of Angoulème

Henry III (1207–72) King of England 1216–72 = Eleanor of Provence

Edward I (1239–1307) King of England 1272–1307 = Eleanor of Castile

Edward II (1284–1327) King of England 1307–27 = Isabella of France

Edward III (1312–77) King of England 1327–77 = Philippa of Hainault

Robert I 'the Bruce' (1274–1329) King of Scots 1306–29 = 1 Isabel of Mar
= 2 Elizabeth de Burgh

David II (1324–71) King of Scots 1329–71

Walter Stewart = Marjorie (d.1316)

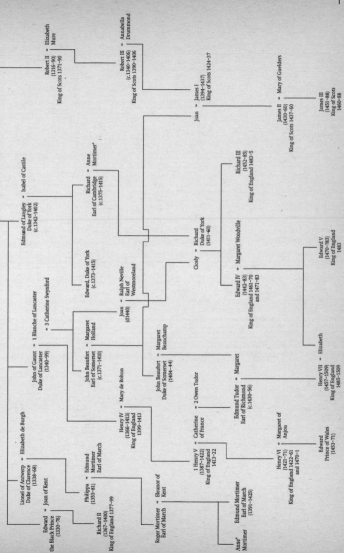

Robert II (1316–90) King of Scots 1371–90 = Elizabeth Mure

Robert III (c.1340–1406) King of Scots 1390–1406 = Annabella Drummond

Joan = James I (1394–1437) King of Scots 1424–37

James II (1430–60) King of Scots 1437–60 = Mary of Guelders

James III (1451–88) King of Scots 1460–88

Edmund of Langley Duke of York (c.1342–1402) = Isabel of Castile

Richard Earl of Cambridge (c.1375–1415) = Anne Mortimer*

Edward, Duke of York (c.1373–1415)

Joan (d.1440) = Ralph Neville Earl of Westmoreland

Cecily = Richard Duke of York (1411–60)

Edward IV (1442–83) King of England 1461–70 and 1471–83 = Margaret Woodville

Richard III (1452–85) King of England 1483–5

Edward V (1470–83) King of England 1483

Lionel of Antwerp Duke of Clarence (1338–68) = Elizabeth de Burgh

Edward the Black Prince (1330–76) = Joan of Kent

Philippa (1355–81) = Edmund Mortimer Earl of March

Richard II (1367–1400) King of England 1377–99

John of Gaunt Duke of Lancaster (1340–99) 1 Blanche of Lancaster = 3 Catherine Swynford

Henry IV (1366–1413) King of England 1399–1413 = Mary de Bohun

John Beaufort Earl of Somerset (1371–1410) = Margaret Holland

John Beaufort Duke of Somerset (1404–44) = Margaret Beauchamp

Margaret = Edmund Tudor Earl of Richmond (c.1430–56) = 2 Owen Tudor = Catherine of France

Henry VII (1457–1509) King of England 1485–1509 = Elizabeth

1 Henry V (1387–1422) King of England 1413–22 = Catherine of France

Roger Mortimer Earl of March

Edmund Mortimer Earl of March (1391–1425) = Eleanor of Kent

Anne* Mortimer

Henry VI (1421–71) King of England 1422–61 and 1470–1 = Margaret of Anjou

Edward Prince of Wales (1453–71)

*denotes the same person occurring in a different part of the tree
1 denotes first marriage; 2, second marriage; 3, third marriage

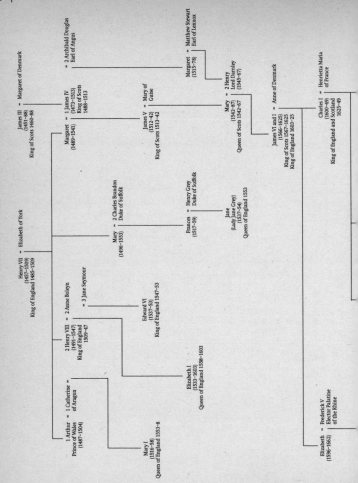

James III = Margaret of Denmark
(1451-88)
King of Scots 1460-88

Henry VII = Elizabeth of York
(1457-1509)
King of England 1485-1509

Margaret = 1 James IV   = 2 Archibald Douglas
(1489-1541)   (1473-1513)   Earl of Angus
King of Scots
1488-1513

Margaret = Matthew Stewart
(1515-78)   Earl of Lennox

James V = Mary of
(1512-42)   Guise
King of Scots 1513-42

Mary = 2 Henry
(1542-87)   Lord Darnley
Queen of Scots 1542-67   (1545-67)

Mary = 2 Charles Brandon
(1496-1533)   Duke of Suffolk

Frances = Henry Grey
(1517-59)   Duke of Suffolk

Jane
(Lady Jane Grey)
(1537-54)
Queen of England 1553

James VI and I = Anne of Denmark
(1566-1625)
King of Scots 1567-1625
King of England 1603-25

Charles I = Henrietta Maria
(1600-49)   of France
King of England and Scotland
1625-49

1 Arthur = 1 Catherine =
Prince of Wales   of Aragon
(1487-1504)

2 Henry VIII = 2 Anne Boleyn
(1491-1547)
King of England
1509-47

= 3 Jane Seymour

Edward VI
(1537-53)
King of England 1547-53

Mary I
(1516-58)
Queen of England 1553-8

Elizabeth I
(1533-1603)
Queen of England 1558-1603

Elizabeth = Frederick V
(1596-1662)   Elector Palatine
of the Rhine

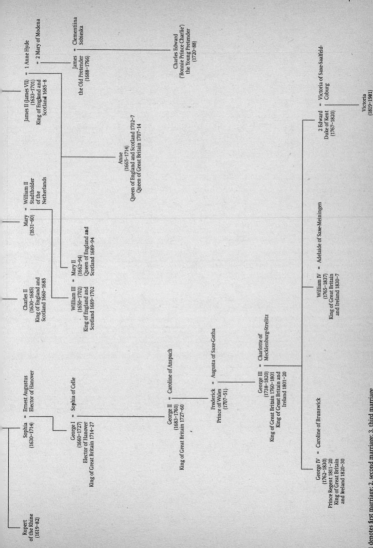

Rupert
of the Rhine
(1619-82)

Sophia = Ernest Augustus
(1630-1714)   Elector of Hanover

Mary = William II
(1531-60)   Stadtholder
of the
Netherlands

Charles II
(1630-1685)
King of England and
Scotland 1660-1685

James II (James VII) = 1 Anne Hyde
(1633-1701)
King of England and
Scotland 1685-8
= 2 Mary of Modena

William III = Mary II
(1650-1702)   (1662-94)
King of England and   Queen of England and
Scotland 1689-1702   Scotland 1689-94

James
the Old Pretender
(1688-1766)
= Clementina
Sobieska

Anne
(1665-1714)
Queen of England and Scotland 1702-7
Queen of Great Britain 1707-14

Charles Edward
('Bonnie Prince Charlie')
the Young Pretender
(1720-88)

George I
(1660-1727)
Elector of Hanover
King of Great Britain 1714-27
= Sophia of Celle

George II = Caroline of Anspach
(1683-1760)
King of Great Britain 1727-60

Frederick = Augusta of Saxe-Gotha
Prince of Wales
(1707-51)

George III = Charlotte of
(1738-1820)   Mecklenburg-Strelitz
King of Great Britain 1760-1801
King of Great Britain and
Ireland 1801-20

George IV = Caroline of Brunswick
(1762-1830)
Prince Regent 1811-20
King of Great Britain
and Ireland 1820-30

William IV = Adelaide of Saxe-Meiningen
(1765-1837)
King of Great Britain
and Ireland 1830-7

2 Edward = Victoria of Saxe-Saalfeld-
Duke of Kent   Coburg
(1767?-1820)

Victoria
(1819-1901)
Queen of Great Britain and Ireland 1837-1901

1 denotes first marriage; 2, second marriage; 3, third marriage

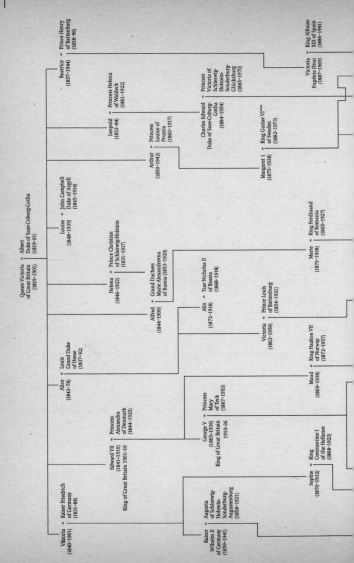

Queen Victoria = Albert
of Great Britain Duke of Saxe-Coburg-Gotha
(1819–1901)   (1819–61)

Victoria = Kaiser Friedrich
(1840–1901) of Germany
(1831–88)

Edward VII = Princess
(1841–1910) Alexandra
King of Great Britain 1901–10 of Denmark
(1844–1925)

Alice = Louis
(1843–78) Grand Duke
of Hesse
(1837–92)

Alfred = Grand Duchess
(1844–1900) Marie Alexandrovna
of Russia (1853–1920)

Helena = Prince Christian
(1846–1923) of Schleswig-Holstein
(1831–1917)

Louise = John Campbell
(1848–1939) Duke of Argyll
(1845–1914)

Arthur = Princess
(1850–1942) Louise
of Prussia
(1860–1917)

Leopold = Princess Helena
(1853–84) of Waldeck
(1861–1922)

Beatrice = Prince Henry
(1857–1944) of Battenberg
(1858–96)

Kaiser = Augusta
Wilhelm II of Schleswig-
of Germany Holstein-
(1859–1941) Sonderburg-
Augustenburg
(1858–1921)

George V = Princess
(1865–1936) Mary
King of Great Britain of Teck
1910–36 (1867–1953)

Maud = King Haakon VII
(1869–1938) of Norway
(1872–1957)

Sophie = King
(1870–1932) Constantine I
of the Hellenes
(1868–1923)

Victoria = Prince Louis
(1863–1950) of Battenberg
(1854–1921)

Alix = Tsar Nicholas II
(1872–1918) of Russia
(1868–1918)

Marie = King Ferdinand
(1875–1938) of Romania
(1865–1927)

Charles Edward
Duke of Saxe-Coburg-
Gotha
(1884–1954)

Princess
Victoria of
Schleswig-
Holstein-
Sonderburg-
Glücksburg
(1885–1970)

Margaret 1 = King Gustav VI****
(1875–1938) of Sweden
(1882–1973)

Victoria
Eugénie (Ena)
(1887–1969)

King Alfonso
XIII of Spain
(1886–1941)

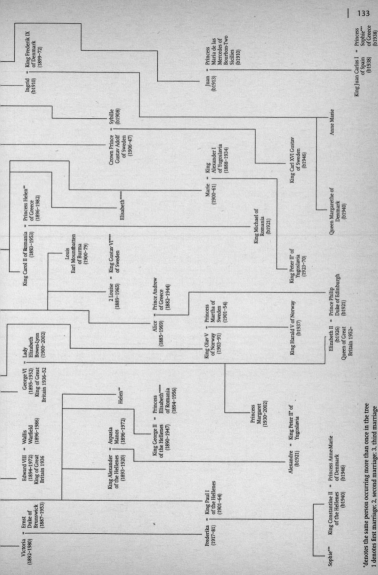

The British royal family today

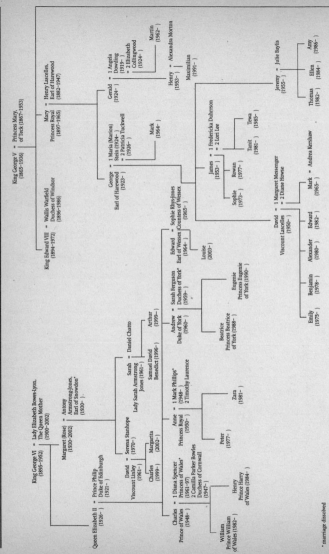

King George V (1865–1936) = Princess Mary of Teck (1867–1953)

King George VI (1895–1952) = Lady Elizabeth Bowes-Lyon, The Queen Mother (1900–2002)

King Edward VIII (1894–1972) = Wallis Warfield Duchess of Windsor (1896–1986)

Mary Princess Royal (1897–1965) = Henry Lascelles, Earl of Harewood (1882–1947)

Queen Elizabeth II (1926–) = Prince Philip Duke of Edinburgh (1921–)

Margaret (Rose) (1930–2002) = Antony Armstrong-Jones, Earl of Snowdon* (1930–)

George Earl of Harewood (1923–) = 1 Maria (Marion) Stein (1924–) = 2 Patricia Tuckwell (1926–)

Gerald (1924–) = 1 Angela Dowding (1919–) = 2 Elizabeth Collingwood (1924–)

Mark (1964–)

Henry (1953–) = Alexandra Morton

Martin (1962–)

Maximilian (1991–)

Charles Prince of Wales (1948–) = 1 Diana Spencer Princess of Wales* (1961–97) = 2 Camilla Parker Bowles Duchess of Cornwall (1947–)

David Viscount Linley (1961–) = Serena Stanhope (1970–)

Lady Sarah Armstrong Jones (1961–) = Daniel Chatto

Anne Princess Royal (1950–) = 1 Mark Phillips* (1948–) = 2 Timothy Laurence

Andrew Duke of York (1960–) = Sarah Ferguson Duchess of York* (1959–)

Edward Earl of Wessex (1964–) = Sophie Rhys-Jones (Countess of Wessex) (1965–)

David Viscount Lascelles (1950–) = 1 Margaret Messenger = 2 Diane Howse

James (1953–) = 1 Fredericka Duhrssen = 2 Lori Lee

Jeremy (1955–) = Julie Baylis

William Prince William of Wales (1982–)

Henry Prince Harry of Wales (1984–)

Charles (1999–)

Margarita (2002–)

Samuel David Benedict (1996–)

Arthur (1999–)

Peter (1977–)

Zara (1981–)

Beatrice Princess Beatrice of York (1988–)

Eugenie Princess Eugenie of York (1990–)

Louise (2003–)

Emily (1975–)

Benjamin (1978–)

Alexander (1980–)

Edward (1982–)

Sophie (1973–)

Rowan (1977–)

Tanit (1981–)

Tewa (1985–)

Mark (1965–) = Andrea Kershaw

Thomas (1982–)

Ellen (1984–)

Amy (1986–)

* marriage dissolved

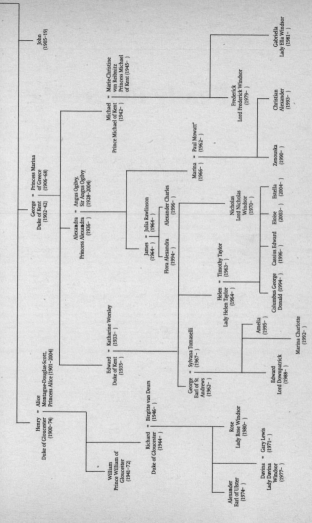

John
(1905–19)

Henry = Alice
Duke of Gloucester   Montague-Douglas-Scott,
(1900–74)   Princess Alice (1901–2004)

George = Princess Marina
Duke of Kent   of Greece
(1902–42)   (1906–68)

Michael = Marie-Christine
Prince Michael of Kent   von Reibnitz
(1942–)   Princess Michael
of Kent (1945–)

Alexandra = Angus Ogilvy,
Princess Alexandra   Sir Angus Ogilvy
(1936–)   (1928–2004)

Frederick
Lord Frederick Windsor
(1979–)

Gabriella
Lady Ella Windsor
(1981–)

Christian
Alexander
(1993–)

James = Julia Rawlinson
(1964–)   (1964–)

Alexander Charles
(1996–)

Martina = Paul Mowatt*
(1966–)   (1962–)

Flora Alexandra
(1994–)

Edward = Katharine Worsley
Duke of Kent   (1933–)
(1935–)

Nicholas
Lord Nicholas
Windsor
(1970–)

Zenouska
(1990–)

Helen = Timothy Taylor
Lady Helen Taylor   (1963–)
(1964–)

Eloise
(2003–)

Estella
(2004–)

George = Sylvana Tomaselli
Earl of St   (1957–)
Andrews
(1962–)

Cassius Edward
(1996–)

Columbus George
Donald (1994–)

Amelia
(1995–)

Edward
Lord Downpatrick
(1988–)

Marina Charlotte
(1992–)

William
Prince William of
Gloucester
(1941–72)

Richard = Birgitte van Deurs
Duke of Gloucester   (1946–)
(1944–)

Rose
Lady Rose Windsor
(1980–)

Alexander
Earl of Ulster
(1974–)

Davina = Gary Lewis
Lady Davina   (1971–)
Windsor
(1977–)

* marriages dissolved

Ready Reference

Rulers of England and Great Britain   137
Rulers of Scotland   139
High Kingship of Ireland   140
British Order of Succession   141

Rulers of England and Great Britain

Saxons and Danes

Egbert	802–39	King of Wessex
Ethelwulf	839–56	Son of Egbert. King of Wessex, Sussex, Kent, Essex
Ethelbald	856–60	Son of Ethelwulf. Displaced his father as King of Wessex
Ethelbert	860–5	Second son of Ethelwulf. United Kent and Wessex
Ethelred I	865–71	Third son of Ethelwulf. King of Wessex
Alfred (the Great)	871–99	Fourth son of Ethelwulf. Defeated the Danes
Edward (the Elder)	899–924	Son of Alfred. United England and claimed Scotland
Athelstan (the Glorious)	924–39	Son of Edward. King of Mercia, Wessex
Edmund I (the Magnificent)	939–46	Third son of Edward. King of Mercia, Wessex
Edred	946–55	Fourth son of Edward
Edwy (the Fair)	955–9	Eldest son of Edmund. King of Wessex
Edgar (the Peaceful)	959–75	Younger son of Edmund. Ruled all England
Edward (the Martyr)	975–8	Son of Edgar. Murdered by step-mother
Ethelred II (the Unready)	978–1016	Second son of Edgar (in exile 1013–14)
Edmund II (Ironside)	1016	Son of Ethelred II. King of London
Canute	1016–35	The Dane. Became ruler by conquest
Harold I (Harefoot)	1037–40	Illegitimate son of Canute
Hardicanute	1040–2	Son of Canute by Emma. King of Denmark
Edward (the Confessor)	1042–66	Younger son of Ethelred II
Harold II	1066	Brother-in-law of Edward the Confessor. Last Saxon King of England

House of Normandy

William I (the Conqueror)	1066–87	Became ruler by conquest
William II (Rufus)	1087–1100	Third son of William I
Henry I	1100–35	Youngest son of William I

House of Blois

Stephen	1135–54	Grandson of William I

House of Plantagenet

Henry II	1154–89	Grandson of Henry I
Richard I (the Lionheart)	1189–99	Third son of Henry II. Crusader
John	1199–1216	Youngest son of Henry II
Henry III	1216–72	Son of John
Edward I (Longshanks)	1272–1307	Son of Henry III
Edward II	1307–27	Son of Edward I. Deposed by Parliament
Edward III	1327–77	Son of Edward II
Richard II	1377–99	Grandson of Edward III. Deposed

House of Lancaster

Henry IV	1399–1413	Grandson of Edward III
Henry V	1413–22	Son of Henry IV. Victor of the Battle of Agincourt 1415
Henry VI	1422–61, 1470–1	Son of Henry V. Two periods of rule

House of York

Edward IV	1461–70, 1471–83	Great grandson of Edward III. Two periods of rule
Edward V	1483	Son of Edward IV. Murdered in the Tower of London
Richard III (Crookback)	1483–5	Brother of Edward IV. Fell at Bosworth Field

House of Tudor

Henry VII	1485–1509	Descendant of Edward III
Henry VIII	1509–47	Son of Henry VII. Created the Church of England
Edward VI	1547–53	Son of Henry VIII by Jane Seymour
Jane	1553	Great-granddaughter of Henry VII; deposed after nine days
Mary I	1553–8	Daughter of Henry VIII by Catherine of Aragón
Elizabeth I	1558–1603	Younger daughter of Henry VIII by Anne Boleyn

House of Stuart

James I (James VI of Scotland)	1603–25	Descendant of Henry VII. First King of Great Britain
Charles I	1625–49	Son of James I. Beheaded

Commonwealth

Oliver Cromwell	1653–8	Lord Protector
Richard Cromwell	1658–9	Lord Protector. Son of Oliver Cromwell

House of Stuart

Charles II	1660–85	Son of Charles I

James II	1685–8	Younger son of Charles I. Deposed
William III	1689–1702	Son of Mary, daughter of Charles I
Mary II	1689–94	Daughter of James II. Ruled jointly with William III
Anne	1702–14	Younger daughter of James II
House of Hanover		
George I	1714–27	Great grandson of James I
George II	1727–60	Only son of George I
George III	1760–1820	Grandson of George II
George IV	1820–30	Eldest son of George III
William IV	1830–7	Third son of George III
Victoria	1837–1901	Granddaughter of George III
House of Saxe-Coburg		
Edward VII	1901–10	Son of Victoria
House of Windsor		
George V	1910–36	Son of Edward VII
Edward VIII	1936	Eldest son of George V. Abdicated
George VI	1936–52	Second son of George V
Elizabeth II	1952–	Daughter of George VI

Rulers of Scotland

House of Alpin

c.843–c.858	Kenneth I MacAlpin
c.858–63	Donald I
863–77	Constantine I
877–8	Aodh
878–89	Eochaid *Joint ruler*
878–89	Giric *Joint ruler*
889–900	Donald II
900–43	Constantine II
943–54	Malcolm I
954–62	Indulf
962–7	Duff
967–71	Colin
971–95	Kenneth II
995–7	Constantine III
997–1005	Kenneth III
1005–34	Malcolm II

House of Dunkeld

1034–40	Duncan I

House of Moray

1040–57	Macbeth
1057–8	Lulach

House of Dunkeld

1058–93	Malcolm III 'Canmore'
1093–4	Donald III Bán (Donaldbane)
1094	Duncan II
1094–7	Donald III Bán (Donaldbane) (*restored*) *Joint ruler*
1094–7	Edmund *Joint ruler*
1097–1107	Edgar
1107–24	Alexander I
1124–53	David I
1153–65	Malcolm IV 'the Maiden'

1165–1214	William I 'the Lion'	*House of Stewart (Stuart)*	
1214–49	Alexander II	1371–90	Robert II
1249–86	Alexander III	1390–1406	Robert III
1286–90	Margaret, 'Maid of Norway'	1406–37	James I
1290–2	*No monarch*	1437–60	James II
1292–6	John de Balliol	1460–88	James III
1296–1306	*English rule*	1488–1513	James IV
		1513–42	James V
House of Bruce		1542–67	Mary, 'Queen of Scots'
1306–29	Robert I 'Robert the Bruce'	1567–1625	James VI (James I of England)
1329–71	David II		

High Kingship of Ireland

A symbolic rather than functional office that united the people of Ireland. The traditional list of those bearing the title High King of Ireland (Ard Rí Érenn) goes back thousands of years, but it is generally accepted that the earlier parts of the list are largely mythical. It is unclear at what point the list begins to refer to historical individuals, although Niall Noígiallach (Niall of the Nine Hostages) is usually regarded as the first. The most successful of the dynasties descended from Niall were the Uí Néill (O'Neill), who as kings of Tara conquered petty kingdoms from the 5th century, and claimed high-kingship over all Ireland in the 9th century.

N = Kings of the Northern Uí Néill S = Kings of the Southern Uí Néill

?–453?	Niall Noígiallach (Niall of the Nine Hostages)	598–604	Áed Slaine (**S**) and Colmán Rímid (**N**)
c.454/6–c.463	Lóegaire	604–12	Áed Uaridnach (**N**)
463/6–482	Ailill Molt	612–15	Máel Cobo (**N**)
c.482–507	Lugaid	615–28	Suibne Menn (**N**)
507–34/6	Muirchertach (**N**)	628–42/3	Domnall (**N**)
534/6–44	Tuathal Máelgarb	642/3–54	Conall Cáel (**N**)
544–64/5	Diarmait I	642/3–56/8	Cellach (**N**) *Co-regent to 654*
564/5–6	Forggus (**N**) and Domnall Ilchelgach (**N**)	656/8–65/6	Diarmait II (**S**) and Blathmac (**S**)
566–9	Ainmire (**N**)	665/6–71	Sechnussach (**S**)
569–72	Báetáin I (**N**) and Eochaid (**N**)	671–5	Cennfáelad (**S**)
		675–95	Finsnechta Fledach (**S**)
572–86	Báetáin II (**N**)	695–704	Loingsech (**N**)
586–98	Áed (**N**)	704–10	Congal Cennmagair (**N**)

710–22	Fergal (**N**)
722–4	Fogartach (**S**)
724–8	Cináed (**S**)
728–34	Flaithbertach (**N**)
734–43	Áed Allán (**N**)
743–63	Domnall Midi (**S**)
763–70	Niall Frossach (**N**)
770–97	Donnchad Midi (**S**)
797–819	Áed Oirdnide (**N**)
819–33	Conchobar (**S**)
833–46	Niall Caille (**N**)
846–62	Máel Sechnaill I (**S**)
862/3–79	Áed Findliath (**N**)
879–916	Flann Sinna (**S**)
916–19	Niall Glúndub (**N**)
919–44	Donnchad Donn (**S**)
944–56	Congalach Cnogba (**S**)
956–80	Domnall ua Néill (**N**)

980–1002	Máel Sechnaill II (**S**)
	(*deposed*)
1002–14	Brian Bóruma (Brian Boru)
1014–22	Máel Sechnaill II (**S**)
	(*restored*)
1022–72	*Interregnum*
1072–86	Toirrdelbach ua Briain
	(Munster)
1086–1119	Muirchertach ua Briain
	(Munster)
1119–21	Domnall mac Lochlainn (**N**)
1121–56	Toirrdelbach ua Conchobair
	(Connacht)
1156–66	Muirchertach mac
	Lochlainn (**N**)
1166–86	Ruaidhrí ua Conchobair
	(Rory O'Connor)
	(Connacht)

British Order of Succession

1 Charles, Prince of Wales
2 Prince William of Wales
3 Prince Henry (Harry) of Wales
4 Prince Andrew, Duke of York
5 Princess Beatrice of York
6 Princess Eugenie of York
7 Prince Edward, Earl of Wessex
8 Lady Louise Windsor
9 Princess Anne, The Princess Royal
10 Mr Peter Phillips
11 Miss Zara Phillips
12 Viscount Linley
13 The Hon Charles Armstrong-Jones
14 The Hon Margarita Armstrong-Jones
15 Lady Sarah Chatto

16 Master Samuel Chatto
17 Master Arthur Chatto
18 The Duke of Gloucester
19 The Earl of Ulster
20 Lady Davina Windsor
21 Lady Rose Windsor
22 The Duke of Kent
23 Lady Marina Charlotte Windsor
24 Lady Amelia Windsor
25 Lady Helen Taylor
26 Master Columbus Taylor
27 Master Cassius Taylor
28 Miss Eloise Taylor
29 Lord Frederick Windsor
30 Lady Gabriella Windsor

Part Two: Monarchs of the World

World Monarchs

Abbas I, known as **Abbas the Great** (1571–1629) The fifth Safavid Shah of Persia. After his accession (1588), he set about establishing a counterweight to the Turkmen tribal chiefs who had constituted the principal political and military powers in the state. From 1598 he was able to recover Azerbaijan and parts of Armenia from the Ottomans, and Khurasan from the Uzbeks. He transferred his capital from Qazvin to Isfahan (Esfahan), and established diplomatic and economic relations with Western Europe.

Abd-ul-Hamid II, nickname **The Great Assassin** (1842–1918) The last Sultan of Turkey (1876–1909). He promulgated the first Ottoman constitution in 1876, but his reign was notable for his cruel suppression of revolts in the Balkans, which led to wars with Russia (1877–8), and especially for the Armenian massacres of 1894–6. A reform movement by the revolutionary Young Turks forced him to summon a parliament in 1908, but he was deposed and exiled in 1909.

Abdullah (ibn Hussein) (1882–1951) First King of Jordan (1946–51), the second son of Hussein ibn Ali and grandfather of King Hussein. Emir of the British mandated territory of Transjordan in 1921, he became king

ABDICATION

Abdication is a political situation which occurs when the ruler of a country gives up the throne or other high office. Most abdications take place under duress: the ruler is forced to abdicate following a wartime defeat, a revolution, or a constitutional crisis. Napoleon Bonaparte was forced to abdicate twice – once in 1814, and again in 1815. Edward VIII of Britain was forced to abdicate in 1936 because of public disapproval of his proposed marriage to a divorcee. Some rulers choose to abdicate, perhaps because of illness or old age, or simply because they feel they have ruled for too long. Queen Wilhelmina of the Netherlands voluntarily abdicated in 1948, as did her daughter, Queen Juliana, in 1980.

when the mandate ended in 1946, but was assassinated by disgruntled Palestinians.

Abd-ul-Medjid (1823–61) Sultan of Turkey from 1839. He continued the Westernizing reforms of the previous reign of Mahmut II (1785–1839), reorganizing the court system and education, and granting various rights to citizens, including Christians. In 1854 he secured an alliance with Britain and France to resist Russian demands, thus precipitating the Crimean War (1854–6).

Achaemenids The first royal house of Persia, founded by the early 7th-century BC ruler, Achaemenes. Its capitals included Parsagadae, Susa, and Persepolis.

Adalberto I (9th-c) Italian ruler, the son of Boniface II, Count of Lucca. He became the first Marquis of Tuscany in 846, supporting antipope Anastasio and taking Pope John VIII prisoner. He was excommunicated, but this was revoked thanks to the intervention of Charles III.

Adalberto II, known as **the Rich** (?–915) Italian ruler, the son of Adalberto I. He was Marquis of Tuscany (889–915), and married Berta, the daughter of Lothar II. A very powerful feudal lord, he took part in the conflicts for the Italian crown, supporting a number of candidates. He consolidated the autonomy of the Tuscany march.

Adelaide, St, Ger. **Adelheid** (931–99) Holy Roman Empress, a daughter of Rudolf II of Burgundy. She married Lothar II of Italy in 947. After his death in 950 she was imprisoned by his successor, Berengar II, but was rescued by King Otto I of Germany, who married her as his second wife in 951. They were crowned emperor and empress in 962. Their son was Otto II. As queen mother, she exercised considerable influence. She became joint regent for her grandson, Otto III, and then sole regent (991–6). Thereafter she retired to a convent in Alsace. Feast day 16 December.

Adelchis (?–c.788) King of the Lombards. The son of Desiderio and Ansa, he was joint ruler with his father (759). He was defeated by Charlemagne's Franks at Chiusa di Val di Susa (773). When Desiderio was taken prisoner at Pavia, Adelchis took refuge in Verona and, after the demise of the Lombard Kingdom, in Constantinople. In 788 he organized an unsuccessful military expedition to regain his kingdom. He is the protagonist of the eponymous tragedy by Manzoni.

Agamemnon King of Argos and commander of the Greek army in the Trojan War. In the *Iliad*, Homer calls him 'king of men'. On his return home he was murdered by his wife Clytemnestra.

Agathocles (361–289 BC) Ruler of Syracuse, born at Terme, Sicily. After seizing power in 317 BC, he clashed with the Carthaginians and was defeated at Ecnomo (310 BC). When the Carthaginians besieged Syracuse, Agathocles brought the war to Africa. After achieving peace, he was left in control of all Sicily apart from Agrigento. At his death, he bequeathed his possessions to the people of Syracuse.

Agesilaus (444–360 BC) King of Sparta (399–360 BC). Called on by the Ionians to assist them in 397 BC against Artaxerxes II, he launched an ambitious campaign in Asia, but the Corinthian War recalled him to Greece. At Coronea (394 BC) he defeated the Greek allied forces, and peace was eventually concluded in favour of Sparta (387 BC). He precipitated the Battle of Leuctra against Thebes (371 BC), a disaster which signified the end of Spartan ascendancy and the beginning of a decade of Theban supremacy in Greece.

Agilulf (?–616) King of the Lombards (590–616). As Duke of Turin, he married Autari's widow, Theodolinda, and succeeded him to the throne. He asserted his authority on rebel dukes, conquered Padua (601), and forced the Byzantine exarch to pay him a tribute. Although an Arian, under the influence of the Catholic Theodolinda he promoted the spread of Catholicism among his people and sustained a policy of conciliation with Pope Gregory I.

Ahab (9th-c BC) King of Israel (c.873–c.852 BC), the son of Omri. He was a warrior king and builder on a heroic scale, extending his capital city of Samaria and refortifying Megiddo and Hazor. He married Jezebel, daughter of the king of Tyre and Sidon, who introduced the worship of the Phoenician god, Baal, in opposition to Yahweh (the God of Israelite religion), and thus aroused the hostility of the prophet Elijah.

Ahmad Shah Durrani (1724–73) Founder and first monarch of Afghanistan. A chieftain of the Durrani clan of the Abdali tribe, and a cavalry general under the Persian emperor Nadir Shah, he was elected King of the Afghan provinces in 1747. He established his capital at Kandahar, and made nine successful invasions of the Punjab. In 1761 he defeated the Marathas decisively at the Battle of Panipat, but was eventually obliged to acknowledge Sikh power in the Punjab.

Akbar the Great, in full **Jalal ud-Din Muhammad Akbar** (1542–1605) Mughal Emperor of India, born in Umarkot, near Hyderabad, Sind province, present-day Pakistan. He succeeded his father, Humayun, in 1556, and assumed power in 1560. The early years of his reign were marred by civil war and rebellion, but after triumphing over his enemies within the empire he turned to foreign conquest, extending his control to the whole of northern India. He reformed the tax system, promoted commerce, encouraged science, literature, and the arts, and abolished slavery. Although brought up a Muslim, he pursued a tolerant and eclectic religious policy.

Akhenaton, also **Akh(e)naten** or

Amenhotep (Amenophis) IV (14th-c BC) Egyptian king of the XVIII dynasty. He renounced the worship of the old gods, introduced a monotheistic solar cult of the sun-disc (Aton), and changed his name. He built a new capital at Amarna (Akhetaton), where the arts blossomed while the empire weakened. One of his wives was Nefertiti.

Akihito (1933–) Emperor of Japan (1989–), born in Tokyo, the son of Hirohito. He studied among commoners at the elite Gakushuin school, and in 1959 married **Michiko Shoda** (1934–), the daughter of a flour company president, who thus became the first non-aristocrat to enter the imperial family. They have three children: **Crown Prince Naruhito** (1960–), **Prince Fumihito** (1963–), and **Princess Sayako** (1969–). An amateur marine biologist, he is also an accomplished cellist. On becoming emperor in 1989, the new *Heisei* ('the achievement of universal peace') era commenced. In 2001 Crown Prince Naruhito and his wife, Masako, celebrated the birth of a baby daughter. Princess Sayako relinquished her royal status when she married commoner Yoshiki Kuroda in 2005.

Alaric I (c.370–410) King of the Visigoths (395–410), born in Dacia. After his election as king, he invaded Greece (395), but was eventually driven out by Flavius Stilicho. In 401 he invaded Italy until checked by Stilicho at Pollentia (402). He agreed to join the Western emperor, Honorius, in an attack on Arcadius, but when Honorius failed to pay the promised subsidy Alaric laid siege to Rome, and in 410 pillaged the city, an event which marked the beginning of the end of the Western Roman Empire. Later that year he set off to invade Sicily, but died at Cosenza.

Alaric II (450–507) King of the Visigoths (485–507), who reigned over Gaul south of the Loire, and over most of Spain. In 506 he issued a code of laws known as the Breviary of Alaric (*Breviarum Alaricianum*). An Arian Christian, he was killed at the Battle of Vouillé, near Poitiers, by the orthodox Clovis, King of the Franks.

Albert I (1875–1934) King of the Belgians (1909–34), born in Brussels, the younger son of Philip, Count of Flanders. At the outbreak of World War 1 he refused a German demand for the free passage of their troops, and after a heroic resistance led the Belgian army in retreat to Flanders. He commanded the Belgian and French army in the final offensive on the Belgian coast in 1918. After the war he took an active part in the industrial reconstruction of the country.

Albert II, in full **Albert Félix Humbert Théodore Chrétien Eugène Marie Wettin** (1934–) King of Belgium (1993–), born in Brussels, the younger son of King Leopold III and the brother of King Baudouin. He was educated privately and in Geneva. Between 1962 and his succession to the throne, he took a particular interest in promoting Belgian exports, holding the post of honorary president of the administrative council of the Belgian Office of External Trade. In 1959 he married **Donna Paola** (1937–), daughter of Principe Don Fulco Ruffo di Calabria, Duca di Guardia Lombarda. Their children are heir apparent **Philippe Leopold Louis Marie, Duke of Brabant** (1960–), **Astrid Josephine Charlotte Fabrizia Elisabeth Paola Marie** (1962–), and **Laurent Benôit Baudouin Marie** (1963–). Since 1991 males and females have equal rights of succession. Prior to 1991 Belgium used Salic law.

Albert, known as **the Bold** (1443–1500) Duke of Saxony, the son of Frederick the Gentle. He was joint ruler with his brother Ernest from 1464 until 1485 when, by the Treaty of Leipzig, they divided their inheritance between them. The two branches of the Wettin family then became known as the *Albertine* and *Ernestine* lines.

Alboin or **Alboino** (?–572) King of the Lombards in Pannonia (present-day Austria and western Hungary) (c.565–72). He succeeded his father Audoin, defeated the Gepidae, and married Rosamond, daughter of their dead King Cunimond (or Cunimund). In 568–9 he took his people from Pannonia to Italy, and conquered Veneto. He established a duchy at Cividale, invaded Lombardy, conquered Milan (569), and entered Pavia (571) after a long siege. He installed himself at Verona, but was killed by Rosamond, who had him poisoned by the squire Elmichi.

Alexander I (1777–1825) Tsar of Russia (1801–25), born in St Petersburg, the grandson of Catherine the Great. The early years of his reign were marked by the promise of liberal constitutional reforms and the pursuit of a vigorous foreign policy. His wars with Turkey (1806–12) and Persia (1804–13) brought territorial gains, including the acquisition of Georgia. In 1805 Russia joined the coalition against Napoleon, but after a series of military defeats was forced to conclude the Treaty of Tilsit (1807) with France. When Napoleon broke the treaty by invading Russia in 1812, Alexander's armies forced the French army's retreat. At the Congress of Vienna (1814–15) he laid claim to Poland. He supported Metternich in suppressing liberal and national movements. During the last years of his reign his increased political reactionism and religious mysticism resulted in the founding of the Holy Alliance of European monarchs. His mysterious death at Taganrog caused a succession crisis which led to the attempted revolutionary coup of the Decembrists.

Alexander I (1888–1934) King of the Serbs, Croats, and Slovenes (1921–9), then King of Yugoslavia (1929–34), born in Cetinje, Montenegro, the second son of Peter I. He tried to build up a strong and unified Yugoslavia, imposing a royal dictatorship in 1929, but was assassinated in Marseille.

Alexander II, known as **Alexander the Liberator** (1818–81) Tsar of Russia from 1855, born in St Petersburg, the son of Nicholas I. He succeeded to the throne during the Crimean War, and signed the Treaty of Paris which ended it in 1856. A determined reformer, the great achievement of his reign was the emancipation of the serfs in 1861 (hence his byname), followed by reform of the legal and administrative systems, and the establishment of elected assemblies in the provinces. Despite his liberal views, his government was severe in repressing peasant unrest and revolutionary movements, and he was assassinated.

Alexander III (1845–94) Tsar of Russia (1881–94), born in St Petersburg, the younger son of Alexander II. He followed a repressive policy in home affairs, especially in the persecution of Jews (the 'pogroms'), thousands of whom emigrated to the UK and USA. Abroad, he consolidated Russia's hold on central Asia to the frontier of Afghanistan, provoking a crisis with Britain (1885).

Alexander the Great (356–323 BC) King of Macedonia (336–323 BC), born at Pella, the son of Philip II and Olympias. He was tutored by Aristotle, and ascended the throne when less than 20 years old. After crushing all opposition at home, he set out to conquer Greece's hereditary enemy, Achaemenid Persia. This he achieved with great rapidity in a series of famous battles: Granicus (334 BC), Issus (333 BC), and Gaugmela (331 BC). By 330 BC, Darius III had fled, and the capitals of Susa, Persepolis, and Ecbatana had been taken. In the next three years, the eastern half of the empire was also conquered, and

Alexander set out for India. He reached the Punjab, and had set his sights on the Ganges, when his troops mutinied and forced his return. He died shortly after at Babylon.

Alexander Severus (205–35) Roman emperor (222–35), the cousin and adopted son of Heliogabalus, whom he succeeded. A weak ruler, under the influence of others (especially his mother), he failed to control the military. Though successful against the Sassanid Ardashir I, he was murdered by mutinous troops during a campaign against the Germans.

Alexandra Feodorovna (1872–1918) German princess, and Empress of Russia as the wife of Nicholas II, born in Darmstadt, Germany, the daughter of Grand Duke Louis of Hesse-Darmstadt and Alice Maud Mary (the daughter of Queen Victoria). She married Nicholas in 1894. Deeply pious and superstitious, she came under the influence of the fanatical Rasputin. During World War 1, while Nicholas was away at the front, she meddled disastrously in politics. When the revolution broke out, she was imprisoned by the Bolsheviks, and shot in a cellar at Yekaterinburg.

Alexey I Mihailovitch or **Alexis I** (1629–76) Second Romanov Tsar of Russia (1645–76), who succeeded his father, Michael Romanov. He waged war against Poland (1654–67), regaining Smolensk and Kiev. His attempts to place the Orthodox Church under secular authority brought him into conflict with the Patriarch, Nikon. By his second wife he was the father of Peter I.

Alexis, in full **Alexey Petrovitch** (1690–1718) Prince, born in Moscow, the eldest son of Peter I. Having opposed the tsar's reforms, he was excluded from the succession, and escaped to Vienna, and thence to Naples. Induced to return to Russia, he was condemned to death, then pardoned, but died in prison a few days after. His son became tsar as Peter II (reigned 1727–30).

Alexius I (Comnenus) (1048–1118) Byzantine emperor (1081–1118), the founder of the Comnenian dynasty, born in Istanbul. He defeated a major invasion mounted by the Normans of Sicily under Robert Guiscard (1081–2) and later under Bohemond I (1083); in alliance with the Cumans he destroyed the Patzinaks at Mount Levounion (1091). He built up a new fleet with the aim of re-establishing Byzantine rule in Asia Minor. This coincided with the arrival of the First Crusade (1096–1100), with which he co-operated to recover Crete, Cyprus, and the west coast of Anatolia. His reign is well known from the *Alexiad*, the biography written by his daughter, Anna Comnena.

Alexius III (Angelus) (?–1211) Byzantine emperor (1195–1203). He became emperor after plotting against his brother Isaac II, but was unable to stop the empire's economic collapse, and was forced to leave Constantinople in 1203 by the arrival of the crusaders. Taken prisoner in 1210 and sent to Italy, he was ransomed by the Genoese and confined to a monastery by his son-in-law, Theodore Lascaris, where he died.

Alexius IV (Angelus) (c.1182–1204) Byzantine emperor (1203–4), born in Constantinople. He was the son of Isaac II and escaped to Italy after his father was dethroned by Alexius III. With the help of Pope Innocent III and Enrico Dandolo's Venetian forces, he returned to Constantinople. When the city fell to the crusaders (1203), he was reinstated to the throne together with his father. Soon after, he was murdered during an insurrection headed by Alexius Ducas (Alexius V).

Alexius V, in full **Alexius Ducas Mourtzouphlos** (?–1204) Byzantine emperor (1204), the son-in-law of Alexius III. In 1204 he overthrew the emperors Isaac II and his son Alexius IV, who had been reinstated as co-emperors (1203) by the Latin crusaders, causing the sack of Constantinople by the army of the Fourth Crusade. He was deposed and killed, and Baldwin I was elected by the crusaders as Latin emperor of Constantinople.

Alfonso I or **Alfonso Henriques**, also spelled **Afonso** (c.1110–85) Earliest King of Portugal (1139–85), born in Guimarães, Portugal. He was only two years old at the death of his father, Henry of Burgundy, the conqueror and first Count of Portugal, so that the management of affairs fell to his mother, Theresa of Castile. Wresting power from her in 1128, he defeated the Moors at Ourique (1139), and pro-claimed himself king. He took Lisbon (1147), and later all Galicia, Estremadura, and Elvas.

Alfonso III, known as **Alfonso the Great** (?–910) King of León, Asturias, and Galicia (866–910). He fought over 30 campaigns and gained numerous victories over the Moors, occupied Coimbra, and extended his territory as far as Portugal and Old Castile.

Alfonso V, known as **the Magnanimous** (1396–1458) King of Aragón, Sicily, and Sardinia (1416–58). King of Naples as Alfonso I (1442–58), he had himself adopted by Queen Giovanna d'Angiò in an attempt to reunite the kingdoms of Naples and Sicily, but was thwarted and forced to return to Spain where he succeeded in blending together Catalans and Castilians. He returned to Italy where he faced the alliance of Florence, Milan, Venice, and Renato d'Angiò. He was captured at Ponza (1435) by Filippo Maria Visconti, but later obtained his support to regain Naples in 1442. As King of Naples, he imple-mented administrative reforms, curbed the power of the aristocracy, and promoted the arts.

Alfonso X, nicknames **Alfonso the Astronomer** and **Alfonso the Wise** (1221–84) King of León and Castile (1252–84), born in Toledo, Spain, the son of Ferdinand (or Fernando) III and Beatrice of Swabia. He captured Cadiz and Algarve from the Moors, and thus united Murcia with Castile. The foun-der of a Castilian national literature,

he caused the first general history of Spain to be composed in Castilian, as well as a translation of the Old Testament to be made by Toledo Jews. His great code of laws (*Siete Partidas*) and his planetary table were of major importance. In 1282, he lost power following a rising under his son, Sancho IV.

Alfonso XI, known as **Alfonso the Just** (1311–50) King of Castile (1312–50), born in Salamanca, Spain. He became king when only one year old, but once of age (1325), he began to restore order in a court fragmented by factions of nobles. He gave new powers to the Cortés and chose officials without aristocratic affiliations. He also made important administrative and legal reforms, and was diplomatic in his dealings with France and England. He is the supposed writer of the first troubadour song recorded in Castilian.

Alfonso XII (1857–85) King of Spain (1874–85), the son of Isabella II. After a period of republican rule following the overthrow of his mother by the army in 1868, he was formally pro-claimed king. In 1876 he suppressed the last opposition of the Carlists (supporters of the Spanish pretender Don Carlos de Bourbon and his suc-cessors), and drafted a new constitu-tion. In 1879 he married **Maria Christina** (1858–1929), daughter of Archduke Charles Ferdinand of Austria, and was succeeded by his son, Alfonso XIII.

Alfonso XIII (1886–1941) King of Spain (1886–1931), the posthumous son of

Alfonso XII. In 1906 he married princess Ena, granddaughter of Queen Victoria. After neutrality during World War 1, the Spanish were defeated by the Moors in Morocco in 1921, and from 1923 he associated himself with the military dictatorship of Primo de Rivera. In 1931 the king agreed to elections, which voted overwhelmingly for a republic. He refused to abdicate, but left Spain, and died in exile.

Ali Bey (1728–73) Egyptian ruler, a slave from the Caucasus who distinguished himself in the service of Ibrahim Katkhuda and rose to be chief of the Mamluks. Victorious in the power-struggle that followed the death of Ibrahim in 1754, he had himself declared sultan (1768) and proceeded to establish in Egypt an adminstration independent of Ottoman overlordship. Defeated by Ottoman forces in 1772, he was forced to take refuge in Syria. Under him Egypt briefly achieved independence for the first time in more than 200 years.

Alice Maud Mary, Princess (1843–78) British princess, the second daughter of Queen Victoria. In 1862 she married **Prince Louis of Hesse-Darmstadt** (1837–92). They had four daughters: the eldest became the mother of Louis, Earl Mountbatten; the youngest, Alexandra, married Nicholas II of Russia.

al-Sabah The ruling dynasty of Kuwait. Dating their authority in Kuwait to the mid-18th century, the al-Sabah sheikhs attempted to maintain their independence among the competing rivalries of European, Ottoman, and local powers. **Mubarak the Great** (reigned 1896–1915) sought

ANGEVINS

The Angevins were three ruling families of the mediaeval county (and later duchy) of Anjou in western France. (1) Henry II, founder of the Angevin or Plantagenet dynasty in England, was a descendant of the earliest counts of Anjou. He established the 'Angevin empire' by taking control of Normandy, Anjou, and Maine (1150–1), acquiring Aquitaine (1152), and succeeding Stephen in England (1154). (2) The French crown had annexed Anjou by 1205, and in 1246 Louis IX's brother Charles, future king of Naples and Sicily, became count. (3) The third line was descended from Charles of Valois, brother of Philip IV, who married Charles of Anjou's granddaughter in 1290. This family died out in 1481.

British protection to forestall Ottoman intervention into Kuwaiti affairs. Since independence in 1961, al-Sabah rule has twice been challenged by Iraq on the disputed grounds that Kuwait once formed part of the province of Basra. Sheikh Jaber al-Ahmad al-Jaber al-Sabah (1926–2006) came to power in 1977, but was seldom seen in public after 2001 following a minor stroke. One of the main crises of his rule was Iraq's invasion of Kuwait (1990). The National Assembly, which had been dissolved by Sheikh Jaber in 1986, was reconstituted in 1992. However, the government of Kuwait remains dominated by members of the al-Sabah family. Crown Prince Saad al-Abdullah al-Salim al-Sabah succeeded to the emir briefly in January 2006, but stepped down due to ill health and was replaced by Sabah al-Ahmad al-Jaber al-Sabah. Sheikh Nawaf al-Ahmad was appointed crown prince.

Amalaric (502–31) King of the Visigoths, the son of Alaric II. He succeeded his step-brother Gesaleic in 511 and was under the guardianship of his grandfather Theodoric until 526. To strengthen his relationship with the Franks, he married Clotilda de Meroving (497–531); when Clotilda was forced to convert to Arianism, she asked her brother Childebert for help and he defeated Amalaric at Narbonne in 531.

Amalasuntha (c.498–535) Queen and regent of the Ostrogoths (526–34). Daughter of Theodoric, she was regent for her son Athalaric from 526, and at his death (534) became Queen of the Ostrogoths. She followed her father's policies and reorganized the kingdom's administration, ruling that the monarch should arbitrate over the election of popes and bishops. Her reign was unstable due to pressure from barbarian tribes and the Goths' discontent. When her son died she shared the throne with her cousin Theodahad, who exiled her to Bolsena and had her killed. This gave Justinian the pretext for the Gothic War.

Amanullah Khan (1892–1960) Ruler of Afghanistan (1919–29), born in Pagman, Afghanistan. After an inconclusive religious war against the British in India (1919–22), independence for Afghanistan was recognized by Britain with the Treaty of Rawalpindi (1922). He assumed the title of king in 1926, but his zeal for Westernizing reforms provoked rebellion in 1928. He abdicated and fled the country in 1929, and went into exile in Rome.

Amenhotep II (15th-c BC) King of Egypt in the XVIII dynasty (c.1426–c.1400 BC), the son of Thuthmose III. He fought successful campaigns in Palestine and on the Euphrates. His mummy was found in the Valley of the Tombs of the Kings, Thebes.

Amenhotep III (c.1411–1379 BC) King of Egypt (c.1390–c.1353 BC), the son of Thuthmose IV. He consolidated Egyptian supremacy in Babylonia and Assyria. In a reign of spectacular wealth and magnificence, he built his great capital city, Thebes, and its finest monuments, including the Luxor temple, the great pylon at Karnak, and the colossi of Memnon.

Ancus Marcius (7th-c BC)
Traditionally, the fourth King of Rome. He is said to have conquered the neighbouring Latin tribes, and settled them on the Aventine.

Anna Comnena (1083–1148)
Byzantine princess and historian, the daughter of the Emperor Alexius I Comnenus. In 1097 she married Nicephorus Bryennius, for whom she tried in vain to gain the imperial crown after her father's death in 1118. She took up literature and, after her husband died (1137), retired to a convent where she wrote the *Alexiad*, a notable account in 15 books of Byzantine history and society for the period 1069–1118.

Anna Paulowna of Russia
(1795–1865) Queen of The Netherlands, born in St Petersburg, the daughter of Tsar Paul I, Grand-Duchess of Russia (Romanov), and sister of Alexander I and Nicholas I. She married King William II of The Netherlands and became Queen of The Netherlands (1840–9). She had four sons (including King William III of The Netherlands) and one daughter. After the death of William II she engaged in charitable activities.

Anne of Austria (1601–66) Queen of France, born in Valladolid, Spain, the eldest daughter of Philip III of Spain and wife of Louis XIII of France, whom she married in 1615.

The marriage was unhappy, and much of it was spent in virtual separation, due to the influence of the king's chief minister Cardinal Richelieu. In 1638, however, they had their first son, Louis, who succeeded his father in 1643 as Louis XIV. Anne was appointed regent for the boy king (1643–51), and wielded power with Cardinal Mazarin as prime minister. After Mazarin's death in 1661, she remained at court, though often visiting the convent of Val de Grâce.

Anne of Brittany (1476–1514) Duchess of Brittany and twice Queen of France. She struggled to maintain Breton independence, but in 1491 was forced to marry Charles VIII of France (reigned 1483–98), whereby Brittany was united with the French crown. In 1499, a year after his death, she married his successor, Louis XII.

Antigonus II, known as **Gonatas** (c.319–239 BC) King of Macedon. He did not mount his throne until 276 BC, seven years after the death of his father, Demetrius Poliorcetes. Pyrrhus of Epirus overran Macedonia in 274 BC, but Antigonus soon recovered his kingdom, and consolidated it despite incessant wars.

Antiochus I, known as **Antiochus Soter** (Greek 'Saviour') (324–261 BC) Seleucid King of Syria (281–261 BC). He was the son of Seleucus I, one of Alexander's generals, whose murder in 280 BC gave him the whole Syrian empire, but left him too weak to assert his right to Macedonia. He gained his surname for a victory over the Gauls, but fell in battle with them.

Antiochus II, known as **Antiochus Theos** (Greek 'God') (286–247 BC) Seleucid King of Syria, the son and successor of Antiochus I. He married Berenice, the daughter of Ptolemy II, exiling his first wife, Laodice, and her children. On his death there followed a struggle between the rival queens. Berenice and her son were murdered, and the succession went to Laodice's son, Seleucus II (reigned 246–226 BC).

Antiochus III, known as **Antiochus the Great** (c.242–187 BC) Seleucid King of Syria, the son of Seleucus II and grandson of Antiochus II, who succeeded his brother, Seleucus III, in 223 BC. He waged war with success against Ptolemy IV Philopator, and though defeated at Raphia near Gaza (217 BC), he obtained entire possession of Palestine and Coele Syria (198 BC). He later became involved in war with the Romans, who had conquered Macedonia. He crossed over into Greece, but was defeated in 191 BC at Thermopylae, and in 190 or 189 BC by Scipio at Magnesia. To raise tribute money, he attacked a rich temple in Elymais, but the people rose against him and killed him.

Antiochus IV, known as **Antiochus Epiphanes** (c.215–163 BC) Seleucid King of Syria, the son of Antiochus III. He succeeded his brother in 175 BC, then fought against Egypt and conquered a great part of it. He twice took Jerusalem, provoking the Jews to a successful insurrection under Mattathias and his sons, the Maccabees.

Antipater (?–4 BC) Judaean prince, the son of Herod the Great by his first wife. He conspired against his half-brothers and had them executed, then plotted against his father, and was himself executed five days before Herod died.

Antoninus Pius, originally **Titus Aurelius Fulvus** (86–161) Roman emperor, born in Lanuvium. He inherited great wealth, and in 120 was made consul. Sent as proconsul into Asia by Emperor Hadrian, in 138 he was adopted by him, and the same year came to the throne. His reign was proverbially peaceful and happy. In public affairs he acted as the father of his people, and the persecution of Christians was partly stayed by his mild measures. In his reign the empire was extended, and the Antonine Wall, named after him, built between the Forth and Clyde rivers. He was called *Pius* for his defence of Hadrian's memory. Marcus Aurelius was his adopted son and successor.

Arcadius (377–408) Emperor of the Eastern Roman Empire, born in Spain. After the death of his father, Emperor Theodosius (395), he received the eastern half of the Roman Empire, the western half falling to his brother Honorius. An ineffectual ruler, he was dominated by his ministers and by his wife (married 395), Empress Eudoxia (?–404).

Ardashir I or **Artaxerxes** (c.211–41)

King of Persia (224–41), and founder of the new Persian dynasty of the Sassanids. He overthrew Artabanus IV, the last of the Parthian kings, in c.226. He entered into battle with Alexander Severus (232), and though Alexander celebrated victory in Rome, Ardashir took Armenia and Persian power was firmly established. He was succeeded by Shapur I.

Arduino (955–c.1015) King of Italy (1002–14), the son of Dodone, Count of Pombia. He became Marquis of Ivrea (c.990) and, with the support of the lay feudal lords, was crowned at Pavia (1002) and recognized as King of Italy in the north and centre of the country. Opposed by the powerful lords of the clergy and by Emperor Henry II, in 1014 he gave up the throne and retired to Fruttuaria Abbey.

Arnulf of Carinthia (c.850–99) German emperor. He was elected King of Germany in 887, defeated the Normans at Louvain, and strengthened his power in Bavaria, Swabia, and Franconia. He was called by Pope Formosus in 894 and intervened in the disputes between Berengario and Guido of Spoleto, the first German king to intervene in Italian events. Crowned emperor in Rome by Pope Formosus in 896, he was later deposed by Berengario and died in Germany.

Arsinoë (316–270 BC) Macedonian princess, the daughter of Ptolemy I, and one of the most conspicuous of Hellenistic queens. She married first (c.300 BC) the aged Lysimachus, King of Thrace, secondly (and briefly) Ptolemy Ceraunus, and finally (c.276 BC) her own brother, Ptolemy II Philadelphus. Several cities were named after her.

Artaxerxes I, known as **Longimanus** ('long-handed') (5th-c BC) King of Persia (465–424 BC), the second son of Xerxes I. In a long and peaceful reign, he sanctioned the Jewish religion in Jerusalem, and appointed Nehemiah as governor of Judea in 445.

Artaxerxes II, Greek **Mnemon** (?–358 BC) King of Persia (404–358 BC), the son and successor of Darius II. Early in his reign, his brother Cyrus the Younger attempted to assassinate him and seize the throne, but Artaxerxes finally crushed him at the Battle of Cunaxa (401 BC), where Cyrus was killed. Artaxerxes was ruled by the will of his wife and mother and relied heavily on his officials. His troubled reign included two failed expeditions against Egypt (385–383 BC and 374 BC), rebellions in Anatolia, and wars against the mountain tribes of Armenia and Iran. He introduced an important change in Persian religious life by reviving the cults of Anahita and Mithra, two deities of the old popular Iranian religion.

Artemisia I (5th-c BC) Ruler of Halicarnassus and the neighbouring islands. She accompanied Xerxes in his expedition against Greece, and distinguished herself at Salamis (480 BC).

Artemisia II (?–c.350 BC) Sister and

wife of Mausolus, ruler of Caria. She succeeded him on his death (c.353–352 BC), and erected a magnificent mausoleum at Halicarnassus to his memory, which was one of the seven wonders of the ancient world. Also known as a botanist, *Artemisia* (wormwood) is named after her.

Arthur, Prince (1187–?1203) Duke of Brittany, and claimant to the throne of England as the grandson of Henry II. He was the posthumous son of Geoffrey, Duke of Brittany, Henry's fourth son, and on the death of his uncle, Richard I (1199), he became a claimant to the throne. The French king, Philip II, upheld Arthur's claim until Richard's brother, John, came to terms with Philip. Arthur was soon in his uncle's hands and was imprisoned, first at Calais and then at Rouen, where he died. It was popularly believed that King John was responsible for his death.

Aśoka or **Ashoka** (3rd-c BC) King of India (c.273–232 BC), the last ruler of the Mauryan dynasty. After his invasion of the Kalinga country, he renounced armed conquest and became a convert to Buddhism, which subsequently spread throughout India and beyond. He adopted a policy called *dharma* (principles of right life), advocating toleration, honesty, and kindness, and had his teachings engraved on rocks and pillars at certain sites. With his death the Mauryan empire declined and his work was discontinued.

Assurbanipal or **Ashurbanipal** (7th-c BC) King of Assyria (669–626 BC), the last of the great Assyrian kings, the son of Esarhaddon and grandson of Sennacherib. A patron of the arts, he founded at Nineveh the first systematically gathered and organized library in the Middle East, containing a vast number of texts on numerous subjects copied from temple libraries throughout his empire.

Astolfo (?–756) King of the Lombards, the son of Penmone, Duke of Friuli. He succeeded his brother Rachis as king in 749, and in 751 took the Exarchate and the Pentapolis from the Byzantines. When he threatened Rome, Pope Stephen II asked Pepin III, King of the Franks, for help. Astolfo was twice (754, 756) defeated by Pepin, and was forced to surrender the territories which formed the core of the Papal States.

Atahualpa (?–1533) Last Inca ruler of Peru. On the death of his father, he received the northern half of the Inca empire, and in 1532 overthrew his brother, Huascar, who ruled the southern half. A year later he was captured by invading Spaniards under Francisco Pizarro. Although his subjects paid a vast ransom to secure his release, Atahualpa was executed.

Ataulphus (?–415) King of the Visigoths. He succeeded his brother-in-law Alaric I (410) and led his people from Italy to Provence. In the service of Emperor Onofrio, he defeated the usurper Giovino, and in 414 married Onofrio's sister, Galla Placidia. He pursued a policy of conciliation with the Romans.

Athanaric (?–381) Prince of the Western Goths, who fought three campaigns against the Roman Emperor Valens (ruled 364–78). He was finally defeated in 369, and driven out by the Huns from the north of the Danube.

Attila, known as **the Scourge of God** (c.406–53) King of the Huns (434–53). He ruled with his elder brother until 445, his dominion extending over Germany and Scythia from the Rhine to the frontiers of China. In 447 he devastated all the countries between the Black Sea and the Mediterranean, defeating Emperor Theodosius II (ruled 408–50). In 451 he invaded Gaul, but was routed by Aëtius, the Roman commander, and Theodoric I, King of the Visigoths, on the Catalaunian Plain. He retreated to Hungary, but then made an incursion into Italy (452), devastating several cities, Rome itself being saved only by the personal mediation of Pope Leo I. The Hunnish empire decayed after his death.

Augusta (1811–90) German empress and Queen of Prussia, born in Weimar, Germany. A princess of Saxony-Weimar, in 1829 she married the future Emperor Wilhelm I, over whom she exercised a strong influence. She was an opponent of Bismarck.

Auguste Viktoria (1858–1921) The last German empress and Queen of Prussia (1888–1918), born in Dolzig, Germany (now Dolsk, Poland). Daughter of Duke Friedrich von Schleswig-Holstein-Sonderburg-Augustenburg, in 1881 she married the future Emperor Wilhelm II.

Augustulus, Romulus, nickname of **Flavius Momyllus Romulus Augustus** (5th-c) Last emperor of the western half of the old Roman Empire (ruled 475–476). His father, Orestes, had risen to high rank under Emperor Julius Neppos, on whose flight he conferred the vacant throne on Augustus (he received his nickname, a diminutive form of Augustus, because he was still a child at the time), retaining power in his own hands. After Orestes was killed by the barbarians, Augustulus was forced to retire to a villa near Naples.

Augustus (Gaius Julius Caesar Octavianus) (63 BC–AD 14) Founder of the Roman Empire, the son of Gaius Octavius, senator and praetor, and great nephew (through his mother, Atia) of Julius Caesar. On Caesar's assassination (44 BC), he abandoned student life in Illyricum and returned to Italy where, using Caesar's money and name (he had acquired both under his will), he raised an army, defeated Antony, and extorted a wholly unconstitutional consulship from the Senate (43 BC). When Antony returned in force from Gaul later that year with Lepidus, Octavian made a deal with his former enemies, joining the so-called Second Triumvirate with them, and taking Africa, Sardinia, and Sicily as his province. A later redivision of power gave him the entire western half of the Roman world, and Antony the eastern. While Antony was distracted there by his military schemes against Parthia, and his liaison with Cleopatra, Octavian consistently undermined him at home. Matters came to a head in 31 BC, and the Battle of Actium followed, Octavian emerging victorious as the sole ruler of the Roman world. Though taking the inoffensive title *princeps* ('first citizen'), he was in all but name an absolute monarch. His new name, Augustus ('exalted'), had historical and religious overtones, and was deliberately chosen to enhance his prestige. His long reign (27 BC–AD 14) was a time of peace and reconstruction at home, sound administration and steady conquest abroad. In gratitude the Romans awarded him the title *Pater Patriae* ('Father of his Country') in 2 BC, and on his death made him a god (*divus Augustus*).

Augustus II, known as **Augustus the Strong** (1670–1733) King of Poland (1697–1706, 1710–33) and Elector of Saxony, born in Dresden, Germany (formerly Saxony). He succeeded to the electorship as Frederick Augustus I in 1694, and became a Roman Catholic in order to secure his election to the Polish throne as Augustus II in 1697. In alliance with Peter the Great of Russia and Frederik IV of Denmark, he planned the partition of Sweden, invading Livonia in 1699. Defeated by Charles XII of Sweden, he was deposed in 1706 and replaced by Stanislaus Leszczynski. After the defeat of the

Swedes by Peter the Great at Poltava (1709), he recovered the Polish throne.

Aurangzeb or **Aurungzib** ('ornament of the throne'), kingly title **Alamgir** (1618–1707) Last of the Mughal emperors of India (1658–1707), the third son of Emperor Shah Jahan. When Shah Jahan became seriously ill in 1657, Aurangszeb defeated his brothers and confined his father, beginning his rule without formal coronation in 1658. During his long reign, the empire remained outwardly prosperous and extended its boundaries, but his puritanical and narrow outlook alienated the various communities, particularly the Hindus, whom he treated with great harshness. Opposed by his own rebellious sons and by the Mahratta empire in the south, he died a fugitive at Ahmadnagar.

Aurelian, in full **Lucius Domitius Aurelianus** (c.215–75) Roman emperor (270–5), born of humble origins in Dacia or Pannonia. Enlisting early as a common soldier he rose rapidly to the highest military offices. On the death of Claudius II (270), he was elected emperor by the army. By restoring good discipline in the army, order in domestic affairs, and political unity to the Roman dominions, he merited the title awarded him by the Senate, *Restitutor Orbis* ('Restorer of the World'). He was assassinated by his own officers during a campaign against the Persians.

Aurelius, in full **Caesar Marcus Aurelius Antoninus Augustus**, originally **Marcus Annius Verus** (121–80) One of the most respected emperors in Roman history, born in Rome. When only 17, he was adopted by Antoninus Pius, who had succeeded Hadrian and whose daughter Faustina was selected for his wife. From 140, when he was made consul, till the death of Antoninus in 161, he discharged his public duties with great conscientiousness, at the same time devoting himself to the study of law and philosophy, especially Stoicism. Peaceful by temperament, his reign suffered from constant wars, and though in Asia, in Britain, and on the Rhine the barbarians were checked, permanent peace was never secured. His death was felt to be a national calamity, and he was retrospectively idealized as the model of the perfect emperor.

Autari (?–590) King of the Lombards. He became king (584) after a long period of anarchy following the death of his father Clefi (574), and married Theodolinda in 589. He reorganized the country's administration and tried to reconcile the different factions. When threatened with an invasion by a Frank–Byzantine alliance, he reached an agreement with the Franks. He left the crown a number of new territories given to him by the dukes.

his father as Count of Flanders (in 1194) and Hainault (in 1195). In 1202 he joined the Fourth Crusade, and in 1204 was chosen the first Latin Emperor of Constantinople. The Greeks, invoking the aid of the Bulgarians, rose and took Adrianople. Baldwin laid siege to the town, but was defeated in 1205 and died in captivity.

Bao Dai (Vietnamese 'keeper of greatness'), originally **Nguyen Vinh Thuy** (1913–97) Indo-Chinese ruler, born in Hué, Vietnam, the son of Emperor Khai Dai. He ruled as Emperor of Annam (1932–45), then in 1949, having renounced his hereditary title, returned to Saigon as chief of the State of Vietnam within the French Union. In 1955 he was deposed and South Vietnam became a republic.

Basil I, known as **Basil the Macedonian** (c.812–86) Byzantine emperor (867–86), born in Thrace. He rose in the imperial service from obscure origins to become co-ruler in 867 with Michael III, whom he murdered in the same year. He formulated the Greek legal code, in a text known as the *Basilica*. The dynasty he founded ruled Constantinople until 1056.

Basil II, known as **Basil Bulgaroctonus** ('slayer of the Bulgars') (c.958–1025) Byzantine emperor who came to the throne as sole ruler in 976. A palace revolution was crushed by his alliance with Vladimir I the Great, Prince of Kiev. Vladimir's troops became the core of

Babar or **Babur** (Arabic 'tiger'), originally **Zahir-ud-din Muhammad** (1483–1530) First Mughal Emperor of India, born in Ferghana, Uzbekistan. After failing to establish himself in Samarkand, he invaded India, defeating Ibrahim Lodi decisively at the Battle of Paniput in 1526, and laying the foundation for the Mughal empire. The following year he defeated the Hindu Rajput confederacy. A soldier of genius, he was also a cultured man with interests in architecture, music, and literature. Himself a Muslim, he initiated a policy of toleration towards his non-Muslim subjects. He was succeeded by his son, Humayun.

Bacciochi, Maria Anna Elisa, *née* **Bonaparte** (1777–1820) Eldest of the sisters of Napoleon, born in Ajaccio, Corsica. She married Felice Bacciochi, and was created a princess by her brother in 1805, and made Grand Duchess of Tuscany in 1809.

Baldwin I (1172–c.1205) Emperor of Constantinople, born in Valenciennes, France. He succeeded

the future Varangian Guard, the elite unit of the Byzantine army. Basil's 15-year war against the Bulgarians culminated in the victory in the Belasica Mountains which earned him his surname. Bulgaria was annexed to the empire by 1018, while the eastern frontier was extended to Lake Van in Armenia.

Battenberg, Prince Alexander of (1820–93) First prince of Bulgaria, and uncle of Earl Mountbatten, born in Verona, Italy. An officer in the Hessian army, he was elected prince of the new principality of Bulgaria in 1879. In 1885 he annexed eastern Romania after an uprising there, thereby provoking the hostility of Serbia. In 1886 he was overpowered by pro-Russian army conspirators in his palace in Sofia, and forced to abdicate.

Baudouin I (1930–93) King of the Belgians (1951–93), born at Stuyvenberg Castle, near Brussels, the elder son of Leopold III and his first wife, Queen Astrid. He succeeded to the throne in July 1951 on the abdication of his father over the controversy of the latter's conduct during World War 2. In 1960 he married the Spanish **Doña Fabiola de Mora y Aragón**. A Roman Catholic, in 1990 he resigned his throne for a day to overcome a constitutional crisis caused by his refusal to sign a law legalizing abortion.

Bayern, Ludwig I von (1786–1868) King of Bavaria, born in Strasbourg, the son of Maximilian I Joseph. He came to the Bavarian throne in 1825, established Munich as a centre for the arts and science, and supported a liberal constitution for Bavaria in 1818 and the cause of Greek liberation. His son, Otto, was crowned King of Greece in 1832. He became unpopular due to his liaison with Lola Montez and abdicated after the revolution of March 1848, in favour of Maximilian II.

Bayezit I, also spelled **Bajazet** or **Bayazid**, nickname **Yildrim** ('Thunderbolt') (c.1354–1403) Sultan of the Ottoman empire. He succeeded his father (1389), and conquered Bulgaria, with parts of Serbia, Macedonia, and Thessaly, and most of Asia Minor. His rapid conquests earned him his nickname. For 10 years he blockaded Constantinople, defeating a large army of crusaders under Sigismund of Hungary (1396). He would have entirely destroyed the Greek empire if he had not been defeated by Timur near Ankara (1402).

Beatrix, in full **Beatrix Wilhelmina Armgard** (1938–) Queen of The Netherlands (1980–), born in Soestdijk, The Netherlands, the eldest daughter of Queen Juliana and Prince Bernhard Leopold. In 1966 she married West German diplomat **Claus-Georg Wilhelm Otto Friedrich Gerd von Amsberg** (1926–2002); their son, **Prince Willem-Alexander Claus George Ferdinand** (1967–) is the first male heir to the Dutch throne in over a century. There are two other sons, **Johan Friso Bernhard Christiaan David** (1968–) and **Constantijn Christof Frederik Aschwin** (1969–).

Prince Johan renounced his right to the throne in order to marry **Mabel Wisse Smit** in 2003. Beatrix acceded to the throne on her mother's abdication in 1980.

Beauharnais, Hortense Eugénie Cécile (1783–1837) Queen of Holland, born in Paris, France, the daughter of Alexandre, Vicomte de Beauharnais. As a child she was a great favourite of her stepfather, Napoleon, and in 1802 married his brother Louis, King of Holland; the youngest of their three children became Napoleon III.

Belshazzar, Greek **Balt(h)asar** (?–539 BC) Son of Nabonidus, King of Babylon (556–539 BC), and ruler after his father was exiled in 550 BC. In the Book of Daniel, mysterious writing appears on the wall of his palace, which Daniel interprets as predicting the fall of the empire to the Persians and Medes. He died during the capture of Babylon.

Berengario I (c.850–924) Duke and Marquis of Friuli (874), then King of Italy (888). He lost the crown when defeated by Guido di Spoleto (889), but reconquered it after Guido and Arnulf of Carinthia died (899). He became emperor in 915 but lost the crown to Rudolph II of Burgundy (923), backed by the feudal lords. Defeated by Rudolph at Fiorenzuola, he was murdered in jail.

Berengario II (c.900–66) Marquis of Ivrea and King of Italy. He was an adviser to Lothar II, and at his death was crowned King of Italy (950). He

was opposed by Otto I, who had himself crowned King of Italy, but then recognized Berengario as king (952). The hostility of the feudal lords, the pope, and Adelaide (Otto's wife) caused Otto to intervene again in 961. Berengario was finally defeated in 964 and died in exile.

Bernhard Leopold, in full **Bernhard Leopold Frederik Everhard Julius Coert Karel Godfried Pieter** (1911–2004) Prince of The Netherlands, born in Jena, Germany, the son of Prince Bernhard Casimir of Lippe. In 1937 he married future Queen Juliana, the only daughter of Wilhelmina, Queen of The Netherlands; they have four daughters. During World War 2, he served as a pilot and commanded The Netherlands Forces of the Interior (1944–5), and his efforts in rebuilding his adopted country after the war earned him the nation's respect. In 1961 he helped establish the World Wildlife Fund, becoming its first president. He is also credited with founding the Bilderberg group – a secretive annual discussion forum for prominent politicians and thinkers. A popular member of the royal family, his image suffered when, in 1976, he was found to have received money for promoting the Dutch purchase of aircraft from the Lockheed Aircraft Corporation.

Bethlen, Gábor, Ger. **Gabriel Bethlen** (1580–1629) King of Hungary (1620–1). Born into a Hungarian Protestant family, he was elected Prince of Transylvania in 1613. In 1619 he invaded Hungary and had himself elected king in 1620. Although he had to come to terms with the Holy Roman Emperor Ferdinand II (ruled 1619–37) the following year, relinquishing his claims to the Hungarian throne, Ferdinand was obliged to grant religious freedom to Hungarian Protestants.

Bhumibol Adulyadej (1927–) King of Thailand, born in Cambridge, Massachusetts. He studied in Bangkok and Switzerland and became monarch as King Rama IX in 1946 after the assassination of his elder brother. He married **Queen Sirikit** in 1950 and has one son, **Crown Prince Vajiralongkorn** (1952–), and three daughters. The longest reigning monarch in Thailand's history, he is a highly respected figure, viewed in some quarters as semi-divine.

Birendra, Bir Bikram Shah Dev (1945–2001) King of Nepal from 1972, the son of King Mahendra, born in Kathmandu. He studied at St Joseph's College, Darjeeling, Eton, and Tokyo and Harvard universities. He married **Queen Aishwarya Rajya Laxmi Devi Rana** in 1970, and had two sons and one daughter. During his reign, there was gradual progress towards political reform, but Nepal remained essentially an absolute monarchy until 1990, when Birendra was forced to concede much of his power. He was shot and killed at the royal palace along with his wife and eight members of his family by his son, Crown Prince Dipendra, who afterwards turned the gun on himself and died three days later.

Bohemond I (c.1056–1111) Prince of Antioch, the eldest son of Robert Guiscard. He led his father's army against Alexius I Comnenus in Thessaly in 1083 but was defeated. He joined the First Crusade (1096), and took a prominent part in the capture of Antioch (1098). While the other crusaders advanced to storm Jerusalem, Bohemond established himself as prince in Antioch. He was taken prisoner by the Turks (1100–3), then returned to Europe to marry Constance, the daughter of Philip I of France (1106). He then collected troops to wage war against Alexius, who agreed to hand over lands to Bohemond in return for peace in 1107.

Bokassa, Eddine Ahmed, originally **Jean Bédel Bokassa** (1921–96) Central African Republic soldier, president (1966–79), and emperor (1977–9), born in Bobangui, Central African Republic. He joined the French army in 1939 and in 1963, after independence, was made army commander-in-chief. He led a coup which overthrew President David Dacko (1965), made himself life-president, and in 1977 was crowned emperor as Bokassa I. He became increasingly dictatorial and was held responsible for the deaths of numerous people. In 1979 he was himself ousted and went into exile, but in 1988 was returned for trial and found guilty of murder and other crimes. His death sentence was eventually commuted.

Bolkiah, Hassanal (1946–) Sultan of Brunei, the son of Sultan Sir Omar Ali Saifuddin. He was educated in

Malaysia, and at Sandhurst Military Academy. Appointed crown prince in 1961, he became sultan in 1967 on his father's abdication. On independence (1984) he also became prime minister and defence minister. As head of an oil- and gas-rich microstate, he is reputed to be the richest individual in the world, with an estimated wealth of $25 billion. A moderate Muslim, he has two wives, **Princess Saleha** (m.1965), and **Mariam Bell** (m.1981), a former air stewardess. His son, Crown Prince Al-Muhtadee Billah Bolkiah, married commoner Sarah Salleh in 2004.

Bonaparte, (Maria Annunciata) Caroline (1782–1839) Queen of Naples (1808–15), born in Ajaccio, Corsica, the youngest sister of Napoleon I. She married **Joachim Murat** in 1800, and brought a brilliant court life to the Neapolitan palaces of Caserta and Portici. After her husband's execution she lived in Austria (1815–24) and Trieste (1824–31) before settling in Florence.

Bonaparte, Jérôme (1784–1860) King of Westphalia (1807–13), born in Ajaccio, Corsica, the youngest brother of Napoleon. He served in the navy (1800–2) and lived in New York (1803–5), marrying **Elizabeth Patterson** (1785–1879) in Baltimore in 1803, a marriage which Napoleon declared null and void. Jérôme was given a high military command by Napoleon in the Prussian campaign of 1806, led an army corps at Wagram in 1809, incurred his brother's displeasure during the invasion of Russia in

1812, but fought with tenacity at Waterloo (1815). After accepting exile in Rome, Florence, and Switzerland, he returned to Paris in 1847. His nephew Napoleon III appointed him governor of the Invalides, and created him a marshal of France.

Bonaparte, Joseph (1768–1844) King of Naples and Sicily (1806–8) and of Spain (1808–13), born in Corte, Corsica, the eldest surviving brother of Napoleon I. He served Napoleon on diplomatic missions and was a humane sovereign in southern Italy, but faced continuous rebellion as a nominated ruler in Spain, where his army was decisively defeated by Wellington at Vittoria (1813). He spent much of his life in exile in New Jersey, but settled in Florence for the last years of his life.

Bonaparte, Louis (1778–1846) King of Holland (1806–10), born in Ajaccio, Corsica, the third surviving brother of Napoleon I. He was a soldier, who married Napoleon's stepdaughter, **Hortense Beauharnais**, in 1802. He ruled Holland as King Lodewijk I, but abdicated because Napoleon complained that he was too attached to the interests of the Dutch. He became Count of Saint-Leu, and settled in Austria and Switzerland, later living in Florence. He was the father of Napoleon III.

Bonaparte, Lucien (1775–1840) Prince of Canino, born in Ajaccio, Corsica, the second surviving brother of Napoleon I. In 1798 he was made a member of the Council of Five

Hundred, and just before the 18th Brumaire was elected its president. He was successful as minister of the interior, and as ambassador to Madrid (1800) undermined British influence. He had never wholly shaken off his early strong republicanism, and having denounced the arrogant policy of his brother towards the court of Rome, he was 'advised' to leave Roman territory. In 1810, on his way to America, he was captured by the English and kept a prisoner until 1814, after which he returned to Italy.

Bonaparte, (Marie-) Pauline
(1780–1825) Princess Borghese, born in Ajaccio, Corsica, the favourite sister of Napoleon I. She married **General Leclerc** in 1797 and accompanied him on the expedition to Haiti (1802), during which he died. In 1803 she married **Prince Camillo Borghese**, her private life soon shocking the patrician family into which she married. She loyally supported Napoleon in his exile on Elba.

Caligula, nickname of **Gaius Julius Caesar Germanicus** (12–41) Roman emperor (37–41), the youngest son of Germanicus and Agrippina, born in Antium. Brought up in an army camp, he was nicknamed Caligula from his little soldier's boots (*caligae*). His official name, once emperor, was Gaius. Extravagant, autocratic, vicious, and mentally unstable, he wreaked havoc with the finances of the state, and terrorized those around him, until he was assassinated. Under him, Hellenistic court practices, such as ritual obeisance, made their first (though not last) appearance in Rome.

Cambyses II, Persian **Kambujiya** (?–522 BC) King of the Medes and Persians, who succeeded his father, Cyrus II, in 529 BC. He put his brother Smerdis to death, and in 527 or 525 BC invaded and conquered Egypt. When news came, in 522 BC, that Gaumáta, a Magian, had assumed Smerdis's character, and usurped the Persian throne, Cambyses marched against him from Egypt, but died in Syria.

Capet, Hugo or **Hugh** (c.938–96) King of France, founder of the third Frankish royal dynasty (the Capetians), which ruled France until 1328. Son of Hugh the Great, whom he succeeded as Duke of the Franks in 956, he was elected king and crowned at Noyon (987). His 40 years in power were marked by constant political intrigue and struggle, both among the feudal aristocracy and with his Carolingian rivals, but his position was invariably saved by the disunity of his enemies.

Caracalla or **Caracallus**, popular name of **Marcus Aurelius Severus Antoninus Augustus**, originally **Septimius Bassianus** (188–217) Roman emperor, born in Lugdunum (Lyon, modern France), the son of the emperor Septimius Severus. He ascended the throne in 211 as joint emperor with his brother **Publius Septimius Antoninius Geta**, whom he soon murdered. His open reliance on the army alienated the senatorial class and earned him an unfavourable reputation in the historical tradition. He campaigned extensively abroad, in Germany, on the Danube, and in the East, and was assassinated while preparing for war against the Parthians. His chief title to fame was the edict of 212, which granted Roman citizenship to all free members of the empire.

Carl XVI Gustaf (1946–) King of Sweden since 1973, born in Stockholm, Sweden, the grandson of King Gustav VI. His father died in an air accident (1947), and he became crown prince from his grandfather's accession (1950). A new constitution restricting monarchical powers was approved by the Swedish parliament just before his accession. In 1976 he married **Silvia Sommerlath**, the daughter of a West German businessman. They have three children: **Victoria** (1977–), **Carl Philip** (1979–), and **Madeleine** (1982–). He is a keen all-round sportsman, proficient in yachting, skiing, and shooting.

Carlo Alberto (1798–1849) King of Sardinia, born in Turin, Italy. The son of Carlo Emanuele of Savoy, Prince of Carignano, he became temporary regent after Vittorio Emanuele I abdicated during the 1821 risings. He granted the Constitution, but when Carlo Felice took over as king he withdrew it; Carlo Alberto was sent to Tuscany in punishment, and undertook not to change Piedmont's absolute regime if he became king. As king (1831) he suppressed liberal movements and protected the absolute power of the king, while reorganizing and strengthening the state's structures. After 1841 he pursued an anti-Austrian policy and moved closer to the liberals. He granted the Statute in 1848, and after the Five Days Milan revolt he declared war on Austria. Defeated at Custoza, he signed the Salasco armistice in August 1848. He resumed the war, but was defeated again at Novara (1849) and abdicated in favour of his son, Vittorio Emanuele II.

Carlo Emanuele I of Savoy
(1562–1630) Duke of Savoia, born in Rivoli, Italy. He succeeded his father, Emanuele Filiberto, as Duke of Savoia in 1580 and married Caterina, daughter of Philip II of Spain, in 1585. To extend his territories he formed alliances with the empire, France and Spain. The Peace of Lyon (1601) gave him the marquisate of Saluzzo, that he had previously occupied, but he had to give other territories to France. He signed the Treaty of Bruzolo (1610) with Henry IV of France, but refuted it after the king's death. Defeated by the French at Susa (1629), he died leaving his country in a situation of decay.

Carlo Emanuele III of Savoy (1701–73) King of Sardinia, born in Turin, Italy. In 1730 he became king following the abdication of his father Vittorio Amedeo II. He concluded a number of alliances to widen his domain, firstly joining France and Spain against Austria, and was rewarded with Novara and Tortona by the Peace of Vienna (1738). During the Austrian War of Succession (1740–8), he supported Austria against France and Spain, and obtained Vigevano and other territories. He promoted industrial and commercial development and founded universities at Cagliari and Sassari.

Carlo Felice (1765–1831) King of Sardinia, born in Turin, Italy. He succeeded his brother Vittorio Emanuele I, who had abdicated following the liberal risings of 1821. Carlo Alberto, regent for the absent Carlo Felice, granted the constitution, but it was retracted by Carlo Felice who asked the Austrians for help in suppressing the insurrection. His rule was characterized by rigid absolutism and total opposition to liberalism.

Carlo II Ludovico (1799–1883) King of Etruria (1803–7), Duke of Lucca (1815–47), and Duke of Parma-Piacenza (1847–9), born in Parma, Italy. The son of Ludovico II of Borbone-Parma, he had little interest in politics, and under pressure from the liberals granted a constitution (1848), and abdicated in favour of his son in 1849.

Carol I (1839–1914) The first King of Romania (1881–1914), born in Hohenzollern-Sigmaringen. He was elected Prince of Romania in 1866 and became king when his country received independence from the Ottoman empire. He promoted economic development and military expansion, and brutally crushed a peasant rebellion in 1907. He married **Princess Elizabeth of Wied** (1869), a prolific writer under the pseudonym Carmen Sylva. At the outset of World War 1 he declared Romanian neutrality, but his successor (his nephew King Ferdinand I) declared for the Allies in 1916.

Carol II (1893–1953) King of Romania (1930–40), born in Sinaia, Romania. He renounced his right of succession (1925) as a result of a love affair (he divorced his second wife, **Princess Helen of Greece** (1928), mother of his son **Michael**, to live with **Elena (Magda) Lupescu**) and went into exile in Paris. He returned through a coup in 1930, proclaiming a dictatorship in 1938. He was forced to abdicate in 1940 in favour of his son and went

into exile in Portugal where he later married Lupescu (1947). In 2003, fifty years after his death, his remains were brought back to Romania for reburial with full national honours.

Carolina (1743–87) Princess of Orange-Nassau, born in Kirchheim-Bolanden, Germany, the daughter of Stadtholder William IV and Anne of Hanover. She married in 1760 Charles Christian, Prince of Nassau-Weilburg (Walram line), who was a general in the States' service, and governor of Maastricht. She was used by regents and others to try to obtain the guardianship of William V in place of the Duke of Brunswick-Wolfenbüttel, but their attempts were unsuccessful. She bore twelve children.

Cassander (c.358–297 BC) Ruler of Macedon after the death of his father Antipater in 319 BC, and its king from 305 BC. An active figure in the power struggle after Alexander's death (323 BC), he murdered Alexander's mother, widow, and son, and contributed to the defeat of Antigonus I Monophthalmos at Ipsus in 301 BC.

Castracani degli Antelminelli, Castruccio (1281–1328) Condottiere and ruler of Lucca, born in Lucca, Italy. A member of the *Bianchi* faction, he was forced into exile in 1300, but returned in 1314. With Uguccione della Faggiuola he defeated the Guelphs at Montecatini (1315) and replaced him as ruler of Lucca (1315). He set himself up as leader of the Ghibellines, conquered Pistoia, and defeated the Florentines at Altopascio (1325). He was appointed imperial vicar and Duke of Lucca by Ludwig the Bavarian (1327). Machiavelli wrote an idealized biography of him in *Viat di Castruccio Castracani* (1520).

Catherine I (1684–1727) Tsarina of Russia (1725–7), who succeeded her husband Peter I, the Great. She was of lowly birth, and was baptized a Roman Catholic with the name of Martha. In 1705 she became mistress to Peter, changing her name to Catherine, and converting to Orthodoxy in 1708. The tsar married her in 1712, and in 1722 passed a law allowing him to nominate a successor. He chose Catherine, having her crowned empress (tsaritsa) in 1724, and after his death Prince Menshikov (c.1660–1729) ensured her succession to the throne. She was succeeded by Peter's grandson, Peter II.

Catherine II, known as **Catherine the Great**, originally **Princess Sophie Friederike Auguste von Anhalt-Zerbst** (1729–96) Empress of Russia (1762–96), born in Szczecin (Stettin), Poland. A German princess, she was the daughter of Christian Augustus, prince of Anhalt-Zerbst. In 1745 she was married to the heir to the Russian throne (later Peter III, reigned 1761–2). Their marriage was an unhappy one, and Catherine (now baptized into the Russian Orthodox Church under that name) spent much of her time in political intriguing, reading, and extramarital affairs. In 1762 a palace coup overthrew her unpopular husband; he was murdered, and she was proclaimed empress.

She carried out an energetic foreign policy and extended the Russian empire south to the Black Sea as a result of the Russo-Turkish Wars (1774, 1792) while in the west she brought about the three partitions of Poland (1772, 1793, 1795). Despite pretensions to enlightened ideas, her domestic policies achieved little for the mass of the Russian people, though great cultural advances were made among the nobility. In 1774 she suppressed the popular rebellion led by Pugachev, and later actively persecuted members of the progressive-minded nobility while curtailing the rights of serfs. She increased Russian control over the Baltic provinces and Ukraine. She secured the largest portion of Poland in successive partitions of that country. Russia became the dominant power in the Middle East through the Treaty of Kuchuk Kainarji (1774). In 1783 she annexed the Crimea and cemented Russia's hold on the northern coast of the Black Sea.

An active patron of the arts and education, she wrote memoirs, comedies, and stories, and corresponded with the French Encyclopaedists, notably Voltaire, Diderot, and d'Alembert. Of her many lovers, Orlov, Potemkin, and P. L. Zubor (1767–1822) were the most influential in government affairs. She was succeeded by her son, Paul I.

Catherine de' Medici (1519–89) Queen of France, the wife of Henry II, and regent (1560–74), born in Florence, Italy, the daughter of Lorenzo de' Medici, Duke of Urbino. Married at 14, she was slighted at the

French court, but during the minority of her sons, Francis II (1559–60) and Charles IX (1560–3), she assumed political influence which she retained as queen mother until 1588. She tried to pursue moderation and toleration, to give unity to a state increasingly torn by religious division between the Catholic Guise faction and the Huguenots, but she nursed dynastic ambitions, and was drawn into political and religious intrigues, conniving in the infamous Massacre of St Bartholomew (1572). After the accession of her third son, Henry III, she continued to rule the court, and unsuccessfully attempted religious reconciliation between the Protestant and Catholic factions.

Cetewayo or **Cetshwayo** (c.1826–84) Ruler of Zululand from 1873, born near Eshowe, South Africa. In 1879 he defeated the British at Isandhlwana, but was himself defeated at Ulundi. He presented his case in London, and in 1883 was restored to part of his kingdom, but soon after was driven out by an anti-royalist faction.

Chandragupta II, also known as **Vikramaditya** (Sanskrit 'sun of valour') (4th-c) Indian emperor (c.380–c.415), the third of the imperial Guptas of northern India. He extended control over his neighbours by both military and peaceful means. A devout Hindu, he tolerated Buddhism and Jainism, and patronized learning. During his reign, art, architecture, and sculpture flourished, and the cultural development of ancient India reached its climax.

Charlemagne or **Charles the Great** (742–814) King of the Franks (joint ruler with his brother from 768; sole ruler, 771–814), and Emperor of the West (800–14), the eldest son of Pepin the Short. He defeated the Saxons (772–804) and the Lombards (773–4), fought the Arabs in Spain, and took control of most of Christian western Europe. In 800 he was crowned emperor by Pope Leo III. In his later years he consolidated his vast empire, building palaces and churches, and promoting Christianity, education and learning, agriculture, the arts, manufacture, and commerce, so much so that the period has become known as the *Carolingian Renaissance*. His reign was an attempt to consolidate order and Christian culture among the nations of the West, but his empire did not long survive his death, for his sons lacked both his vision and authority.

Charles I of Anjou (1226–85) King of Naples and Sicily, the son of Louis VIII of France, and Count of Anjou and Maine, Provence and Ventimiglia. Offered the crown of Sicily against Manfredi by the Italian Guelphs and Pope Urban IV, he was crowned in Rome (1265), defeated Manfredi at Benevento (1266) and Corradino at Tagliacozzo (1268). His expensive foreign policy, including the crusade against Tunis and conquest of Achaea, led to the Sicilian Vespers and a war against the Aragonese. Defeated at Naples in 1284, he died soon after.

Charles I (1887–1922) Emperor of Austria (1916–18, as **Karl I**) and king of

Hungary (1916–19, as **Kàroly IV**), born at Persenbeug Castle, central Austria. The last of the Habsburg emperors, he succeeded his grand-uncle, Francis Joseph, in 1916, and became heir presumptive on the assassination at Sarajevo (1914) of his uncle, Archduke Francis Ferdinand. In 1919 he was deposed by the Austrian parliament and exiled to Switzerland. Two attempts to regain his Hungarian throne in 1921 failed.

Charles II of Anjou, known as **the Lame** (1248–1309) King of Naples and Sicily, the son of Charles I, Prince of Salerno. Captured by the Aragonese during the Vespers Wars, he was then freed by the Treaty of Campofranco (1288) and crowned king by Pope Niccolò IV (1289). He succeeded in obtaining the crown of Hungary for his son, Charles Martel, but lost Sicily to the Aragonese by the Peace of Caltabellotta (1302).

Charles II (1661–1700) King of Spain (1665–1700), the last ruler of the Spanish Habsburg dynasty, born in Madrid. The congenitally handicapped son of Philip IV (reigned 1621–65), he presided over the final decline of Spanish hegemony. Under him Spain joined the League of Augsburg (1686) and the ensuing hostilities against France. To prevent the dismemberment of his patrimony, he bequeathed the entire Spanish Habsburg inheritance to Louis XIV's younger grandson, Philip of Anjou, in 1700, although his intentions were subsequently thwarted by the War of the Spanish Succession and the territorial settlement of Utrecht (1713).

Charles III (1716–88) King of Naples and Sicily (1734–59) before becoming King of Spain (1759–88), born in Madrid. Generally regarded as an archetypal enlightened despot, he was driven by the belief that the Spanish monarchy and the colonial empire were in need of political, economic, and cultural reform. He encouraged commercial reforms in the colonies, and encouraged an ambitious building programme at home, undertook agricultural improvements, and brought the Roman Catholic Church under state control. In the Seven Years War (1756–63) he sided with France and against Great Britain, receiving Louisiana from his ally while conceding Florida to Britain in return for Havana and Manila (1763). Later, however, by joining the anti-British coalition in support of the Americans, he regained Florida by the Treaty of Paris (1783).

Charles IV (1316–78) Holy Roman Emperor (1355–78), German king (1347–78), and King of Bohemia (1346–78). He was raised at the French court and was crowned emperor at Rome by a papal legate. A skilful diplomat, he acquired Brandenburg (1373) and added to his territories in Silesia and Lusatia. His building projects included Charles University in Prague (1348) and the renovation of the cathedral of St Vitus, and he also introduced laws to protect the lower classes and encouraged the development of a wine industry. His reign was marked by the issuing of the Golden Bull (1356) ending papal interference in the method of imperial election. He had four wives and many children, one of which, Anne of Bohemia, married Richard II of England.

Charles IV (1748–1819) King of Spain (1788–1808), born in Portici, Italy, the son of Charles III (reigned 1759–88). His government was largely in the hands of his wife, **Maria Luisa** (1751–1819) and her favourite, Manuel de Godoy. Nelson destroyed his fleet at Trafalgar (1805), and in 1808 he abdicated under pressure from Napoleon. He spent the rest of his life in exile.

Charles V (of France), known as **Charles the Wise** (1338–80) King of France, born in Vincennes, France. He came to the throne in 1364, and in a series of victories regained most of the territory lost to the English in the Hundred Years War.

Charles V (1500–58) Holy Roman Emperor (1519–56), born in Ghent, Belgium, the son of Philip of Burgundy and Joanna of Spain. He was made joint ruler of Spain (as **Charles I**) with his mother (1517), and was elected to the Holy Roman Empire (1519). His rivalry with Francis I of France dominated west European affairs, and there was almost constant warfare between them. In 1525 the defeat of Francis led to the formation of the Holy League against Charles by Pope Clement VII, Henry VIII, Francis, and the Venetians. In 1527 Rome was sacked and the pope

imprisoned, and although Charles disclaimed any part of it, the Peace of Cambrai (1529) left him master of Italy. At the Diet of Augsburg (1530) he confirmed the 1521 Edict of Worms, which had condemned Luther, and the Protestants formed the League of Schmalkald. After further battles, in 1538 the pope, Francis, and Charles agreed at Nice to a 10 years' truce. Charles's league with the pope drove the Protestants to rebellion. They were crushed at Mühlberg (1547); but in 1552 Charles was defeated by Maurice of Saxony, and Protestantism received legal recognition. In 1555 he divided the empire between his son (Philip II of Spain) and his brother (Emperor Ferdinand I), retiring to the monastery of Yuste in Spain.

Charles VI, known as **Charles the Foolish** (1368–1422) King of France, born in Paris, who came to the throne as a young boy in 1380. He was defeated by Henry V at the Battle of Agincourt (1415). From 1392, he suffered from fits of madness.

Charles VII (of France), known as **Charles the Victorious** (1403–61) King of France (1422–61), born in Paris. At his accession, the north of the country was in English hands, with Henry VI proclaimed King of France, but after Joan of Arc roused the fervour of both nobles and people, the siege of Orléans was raised (1429), and the English gradually lost nearly all they had gained in France. Under his rule France recovered in some measure from her calamities.

Charles VIII (1470–98) King of France (1483–98), born in Amboise, France, the son of Louis XI and Charlotte of Savoy. His sister Anne served as regent (1483–91) until he began to rule in his own right. Through his marriage to Anne of Brittany (1491) the province became united to France. The chief event of his reign was his invasion of Italy (1494) and the brief occupation of Naples (1495), but the states of Italy united to defeat him and he fled back to France. The history of his reign was recorded by his contemporary, Philippe de Comines.

Charles IX (1550–74) King of France (1560–74), born in St Germain-en-Laye, France. The second son of Henry II and Catherine de' Medici, he succeeded his brother Francis II. His reign coincided with the Wars of Religion. He was completely subject to his mother, whose counsels drove him to authorize the massacre of Huguenots on St Bartholomew's Day (1572), the memory of which was said to have haunted him until his death.

Charles X (1757–1836) The last Bourbon King of France (1824–30), born at Versailles, France. The grandson of Louis XV, he received the title of Comte d'Artois, and in 1773 married Maria Theresa of Savoy. He lived in England during the French Revolution, returning to France in 1814 as lieutenant-general of the kingdom. He succeeded his brother Louis XVIII, but his repressive rule led to revolution, and his eventual abdication and exile after the July Revolution (1830).

Charles XII (1682–1718) King of Sweden (1697–1718), born in Stockholm, the son of Charles XI. Following an alliance against him by Denmark, Poland, and Russia, he attacked Denmark (1699), and compelled the Danes to sue for peace. He then defeated the Russians at Narva (1700), and dethroned Augustus II of Poland (1704). He invaded Russia again in 1707, and was at first victorious, but when Cossack help failed to arrive, he was defeated at Poltava (1709). He escaped to Turkey, where he stayed until 1714. He then formed another army and attacked Norway, but was killed at the siege of Halden. After his death, Sweden, exhausted by his wars, ceased to be numbered among the great powers.

Charles XIV, originally **Jean Baptiste Jules Bernadotte** (1763–1844) King of Sweden (1818–44), born a lawyer's son in Pau, France. He joined the French army in 1780, and fought his way up to become marshal (1804). In 1799 he was minister of war, and for his conduct at Austerlitz was named Prince of Pontecorvo (1805). He fought in several Napoleonic campaigns (1805–9), then was elected heir to the throne of Sweden (1810), turning Protestant, and changing his name to Charles John. He refused to comply with Napoleon's demands, and was soon involved in war with him, taking part in the final struggle at Leipzig (1813). In 1814 he was rewarded with the Kingdom of Norway, recreating the union of the two countries. Thereafter he had a peaceful reign, though his conservative rule led to opposition at home in the 1830s.

Charles Martel (Old French, 'the hammer') (c.688–741) Mayor of the palace for the last Merovingian kings of the Franks, the illegitimate son of Pepin of Herstal, and the undisputed head of the Carolingian family by 723. He conducted many campaigns against the Frisians and Saxons, as well as in Aquitaine, Bavaria, and Burgundy. He halted Muslim expansion in western Europe at the Battle of Poitiers (732). Established as effective ruler of much of Gaul, but never crowned king, he left the kingdom to his sons, Carloman and Pepin, and in 751 Pepin was anointed as the first Carolingian king of the Franks.

Cheops, Greek form of **Khufu** (26th-c BC) King of Memphis in Egypt, second ruler of the IV dynasty. He is famous as the builder of the Great Pyramid. The *Ship of Cheops* is a funeral ship found dismantled at Giza in 1954 in one of five boat pits around the pyramid.

Christian IV (1577–1648) King of Denmark (1596–1648), born at Frederiksborg Castle, Hillerød, Denmark, the son of King Friedrich II and Sophie of Mecklenburg. Only 11 years old when his father died (1588), Denmark was ruled by a regency until he was crowned in 1596. His long reign was one of the most important in Denmark's history, but his foreign policy led to two unsuccessful wars against Sweden and brought his country disastrously into the Thirty Years War. He founded several forti-fied new towns and harbours, including Kristianstad, and built a number of fine buildings in a semi-Dutch style that was named after him.

Christian IX (1818–1906) King of Denmark (1863–1906), born in Gottorp, Schleswig-Holstein, Germany, the son of Duke William of Glücksburg. Not in direct line to the Danish throne, he belonged to a younger branch of the reigning Oldenburg dynasty, and on his father's death (1831) was cared for by his uncle, King Frederic VI. Christian began a career in the Danish army, but on Frederic's death (1863) was named his successor. A dispute between Denmark and Prussia over the status of Schleswig-Holstein led to war (1863), after which he resisted the growing democratic forces in Denmark. He finally submitted to them in 1901 by appointing a majority cabinet, a change which brought full parliamentary government to Denmark. His eldest daughter, Alexandra, became the consort of King Edward VII of Great Britain.

Christian X (1870–1947) King of Denmark (1912–47), born in Charlottenlund, Denmark. During his reign, Denmark's link with Iceland was severed (1918, 1944), but North Schleswig was recovered from Germany (1920). During the German occupation (1940–5), he attracted great acclaim by remaining in Denmark, seeking with some success to save the country, without undue collaboration, from the harshest effects of occupation.

Christina (1626–89) Queen of Sweden (1632–54), born in Stockholm, Sweden, the daughter and successor of Gustav II Adolf. She was educated as a prince on her father's orders during her minority, when the affairs of the kingdom were ably managed by Axel Oxenstierna. When she came of age (1644) she negotiated the Peace of Westphalia, bringing to an end the Thirty Years War (1648). She patronized the arts and attracted some of the best minds in Europe, such as Hugh Grotius, Salamasius, and Descartes, to her court. In 1654 she suddenly abdicated and proclaimed Charles X Gustav her successor. She was received into the Catholic Church (proscribed in Sweden) and went to Rome. She aspired to the throne of Poland vacated by her cousin, John Casimir (1667), but failed. For the rest of her life she lived in Rome as a pensioner of the pope, and was a generous and discerning patron of the arts. She founded the Accademia dell'Arcadia for philosophy and literature, and sponsored the sculptor Bernini and the composers Corelli and Scarlatti.

Christophe, Henry (1767–1829) Haitian revolutionary, born a slave on the island of Grenada. He joined the black insurgents on Haiti against the French (1790), and became one of their leaders, under Toussaint L'Ouverture. He was appointed resident in 1807, and despite civil war was proclaimed king in the northern part of the island as Henry I in 1811. He ruled with vigour, but his avarice and cruelty led to an insurrection, and he shot himself.

Chulalongkorn, Phra Paramindr Maha (1853–1910) King of Siam (1868–1910, as **Rama V**), born in Bangkok. His father, **Mongkut (Rama IV)**, was the model for the oscar-winning film *The King and I* (1956), drawn from the reminiscences of Chulalongkorn's governess, Anna Leonowens (1834–1914). He was educated by English teachers, acquiring Western linguistic and cultural skills, after which he went to a Buddhist monastery until he was 20. He completed the reforms Mongkut had begun to modernize Siam (today Thailand). He abolished slavery, proclaimed liberty of conscience, and introduced modern buildings, transport systems, and communications. He sent his crown prince to study in Britain, and ultimately paid for his Westernization by being forced to accept treaties with France and with Britain.

Claudius, in full **Tiberius Claudius Caesar Augustus Germanicus** (10 BC–AD 54) Roman emperor (41–54), the grandson of the Empress Livia, the brother of Germanicus, and the nephew of the Emperor Tiberius. Kept in the background because of his physical disabilities, he devoted himself to historical studies, and thus survived the vicious in-fighting of the imperial house. Becoming emperor largely by accident in the chaos after Caligula's murder, he proved to be an able and progressive ruler, despite his gross and sometimes ridiculous indulgence of his wives and freedmen. Through his lavish public works and administrative reforms, he made a lasting contribution to the government of Rome and the empire, and through the annexation of Britain, Mauretania, and Thrace, a significant extension of its size. He died poisoned, it was widely believed, by his fourth wife **Agrippina**.

Cleopatra VII (69–30 BC) Queen of Egypt (51–48 BC, 47–30 BC), the daughter of Ptolemy Auletes. A woman of great intelligence, she made the most of her physical charms to strengthen her own position within Egypt, and to save the country from annexation by Rome. Thus, Julius Caesar, to whom she bore a son **Caesarion**, supported her claim to the throne against her brother (47 BC), while Antony, by whom she had three children, restored to her several portions of the old Ptolemaic empire, and even gave to their joint offspring substantial areas of the Roman East (34 BC). Defeated along with Antony at Actium (31 BC), she preferred suicide to being captured and exhibited at Rome in Octavian's victory parade. The asp, which she used to cause her death, was an Egyptian symbol of royalty.

Clotilde or **Clotilda, St** (474–545) Queen consort of Clovis I, King of the Franks, and daughter of Chilperic, King of Burgundy. She married in 493, and after Clovis's death lived a life of austerity and good works at the Abbey of St Martin at Tours. Feast day 3 June.

Clotilde of Savoy (1843–1911) Princess, born in Turin, Italy, the daughter of Vittorio Emanuele II, King of Sardinia and Maria Adelaide. She was given in marriage to Jérôme Napoleon Bonaparte, to strengthen the alliance between France and Piedmont, as agreed at Plombières.

Clovis I, Ger. **Chlodwig** or **Chlodovech** (c.465–511) Merovingian king, who succeeded his father, Childeric (481), as King of the Franks. He overthrew the Gallo-Romans, and took possession of the whole country between the Somme and the Loire by 496. In 493 he married (St) **Clotilde**, and was converted to Christianity along with several thousand warriors after routing the Alemanni. In 507, he defeated the Visigoth, Alaric II, captured Bordeaux and Toulouse, but was checked at Arles by the Ostrogoth, Theodoric. He then took up residence in Paris.

Commodus, Lucius Aurelius (161–92) Roman emperor from 180, the son of Marcus Aurelius and Faustina. His reign was one of the worst chapters of Roman imperial despotism. After the discovery of his sister Lucilla's plot against his life in 183, he gave uncontrolled vent to his savagery. At length his mistress, Marcia, had him strangled by Narcissus, a famous athlete. His death brought to an end the dynasty of the Antonine emperors.

Conrad IV of Swabia (1228–54) King of Germany, born in Andria, Puglia, Italy. The son of Frederick II, he defended his right to the German throne but was defeated by William of Holland with the support of Pope Innocent IV. After his father's death in 1250, he renounced the German crown, and in 1251 crossed the Alps to claim the Kingdom of Sicily which was ruled by his stepbrother, Manfredi. He conquered Naples but failed to win the support of Pope Innocent. He died suddenly, leaving his son, Corradino, under Innocent's guardianship.

Constantijn Christof Frederik Aschwin (1969–) Prince of The Netherlands, and Prince of Orange-Nassau, born in Utrecht, The Netherlands, the third and youngest son of Queen Beatrix of The Netherlands and Prince Claus. He became assistant to the European Commissioner Hans van den Broek in Brussels.

Constantine I, known as **the Great**, originally **Flavius Valerius Constantinus** (c.274–337) Roman emperor, born in Naissus, Moesia (Nis in modern Serbia), the eldest son of Constantius Chlorus. Though proclaimed emperor by the army at York on his father's death in 306, it was not until his defeat of Maxentius at the Milvian Bridge in Rome (312) that he became emperor of the West; and only with his victory over Licinius, the emperor of the East, that he became sole emperor (324). Believing that his victory in 312 was the work of the Christian God, he became the first emperor to promote Christianity, from which came the byname 'Great'. His Edict of Milan (313), issued jointly with Licinius, brought toleration to Christians throughout the empire, and his new capital at Constantinople, founded on the strategically important site of Byzantium (324), was from the outset a Christian city.

Constantine I (1868–1923) King of Greece (1913–17, 1920–2), born in Athens. He played a leading part in Greece's victories in the Balkan Wars (1912–13), and succeeded his father, George I, as king. During World War 1, his policy of neutrality led to bitter conflict with interventionist forces led by liberal politician Venizelos, culminating (1916–17) in virtual civil war, Anglo-French intervention, and his abdication. Restored after the war, he abdicated once again (1922) following Greece's defeat by Turkey and an internal military revolt.

Constantine II (1940–) King of

CONDÉ

Condé is the name given to the junior branch of the French royal line, the House of Bourbon, which played a prominent role in French dynastic politics, particularly in the 16th–17th centuries. Ten generations bore the title of **Prince de Condé**, the most eminent being Louis II de Bourbon (1621–86), better known as the **Great Condé**.

Greece (1964–73), born near Athens, who succeeded his father Paul I. In 1964 he married **Princess Anne-Marie of Denmark** (1946–), and has two sons and a daughter. He fled to Rome in 1967 after an abortive coup against the military government which had seized power, and was deposed in 1973. The monarchy was abolished by a national referendum in 1974.

Constantius Chlorus (c.250–306) Roman emperor, the nephew of Claudius II Gothicus and the father of Constantine the Great. He took the title of Caesar in 292, had Britain, Gaul, and Spain as his government, and, after re-establishing Roman power in Britain and defeating the Alemanni, took the additional title of Augustus in 305.

Cornaro, Caterina (1454–1510) Queen of Cyprus, born in Venice. She was the wife of Giacomo II dei Lusignano, King of Cyprus. When he died (1473), she kept the crown in spite of various attempts by the Venetians to oust her. She was deposed by Venice, who annexed Cyprus in 1489, and was made ruler of Asolo. There she created a cultured and sophisticated court, described by Bembo in *Gli Asolani*.

Cosimo de' Medici (1389–1464) Financier, statesman, and philanthropist, born in Florence. Known posthumously as 'father of his country', he began the glorious epoch of the Medici family. As ruler of Florence he procured for the city (nominally still republican) security abroad and peace from civil dissensions. He employed his wealth in encouraging art and literature, building the Medici library, the first public library in Europe, as well as many other magnificent buildings, and made Florence the centre of the new learning.

Costanza d'Altavilla (1146–98) Holy Roman Empress, the daughter of Ruggero II, King of Sicily. In 1186 she married Henry VI, heir to Frederick Barbarossa. She was imprisoned by her nephew, Tancredi, who staked a claim on the Sicilian crown, but was freed by Pope Celestine III. After Henry's death (1195) she tried to oppose German influence; she had Frederick II crowned King of Sicily in 1198 and made Pope Innocent III his guardian.

Croesus (?–c.546 BC) The last King of Lydia (c.560–546 BC), who succeeded his father, Alyattes. He made the Greeks of Asia Minor his tributaries, and extended his kingdom east from the Aegean to the Halys. His conquests and mines made his wealth proverbial. Cyrus II defeated and imprisoned him (546 BC), but his death is a mystery.

Cuauhtémoc (c.1495–1525) The last Aztec ruler, successor to Montezuma, who resisted the Spaniards under Cortés at the siege of Tenochitlán (now Mexico City) in 1521. He was later executed while on an expedition with Cortés to Honduras.

Cyrus II, known as **the Great** (?–529 BC) The founder of the Achaemenid Persian empire, the son of Cambyses I. He became King of Persia (559 BC), defeated the Medes (549 BC), and took Lydia (c.546 BC) and Babylon (539 BC). His empire eventually ran from the Mediterranean to the Hindu Kush. He had a policy of religious conciliation: the nations which had been carried into captivity in Babylon along with the Jews were restored to their native countries, and allowed to take their gods with them.

into a state religion, he showed an unusual respect for the religions of his subjects.

Darius III, also known as **Codommanus** (?–330 BC) King of Persia (336–330 BC), the last ruler of the Achaemenid dynasty. He was placed on the throne by the eunuch Bagoas, who had poisoned the two previous kings, Artaxerxes III and his son, Arses. When Darius asserted his independence, Bagoas tried to poison him too, but Darius forced him to drink it himself. In 334 BC, Alexander the Great invaded Persia; Darius was unprepared, and his army was defeated at Issus (333 BC) and at Gaugamela (331 BC). He fled to Ecbatana and then to Bactria, where he was murdered by Bessus, satrap of Bactria.

Darius I, known as **the Great** (548–486 BC) King of Persia (521–486 BC), one of the greatest of the Achaemenids. He is noteworthy for his administrative reforms, military conquests, and religious toleration. His division of the empire into provinces called *satrapies* outlasted the Achaemenids. His conquests, especially in the East and Europe (Thrace and Macedonia) consolidated the frontiers of the empire. Patriotic Greek writers made much of the failure of his two punitive expeditions against Athens, the first miscarrying through the wreck of his fleet off Mt Athos (492 BC), the second coming to grief at Marathon (490 BC); but in Persian eyes they were probably not very important. Although a worshipper himself of Ahura Mazda, turning Zoroastrianism

David (?–c.961 BC) Second King of Israel, and the first of the dynasty that governed Judah and Israel until the exile, the youngest son of Jesse of Bethlehem. According to Jewish tradition he is the author of several of the Psalms, and according to some Christian traditions he is the ancestor of Jesus. He was a warrior under King Saul (and his son-in-law), but his successes against the Philistines

DAUPHIN
Dauphin is the title which was given to the eldest son of the reigning French monarch in the period 1350–1830. It was acquired in 1349, when the future King Charles V purchased the lands known as Dauphiné.

(including the killing of Goliath) caused the king's jealousy, and he was forced to become an outlaw. After Saul's death, he became king over Judah in Hebron, and later was chosen king of all Israel. He made Jerusalem the political and religious centre of his kingdom, building a palace for himself on its highest hill, Zion (the 'city of David'), and placing the Ark of the Covenant there under a tent. He united the many tribes of Israel, and extended his territory from Egypt to the Euphrates. The later part of his reign was troubled by the revolts of his sons **Absalom** and **Adonijah**. He was succeeded by Solomon, his son by Bathsheba.

Decius, in full **Caius Messius Quintus Trajanus Decius** (c.200–251) Roman emperor, born in Lower Pannonia. He was sent by Emperor Philip the Arab (ruled 244–9) to reduce the rebellious army of Moesia (249). The soldiers proclaimed him emperor against his will, and he defeated and killed Philip near Verona. Decius' brief reign was one of warring with the Goths, and he was killed near Abricium in 251. Under him the Christians were persecuted with great severity.

Desiderio (?–774) Last King of the Lombards (757–74). The Duke of Tuscia, he succeeded Astolfo in 756 with the support of the pope against Rachis. At first he achieved a good relationship with the Franks by marrying his two daughters to Pepin III's sons, Charlemagne and Carloman. This ended when he adopted a policy of aggression towards the Papal States, invading Rome in 772. Pope Hadrian I asked Charlemagne – who had repudiated his wife Ermengarda (Desiderio's daughter) – for help. Desiderio was defeated at Susa and besieged at Pavia, while his son Adelchis was defeated at Verona. Desiderio surrendered and abdicated in favour of Charlemagne. He was then confined to a French monastery, where he died.

Dessalines, Jean Jacques (c.1758–1806) Emperor of Haiti (1804–6), born a slave probably in Grande Rivière du Nord, Haiti (formerly Saint Domingue). In the slave insurrection of 1791 he was second only to Toussaint L'Ouverture. After compelling the French to leave Haiti (1803), he was created governor and crowned emperor as Jacques I, but his despotic behaviour alienated his adherents and he was assassinated.

Diane de Poitiers (1499–1566) Mistress of Henry II of France. She was married at 13, and left a widow at 32. She then won the affections of the boy dauphin, already wedded to Catherine de' Medici. On his accession (1547) Diane became a friend and patron of poets and artists, and enjoyed great influence. She was made Duchess of Valentinois and, after the king's death (1559), retired to her Château d'Anet.

Didius Julianus, Marcus (c.135–193) Roman soldier and emperor. A former governor of Gaul, he purchased power on 28 March 193 by bribing the praetorian guard in a famous 'auction of the empire' held after the murder of

Pertinax (who ruled for three months in 193). He did not hold power for long, as the Senate soon declared for his rival Lucius Septimius Severus and deposed him, and he was murdered in his palace.

Diocletian, in full **Gaius Aurelius Valerius Diocletianus** (245–316) Roman emperor (284–305), a Dalmatian of humble birth, born in Diocles. He rose through the ranks of the army to become the greatest of the soldier emperors of the 3rd century. He saw the answer to the empire's problems in a division of power at the top and a reorganization of the provincial structure below. In 286 the empire was split in two, with Diocletian retaining the East, and Maximian, a loyal friend, taking the West. Further refinement followed in 293 when, under the famous tetrarchy, the empire was divided into four. Towards the end of his reign he initiated a fierce persecution of Christians throughout the empire. He abdicated in 305.

Dionysius the Elder (c.431–367 BC)

Tyrant of Syracuse (405–367 BC) and ruler of half of Sicily, whose influence extended over most of southern Italy. His reign was dominated by intermittent warfare with the Carthaginians, his chief rivals for power in Sicily. A patron of the arts, he invited Plato to his court, and even won a prize himself for tragedy at one of the great Athenian dramatic festivals.

Dionysius the Younger (c.397–? BC) Tyrant of Syracuse (367–357/6 BC, 347/6–344 BC), the son and successor of Dionysius the Elder. Groomed by Plato as a potential philosopher-king, he turned out to be a rake and an oppressor. Twice overthrown, he ended his days in exile at Corinth.

Dipo Negoro, originally **Ario Wirio** (c.1785–1855) Javanese prince, son of the Sultan of Jogja, whom he supported in his war with the Sultan of Sepu. After he was passed over for the sultanate as the son of a lesser wife, and rejected as guardian of the 10-year-old sultan by Raffles, he returned to his estates and became famous as a holy man and miracle worker. When

DIVINE RIGHT OF KINGS

The Divine Right of Kings was a concept of the divinely ordained authority of monarchs, widely held in the mediaeval and early modern periods in part as a reaction to papal intrusions into secular affairs. It is often associated with the absolutism of Louis XIV of France and the assertions of the Stuarts, Charles I being executed for refusing to accept parliamentary control of his policies.

road-construction disturbed a holy tomb, he raised a revolt against the Dutch, gaining much support, both popular and from the princes, and led what became known as the Java War (1825–30). He was taken prisoner during negotiations by General De Kock, and exiled to Macassar, where he died.

Dmitri, also known as **Demetrius** (1583–91) Russian prince, the youngest son of Tsar Ivan the Terrible. He was murdered by the regent Boris Godunov, but about 1603 was impersonated by a runaway Moscow monk, Grigoriy Otrepieff, the 'false Dmitri', who was crowned tsar by the army in 1605 but killed in 1606 in a rebellion.

A second and a third 'false Dmitri' arose within the next few years, but their fate was no better.

Domitian, in full **Titus Flavius Domitianus** (51–96) Roman emperor (81–96), the younger son of Vespasian, and the last of the Flavian emperors. An able but autocratic ruler, he thoroughly alienated the ruling class by his rapacity and tyrannical ways. Becoming paranoid about opposition after the armed revolt of Saturninus, the Governor of Upper Germany (89), he unleashed a reign of terror in Rome which lasted until his own assassination.

Elena of Savoy (1873–1953) Queen of Italy, born in Cetinje, Montenegro, the daughter of King Nicholas I of Montenegro. She married the future Vittorio Emanuele III in 1896 and went into exile with him after 8 September 1943.

Eleonora of Arborea (c.1350–1404) Sardinian ruler, regarded as the national heroine of Sardinia, the daughter of a district chieftain (*giudice*). In 1383 she defeated an incursion from Aragón, and became regent of Arborea for her infant son, **Frederick**. In 1395 she introduced a humanitarian code of laws, *Carta di logu*, which was far ahead of its time. Her statue stands in the Piazza Eleonora in Oristano. She gave special protection to hawks and falcons, and *Eleonora's falcon* is named after her.

Elizabeth of Bohemia (1596–1662) Queen of Bohemia, the eldest daughter of James I (of England) and Anne of Denmark. She married **Frederick V**, Elector Palatine, in 1613. Driven from Prague and deprived of the Palatinate by Maximilian of Bavaria, the couple lived in exile in The Hague with their numerous children, continually beset by financial difficulties. Frederick died in 1632, but Elizabeth outlived him by 30 years. Her son, **Charles Louis**, was restored to the Palatinate in 1648, but his mother remained in Holland. She died in London in 1662 while on a visit to her nephew, the newly restored Charles II of England.

Elizabeth, St (1207–31) Hungarian princess, born in Pressburg, Hungary (now Bratislava, Slovak Republic), the daughter of Andreas II. At the age of four she was betrothed to **Louis IV, Landgrave of Thuringia**, whom she

ELECTORS
Electors were the members of the electoral college that chose Holy Roman Emperors. By the 13th century, membership was limited to seven – the Duke of Saxony, King of Bohemia, Count Palatine of the Rhine, Margrave of Brandenburg, and Archbishops of Cologne, Mainz, and Trier. The Golden Bull (1356) of Emperor Charles IV permanently granted the right of election to the seven.

married in 1221. Louis died on his way to the Sixth Crusade in 1227, whereupon Elizabeth was deprived of her regency by her husband's brother. She renounced wealth, and devoted the rest of her life to the service of the poor, building a hospice at Marburg. She was canonized by Pope Gregory IX in 1235. Feast day 17 November.

Elizabeth Petrovna (1709–62)
Empress (tsaritsa) of Russia (1741–62), the daughter of Peter the Great and Catherine I, born in Kolomenskoye, near Moscow. She was passed over for the succession in 1727, 1730, and 1740, but finally became empress on the deposition of Ivan VI. She was guided by favourites throughout her reign. A war with Sweden was brought to a successful conclusion, and her animosity towards Frederick the Great led her to take part in the War of the Austrian Succession and in the Seven Years War.

Emanuel or **Manuel I**, known as **the Great** or **the Fortunate** (1469–1521)
King of Portugal (1495–1521), born in Alcochete, Portugal. He consolidated royal power, and his reign, which was marred by his persecution of the Jews, was the Golden Age of Portugal. He prepared the code of laws which bears his name, and made his court a centre of chivalry, art, and science. He sponsored the voyages of Vasco da Gama, Cabral, and others, which helped to make Portugal the first naval power of Europe and a world centre of commerce. He promoted a religious crusade against the Turks, and expelled all of Portugal's Jews in 1497–8.

Emma, in full **Adelheid Emma Wilhelmina Theresia, Princess of Waldeck Pyrmont** (1858–1934)
Queen of The Netherlands, the second wife of King William III of The Netherlands and mother of the future Queen Wilhelmina, born in Arolsen, Germany. She married William in 1879, and became regent during the last days of his life, and for Queen Wilhelmina until her majority in 1898. She was a very highly regarded member of the Dutch royal family, and her popularity contributed appreciably to the respect felt for royalty in The Netherlands.

Enzo, known as **Heinz** (c.1220–72)
King of Sardinia. He was the illegitimate son of Frederick II, who made him King of Sardinia after his marriage in 1239 to Adelasia, the widow of Ubaldo Visconti, a magistrate on the island. He fought against the Guelphs, and was excommunicated by Pope Innocent IV (1241) for taking captive a group of prelates bound for Rome and the council that was supposed to remove Frederick from the throne. Enzo was captured at Fossalta (1249) and confined till his death in the *podestà*'s palace, which is now called 'King Enzo's palace'.

Erik the Saint (12th-c) Patron saint of Sweden. He became King of Sweden c.1150, and is said to have led a Christian crusade for the conversion of Finland. He is thought to have been murdered at Mass in Uppsala by a Danish pretender to his throne. He was married to **Kristina**, and became father of **King Knut Eriksson** (died c.1195).

Ermengarda, also known as **Desiderata** (?–c.772) The daughter of Desiderio, King of the Lombards. She was given in marriage to Charlemagne as a pledge of the peace between the Franks and Lombards, in accordance with the wishes of Bertrada, Charlemagne's mother. She was repudiated by him when Desiderio supported Carloman's sons against Charlemagne. She is one of the characters in Manzoni's *Adelchi*.

Esarhaddon (?–669 BC) King of Assyria (681–669 BC), the son of Sennacherib and father of Assurbanipal. He is best known for his conquest of Egypt (671 BC).

Eudocia, originally **Athenais** (401–65) Byzantine princess, born in Athens, Greece, the wife of the Eastern Roman emperor Theodosius II (ruled 408–50). She was baptized a Christian and changed her name before her marriage in 421. After a quarrel with her sister-in-law, Pulcheria, she retired to Jerusalem in 443, where she supervised the building of several churches. She wrote a panegyric on Theodosius's victories over the Persians (422), paraphrases of Scripture, hymns, and poetry.

Ezzelino da Romano (1194–1259) Italian politician and ruler of Vicenza, Verona, and Padua, born in Onara, Italy. The son of Ezzelino II da Romano, he strongly supported Frederick II, whose daughter Selvaggia he married in 1238. He conquered Verona and Bassano in 1232, received Vicenza from Frederick (1236), and seized Padua and Treviso (1236–7). Leader of the Ghibellines, in 1254 he was excommunicated by Pope Innocent IV. He was defeated at Cassano d'Adda by the Guelphs and, captured and wounded, let himself die. He is featured in Dante and in other literary works as a cruel tyrant.

Fahd (ibn Abd al-Aziz al Saud)
(1923–2005) Ruler of Saudi Arabia
(1982–2005), born in Riyadh, Saudi
Arabia. He was one of seven sons of the
founder of Saudi Arabia, King Abd-Aziz
ibn Saud, and his favourite wife, Hassa.
Effectively ruler since the assassination
of his older half-brother **Faisal** in 1975,
he became king on the death of his
other half-brother, **Khaled**. As king,
he ruled as a traditional Arab monarch
but continued the modernizing work
of his elder brother in transforming
Saudi Arabia from a backwater in the
Arab world into the regional power
that it is today. In 1986 he added the
title Custodian of the Two Holy
Mosques to his name. His rule wit-
nessed such crises as the Iranian
Revolution (1979) and the Iran–Iraq
War (1980–8), and in 1990 he invited
US troops into Saudi Arabia to counter
the threat of Iraqi invasion. The ensuing Gulf War (1991) ended in the
eviction of Iraq from Kuwait. A series
of strokes in 1995 forced him to hand
over most of his powers to his half-
brother, Crown Prince Abdullah (ibn
Abd al-Aziz) (1924–), who succeeded
him in 2005. On his death, Fahd was
buried in a simple unmarked grave as is
customary of the Wahhabi sect to
which he belonged. King Abdullah's
brother, Sultan ibn Abd al-Aziz, was
named as Crown Prince.

Faisal I, also spelled **Faysal**
(1885–1933) King of Iraq (1921–33), born
in Ta'if, Hejaz, son of Hussein ibn Ali,
sharif of Mecca. He played a major
role in the Arab revolt of 1916, and was
for a short while King of Syria after
World War 1. Installed as King of Iraq
by the British, he laid the foundations
of Iraqi independence.

Faisal II, also spelled **Faysal** (1935–58)
King of Iraq (1939–58), born in
Baghdad, the great-grandson of
Hussein ibn Ali. He succeeded his
father, King Ghazi, who was killed in
an accident, and after an education at
Harrow school in England was
installed as king. In February 1958 he
concluded with his cousin King
Hussein of Jordan a federation of the
two countries in opposition to the
United Arab Republic of Egypt and
Syria. In July that year, he and his
entire household were assassinated
during a military coup, and Iraq
became a republic.

Faisal (ibn Abd al-Aziz), also spelled
Faysal (1904–75) King of Saudi Arabia
(1964–75), born in Riyadh, Saudi
Arabia. Appointed Viceroy of Hejaz in
1926, he became minister for foreign
affairs in 1930, crown prince in 1953,
and succeeded his half-brother Saud as
king. He was assassinated in the royal
palace in Riyadh by his nephew Faisal
ibn Musaid.

Farouk (1920–65) Last reigning King of Egypt (1936–52), born in Cairo, the son of Fuad I. He was educated in England, and studied at the Royal Military Academy, Woolwich. After World War 2 he turned increasingly to a life of pleasure. The defeat of Egypt by Israel (1948) and continuing British occupation led to increasing unrest, and the Free Officers' coup (1952) forced his abdication and exile, and in 1959 he became a citizen of Monaco. He was succeeded by his infant son as **Fuad II**, but the establishment of a Regency Council was forestalled by the formation of a republic some months later. He died in Rome.

Ferdinand I, known as **Ferrante** (1431–94) King of Naples (from 1458), born in Valencia, Spain, the illegitimate son of Alfonso V of Aragón. He faced opposition from the pro-Angio aristocracy, but he defeated them, thanks to Pius II's recognition and the help of Francesco Sforza. He abolished feudal practices and promoted commerce, and embarked on a series of alliances with Milan, the papacy, and Florence to maintain the political status quo. His ruthless repression of the 'barons' plot' in 1485 led to Pope Innocent VIII declaring him dethroned (1489). He died while trying to prevent Charles VIII's intervention.

Ferdinand I (1503–64) King of Bohemia and Hungary (1526), King of Germany (1531), and Holy Roman Emperor (from 1556). In 1521 he received the Austrian hereditary countries from his brother Charles V and was appointed his representative and successor in Germany. He worked towards an agreement between Catholics and Protestants, the Augsburger Religionsfriede (1555).

Ferdinand I (1751–1825) King of Naples, as **Ferdinand IV** (1759–99, 1799–1806) and of the Two Sicilies (1816–25), born in Naples. He joined England and Austria against France in 1793, and suppressed the French-supported Roman Republic (1799), but in 1801 was forced to make a treaty with Napoleon. In 1806 he took refuge in Sicily, under English protection, being reinstated by the Congress of Vienna (1815). In 1816 he united his two states into the Kingdom of the Two Sicilies and, despite demands for constitutional government, retained a harsh absolutism.

Ferdinand I, in full **Ferdinand Karl Leopold Maria** (1861–1948) King of Bulgaria, born in Vienna, Austria. The youngest son of Prince Augustus of Saxe-Coburg and Princess Clementine of Orléans, he served in the Austrian army. On the abdication of Prince Alexander of Bulgaria, Ferdinand was offered, and accepted, the crown in 1887. In 1908 he proclaimed Bulgaria independent, and took the title of king or tsar. Allying himself with the Central Powers, he invaded Serbia in 1915. His armies were routed, and he abdicated in 1918, his son **Boris III** (1894–1943) succeeding him.

Ferdinand II di Borbone (1810–59) King of the Two Sicilies (from 1830), born in Palermo, Sicily, the son of

Francesco I and Maria Isabella di Borbone. He implemented a number of reforms at first, but then his rule turned reactionary. The Sicilian risings forced him to grant a constitution in 1848, but soon he re-established an absolutist regime and dissolved parliament. He also recalled the troops, headed by Guglielmo Pepe, that had gone north to help in the Independence War, and ferociously suppressed any revolts.

Ferdinand III (1201–52) King of Castile (1217–52) and León (1230–52), the son of Alfonso IX of León and Berengaria of Castile. He permanently united the kingdoms of Castile and León. During his important reign, he campaigned against the Moors, taking Córdoba (1236), Jaén (1246), and Seville (1248), and occupied Murcia, thus completing the reconquest of Spain, except for the kingdom of Granada which became a vassal state. He was succeeded by his son, Alfonso X. Ferdinand was canonized by the Roman Catholic Church in 1671. Feast day 30 May.

Ferdinand, known as **the Catholic** (1452–1516) King of Castile as **Ferdinand V** (from 1474), of Aragón and Sicily as **Ferdinand II** (from 1479), and of Naples as **Ferdinand III** (from 1503), born in Sos, Aragón, Spain. In 1469 he married **Isabella**, sister of Henry IV of Castile, and ruled jointly with her until her death. He introduced the Inquisition (1478–80), and in 1492, after the defeat of the Moors, expelled the Jews. Under him, Spain gained supremacy following the discovery of America, and in 1503 he took Naples from the French, with the help of the Holy League. After Isabella's death (1504) he was regent of Castile for his insane daughter **Juana**, and in 1512 gained Navarre, thus becoming monarch of all Spain. To him and Isabella, Spain owed her unity and greatness as a nation and the foundation of her imperial influence.

Ferdinand VII, known as **the Desired** (1784–1833) King of Spain (1808 and 1814–33), born in El Escorial, Spain, the son of Charles IV and Maria Luisa of Parma. He became involved in intrigues against the chief minister and favourite, Manuel de Godoy, and sought the support of Napoleon I. When Godoy let French troops enter Spain, Charles was overthrown by the Revolt of Aranjuez (1808), and abdicated in favour of Ferdinand, who was acclaimed by the people. Napoleon summoned Ferdinand to France and forced him to return the throne to his father. He in turn granted it to Napoleon, who then made his brother, Joseph, King of Spain and held Ferdinand prisoner during the Peninsular War (1808–14). In support of Ferdinand, the Spanish people rose against the French invaders, and the Constitution of Cadiz was proclaimed (1812). Napoleon released Ferdinand, who was restored in 1814. In 1830, Ferdinand's fourth wife, Maria Christina, gave birth to his only child, the future Isabella II.

Floris I (?–1061) Early Dutch ruler, who succeeded his brother Dirk IV as

Count of Holland in 1049. He married c.1050 Gertrude of Saxony and continued his brother's expansion of the county southwards. In 1061 he defeated Ecbert I of Friesland at Nederhemert, but was ambushed and murdered on his way home. He was succeeded by his son, Dirk V. His daughter Bertha married Philip I of France.

Floris III (?–1190) Early Dutch ruler, the eldest son of Dirk VI, who succeeded him as Count of Holland in 1157. In 1162 he married Ada, sister of the King of Scotland. After campaigning with Frederick Barbarossa in Italy, he signed the Treaty of Bruges between Holland and Flanders in 1167, giving joint administration of the disputed land west of the Scheldt to both counts, and ensuring comparatively peaceful relations for the next century. In 1180 he fought against the West Frisians. While on the Third Crusade (1189–92) he distinguished himself in the capture of Iconium, and died in 1190 in Antioch.

Floris V, nickname **Der Keerlen God** (the Peasants' God) (1254–96) Early Dutch ruler, who succeeded his father William II in 1256 at the age of 18 months as Count of Holland and Zeeland. He ruled with regents, first his uncle Floris (the Regent) until 1258, then his aunt Aleida of Hainault and Holland, who was ousted by Otto II of Gelre. To end the Gelre hegemony, Floris was declared to have reached his majority in 1266. He became a very popular ruler. Influenced by his aunt he sided with Avesnes against

Dampierre, despite his marriage to Beatrix of Dampierre, daughter of Guy of Flanders, in 1270. He had problems with the West Frisians and Kennemers, who were supported by Utrecht, but arranged a treaty of neutrality with Utrecht and settled the north by concessions. In 1277 he switched from Avesnes and made up with Flanders, brought Jan van Nassau under his influence, and finally subdued the West Frisians. In 1287 the Diet declared invalid the Holland/ Flanders treaty which had been agreed by Floris the Regent in 1256. Guy of Flanders conspired with the Zeeland nobles and captured Floris V, who refused to honour the strict conditions of his release and started a new war with Flanders. An English alliance (two of his children were betrothed to Edward I's children) did not bring the expected results, so he switched to France. As a result Guy and Edward conspired to have him murdered.

Francesco I of Bourbon (1777–1830) King of the Two Sicilies, born in Naples, the son of Ferdinand I and Maria Carolina of Austria. He escaped to Sicily with his father when the French army entered Naples (1806), and was viceroy of Sicily (1815–20). Apparently well disposed towards revolutionary rising, he turned into a reactionary on becoming king in 1825.

Francesco II of Bourbon (1836–94) King of the Two Sicilies, born in Naples. The son of Ferdinand II and Maria Cristina of Savoy, he inherited the throne in 1859. A weak character, he failed to take the country out of its political stagnation. Garibaldi's landing forced him to grant a constitution, but he was unable to stop the collapse of the kingdom. He escaped to Rome, where he lived until 1870, and then to Paris.

Francis I (1494–1547) King of France (1515–47), born in Cognac, France. He was Count of Angoulême and Duke of Valois before succeeding Louis XII as king and marrying his daughter, **Claude**. He combined many of the attributes of mediaeval chivalry and the Renaissance prince, the dominant feature of his reign being his rivalry with the Emperor Charles V, which led to a series of wars (1521–6, 1528–9, 1536–8, 1542–4). After establishing his military reputation against the Swiss at Marignano (1515) in his first Italian campaign, he later suffered a number of reverses, including his capture at Pavia (1525) and imprisonment in Madrid. Though he avoided religious fanaticism, he became increasingly hostile to Protestantism after 1534. A patron of the arts and learning, the palace of Fontainebleu was rebuilt during his reign, and the artists Leonardo da Vinci, Benvenuto Cellini, and Andrea de Sarto worked at his court.

Francis II (1768–1835) Last Holy Roman Emperor (1792–1806), the first emperor of Austria (Francis I, 1804–35), and king of Hungary (1792–1830) and Bohemia (1792–1835), born in Florence. Defeated on several occasions by Napoleon (1797, 1801, 1805, 1809), he made a short-lived alliance with him, sealed by the marriage of his daughter, **Marie Louise**, to the French emperor.

Later he joined with Russia and Prussia to win the Battle of Leipzig (1813). By the Treaty of Vienna (1815), thanks to Metternich, he recovered several territories (eg Lombardy–Venetia).

Francis Joseph I, Ger. **Franz Josef I** (1830–1916) Emperor of Austria (1848–1916) and King of Hungary (1867–1916), born near Vienna, the grandson of Emperor Francis I. During his reign the aspirations of the various nationalities of the empire were rigorously suppressed. He was defeated by the Prussians in 1866, and established the Dual Monarchy of Austria–Hungary in 1867. His annexation of Bosnia-Herzegovina in 1908 agitated Europe; and his attack on Serbia in 1914 precipitated World War 1.

Frederick I, known as **Frederick Barbarossa** ('Redbeard') (c.1123–90) Holy Roman Emperor, born of the Hohenstaufen family. He succeeded his uncle, Conrad III, in 1152. His reign was a continuous struggle against unruly vassals at home, the city republics of Lombardy, and the papacy. He went on several campaigns in Italy, and though severely defeated at Legnano (1176), he quelled Henry the Lion of Bavaria, and asserted his feudal superiority over Poland, Hungary, Denmark, and Burgundy. He led the Third Crusade against Saladin (1189), and was victorious at Philomelium and Iconium.

Frederick I, Ger. **Friedrich** (1657–1713) King of Prussia (1701–13), born in Königsberg, Prussia (now Kaliningrad,

Russia). He succeeded to the electorate of Brandenburg in 1688 (as Frederick III) and was made the first King of Prussia for his loyalty to Emperor Leopold against the French. He maintained a large court, established a standing army, and was a great patron of the arts and learning.

Frederick II (1194–1250) Holy Roman Emperor, born in Jesi, near Ancona, Italy, the grandson of Frederick I. He succeeded Henry VI in 1220, and was the last emperor of the Hohenstaufen line. He was also King of Sicily (1198) and of Germany (1212). He keenly desired to consolidate imperial power in Italy at the expense of the papacy, and devoted himself to organizing his Italian territories, but his plans were frustrated by the Lombard cities and by the popes. Embarking on the Sixth Crusade in 1228, he took possession of Jerusalem, and crowned himself king there (1229). Returning to Italy, he continued his struggles with the papacy until his death.

Frederick II (1534–88) King of Denmark and Norway (1559–88), born in Haderslev, Denmark, the son of King Christian III. His competition with Sweden for supremacy in the Baltic developed into open warfare and began the Seven Years War of the North (1563–70). He failed in his attempt to take full control of the Baltic and reluctantly signed the Peace of Stettin (1570) with Sweden, in which both countries agreed to share control of Baltic coastal territories.

Frederick II, Ger. **Friedrich**, known

as **the Great** (1712–86) King of Prussia (1740–86), born in Berlin, the son of Frederick William I and Sophia Dorothea, daughter of George I of Great Britain. His childhood was spent in rigorous military training and education. In 1733 he married, and lived at Rheinsberg, where he studied music and French literature, and himself wrote and composed. As king, he fought to oppose Austrian ambitions, and earned a great reputation as a military commander in the War of the Austrian Succession (1740–8). He seized Silesia, and defeated the Austrians at Mollwitz (1741) and Chotusitz (1742). The second Silesian War (1744–5) left him with further territories which, by good luck and great effort, he retained after fighting the Seven Years War (1756–63). In 1772 he shared in the first partition of Poland. Under him, Prussia became a leading European power. An enlightened despot, he believed that a ruler should exercise absolute power; he established full religious toleration, abolished torture, and freed the serfs on his estates. He also built the rococo palace of Sans Souci at Potsdam, composed music, and was the patron of composers and men of letters such as Voltaire. When he died, he had doubled the area of his country, and given it a strong economic foundation.

Frederick IX (1899–1972) King of Denmark (1947–72), born near Copenhagen, the son of Christian X. He married **Ingrid**, the daughter of King Gustav VI Adolf of Sweden, in 1935, and they had three daughters, **Margrethe** (later Queen Margrethe

II), **Benedikte**, and **Anne-Marie**, who married the former King Constantine II of Greece. During World War 2, Frederick encouraged the Danish resistance movement, and was imprisoned by the Germans (1943–5).

Frederick Henry, Dutch **Frederik Hendrik, Prins van Oranje** (1584–1647) Prince of Orange, born in Delft, The Netherlands, the youngest son of William of Orange and his third wife Louise de Coligny. A leading general in the Eighty Years War (1568–1648), he avoided pitched battles, but was very effective at sieges and acquired the soubriquet of **Stedendwinger** (Town Enforcer). He married Amalia of Solms in 1625, and arranged the marriage of his son William II to Mary Stuart, daughter of Charles I of England, and of his daughter Louise Henrietta to the Great Elector, Frederick William of Brandenburg. His second daughter, Albertine Agnes, married William Frederick, the future Stadtholder of Friesland, which assured the future of the Orange line. In 1625 he became stadtholder of Holland, Zeeland, Utrecht, Gelderland, and Overijssel, and captain-general of the Union, adding the stadtholderships of Groningen and Drenthe in 1640. His military successes brought North Brabant and most of Limburg into the Union. He was the first stadtholder to hold a court.

Frederick William III, Ger. **Friedrich Wilhelm** (1770–1840) King of Prussia (1797–1840), the son of Frederick William II (1744–97), born in Potsdam, Germany. At first cautiously neutral towards Napoleon's conquests, he eventually declared war (1806) and was severely defeated at Jena and Auerstadt, with the loss of all territory west of the Elbe. To further Prussia's recovery, he sanctioned the reforms of Hardenburg and Stein, and the military reorganization of Scharnhorst and Gneisenau, sharing in the decisive victory of Leipzig with Alexander I (1813). By the Treaty of Vienna (1815) he recovered his possessions, and thereafter tended to support the forces of conservatism.

Frederick William IV, Ger. **Friedrich Wilhelm** (1795–1861) King of Prussia, born in Cologne, Germany. He succeeded his father, Frederick William III, in 1840, and began his reign by granting minor reforms and promising radical changes, but always evaded the fulfilment of these pledges. He survived the revolution of 1848, and refused the imperial crown offered him by the Liberal Frankfurt Diet in 1849. In 1857, after suffering a stroke, he resigned the administration to his brother, who from 1858 acted as regent till his accession, as William I, on Frederick William's death.

Fuad I (1868–1936) King of Egypt (1922–36), the son of Khedive Ismail Pasha, born in Cairo. He was Sultan of Egypt from 1917, and became king when the British protectorate was ended. In an attempt to control the nationalist Wafd Party, he suspended the constitution in 1931, but was forced to restore it in 1935. He was succeeded by his son Farouk.

Gaiseric or **Genseric** (c.390–477) King of the Vandals and Alans (428–77), who led the Vandals in their invasion of Gaul. He crossed from Spain to Numidia (429), captured and sacked Hippo (430), seized Carthage (439), and made it the capital of his new dominions. He built up a large maritime power, and his fleets carried the terror of his name as far as the Peloponnese. He sacked Rome in 455, and defeated fleets sent against him. The greatest of the Vandal kings, he was succeeded by his son Huneric.

Galba, Servius Sulpicius (3 BC–AD 69) Roman emperor (68–9). He became consul in 33, and administered Aquitania, Germany, Africa, and Hispania Tarraconensis with competence and integrity. In 68 the Gallic legions rose against Nero, and in June proclaimed Galba emperor. But he soon made himself unpopular by favouritism, ill-timed severity, and avarice, and was assassinated by the praetorians in Rome.

Galerius, in full **Gaius Galerius Valerius Maximus** (c.250–311) Roman emperor (305–11), born near Serdica, Dacia. He was a Roman soldier of humble extraction who rose from the ranks to become deputy ruler of the eastern half of the empire under Diocletian (293), and chief ruler after Diocletian's abdication in 305. He was a notorious persecutor of the Christians (303–11) until near the end of his reign, when after an illness he granted them some toleration.

Gallienus, Publius Licinius Egnatius (c.218–68) Roman emperor, from 253 colleague and from 260 successor to his father, Valerian. His authority was limited to Italy, for in the provinces the legions frequently revolted, and proclaimed their commanders Caesars. In 268, while besieging one of his rivals in Milan, he was murdered by some of his officers. A hostile tradition perhaps misrepresents his achievements.

Gaozu, also spelled **Kao-tsu**, originally **Liu Bang** (247–195 BC) First Han dynasty emperor of China. A bandit leader and former prison guard from eastern peasant stock, he seized the throne from the Qin by conquest (202 BC, but he backdated it to 206). He consolidated Qin achievements, building a new capital at Chang-an (modern Xian), re-established suzerainty over the south, and reorganized the empire into 13 provinces. One of only two commoners in Chinese history to found a major dynasty, he showed contempt for the scholar-aristocracy by urinating in their hats. Dying of septicaemia because he despised doctors, he was succeeded by his widow, Empress Lü.

Gaozu, also spelled **Kao-tsu**, originally **Li Yuan** (566–635) First emperor of the Tang dynasty in China (618–26). An official related to the Sui emperors (590–618) and the Turks, he captured Chang-an (Xian) in 617, encouraged by his son Li Shimin. He suppressed 11 other claimants, each with an army ruling part of China, then abdicated in favour of Li Shimin (Emperor Taizong).

George I (1845–1913) King of Greece (1863–1913), born in Copenhagen, Denmark, the second son of King Christian IX of Denmark (reigned 1863–1906). He served in the Danish navy. On the deposition of Otto (King of Greece, 1832–62) he was elected king in 1863 by the Greek National Assembly, and married in 1867 the Grand Duchess Olga, niece of Tsar Alexander II of Russia. His reign saw the consolidation of Greek territory in Thessaly and Epirus, and the suppression of a Cretan insurrection (1896–7). Involved in the Balkan War (1912–13), he was assassinated at Salonika (Thessaloniki), and was succeeded by his son Constantine I.

George II (1890–1947) King of Greece (1922–4, 1935–47), born near Athens. He first came to the throne after the second deposition of his father, Constantine I. He was himself driven out in 1924, but was restored in late 1935 after a plebiscite. When Greece was overrun by the Nazis, he withdrew to Crete, then to Egypt and Britain. After a plebiscite in 1946 in favour of the monarchy, he re-ascended the Greek throne, and died in Athens.

Giovanna (Joanna) I of Anjou (1326–82) Queen of Naples, born in Naples, the daughter of Carlo, Duke of Calabria, and Margherita of Valois. She succeeded her grandfather Roberto in 1343, but in 1347 fled to Avignon to escape Louis of Hungary who blamed her for the death of his brother (Giovanna's first husband). Declared innocent by the pope, in exchange for Avignon, she returned to Naples in 1352. She gave up the Angiò's claims over Sicily in 1371. She then sided with antipope Clemente VII and was excommunicated by Urban VI in 1380. Carlo III of Durazzo invaded her kingdom, and had her jailed and then murdered.

Giovanna (Joanna) II of Anjou-Durazzo (1371–1435) Queen of Naples, born in Naples, the daughter of Carlo III and Margherita of Durazzo. She succeeded her brother Ladislao (Lancelot) to the throne in 1414, and married Giacomo II di Borbone who threw her into jail. A popular rising (1419) forced him to flee and she regained power. She made first Alfonso of Aragón (1421) and then Louis of Anjou (1423) her heir. This caused a contest for her succession which was finally won by Alfonso.

Godfrey of Bouillon (c.1061–1100) Duke of Lower Lorraine (1089–95), and leader of the First Crusade, born in Baisy, Belgium. He served under Emperor Henry IV against Rudolph of

Swabia, and in 1084 in the expedition against Rome. He was elected one of the principal commanders of the First Crusade, and later became its chief leader. After the capture of Jerusalem (1099) he was proclaimed king, but he refused the crown, accepting only the title Defender of the Holy Sepulchre.

Godfrey the Norman, Dutch **Godfried de Noorman** (?–885) Early Dutch ruler, probably a relative of Rorik, the Danish ruler of Friesland. He controlled at one time Flanders, Friesland, and the Rhine estuary, including Utrecht, Holland, and Zeeland. He converted to Christianity in 882 and married Gisela, daughter of Lothaire II, and was officially made Lord of Friesland by the Emperor Charles III. He was planning further conquests in Lotharingia when he was assassinated. His realm broke up, one part later developing into the country of Holland under Gerolf – one of his assassins.

Godunov, Boris (Fyodorovich) (c.1552–1605) Tsar of Russia (1598–1605). Of Tartar stock, he became an intimate friend of Ivan IV (the Terrible), who entrusted to Boris the care of his imbecile elder son, Fyodor. Ivan's younger son, Dmitri, had been banished to the upper Volga, where he died in 1591 – murdered, it was said, at Boris's command. During the reign of Tsar Fyodor (1584–98), Godunov was virtual ruler of the country, with the title of 'the Great Sovereign's brother-in-law', becoming tsar himself on Fyodor's death in 1598. He continued the expansionist pol-

icies of Ivan, going to war against both Poland and Sweden. At home, he disposed finally of the Tartar threat, but was embroiled in the last years of his reign in a civil war against a pretender who claimed to be Dmitri, and who was eventually crowned in 1605 after Boris's death. Boris's life is the subject of a drama by Pushkin that was the basis for Moussorgsky's popular opera.

Gonzaga, Gianfrancesco (1395–1444) The first Marquis of Mantua, born in Mantua, Italy, the son of Francesco Gonzaga and Agnese Visconti. He became ruler of the city in 1407 on the death of his father, and was given the title by Ludwig the Bavarian in 1433. At first he allied himself with Venice and managed to extend his domains. Later on he switched to Ludovico Maria Visconti (1438), and fought against Venice, losing some of his gains. Under his rule, Mantua became a powerful political and cultural force.

Gratian, in full **Flavius Augustus Gratianus** (359–83) Roman emperor from 375, the son of Valentinian I, born in Sirmium, Italy. In 367 his father made him Augustus in Gaul, and on Valentinian's death he became emperor of the West, which he shared with his brother Valentinian II. He appointed Theodosius emperor in the East on the death of his uncle Valens (378). He was much influenced by St Ambrose, and dropped the phrase *Pontifex Maximus* ('Supreme Priest') from his title as a mark of respect for Christianity. He was eventually overthrown by the usurper Magnus Maximus (who ruled the Western empire, 383–8), and was murdered at Lyon.

Grimoald (c.600–71) King of the Lombards, born in Friuli, Italy. The son of Gisulf, Duke of Friuli, he became Duke of Benevento in 647. He took advantage of discord between Aripert's heirs to take possession of the Lombard crown (663–71). He managed to repel the attempts by the Byzantines to reconquer Benevento and the Franks, and suppressed a revolt in Friuli with the help of the Avars. He also added a number of new laws to Rotari's edict.

Guangxu or **Kuang-hsu**, reign-title of **Zai Tian** (also spelled **Tsai-t'ien**) (1871–1908) Ninth emperor of the Qing dynasty (1875–1908), who remained largely under the control of the Empress Dowager Ci-Xi. In 1898, after the defeat of China by Japan (1894–5), he was determined to reform and strengthen China, and threatened to abdicate if not given full authority. He issued a series of reforming edicts; but his attempts to gain power precipitated a coup, after which he was confined to his palace until his mysterious death one day before the death of the Empress Dowager.

Guglielmo II, known as **il Buono** (the Good) (c.1153–89) Duke of Puglia and King of Sicily. He succeeded his father Guglielmo I in 1166, with his mother, Margherita of Navarra, as regent. He sided with the pope, and joined the Lombard league against Frederick

Barbarossa. After the emperor's troops were defeated at Legnano, he signed a peace treaty (1177). He also agreed (1186) to the marriage between his aunt and heir, Costanza, and Frederick's son, Henry, which would bring the Swabian dynasty to Sicily.

Guglielmo VII (c.1240–92) Marquis of Monferrato. He succeeded his father, Boniface II, in 1253. He joined forces first with the Anjous and subsequently with their enemies, and became ruler of a number of territories, including Alessandria, Vercelli, and Milan. Attacked by a coalition of Visconti and Savoy, he was defeated and taken prisoner in 1290, and left to die of starvation.

Guido di Spoleto (?–894) Duke of Spoleto, King of Italy, and emperor. He defeated Berengario I in the Battle of Trebbia (889), and was elected King of Italy at Pavia in 889. In 891 Pope Stephen V crowned him emperor in Rome. He worked closely with counts and bishops to centralize government.

Gustav I, originally **Gustav Eriksson Vasa** (1496–1560) King of Sweden (1523–60), the founder of the Vasa dynasty, born into a gentry family in Lindholmen, Sweden. In 1518 he was carried off to Denmark as a hostage, but escaped to lead a peasant rising against the occupying Danes, capturing Stockholm (1523) and driving the enemy from Sweden. He was elected king by the Diet and, despite several rebellions, his 40-year rule left Sweden a peaceful realm.

Gustav II Adolf or **Gustavus Adolphus** (1594–1632) King of Sweden (1611–32), born in Stockholm, the son of Charles IX. On ascending the throne, he reorganized the government with the assistance of Chancellor Oxenstierna, raised men and money, and recovered his Baltic provinces from Denmark. He ended wars with Russia (1617) and Poland (1629), and carried out major military and economic reforms at home. In 1630 he entered the Thirty Years War, leading the German Protestants against the Imperialist forces under Wallenstein, and won several victories, notably at Breitenfeld (1631). He was killed during the Swedish victory at Lützen, near Leipzig.

Gustav III (1746–92) King of Sweden (1771–92), born in Stockholm. His reign was known as the 'Gustavian Era' or the age of 'the Swedish Enlightenment'. His first political act was to reassert royal authority, subordinating the parties in the Riksdag and thereby halting the so-called Age of Freedom (1720–71). He followed this with administrative, economic, religious, and press reforms, strengthening the navy, increasing trade, and improving the poor law. He encouraged agriculture, commerce, and science, and granted religious toleration, but also created a secret police system and introduced censorship. A committed patron of the arts, he founded the Royal Opera House (1782), the Swedish Academy (1786), and the Royal Dramatic Theatre (1788). Poor harvests and a failing economy created discontent, and as a diversion he launched into a war against Russia (1788–90) that proved unpopular. The war produced an aristocratic conspiracy in Finland, the League of Anjala, before the Swedish fleet was finally victorious at Svensksund (1790). He continued to reduce the powers of the nobility, but aristocratic plots continued, and he was shot and mortally wounded by a Swedish army officer during a masked ball at the Royal Opera House.

Gustav IV Adolf (1778–1837) King of Sweden (1792–1809), the son of Gustav III. During his minority, the regent was his uncle Karl, Duke of Sudermania. In the first years of his reign as an absolute monarch, he did much to improve Swedish agriculture with a General Enclosure Act (1803). He joined the European coalition against Napoleon in 1805, but after Russia sided with France in 1807, Sweden was attacked by Denmark. His policies provoked a military coup, and he and his family went into exile in 1809, eventually settling in Switzerland.

Gustav V (1858–1950) King of Sweden (1907–50), born in Stockholm. Shy and reserved by nature, he disliked pomp and spectacle, and refused a coronation ceremony, thus becoming the first 'uncrowned king' on the Swedish throne. He reigned as a popular constitutional monarch, and in World War 2 came to symbolize the unity of the nation, maintaining its neutrality. During his reign great social advances were made, such as reduced working hours, improved child welfare, and state housing programmes. He was the longest-reigning king in Swedish history.

Gustav VI Adolf (1882–1973) King of Sweden (1950–73), born in Stockholm, the son of Gustav V. He studied at the University of Uppsala, and was respected as a scholar, archaeologist, and authority on Chinese art. During his reign a new constitution was under preparation, and the king worked to transform the crown into a democratic monarchy, which helped to preserve it against political demands for a republic. His eldest son, **Gustav Adolf** (1906–47), having been killed in an air-crash, he was succeeded by his grandson, Carl XVI Gustaf.

Guy de Lusignan (?–1194) French crusader. He became King of Jerusalem in 1186 as consort of Sibylla, the daughter of Amalric I, but was defeated and captured at Hattin (1187) by Saladin, who overran most of the kingdom. On the death of his wife in 1190, he fought with Conrad of Montferrat for the throne. He ceded the throne to Richard I of England in 1192, and in exchange received Cyprus, where his family ruled until 1474.

H h

Haakon IV, known as **the Old** (1204–63) King of Norway (1217–63), born in Norway. The acknowledged illegitimate son of Haakon III, he was raised at the court of Inge II and proclaimed king on Inge's death. He overcame the rival claim of Inge's brother, Earl Skuli Baardsson, and was eventually crowned with great ceremony in 1247 at Bergen by a papal legate. As ruler, he consolidated the power of the monarchy, acquired Greenland and Iceland, and introduced legal and other reforms. He died at Kirkwall in the Orkney Is when campaigning against Scotland, and was succeeded by his son, Magnus VI.

Haakon VII (1872–1957) King of Norway (1905–57), born in Charlottenlund, Denmark. He became king when Norway voted herself independent of Sweden in 1905, dispensed with regal pomp, and emerged as the 'people's king'. During World War 2, he remained active in Norwegian resistance to Nazi occupation from England.

Habsburg, Albrecht I von (1255–1308) German ruler, born in Reuß bei Brugg, the son of Rudolf I von Habsburg, Duke of Austria (1282) and Styria. He fought for the crown of the Holy Roman Empire and the power of the Habsburg dynasty. He challenged his predecessor Adolf von Nassau who fell in battle at Göllheim, near Worms in 1298, and was elected king that year. He renewed his alliance with Philippe IV of France at Quatrevaux and built up a strong military force aimed at expansion to the eastern part of central Europe, placing his short-lived son, Rudolf, on the Bohemian throne. Albrecht was murdered by his nephew, Johann Parricida, whom he had disinherited.

Habsburg, Albrecht II von (1397–1439) King of Bohemia and Hungary (1437–9), born in Neszmely bei Komarom, Hungary. Duke Albrecht V of Austria since 1404, he was elected king in 1437 in succession to his father-in-law, Sigismund. In 1438 he was also elected German king but was never crowned. Under his rule, Austria, Bohemia, and Hungary were united for the first time. A persecutor of the Hussites and Jews, he died after his campaign against the Turks.

Habsburg, Friedrich III von (1415–93) German emperor, born in Innsbruck, Austria, the son of Duke Ernst der Eiserne of Austria. He succeeded Albrecht II von Habsburg in 1440 and was the last German emperor to be crowned by the pope in Rome (1452). In 1448 he signed the Wiener Konkordat with Pope Nicholas V which regulated Church relations until secularization in 1806, with the decline of the Holy Roman Empire. He gained Lower Austria (1458), Upper Austria (1463), and Lorraine (1475), and lost Bohemia to Georg von Podiebrad (1452) and Hungary to Matthias Corvinus (1457) on the death of Ladislaus. The engagement of his son Maximilian, later Emperor Maximilian I, in 1477 to Marie, daughter of Charles the Bold, brought a large portion of the Burgundian domains under Habsburg rule, thus making Austria a major power.

Habsburg, Friedrich der Schöne von (1286–1330) Duke of Austria, as Friedrich II (from 1306), the son of Albrecht I von Habsburg. He was crowned German king in opposition to Ludwig IV von Wittelsbach in 1314. In his campaign for the throne, Friedrich was defeated at Mühldorf am Inn (1322) and taken prisoner. He was pardoned in 1325 on renouncing his claim.

Hadrian, in full **Publius Aelius Hadrianus** (76–138) Roman emperor (117–38), ward, protégé, and successor of the Emperor Trajan, a fellow-Spaniard and relation by marriage. Coming to power in ambiguous circumstances, Hadrian was always unpopular in Rome, and even the object of a serious conspiracy there (118). He spent little of his reign in Rome, but toured the empire, consolidating the frontiers (as in Britain, where he initiated the building of the wall named after him), visiting the provinces, and promoting urban life.

Haidar Ali, also spelled **Hyder Ali** (1722–82) Muslim ruler of Mysore, born in Budikote, India. Having conquered Calicut and fought the Marathas, he

HABSBURGS, also spelled HAPSBURGS

One of the principal dynasties of modern Europe, pre-eminent in central Europe fom the mediaeval period as sovereign rulers of Austria, from which the family extended its territories and influence to secure the title of Holy Roman Emperor (1452–1806). The zenith of Habsburg power was reached under Charles V (1500–58), who presided over an empire stretching from the Danube to the Caribbean. After Charles' retirement (1556) his inheritance was divided between his son and brother, thus creating the **Spanish Habsburg** line, rulers of Spain until 1700, and the **Austrian Habsburgs**, whose descendants retained the imperial title and ruled the Habsburg possessions in central Europe until 1918.

waged two wars against the British, in the first of which (1767–9) he won several gains. In 1779 he and his son, Tippoo, again attacked the British, initially with great success; but in 1781–2 he was defeated.

Haile Selassie I, originally **Prince Ras Tafari Makonnen** (1892–1975) Emperor of Ethiopia (1930–6, 1941–74), born near Harer, Ethiopia. He led the revolution in 1916 against Lij Yasu, and became regent and heir to the throne, Westernizing the institutions of his country. He settled in England after the Italian conquest of Abyssinia (1935–6), but in 1941 was restored after British liberation. In the early 1960s he helped to establish the Organization of African Unity. The disastrous famine of 1973 led to economic chaos, industrial strikes, and mutiny among the armed forces, and he was deposed (1974) in favour of the crown prince. Accusations of corruption levelled at him and his family have not destroyed the reverence in which he is held by certain groups, notably the Rastafarians.

Hammurabi (18th-c BC) Amorite king of Babylon (c.1792–1750 BC), best known for his Code of Laws. He is also famous for his military conquests that made Babylon the greatest power in Mesopotamia.

Harald I Halfdanarson, nickname **Harald Fairhair** or **Finehair** (c.860–c.940) King of Norway (c.890–c.940), the first ruler to claim sovereignty over all Norway. The son of Halfdan the Black (King of Vestfold), he fought

his way to power with a crushing defeat of his opponents at the naval Battle of Hafursfjord, off Stavanger, in c.890. His authoritarian rule caused many of the old aristocratic families to emigrate west to the Orkneys, Hebrides, and Ireland, and to newly settled Iceland.

Harald III Sigurdsson, nickname **Harald Hardrada** ('the Ruthless') (1015–66) King of Norway (1045–66). The half-brother of Olaf II (St Olaf), he was present at the Battle of Stiklestad in 1030 where St Olaf was killed, and sought refuge in Kiev at the court of Prince Yaroslav the Wise. He fought as a Viking mercenary with the Varangian Guard in Constantinople, and returned to Norway in 1045, shared the throne with his nephew Magnus, and became sole king in 1047. After long and unrelenting wars against Sweyn II of Denmark, he invaded England in 1066 to claim the throne after the death of Edward I, but was defeated and killed by Harold II at Stamford Bridge.

Harold I Gormsson, nickname **Harold Bluetooth** (c.910–c.985) King of Denmark from c.940. The son of Gorm the Old and father of Sweyn Forkbeard, he was the first king to unify all the provinces of Denmark under a single crown. He was converted to Christianity in c.960, made Christianity the state religion of Denmark, and made his parents' burial mound at Jelling the site of a Christian church. He strengthened the unity and central administration of the country, and repelled attacks from Norway and the German states, bringing most of Norway under his control. He was eventually deposed in c.985 by his son, Sweyn, and died in exile soon afterwards.

Hassan II (1929–99) King of Morocco (1961–99), born in Rabat, Morocco, the eldest son of Sultan Mulay Mohammed Bin Yusuf, who was proclaimed king as Mohammed V in 1957. He was 20th of the Filali line of sharifs, or descendants of the Prophet, who have ruled Morocco since 1631. Having studied in France at Bordeaux University, Crown Prince Hassan served his father as head of the army and, on his accession as king in 1961, also became prime minister. He suspended parliament and established a royal dictatorship in 1965 after riots in Casablanca. Despite constitutional reforms (1970–2), he retained supreme religious and political authority. His

forces occupied Spanish (Western) Sahara in 1975, and he mobilized a large army to check the incursion of Polisario guerrillas across his western Saharan frontier (1976–88). Unrest in the larger towns led Hassan to appoint a coalition 'government of national unity' under a civilian prime minister in 1984. He helped form the Arab Maghreb Union in 1989, and was chairman of its Presidential Council in 1991.

Hatshepsut (c.1540–c.1481 BC) Queen of Egypt of the XVIII dynasty, the daughter of Thutmose I. She was married to Thutmose II, on whose accession (1516 BC) she became the real ruler. On his death (1503 BC) she acted as regent for his son, Thutmose III, then had herself crowned as Pharaoh. Maintaining the fiction that she was male, she was represented with the

HASHEMITES

The Hashemites are an Arab princely family of sharifs, or descendants of the Prophet, who ruled parts of Arabia and the Fertile Crescent in the 20th century, including the current royal family of Jordan. **Husayn ibn Ali** (c.1852–1931), Sharif of Mecca, won British support for the Arab Revolt (1916–18) against Ottoman rule, and was subsequently recognized as king of the Arabian province of the Hejaz. Of his four sons, three came to occupy Arab thrones. **Ali** (1879–1935) succeeded his father for one year before the Saudi conquest of the Hejaz in 1925; **Faisal** (1884–1933) reigned in Syria until 1920 and thereafter in Iraq (1921–33); and **Abdullah** (1882–1951) ruled in Jordan from 1920 until his assassination in Jerusalem.

regular pharaonic attributes, including a beard.

Heinrich I (c.875–936) German king (919–36), the founder of the Saxon dynasty. He fought a victory against the Slavs (928–9), then conquered Brandenburg and defeated the Hungarians (933).

Heinrich II, also known as **Sankt Heinrich** (973–1024) King of Germany (1002) and Holy Roman Emperor, crowned in Rome (1014). He supported the Church and thus secured his power as king. In 1007 he founded the bishopric of Bamberg and was canonized in 1146.

Heinrich III (1017–56) Holy Roman Emperor (1039–56), born in Osterbeck, Germany. He became King of the Germans (1026), Duke of Bavaria (1027), Duke of Schwaben (1038), and Emperor of Rome (1039). In 1043 he married Agnes von Poitou, and by repeated campaigns in Hungary established the supremacy of the empire in 1044. He supported the efforts of the Cluniac monks to reform the ecclesiastical system of Europe, and elected Clement II as pope (1046). He promoted learning and the arts, and founded many monastic schools and churches.

Heliogabalus, divine name of **Caesar Marcus Aurelius Antonius Augustus**, originally **Varius Avitus Bassianus** (204–22) Roman emperor, born in Emesa, Syria. As a child he was appointed high priest of the Syro-Phoenician Sun-god Elagabal, and he assumed the name of that deity. In 218, he was proclaimed emperor by the soldiers. He defeated his rival Macrinus on the borders of Syria and Phoenicia. His brief reign was marked by extravagant homosexual orgies and intolerant promotion of the god Baal. He was murdered by the praetorians in a palace revolution.

Hendrik II or **Henry Casimir II** (1657–97) Prince of Nassau Dietz, Count of Katzenelnbogen, the son of William Frederick and Albertine Agnes, Princess of Orange-Nassau. He succeeded his father as stadtholder in 1664 under his mother's regency. He was wounded in 1674 at Seneffe as colonel in the States' infantry, and took up his office in 1677. He disliked his cousin William III of Orange, and in the war with France (1672–8) rejected his authority, starting separate negotiations with Louis XIV, but the Grand Pensionary of Holland, Heinsius, managed to arrange an accommodation in 1694. In 1689 Hendrik was made third field-marshal by the States and fought at Fiennes and Steenkerken, and left the service in 1693. He had seven daughters and one son, Johan Willem Friso.

Hendrik or **Henry, Duke of Mecklenburg-Schwerin** (1876–1934) Prince of The Netherlands, the son of Friedrich Franz II, grand-duke of Mecklenburg-Schwerin and his third wife, Marie of Schwarzburg-Rudolstadt, born in Schwerin, Germany. He became prince on his marriage to Queen Wilhelmina of The Netherlands in 1901; by special decree their only daughter, Juliana, was given her mother's family name. He did not involve himself with politics.

Henry II, also known as **Enrique, Conde de Trastámara** (1333–79) King of Castile (1369–79), and founder of the house of Trastámara, which continued until 1504. The illegitimate son of Alfonso XI of Castile, he rebelled against his younger half-brother, Peter I (known as Peter the Cruel), and with French help was crowned king at Burgos. Peter sought aid from the English, and Henry was routed at Najera (1367) by Edward the Black Prince. Henry later captured and murdered Peter (1369). He continued to crush opposition, created the class of grandees from his relatives and supporters, and was succeeded by his son, John (Juan) I of Castile and León.

Henry II (1519–59) King of France (1547–59), born near Paris, the second son of Francis I. In 1533 he married Catherine de' Medici. Soon after his accession, he began to oppress his Protestant subjects. Through the influence of the Guises he formed an alliance with Scotland, and declared war against England, which ended in 1558 with the taking of Calais. He continued the long-standing war against the Emperor Charles V, gaining Toul, Metz, and Verdun, but suffered reverses in Italy and the Low Countries, which led to the Treaty of Cateau-Cambrésis (1559).

Henry III (1551–89) King of France (1574–89), born in Fontainebleau, France, the third son of Henry II. In 1569 he gained victories over the Huguenots, and took an active share in the massacre of St Bartholomew (1572). In 1573 he was elected to the crown of Poland, but two years later succeeded his brother, Charles IX, on the French throne. His reign was a period of almost incessant civil war between Huguenots and Catholics. In 1588 he engineered the assassination of the Duke of Guise, enraging the Catholic League. He joined forces with the Huguenot Henry of Navarre, and while marching on Paris was assassinated by a fanatical priest. The last of the Valois line, he named Henry of Navarre as his successor.

Henry IV (1050–1106) Holy Roman Emperor (1084–1105). He was crowned King of Germany while still an infant (1053), under the regency of his mother. He came of age in 1066, and began to assert his own authority soon afterwards. Twice excommunicated (1076, 1080) by Pope Gregory VII, he attacked Rome and installed an antipope (Clementine III) and had himself proclaimed emperor. Meanwhile, his son Conrad had been elected king in Germany and rebelled unsuccessfully against him. Conrad was replaced by Henry's second son, Henry V, who promptly imprisoned his father and forced him to abdicate.

Henry IV, originally **Henry of Navarre** (1553–1610) The first Bourbon King of France (1589–1610), born in Pau, France, the third son of Antoine de Bourbon. Brought up a Calvinist, he led the Huguenot army at the Battle of Jarnac (1569), and became leader of the Protestant Party. He married Marguerite de Valois in 1572. After the massacre of St Bartholomew (1572), he was spared by professing himself a Catholic, and spent three years virtually a prisoner at the French court. In 1576 he escaped, revoked his conversion, and resumed command of the army in continuing opposition to the Guises and the Catholic League. After the murder of Henry III, he succeeded to the throne. In 1593 he became a Catholic again, thereby unifying the country, and by the Edict of Nantes Protestants were granted liberty of conscience. His economic policies, implemented by his minister, Sully, gradually brought new wealth to the country. He was assassinated in Paris by a religious fanatic.

Henry V (1081–1125) King of Germany and Holy Roman Emperor, the son of Henry IV and Berta of Savoy. He forced his father to abdicate. He clashed with the pope in the 'investiture contest', but with the Sutri accord (1111) relinquished any rights to elect bishops. He was also promised that the properties received by the church from Charlemagne would be returned. Crowned emperor by the pope (1111), he was subsequently excommunicated and the accord reneged. Henry supported antipope Gregory VIII, but finally reached an agreement with new pope Callisto II (Worms concordat, 1122).

Henry VI (1165–97) King of Germany, Italy, and Burgundy, and Holy Roman Emperor, born in Nijmegen, The Netherlands. The son of Frederick I

Barbarossa and Beatrice of Burgundy, he married Costanza d'Altavilla in 1186. At his father's death he faced opposition from Tancredi of Lecce, who was supported by the Sicilian barons, the pope, the German princes, and Richard the Lionheart, King of England. He succeeded in getting Celestine III to crown him emperor (1191) and obtained the Sicilian throne after Tancredi's death in 1194.

Henry VII (c.1275–1313) King of Germany and Holy Roman Emperor, the son of Henry III, Count of Luxemburg. He became King of Germany in 1308 with the support of the German princes. Called to re-establish order among Italian political factions, he crossed the Alps in 1311 and clashed with Robert of Anjou's Guelph troops. In 1312 he was crowned emperor in Rome, but died from malaria soon after.

Henry the Fowler (c.876–936) King of Germany as Henry I from 919. The founder of the Saxon dynasty, he was Duke of Saxony from 912. He brought Swabia and Bavaria into the German confederation, regained Lotharingia (Lorraine, 925), defeated the Wends in 928 and the Hungarians in 933, and seized Schleswig from Denmark in 934. He is said to have been laying bird snares when informed of his election as king, hence his nickname.

Henry the Navigator (1394–1460) Portuguese prince, the third son of John I, King of Portugal, and Philippa, daughter of John of Gaunt, Duke of Lancaster. He set up court at Sagres,

Algarve, and erected an observatory and school of scientific navigation. He sponsored many exploratory expeditions along the West African coast, and the way was prepared for the discovery of the sea route to India.

Heraclius (c.575–641) Byzantine emperor (610–41), born in Cappadocia, the son of the Roman governor of Africa. Responding to an appeal to free Constantinople from the terror of the tyrant Phocas (ruled 602–10), his father made him leader of a force that ultimately overthrew Phocas and crowned Heraclius emperor. The empire was threatened by the Avars, and by the Persians under Chosroes II (ruled 588–627), who overran Syria, Egypt, and Asia Minor. Heraclius carried out far-reaching reorganizations of the army, the provincial government, and the empire's finances, and made Greek its official language. These reforms enabled him to defeat the Persians in a series of campaigns which restored the lost territories (628–33). However, he failed to resolve the differences between the Orthodox and Monophysite parties in the Church, and from 634 the recent gains in the East were almost completely lost to the Arabs and Islam.

Herod, known as **the Great** (c.73–4 BC) King of Judea, the younger son of the Idumaean chieftain, Antipater. He owed his initial appointment as Governor of Galilee (47 BC) to Julius Caesar, his elevation to the kingship of Judea (40 BC) to Marcus Antonius, and his retention in that post after

Actium (31 BC) to Octavian, later Augustus. Judea was annexed by Rome in 6 BC. Besides being a loyal and efficient Roman client king, who ruthlessly kept all his subjects in check, he was also an able and far-sighted administrator who did much to develop the economic potential of his kingdom, founding cities, and promoting agricultural projects. Life at court was marked by constant and often bloody infighting between his sister, his various wives, and their many offspring. Undoubtedly he was cruel, and this is reflected in the Gospel account of the Massacre of the Innocents.

Herod Agrippa I (10 BC–AD 44) King of Judaea (41–4), the grandson of Herod the Great. Reared at the court of the Emperor Augustus, Agrippa's early contacts with the imperial family stood him in good stead later on. Caligula gave him two-thirds of the former kingdom of Herod the Great, while Claudius added the remaining third, the Judaean heartland (41). Loved by the Jews, despite being a Roman appointee, and an active Hellenizer, he was no friend to the Christians, executing St James and imprisoning St Peter.

Herod Agrippa II (c.27–100) King of Chalcis (49/50–3), ruler of the Ituraean principality (53–100), the son of Herod Agrippa I. He was not permitted by Rome to succeed to his father's Judaean kingdom in 44, but was given various minor territories to the north, mostly Arab. A supporter of Rome in the Jewish War (66–70), he was rewarded for it afterwards with grants of land in Judaea and public honours in Rome. It was before him that St Paul made his defence and was found innocent.

Herod Antipas (?–39) The son of Herod the Great and ruler (tetrarch) of Galilee and Peraea (4–39), after Herod's death. An able client of the Romans, he enjoyed an especially good relationship with the Emperor Tiberius, but fell foul of his successor, Caligula, largely through the machinations of his nephew, Herod Agrippa. In the Christian tradition he looms large as the capricious murderer of John the Baptist.

Holland, Wilhelm von (1227/8–56) Roman king from 1247. After the death of Heinrich Raspe, he was nominated anti-king to Frederick II (3 October 1247) and crowned (1 November 1248) in Aachen. After the death of Konrad IV he became widely recognized. He died in battle against the Frisians near Alkmaar.

Hongwu, also spelled **Hung-wu**, originally **Zhu Yuanzhang** (1328–98) First emperor of the Chinese Ming dynasty (1368–1644), known posthumously as **Taizu**. His rise has few world history parallels. Born into a poor Nanjing family and orphaned at 16, he was in turn Buddhist novice, beggar, White Lotus secret society member, and Red Turban rebel. Setting up his own organization, he seized Nanjing (1356), overran the Yangtze basin, took Beijing, overthrew the Yuan dynasty (1368), established a Ming ('brilliant') dynasty at Nanjing,

HOLY ROMAN EMPIRE

The Holy Roman Empire is the revived mediaeval title of the Roman Empire, dating from the 9th century, when the papacy granted the title to Charlemagne, King of the Franks. It was later bestowed upon German princely families, including the Hohenstaufens, Luxemburgs, and Habsburgs. After Charlemagne, imperial power was greatest under the Hohenstaufens in the 12th–13th centuries: the full title 'Holy Roman Empire' (*sacrum Romanum imperium*) was used from the reign of Frederick I ('**Barbarossa**'); and Frederick II came close to uniting diverse imperial territories that covered much of central Europe and Italy. From the 14th century, the empire's power declined with the rise of princely power and city-states. In 1806 the imperial crown was surrendered to Napoleon. It was not revived after his downfall.

and took the reign name **Hongwu** ('vast military power'). He then drove the Mongols out of China, Korea, Manchuria, and beyond the Tien Shan. He bloodily suppressed secret societies and subversives, set up a special police with torture prisons, and concentrated all power in his own hands. Grotesque in appearance with a snout-like face, he was known as 'pig emperor': puns about it were risky.

Honorius, Flavius (384–423) Roman Emperor of the West (395–423), the younger son of Theodosius I. A young and feeble ruler, he abandoned Britain to the barbarians, and cowered in Ravenna while Alaric and the Goths besieged and sacked Rome (408–10). From 395 to 408, power was effectively in the hands of Stilicho.

Humayun (1507–56) Second Mughal Emperor of India (1530–40, 1555–6), the son and successor of Babar. He was opposed by Sher Shah in Bihar who overran Bengal (1537), routed Humayun at Chausa (1539) and defeated him at Kanauj (1540). Humayun fled to Sind and found refuge with Shah Tahmasp of Persia (1544). After the death of Sher Shah's son, Humayun invaded India with Persian support (1555) and restored Mughal authority. He died soon after, and was succeeded as emperor by his son, Akbar.

Hussein (ibn Talal) (1935–99) King of Jordan (1952–99), born in Amman, Jordan, a member of the Hashemite dynasty. He studied at Alexandria, Harrow, and Sandhurst Military Academy. He steered a middle course in the face of the political upheavals inside and outside his country, favouring the Western powers, particularly Britain, while supporting Arab nationalism. In 1967 Jordan joined Egypt and Syria in their war against Israel. Thereafter, the Palestine Liberation Organization (PLO) made increasingly frequent raids into Israel from Jordan, their power developing to such an extent that he ordered the Jordanian army to move against them, and after a short civil war (Black September, 1970), the PLO leadership fled abroad. His decision to cut links with the West Bank (1988) prompted the PLO to establish a government in exile. Alone among the Arab Middle-East States he was forced by domestic pressure to give verbal support to Iraq during the Gulf War (1990–1), and for a time lost Western aid for Jordan. In 1994 he signed an official peace with Israel. He was married four times; his second wife, Toni Gardiner, was an Englishwoman, by whom he had a son, Abdullah, in 1962, whom he named his heir in 1999. (Until that time his brother Hassan had been Crown Prince.)

Hussein ibn Ali (1856–1931) King (1916–24) of the Hejaz (now a province in western Saudi Arabia), and founder of the modern Arab Hashemite dynasty, the great-grandfather of King Hussein of Jordan and father of King Faisal I. He was Sharif of Mecca (1908–16), and after first siding with the Turks and Germans in World War 1, under British encouragement came over to the side of the Allies, fighting for Arab independence (1916 against the Ottoman empire), and was chosen first King of the Hejaz. He was forced to abdicate in 1924 when his country was invaded by Saudi forces and he lost British support, and went into exile in Cyprus.

Hyrcanus I, John (2nd-c BC) High priest of Israel, and perhaps also a king subject to Syrian control (c.134–104 BC), the son of the high priest Simon, and in the line of Hasmonean priestly rulers. He consolidated his own hold over Israel, destroyed the Samaritan temple on Mt Gerizim, and forced the Idumeans (residents of southern Judaea) to adopt Judaism. Eventually he supported the Sadduceans against the Pharisees, who opposed his combination of political and religious leadership.

Hyrcanus II (?–30 BC) Jewish high priest and ruler. On the death of his father (76 BC) he was appointed high priest by his mother, Alexandra, who ruled Judaea until her death (67 BC). He then warred for power with his younger brother Aristobulus, with varying fortune until Aristobulus died from poisoning (49 BC). In 47 BC Caesar made Antipater Procurator of Judaea with supreme power, and a son of Aristobulus, with Parthian help, captured Hyrcanus, and carried him off to Seleucia. But when Herod the Great, son of Antipater, came to power, the aged Hyrcanus was invited home to Jerusalem. He lived there in peace until, suspected of intriguing against Herod, he was put to death in 30 BC.

A series of treaties with neighbouring Arab countries led to the formation in 1945 of the Arab League, of which Ibn Saud was a founder. His son, **Saud** (1902–69) had been prime minister for three months when he succeeded his father (1953). In 1964 he was peacefully deposed by the council of ministers, and his brother **Faisal** became king and absolute ruler of Saudi Arabia until his assassination in 1975.

Ibn Saud, Abdul Aziz, in full **Abdul Aziz ibn Abd al-Rahman al Saud** (1880–1953) The first King of Saudi Arabia (1932–53), born in Riyadh, Saudi Arabia. He followed his family into exile in 1890 and was brought up in Kuwait. A leader of the Wahhabis, a fundamentalist Muslim sect, he succeeded his father in 1901, and set out to reconquer former Saudi territory from the Rashidi rulers, an aim which he achieved with British recognition in 1927. He changed his title from Sultan of Nejd to King of Hejaz and Nejd in 1927, and in 1932 to King of Saudi Arabia. After the discovery of oil (1938), he granted substantial concessions to British and US oil companies.

Irene (752–803) Byzantine empress, the wife of the emperor Leo IV. After 780 she ruled as regent for her son, Constantine VI. When Constantine attempted to deprive her of power, she imprisoned and blinded him and her husband's five brothers, and ruled in her own right as emperor from 797. She was deposed and banished to Lesbos in 802. For her part in the restoration of the use of icons (forbidden in 730) at the Council of Nicaea (787), she was recognized as a saint by the Greek Orthodox Church.

Irene, in full **Princess Irene Emma Elisabeth, Princess of The Netherlands, Princess of Orange, Princess of Lippe-Biesterfeld**

INTERREGNUM

An interregnum is the period between the death, abdication, or deposition of a ruler and the installation of a successor. In the Holy Roman Empire it signfied the time between the death of Konrad IV (1254) and the election of Rudolf I (1273). The *Goldene Bulle* of 1356 regulated the administration of the empire during an interregnum.

(1939–) The second daughter of Princess Juliana and Prince Bernhard of The Netherlands, born in Soestdijk, The Netherlands. She became a Catholic and married Charles Hugo, Prince of Bourbon Parma, in 1964 without officially asking the government for permission, so that she forfeited her rights to the throne. Her conversion and marriage were unpopular in Protestant circles. The couple divorced in 1981 and have four children: **Carlos Javier Bernardo** (1970), twins **Jaime Bernardo** and **Margarita Maria Beatriz** (1972), and **Maria Carolina Christina** (1974). She has published books on the problems of women in society and on environmental issues. In World War 2 the Dutch troops raised in England from those who had escaped from The Netherlands were formed into the Princess Irene Brigade, which took part in the liberation of The Netherlands.

Isaac II (Angelus) (c.1135–1204) Byzantine emperor (1185–95, 1203–4), the great grandson of Alexius I. He was proclaimed emperor by the Constantinople mob that had killed his cousin, the unpopular Andronicus I Comnenus. He repulsed an invasion by the Normans (1185), but failed to crush a revolt of Bulgarians and Walachians and was forced to recognize the second Bulgarian empire (1187). Corruption in public office was rife during his reign, and he was deposed (1195) and blinded by his brother, Alexius III, who became emperor. Isaac's son (later Alexius IV) appealed to the Latins of the Fourth

Crusade, and in 1203 father and son were restored as co-emperors. They were overthrown during a revolution in Constantinople (1204) led by Alexius Ducas (Alexius V), in which Alexius IV was killed; Isaac died soon after.

Isabella I, also known as **Isabella the Catholic** (1451–1504) Queen of Castile (1474–1504), born in Madrigal de las Altas Torres, Spain, the daughter of John II, King of Castile and León. In 1469 she married Ferdinand V of Aragón, with whom she ruled jointly from 1479. During her reign, the Inquisition was introduced (1478), the reconquest of Granada completed (1482–92), and the Jews expelled (1492). She sponsored the voyage of Christopher Columbus to the New World.

Isabella II (1830–1904) Queen of Spain (1833–68), born in Madrid, Spain, the daughter of Ferdinand VII and his fourth wife, Maria Christina. Under the regency of her mother, she succeeded to the throne at the death of her father (1833), thus setting aside the rule of Salic Law. Her troubled reign was marked by intrigues, party conflicts, and civil strife. An insurrection in favour of her uncle, Don Carlos, was defeated in 1839, and she was finally deposed after frequent rebellions culminated in the revolution of 1868. She fled to France and in 1870 abdicated in favour of her son, Alfonso XII.

Ismail Pasha (1830–95) Khedive of Egypt, born in Cairo, the second son of Ibrahim Pasha. Educated at St Cyr, France, he worked briefly for the Ottoman sultan in Istanbul, and was granted the title of khedive (viceroy) in 1866. His massive development programme included the building of the Suez Canal, which was opened in splendour in 1869. The accumulation of a large foreign debt led to European intervention; he was deposed under European pressure by the Ottoman sultan in 1879, and replaced by his eldest son, Tewfik.

Ivan III, known as **the Great** (1440–1505) Grand Prince of Moscow (1462–1505), born in Moscow. He succeeded in ending his city's subjection to the Tartars, and gained control over several Russian principalities. In 1472 he assumed the title of 'Sovereign of all Russia', and adopted the emblem of the two-headed eagle of the Byzantine Empire.

Ivan IV, known as **the Terrible** (1530–84) Grand prince of Moscow (1533–84), born near Moscow, the first to assume the title of 'tsar' (Latin *Caesar*) in 1547. He subdued Kazan (1552) and Astrakhan (1556), made the first inroads into Siberia (1581–3), and established commercial links with England (1550). In 1564 the treachery of some of his counsellors caused him to see treachery everywhere, and he embarked on a reign of terror, directed principally at the feudal aristocracy (boyars) and the Church. He nonetheless did much for Russian commerce, and printing was introduced into Russia during his reign.

Jehu (9th-c BC) King of Israel (c.842–815 BC). He was a military commander under King Ahab, but after Ahab was killed he led a military coup against Jehoram, Ahab's son, and slaughtered the royal family, including Ahab's wife Jezebel. Having seized the throne for himself, he founded a dynasty that presided over a decline in the fortunes of Israel.

Jeroboam I (10th-c BC) First king of the divided kingdom of Israel. Solomon made him superintendent of the labours and taxes exacted from his tribe of Ephraim at the construction of the fortifications of Zion. The growing disaffection towards Solomon fostered his ambition, but he was obliged to flee to Egypt. After Solomon's death he headed the successful revolt of the northern tribes against Rehoboam, and, as their king, established shrines at Dan and Bethel as rival pilgrimage centres to Jerusalem. He reigned for 22 years.

Jahangir, originally **Salim** (1569–1627) Mughal Emperor of India (1605–27), born in Fatehpur Sikri, India, the son of Akbar the Great. The earlier part of his reign was a period of peace and great prosperity for the empire, with a steady growth of trade and commerce and a great flowering of the arts. The later part of the reign was characterized by continual rebellions against his rule, principally on behalf of his various sons, and he was able to survive as ruler only by dint of the courage and vigour of the empress, Nur Jahan. He was, however, a just and tolerant man, and a consistent patron of the arts.

Jezebel (?–c.843 BC) Phoenician princess, the daughter of Ethbaal, King of Tyre and Sidon, and wife of King Ahab

JAGIELLONS

The Jagiellons were the ruling dynasty of Poland–Lithuania, Bohemia, and Hungary, which dominated eastern and central Europe from the Baltic to the Danube in the 15th–16th centuries. Founded when Jagiello, Grand Duke of Lithuania, became King of Poland (1386–1434), it flourished under his acquisitive successors until Sigismund II Augustus (reigned 1548–72) died without heirs.

of Israel (869–850 BC). She introduced Phoenician habits (and religion) to the capital, Samaria, thus earning the undying enmity of the prophet Elijah and his successors. After Ahab's death, Jezebel was the power behind the throne of her sons until the usurper Jehu seized power in an army coup. He had Jezebel thrown from a window, and trampled her to death under his chariot.

Johan Willem Friso (1687–1711) Dutch stadtholder, Prince of Orange, born in Dessau, Germany, the son of Henry Casimir II and Henriëtte Amalia of Anhalt Dessau. He was stadtholder of Friesland, Groningen, and Drenthe (1696) under his mother's regency, and declared heir of William III of Orange in 1702, with the title of Prince of Orange. He married Maria Louise of Hessen-Kassel in 1709. He fought in the War of the Spanish Succession and was installed as stadtholder at the age of 20, after which he commanded all the Dutch troops, though subject to the overall command of Marlborough. He distinguished himself at Oudenarde (1708) and commanded the right wing at Malplaquet (1709). He was drowned in the Moerdijk on the way to defend his inheritance against the claims of the King of Prussia, the Nassau-Siegen family, and the Conti family, who were descendants of the De Chalons. He had one posthumous son, eventually to become William IV of Orange.

Johan Willem Friso, known as **Friso** (1968–) Prince of The Netherlands and Prince of Orange-Nassau, Jonkheer

van Amsberg, born in Utrecht, The Netherlands, the second son of Queen Beatrix of The Netherlands and Prince Claus, and second in line to the throne. He was educated at lyceums in Baarn and The Hague and studied mechanical engineering at Berkeley, California, followed by air and space travel technology at Delft University, and business economics at Rotterdam. He currently works with McKinsey & Co in Amsterdam. In 2003 he renounced his right of succession to the throne after the Dutch government refused to support his forthcoming marriage to human rights activist Mabel Wisse Smit.

John I (1358–90) King of Castile and León (1379–90), the son of Henry II of Castile. He attacked Portugal to defeat the alliance created by King Ferdinand of Portugal and John of Gaunt, who had a claim to the throne of Castile through his wife. Ferdinand made peace in 1382 and gave his daughter to John I in marriage. After Ferdinand's death (1383), John I again made war with Portugal, but was defeated at Aljubarrota (1385). He appeased John of Gaunt by arranging the marriage between his own son, the future King Henry III of Castile and León, and one of John's daughters.

John or **Jan I, Duke of Brabant and Limburg** (1254–94) Dutch ruler, the second son of Henry III of Brabant and Aleidis of Burgundy. He succeeded his brother Henry IV on his retirement in 1267. He married Margaret of France in 1270, and after her death in 1271 Margaret of Dampierre, the daughter of Guy of Flanders. He tried to expand his control of the trade route along the great rivers, and consequently fought against Cologne and Gelre. In 1288 he was victorious at the Battle of Woeringen, north of Cologne, and was awarded Limburg by Philip IV of France. The towns supported him financially in return for privileges, as his policies of controlling the Rhine suited their commercial interests. He is also credited with the authorship of several love poems in Middle Dutch. He was killed in a tournament in Antwerp.

John II, known as **John the Good** (1319–64) King of France (1350–64), the son of Philip VI, born near Le Mans, France. In 1356 he was taken prisoner by Edward the Black Prince at the Battle of Poitiers, and brought to England. After the Treaty of Brétigny (1360) he returned home, leaving his second son, the Duke of Anjou, as a hostage. When the duke broke his parole and escaped (1363), John chivalrously returned to London, and died there.

John or **Jan II, Duke of Brabant and Limburg** (1276–1312) Dutch ruler, the son of John I and Margaret of Dampierre. He married Margaret of York, daughter of Edward I of England. He was neutral towards England, a policy which encouraged English wool imports and cloth exports to France. He suppressed the rebellious trade guilds, but was forced by financial pressure to grant the Charter of Kortenberg in 1312, giving the towns some say in the government of the Duchy.

John or **Jan III, Duke of Brabant and Limburg** (1300–55) Dutch ruler, the only son of Jan II. He married Mary of Evreux. He was forced to grant the 'Walloon charters' in 1314, giving great political and financial independence to the towns, in return for a grant of £40 000 for Tours, which he needed for his wars with neighbouring rulers. In the Hundred Years War he first supported England, to protect the wool trade, but in 1340, when Jacob van Artevelde recovered the wool staple for Bruges, he switched to France. He died in 1355, leaving the succession to his daughter Johanna, resulting in the War of the Brabant Succession with Flanders and Gelre.

John or **Jan IV, Duke of Brabant and Limburg** (1403–72) Dutch ruler, born in Arras, France, the eldest son of Antony of Burgundy and Johanna de Saint Pol. He married Jacqueline of Bavaria in 1418, but she left him after two years, as he did not defend her interest in Holland and Zeeland against her uncle John of Bavaria. In subsequent conflicts he gathered the towns on his side by granting the 'New Regiment' in 1422, which increased the power of the States. He gained Hainault, and was recognized as count in Holland and Zeeland, but was unable to control them and had to appoint Philip the Good as 'steward', marking the beginning of Burgundian rule in The Netherlands. He founded the first university in the Low Countries at Louvain in 1425.

John V Palaeologus (1332–91) Byzantine emperor (1341–91), the son of Andronicus III and Anna of Savoy. He succeeded to the throne at age nine, and was crowned co-emperor with John Cantacuzenus, chief minister under Andronicus. Despite John V's marriage to Helen, daughter of Cantacuzenus, he allied with the Venetians against Cantacuzenus and forced him to abdicate (1354). When the Ottoman Turks occupied Gallipoli and threatened Constantinople, John V appealed to the West for help and was aided by Amadeus VI. Wars with the Serbs and Turks continued, and in 1371 he was forced to recognize the suzerainty of the Turks when they gained most of Macedonia. After he was deposed and imprisoned (1376) by his son, the Turks helped him regain the throne (1379), but at his death he left his heir, Manuel, an empire greatly reduced in size and strength.

John VIII Palaeologus (1390–1448) Byzantine emperor (1425–48), the son and successor of Manuel II. By the time of his accession, the Byzantine empire had been reduced by the Turks to the city of Constantinople. John sought vainly to secure aid from the West by agreeing at the Council of Florence (1439) to the union of the Eastern and Western churches. He was succeeded (1449) by his brother, Constantine XI, the last Byzantine emperor.

John VIII, Count of Nassau-Siegen, known as **the Youngest**, Dutch **Johan VIII de Jongste** (1583–1638) Dutch ruler, born in Dillenburg, Germany, the second son of John VII. Educated in Geneva, he fought for the empire against the Turks, and joined Prince Maurice of Orange's army in 1609. In 1613 he converted to the Catholic faith, joined the service of the Archdukes Albert and Isabella and married Ernestine, Princess de Ligne. After the Twelve-Year Truce he fought in Spanish service as a field marshal against the United Netherlands and against France until his death. His brother William was a field-marshal on the Dutch side.

John of Avesnes (1248–1304) Dutch ruler, born in Mons, Belgium, the eldest son of John of Avesnes and Aleidis of Holland. He succeeded his grandmother Margaret of Constantinople as Count John I of Hainault (from 1280) and became John (Jan) II of Holland and Zeeland from 1299. He opposed the Dampierres in Flanders and favoured France, encouraging Floris V of Holland, who was also at odds with Flanders, to take the French side also. He was invited by the towns of Holland to become regent of Holland in 1299, and on the death of the young Count John (Jan) I, he took over the country two weeks later as Floris V's nearest male relative. He put down revolts in Zeeland and had his brother made Bishop of Utrecht. In 1302 he was attacked by Flanders under Guy of Namur, supported by John II of Brabant, but he restored his authority in Holland and Zeeland by winning the naval battle of Zierikzee with a Dutch/French fleet.

John of Bohemia (1296–1346) King of Bohemia and Count of Luxemburg, the son of Henry V of Luxemburg (the later Emperor Henry VII) and Margaret of Brabant. In 1310 he married Elizabeth, heiress of Bohemia, which he expanded at the expense of Poland. He fought repeatedly against John III of Brabant, who was the most important supporter of England in the Low Countries at the time, and also against Ludwig of Bavaria. In 1339 he went blind. He managed to get his son, Charles IV, elected as the opposition candidate to Ludwig in 1346. He was a vassal of Philip VI of France and was killed at Crécy.

John, Duke of Burgundy, known as **the Fearless** (1371–1419) Duke of Burgundy from 1404, born at Dijon, France, the son of Philip the Bold. He married Margaret of Bavaria (1385). He went on crusade with Emperor Sigismund against the Turks, was captured at Nicopolis, and had to be ransomed by the towns of Flanders. On his succession he regarded his interests in The Netherlands as of less importance than his French ones, where he was co-regent for Charles VI of France with Louis of Orléans, whom he had assassinated in 1407. He strengthened his position by supporting John of Bavaria against Liège, and helped his brother Anthony in Brabant and Luxemburg. He humoured the Flemish towns, whose money he needed for his French policies, restoring the privileges of Bruges (the 'calfskin') and authorizing Flemish as the language in the Council of Flanders. He was assassinated in 1419.

Joseph I (1678–1711) King of Hungary (1687), King of the Romans (1690), and Holy Roman Emperor (1705–11), the son of Leopold I. He successfully pursued the Spanischer Erbfolgekrieg and restored his imperial power. He created Kurfürsten (*see panel* p.255) in Cologne and Bavaria.

Joseph II (1741–90) Holy Roman Emperor (1765–90), born in Vienna, the son of Francis I and Maria Theresa. Until his mother's death (1780) he was co-regent, and his power was limited to the command of the army and the direction of foreign affairs. A sincere enlightened despot, he was known as 'the revolutionary emperor' for his programme of modernization. He was determined to assert Habsburg leadership, but some of his ambitious plans were thwarted variously by the diplomatic obstruction of France, Prussia, the United Provinces, and Britain, by war (with Prussia in 1778–9 and Turkey in 1788), and by insurrection (in The Netherlands in 1787, Hungary in 1789, and the Tyrol in 1790).

Josiah (7th-c BC) Biblical character, king of Judah (c.640–609 BC), a favourite of the Deuteronomistic historians because of his religious reforms (2 *Kings* 22–3, 2 *Chron* 34–5), allegedly based on the discovery of 'the book of the law' in the 18th year of his reign. He is credited with destroying pagan cults and attempting to centralize worship in Jerusalem and the Temple. He died in battle against the Egyptians at Megiddo.

Jovian, in full **Flavius Claudius Jovianus** (c.331–64) Roman emperor

(363–4), appointed by the army in Mesopotamia on Julian's death in battle. He was immediately forced to make a humiliating peace with Shapur II, ceding great tracts of Roman territory to Sassanian Persia, and agreeing to pay a subsidy.

Juan Carlos I (1938–) King of Spain (1975–), born in Rome, the son of **Don Juan de Borbón y Battenberg, Count of Barcelona** (1908–93), and the grandson of Spain's last ruling monarch, Alfonso XIII. He studied in Switzerland and from 1948 in Spain (by agreement between his father and General Franco). He earned commissions in the army, navy, and air force (1955–9), and studied at the University of Madrid (1959–61). In 1962 he married **Princess Sophia of Greece** (1938–), and they have three children: **Princess Elena** (1963–), **Princess Christina** (1965–), and heir apparent **Crown Prince Felipe** (1968–). Prince Felipe married Letizia Ortiz in 2004; they have a daughter **Leonor** (2005–). In 1969 Franco named him as his eventual successor, and he was proclaimed king on Franco's death in 1975. Instead of upholding the Franco dictatorship (as had been intended), he decisively presided over Spain's democratization, helping to defeat a military coup (1981) and assuming the role of a constitutional monarch.

Jugurtha (c.160–104 BC) King of Numidia (118–105 BC), after whom the **Jugurthine War** (112–104 BC) is named. Rome's difficulty in defeating him provided Marius with a launching pad for his career, and led to important reforms in the Roman army. Jugurtha's surrender to Marius's deputy, Sulla, ended the war, but was the starting point of the deadly feud between Marius and Sulla which plunged Rome into civil war 20 years later.

Julian, in full **Flavius Claudius Julianus**, known as **Julian the Apostate** (332–63) Roman emperor (361–3), the son of a half-brother of Constantine the Great. Appointed deputy emperor in the West by his cousin, Constantius II (355), he served with great distinction on the Rhine, and was proclaimed emperor by his adoring troops in 360. As emperor, he publicly proclaimed himself a pagan (hence his nickname) and initiated a vigorous policy of reviving the old pagan cults, though without persecuting Christians. He was killed in battle against the Sassanid Persians.

Juliana, in full **Juliana Louise Emma Marie Wilhelmina** (1909–2004) Queen of The Netherlands (1948–80), born in The Hague. She studied at Leiden, became a lawyer, and in 1937 married Prince Bernhard zur Lippe-Biesterfeld; they had four daughters. On the German invasion of Holland (1940), Juliana escaped to Britain and later resided in Canada. She returned to Holland in 1945, and became queen on the abdication of her mother, Wilhelmina. She herself abdicated in favour of her eldest daughter, Beatrix.

Justinian, in full **Flavius Petrus Sabbatius Justinianus** (c.482–565) Roman emperor (527–65), the protégé of his uncle, the Byzantine emperor, Justin (reigned 518–27). At first co-emperor with Justin, on his death he became sole ruler. Along with his wife Theodora, he presided over the most brilliant period in the history of the late Roman Empire. Through his generals, Belisarius and Narses, he recovered North Africa, Spain, and Italy, and carried out a major codification of the Roman law (begun 529).

Kamehameha I, known as **'the one set apart'**, originally **Paiea** (?1758–1819) Hawaiian unifier and king, born on Kohala, District of Hawaii, USA (formerly the Sandwich Is). Following the death of the chief of Hawaii, his uncle Kalaniopu'u (1782), Kamehameha conquered the island. After other victories on Maui, Oahu, Kauai, and the other islands, he formed the Kingdom of Hawaii by 1810. He stimulated Hawaiian trade, but kept intact the customs and the religion of his people. His statue is in the US Capitol.

Kangxi, also spelled **K'ang-hsi**, originally **Xuanye** (1654–1722) Fifth emperor of the Manchurian Qing dynasty, and the second to rule China. He succeeded at the age of eight, and ruled personally at 16, cultivating the image of an ideal Confucian ruler, and stressing traditional morality. He organized the compilation of a Ming history, a 50 000-character dictionary, and (1726) a 5000-volume encyclopedia. He adopted the Western calendar, and permitted an East India Company trading post (1699). A pro-Ming revolt was crushed in the southeast (1673–81), and he conquered Taiwan (1683), Outer Mongolia (1696), western Mongolia, and Turkestan (from 1715), and established a Tibetan protectorate (1720). A man of wide personal interests, he published three volumes of essays.

Karl VI (1685–1740) Holy Roman Emperor (1711), born in Vienna, the second son of Habsburg Emperor Leopold I. He became emperor on the death of his brother, Emperor Joseph I, and, as Charles [Karl] III, became Archduke of Austria and King of Hungary (1712). Following the War of

---

KAISER

'Kaiser' (Latin *caesar*) was the title assumed (December 1870) by the Prussian king, William (Wilhelm) I, following the unification of Germany and the creation of the German Second Empire. He was succeeded on his death in 1888 by his son Frederick (Friedrich) III, who survived him by only three months, and then by his grandson William (Wilhelm) II, who ruled until his enforced abdication in 1918.

the Spanish Succession (1701–13), Charles' claim to the Spanish throne was rejected in favour of Philip V of Bourbon. Charles issued the *Pragmatic Sanction* (1713) enabling his daughter, Maria Theresa, to succeed him after the extinction of a direct male Habsburg line, which was accepted only after the War of the Polish Succession (1733–8). During his reign he gained (1716–18) and lost (1737–9) territories in Serbia and Hungary from the Ottoman Turks.

Kinmei (?–571) Yamato period ruler in Japan. His linking of the Yamato ruling clan (*uji*) with the Soga *uji* through marriage led to the later ascendancy of Shotoku (early 7th century). In Kinmei's reign (540–71), Buddhism was introduced.

Konrad I, Eng. **Conrad** (?–918) German king (911–18), a member of the Franconian dynasty the Konradiner, in succession to Louis the Child (Ludwig IV, das Kind), the last of the East Frankish Carolingians. He failed in his attempts to uphold the traditions of Carolingian kingship against the powerful Saxon, Bavarian, and Swabian dukes, and is said to have proposed his opponent, the Liudolfing Henry of Saxony, as his successor.

Konrad II, Eng. **Conrad** (c.990–1039) German king (1024–39), King of the Langobards (Italy) (1026), and Holy Roman Emperor (1027–39), the son of the Duke of Franconia. He founded the Salian dynasty and was successor of the Liudolfing Henry II. In 1026 he crossed the Alps, crushed a rebellion in Italy, was crowned at Milan. He was soon recalled to Germany to put down four revolts, which he achieved by

KONRADINER

The Konradiner was a Franconian dynasty from the area of the Moselle and the Maas, named after Karl der Große. First in line was Arnulf, Bishop of Metz. From 639 the Konradiner were seneschals to the Merowinger in Austrien, and through this position were the holders of power in the Reich. In 751 Pippin der Jüngere (714–68) dethroned the Merowingian Childerich III and made himself king with the support of the pope. The Konradiner achieved prominence in Europe with the coronation of Charlemagne as emperor. His grandchildren split the dynasty into three lines, one of which ruled in Italy until 875, in Germany until 911, and in France until 987. With the Konradiner the power base in western Europe shifted from the Mediterranean to France and Germany.

1033, and in the same year was crowned King of Burgundy, which he acquired through the dynastic connections of his wife Gisela. Apart from his successful border politics towards Hungary and Poland, he also tried to strengthen the ties of Italy to the Reich.

Konrad III, Eng. **Conrad** (1093/4–1152) The first king of the Staufer (Hohenstaufen) dynasty, the son of Frederick of Swabia. In 1125 he unsuccessfully contested the crown of Italy with Emperor Lothar III; when the emperor died, the princes of Germany offered Konrad the throne, and he was crowned at Aachen (7 March 1138). His reign saw the beginning of the conflict between Welfen and Staufer dynasties. When St Bernard of Clairvaux preached a new crusade, Konrad travelled to Palestine with a large army (1148), but the enterprise failed. Konrad nominated his nephew Frederick I Barbarossa as his successor.

Konrad IV, Eng. **Conrad** (1228–54) Mediaeval German ruler, the son of Frederick II. As Konrad III he became Duke of Swabia (1235) and was elected Roman King (1237). After the ban on his father (1245), he was greatly troubled by various anti-kings.

Kublai Khan (1214–94) Mongol emperor of China (1279–94), the grandson of Genghis Khan. He was acclaimed Great Khan in 1260, with suzerainty from the Pacific to the Black Sea. An energetic prince, he suppressed his rivals, adopted the Chinese mode of civilization, encouraged mathematicians and men of letters, and made Buddhism the state religion. He established himself at Cambaluc (modern Beijing), the first foreigner ever to rule in China, and ruled an empire which extended as far as the River Danube. Recognizing China's importance, he made it a separate realm within the Mongol empire. The splendour of his court was legendary.

KURFÜRSTEN

The Kurfürsten were the seven electors or princes of the Holy Roman Empire who (from 1257) enjoyed the sole right of electing the German king. Their position was regulated in the Golden Bull (1356), which confirmed that the election right attached to the location and not to the person. Originally they comprised three spiritual (archbishops of Mainz, Cologne, and Trier) and four temporal Kurfürsten (the Count Palatine of the Rhine, the Duke of Saxony, the Margrave of Brandenburg and, since 1289, the King of Bohemia). By the time of their dissolution in 1806, their composition had changed and they numbered ten.

L

nition as the only King of Naples in 1413.

Leo III, known as **Leo the Isaurian** (c.680–741) Byzantine emperor from 717, born in Syria, his byname coming from the region of his birth. He reorganized the army and financial system, and in 718 repelled a formidable attack by the Saracens. In 726 he issued an edict prohibiting the use of images in public worship. In Italy the controversy raised by the edict rent the empire for over a century. In 728 the exarchate of Ravenna was lost, and the eastern provinces became the prey of the Saracens, over whom he won a great victory in Phrygia.

Leonidas (?–480 BC) King of Sparta (c.489–480 BC), and Greek hero. In 480 BC his small command resisted the vast army of Xerxes, King of Persia, at Thermopylae. After two days he dismissed his troops, and with only his 300-strong Spartan royal guard, fought to the last man. The legend that Spartans never surrender emanated from his heroism.

La Vallière, Louise-Françoise de La Baume le Blanc, duchesse de (Duchess of) (1644–1710) Mistress of Louis XIV, born in Tours, France. Brought to court by her mother, she became the king's mistress in 1661 and bore him four children. When the Marquise de Montespan superseded her, she was publicly humiliated, then compensated by being made a duchess (1667). After one escape attempt, she retired to a Carmelite nunnery in Paris (1674), where she lived in penitence for 36 years.

Ladislao of Anjou, known as **the Magnanimous** (1377–1414) King of Naples, born in Naples. He succeeded his father, Charles III of Anjou-Durazzo, in 1386, with his mother, Margherita of Durazzo, as regent, but had to fight to take his crown back from Louis II of Anjou. Styling himself as the pope's advocate, he occupied Rome and took Umbria and Latium. He was defeated by Louis II at Roccasecca in 1411, and had to relinquish to antipope John XXIII the territories he had taken from the Papal States, but managed to obtain recog-

Leopold I (1640–1705) Holy Roman Emperor (1658–1705), born in Vienna, the second son of Ferdinand III and the Infanta Maria Anna. He was elected to the crowns of Hungary (1655) and Bohemia (1656), and succeeded to the imperial title in 1658. In 1666 he married his niece, **Margaret Theresa**, the second daughter of Philip IV of Spain, and after her death (1673) he took a second Habsburg bride, **Claudia Felicitas**, before his third marriage (1676) to **Eleonore of**

Palatinate-Neuberg, by whom he had two sons, the future emperors Joseph I and Charles VI. Committed to the defence of the power and unity of the House of Habsburg, he faced constant threats from the Ottoman Turks and the King of France, as well as the hostility of the Hungarian nobility. Treaties of neutrality (1667, 1671) between Leopold and Louis XIV of France gave way to military conflict over the Rhine frontier (1674–9, 1686–97), and to substantiate the rights of his son, Charles, against the French claimant, he took the empire into the Grand Alliance (1701). He died during the War of the Spanish Succession (1701–13) and the Hungarian revolt of Rákóczi (1703–11).

Leopold I (1790–1865) First king of Belgium (1831–65), born in Coburg, Germany, the son of Francis, Duke of Saxe-Coburg, and uncle of Queen Victoria. In 1816 he married **Charlotte**, daughter of the future George IV of England, and lived in England after her death in 1817. He declined the crown of Greece (1830), but in 1831 he was elected King of the Belgians. His second marriage, to **Marie Louise of Orléans**, daughter of Louis-Philippe, ensured French support for his new kingdom against the Dutch, and he was an influential force in European diplomacy and in domestic reform.

Leopold II (1747–92) Emperor, born in Vienna, the son of Emperor Francis I and Maria Theresa. As Leopold I he became Grand Duke of Tuscany (1765–90), where he pursued a Josephine (anti-curia) policy, and succeeded his brother Joseph II as emperor, King of Bohemia (1790), and King of Hungary (1791). He successfully put down insurrection in Hungary and Belgium, brought an end to the Turkish War by the Peace of Sistowa (1791), and concluded a pact against the French with Frederick William III of Prussia in 1792.

Leopold II (1835–1909) King of Belgium (1865–1909), born in Brussels, the eldest son of Leopold I. He married **Maria Henrietta**, daughter of the Austrian Archduke Joseph in 1853. In 1885 he became king of the newly independent Congo Free State, which became a Belgian colony in 1908. He proceeded to amass great personal wealth from its rubber and ivory trade at enormous cost of Congolese lives. His mistreatment of the Congo native population became an international scandal (1904), and he was forced (1908) to hand over the territory to his parliament. He strengthened his country by military reforms, and under him Belgium developed commercially and industrially.

Leopold II of Habsburg-Lorena (1747–92) Grand-duke of Tuscany (as Pietro Leopoldo I) and Holy Roman Emperor, born in Vienna, the son of Maria Theresa of Habsburg and Francis I. He was grand-duke of Tuscany (1765–90) when he became emperor. In Tuscany he was an enlightened ruler, implementing economic, administrative, and legal reforms, and promulgated (1786) a new criminal code which was called **Leopoldine**

after him. As emperor, he ended the war with Turkey (1791) and signed the Pilnitz declaration (1791).

Leopold III (1901–83) King of Belgium (1934–51), born in Brussels. He was the son of Albert I, and he married **Princess Astrid of Sweden** in 1926. He is especially known for his brave decision in 1940 to prolong the resistance of the Belgian army to the German invasion for a further two days, thus enabling the British evacuation at Dunkirk to succeed. (At the time, his action was vilified as treachery by French prime minister Reynaud, a misinterpretation which remained publicly uncorrected by Churchill, with the result that criticism of Leopold's action continued to be made for several decades.) He remained a prisoner in his own palace at Laeken until 1944, and afterwards in Austria. On returning to Belgium in 1950, he was finally forced to abdicate in favour of his son, Baudouin.

Liutprand (d.744) King of the Lombards, under whose reign the Lombards' domination of Italy reached its peak. He kept in check attempts to shake off his rule by the dukes of Spoleto and Benevento, and took advantage of discord between the pope and the Byzantines to occupy the exarchate, the pentapolis, and the Roman duchy. He reached a compromise with Pope Gregory II, and gave him the castle of Sutri (728), the first nucleus of the Papal States. Helping Charles Martel against the Arabs, he concluded the Terni agreement (742) with Pope Zachary to

guarantee a 20-year truce with the papacy. He revised Rotari's edict by writing a body of laws in 153 chapters (713–35).

Livia Drusilla (58 BC–AD 29) Roman empress, the third wife of the emperor Augustus, whom she married in 39 BC after divorcing her first husband Tiberius Claudius Nero. From her first marriage she had two children: Tiberius and Nero Claudius Drusus. She was influential with Augustus, and conspired maliciously to ensure Tiberius's succession, gaining the nickname 'Ulysses in Petticoats'. Relations with Tiberius after his accession became strained, and when she died he did not execute her will or allow her to be deified.

Lorenzo de' Medici, known as **the Magnificent** (1449–92) Florentine ruler, born in Florence, Italy, the son of Pietro I Medici and grandson of Cosimo de' Medici. He succeeded as head of the family upon the death of his father in 1469, and was an able if autocratic ruler, who made Florence the leading state in Italy. In 1478 he thwarted an attempt by malcontents, with the encouragement of Pope Sixtus IV, to overthrow the Medici, although the rising led to the assassination of his brother, **Giuliano** (1453–78). A distinguished lyric poet, he was, in the words of Machiavelli, 'the greatest patron of literature and art that any prince has ever been'.

Lothar I (795–855) Holy Roman Emperor and King of Italy (818–55), the son of Ludwig the Pious. In 824, during one of his trips to Italy, he promulgated the *Constitutio romana* ('Roman constitution') which sanctioned the superiority of the emperor over the pope. At the death of his father (840), he inherited the imperial crown, but was challenged by his brothers Ludwig II 'the German' and Charles the Bald. Although defeated by them, he was recognized as emperor and King of Italy.

Lothar II (?–950) King of Italy (931–50), who co-ruled (931–47) with his father, Hugh of Arles. Harassed by the powerful Berengar II of Ivrea, Hugh fled to Provence, where he died in 947. That same year Lothar married Adelaide, the 16-year-old daughter of Rudolf II of Burgundy, in the hope of strengthening his position, but instead became only a figurehead, while Berengar exerted control. Lothar died in 950, possibly poisoned by Berengar.

Lothar III (1060–1137) King of Germany (as Lothar II) and of Italy. He clashed repeatedly with Conrad of Swabia for the throne. He supported Innocent II against antipope Anacleto II, who was backed by the Norman king Ruggero II. Lothar was crowned emperor by Innocent in 1133; he then defeated Conrad in Germany (1135) and Ruggero (1136) in Italy.

Lothar III von Supplinburg (c.1075–1137) King of Germany (1125–37) and Holy Roman Emperor (from 1133). In continuation of the Eastern politics of Otto der Große, Lothar managed to assert the sover-

eignty of the Reich over Poland, Bohemia, and Denmark.

Louis I, known as **the Pious** (778–840) King of Aquitaine (781–814) and emperor of the Western or Carolingian empire (814–40), the son of Charlemagne. His reign was marked by reforms of the Church in collaboration with the monk St Benedict of Aniane, and by the raids of the Norsemen in the north-west of the empire, especially the Seine and Scheldt basins. After his death the empire disintegrated while his sons fought for supremacy.

Louis IX, St (1215–70) King of France (1226–70), born in Poissy, near Paris, the son of Louis VIII and Blanche of Castile. He was 11 years old when his father died, and his mother acted as regent (1226–34). At age 19 he married Marguerite of Provence, by whom he had 11 children. Through his victories he compelled Henry III of England to acknowledge French suzerainty in Guienne (1259). He led the Seventh Crusade (1248), but was defeated in Egypt, taken prisoner, and ransomed. After returning to France (1254) he carried out several legal reforms, and fostered learning, the arts, and literature. Also known for his charitable works, he founded many hospitals and homes. He embarked on a new crusade in 1270, and died of plague at Tunis. He was canonized in 1297. Feast day 25 August.

Louis XI (1423–83) King of France (1461–83), born in Bourges, France. He made two unsuccessful attempts to depose his father, Charles VII, but eventually succeeded to the throne on his father's death. During his reign he broke the power of the nobility, led by Charles the Bold of Burgundy, who was killed in 1477. By 1483 he had succeeded in uniting most of France under one crown (with the exception of Brittany), and laid the foundations for absolute monarchy in France. He patronized the arts and sciences, and founded three universities.

Louis XII (1462–1515) King of France (1498–1515), born in Blois, France, the son of Charles, duc d'Orléans, to whose title he succeeded in 1465. He commanded the French troops at Asti during Charles VIII's invasion of Italy (1494–5), before succeeding him to the French throne (1498), and marrying his widow, Anne of Brittany. He proved a popular ruler, concerned to provide justice and avoid oppressive taxation. Through the League of Cambrai (1508), his Italian ambitions brought him into diplomatic and military involvement with Ferdinand II of Aragón who finally outmanoeuvred Louis with the formation of the Holy League (1511). Meanwhile, Louis had foiled the Emperor Maximilian's dynastic designs on Brittany, but paid the price when his forces were driven from Italy (1512), and was then defeated by an Anglo–Imperial alliance at the Battle of Guinegate (1513). To guarantee peace, Louis married Mary Tudor, the sister of Henry VIII (1515), but died in Paris shortly afterwards.

Louis XIII (1601–43) King of France (1610–43), born in Fontainebleau, France, the eldest son of Henry IV and Marie de Médicis. He succeeded to the throne on the assassination of his father (1610), but was excluded from power, even after he came of age (1614), by the queen regent. She arranged Louis' marriage to Anne of Austria, the daughter of Philip III of Spain (1615). In 1617 Louis took over the reins of government, and exiled Marie de Médicis to Blois (1619–20). By 1624 he was entirely dependent upon the political acumen of Richelieu, who became his chief minister. Various plots to oust the Cardinal were foiled by the king's loyalty to his minister, whose domestic and foreign policies seemed to fulfil the royal ambition for great achievements. Louis' later years were enhanced by French military victories in the Thirty Years War against the Habsburgs, and by the birth of two sons in 1638 and 1640, including the future Louis XIV.

Louis XIV, known as **le Roi soleil** ('the Sun King') (1638–1715) King of France (1643–1715), born in St Germain-en-Laye, France, the son of Louis XIII, whom he succeeded at the age of five. During his minority (1643–51) France was ruled by his mother, Anne of Austria, and her chief minister, Cardinal Mazarin. In 1660 Louis married the Infanta Maria Theresa, the elder daughter of Philip IV of Spain, through whom he was later to claim the Spanish succession for his second grandson.

In 1661 he assumed sole responsibility for government, advised by various royal councils. His obsession with France's greatness led him into aggressive foreign and commercial policies, particularly against the Dutch. His patronage of the Catholic Stuarts also led to the hostility of England after 1689; but his major political rivals were the Austrian Habsburgs, particularly Leopold I. From 1665 Louis tried to take possession of the Spanish Netherlands, but later became obsessed with the acquisition of the whole Spanish inheritance. His attempt to create a Franco-Spanish Bourbon bloc led to the formation of the Grand Alliance of England, the United Provinces, and the Habsburg empire, and resulted in the War of the Spanish Succession (1701–13). In later years Louis was beset by other problems. His determination to preserve the unity of the French state and the independence of the French Church led him into conflict with the Jansenists, the Huguenots, and the papacy, with damaging repercussions. His old age was overshadowed by military disaster and the financial ravages of prolonged warfare.

Yet Louis was the greatest monarch of his age, who established the parameters of successful absolutism. In addition, his long reign marked the cultural ascendancy of France within Europe, symbolized by the Palace of Versailles. He was succeeded by his great-grandson as Louis XV.

Louis XV, known as **Louis le Bien-Aimé** ('Louis the Well-Beloved') (1710–74) King of France (1715–74), born in Versailles, France, the son of Louis, duc de Bourgogne and Marie-Adelaide of Savoy, and the great-grandson of Louis XIV, whom he succeeded at the age of five. His reign coincided with the great age of decorative art in the Rococo mode (dubbed the *Louis XV style*). Until he came of age (1723) he was guided by the regent, Philippe d'Orléans, and then by the Duc de Bourbon, who negotiated a marriage alliance with **Maria Leszczynska**, daughter of the deposed King Stanislas I of Poland. In 1726 Bourbon was replaced by the king's former tutor, the elderly Fleury, who skilfully steered the French state until his death (1744). Thereafter Louis vowed to rule without a First Minister, but allowed the government to drift into the hands of ministerial factions, while indulging in secret diplomatic activity, distinct from official policy, through his own network of agents. This system – *le secret du roi* – brought confusion to French foreign policy in the years prior to the Diplomatic Revolution (1748–56), and obscured the country's interests overseas. Instead, France was drawn into a trio of continental wars during Louis's reign, which culminated in the loss of the French colonies in America and India (1763). In 1771 Louis tried to introduce reforms, but these came too late to staunch the decline in royal authority. He was succeeded by his grandson, Louis XVI.

Louis XVI (1754–93) King of France (1774–93), born in Versailles, France, the third son of the dauphin Louis and Maria Josepha of Saxony, and the grandson of Louis XV, whom he succeeded in 1774. He was married in 1770 to the Archduchess Marie Antoinette, daughter of the Habsburg Empress Maria Theresa, to strengthen the Franco–Austrian alliance. He failed to give consistent support to ministers who tried to reform the outmoded financial and social structures of the country, such as Turgot (1774–6) and Necker (1776–81). He allowed France to became involved in the War of American Independence (1778–83), which exacerbated the national debt. Meanwhile, Marie Antoinette's propensity for frivolous conduct and scandal helped to discredit the monarchy. To avert the deepening social and economic crisis, he agreed in 1789 to summon the States General. However, encouraged by the queen, he resisted demands from the National Assembly for sweeping reforms, and in October was brought with his family from Versailles to Paris as hostage to the revolutionary movement. Their attempted flight to Varennes (June 1791) branded the royal pair as traitors. Louis reluctantly approved the new constitution (September 1791), but his moral authority had collapsed. In August 1792 an insurrection suspended Louis's constitutional position, and in September the monarchy was abolished. He was tried before the National Convention for conspiracy with foreign powers, and was guillotined in Paris.

Louis (Charles) XVII (1785–95) Titular King of France (1793–5), born in Versailles, France, the second son of Louis XVI and heir to the throne from June 1789. After the execution of his father (January 1793) he remained in the Temple prison in Paris. His death there dealt a blow to the hopes of Royalists and constitutional monarchists. The secrecy surrounding his last months led to rumours of his escape, and produced several claimants to his title.

Louis XVIII, originally **Louis Stanislas Xavier, comte de** (Count of) **Provence** (1755–1824) King of France in name from 1795 and in fact from 1814, born in Versailles, France, the younger brother of Louis XVI. He fled from Paris in June 1791, finally taking refuge in England, becoming the focal point for the Royalist cause. On Napoleon's downfall (1814) he re-entered Paris, and promised a Constitutional Charter. His restoration was interrupted by Napoleon's return from Elba, but after Waterloo (1815) he again regained his throne. His reign was marked by the introduction of parliamentary government with a limited franchise.

Louis Napoleon, Dutch **Lodewijk Napoleon** (1778–1846) King of The Netherlands, born in Ajaccio, Corsica, the brother of the French Emperor Napoleon. In 1802 he married Napoleon's stepdaughter, Hortense de Beauharnais, and was the father of the later Napoleon III. He accompanied Napoleon on his Italian and Egyptian campaigns and was made King of The Netherlands in 1806, but was removed in 1810 because of his half-hearted promotion of French interests and Napoleon's continental system. After leaving The Netherlands he joined the

Austrians under the title of Comte de Saint-Leu, in the hope of recovering his throne. He ended his days in exile in Florence.

Louis-Philippe, known as **the Citizen King** (1773–1850) King of the French (1830–48), born in Paris, the eldest son of the duc d'Orléans, Philippe Egalité. At the Revolution he entered the National Guard, and with his father renounced his titles to demonstrate his progressive sympathies. He joined the Jacobin Club (1790), and fought in the Army of the North before deserting to the Austrians (1793). He lived in Switzerland (1793–4), the USA, and England (1800–9), and in 1809 moved to Sicily and married **Marie Amélie**, daughter of Ferdinand I of Naples and Sicily. He returned to France in 1814, but fled to England again in the Hundred Days. On the eve of Charles X's abdication (1830) he was elected lieutenant-general of the kingdom, and after the July Revolution was given the title of King of the French. He strengthened his power by steering a middle course with the help of the upper bourgeoisie; but political corruption and industrial and agrarian depression (1846) caused discontent, and united the radicals in a cry for electoral reform. When the Paris mob rose (1848), he abdicated, and escaped to England.

Ludovico I (of Bourbon) (1773–1803) King of Etruria, born in Colorno, Italy, the son of Ferdinando di Borbone, Duke of Parma and Piacenza. After the Treaty of Lunéville (1801) he relinquished his title to the duchy, and

with the Treaty of Aranjuez (1801) was given by Napoleon the former grand-duchy of Tuscany with the title of King of Etruria. He was an ineffectual ruler and was influenced by his wife, Maria Luisa. Instead of implementing reforms, with the Sabatina decree he repealed the *codice leopoldino*, the enlightened penal code issued by Pietro Leopoldo I (Leopold II of Habsburg-Lorena).

Ludwig II, nickname **Mad King Ludwig**, also known as **Louis II** (1845–86) King of Bavaria (1864–86), born in Munich, the son and successor of Maximilian II. A German patriot of Romantic disposition, he devoted himself to patronage of Wagner and his music, and built Neuschwanstein castle in the Bavarian mountains. Siding with Prussia (1870–1) against France, he took Bavaria into the new German Second Reich. Later he adopted the life of a recluse, and in 1886 was declared insane; shortly after, he drowned himself in the Starnberger Lake, near his castle of Berg.

Ludwig III, known as **the Blind** (880–928) King of Provence, King of Italy, and Holy Roman Emperor, born in Autun, France. He was the son of Boso, King of Provence, and Irmingard, the daughter of Lothar II. In 900 he was crowned King of Italy, in opposition to Berengario I, and the following year was anointed emperor by Pope Benedict IV. He was defeated by Berengario in 905, dethroned, and blinded, but remained emperor, if only in name, until Berengario's crowning in 915.

Ludwig IV, der Bayer (1282–1347) German emperor, born in Munich. Duke of Upper Bavaria (1294) and United Bavaria (1340–7), he was elected German king (1314) in favour of the Habsburg King Frederick the Fair (Friedrich der Schöne), whom he defeated at Mühldorf (1322) in a lengthy campaign over the succession. He deposed Pope John XXII in 1324 following a protracted dispute over imperial rights in Italy, appointed an antipope, and was crowned Holy Roman Emperor in 1328. Karl IV of the House of Luxemburg was appointed as anti-king in 1346, but Ludwig died before he could challenge the decision.

Luxemburg, Heinrich VII von (1274/6–1313) Emperor, Count of Luxemburg, and German king (1308). He also acquired the kingdom of Bohemia for his family and thus laid the foundation of the House of Luxemburg. He led a campaign in Italy (1310–13) and was crowned King of Italy in Milan (1311) and emperor (1312) in the Lateran by three cardinals, but failed in his attempt to maintain his position, dying on the return journey in Buonconvento, Siena.

Luxemburg, Karl IV von (1316–78) King of Bohemia (1346) and Holy Roman Emperor (1355), born in Prague, Czech Republic. Originally named Wenzel, he was the son of Johannes, King of Bohemia from the House of Luxemburg. Elected Holy Roman Emperor (1346) initially as anti-king to Ludwig IV, he was

crowned in Rome (1355) and published the Golden Bull (1356). His reign was characterized by a drive for peace and the construction of buildings in Prague, where he founded the first German university in 1348.

Luxemburg, Sigismund von (1368–1437) Holy Roman Emperor (1410), born in Nuremberg, Germany, the son of Emperor Karl IV and the last emperor of the House of Luxemburg. After his marriage to Maria of Hungary, he became King of Hungary (1387), German king (1411), King of Bohemia (1419), and Lombard king (1431). He suffered defeat by the Turks at Nicopolis (1396), participated in the Hussite Wars in Bohemia, and was instrumental in settling the Western Schism.

Luxemburg, Wenzel von (1361–1419) Emperor, born in Nuremberg, Germany, the son of Emperor Karl IV. He was crowned King of Bohemia (as Wenceslas IV) in 1363, as German king (1376), and emperor (1378) in succession to his father. His reign was marked by feuds with the Bohemian nobility, and he was finally deposed by Electors of the Rhine in 1410.

Lysimachus (c.355–281 BC) Macedonian general of Alexander the Great. He acted as his bodyguard during the conquest of Asia, and became King of Thrace, to which he later added north-west Asia Minor and Macedonia. He was defeated and killed at Koroupedion by Seleucus.

Mafalda of Savoy (1902–44) Princess of Hessen, born in Rome, Latium, Italy, the second-born of Victor Emmanuel III, King of Italy. She married Philip of Hessen in 1925. She was arrested by the Germans in Rome in 1943 and sent to Buchenwald concentration camp, where she died.

Mahmud of Ghazna (971–1030) Muslim Afghan conqueror of India. The son of **Sebuktigin**, a Turkish slave who became ruler of Ghazna (modern Afghanistan), he succeeded to the throne in 997. He invaded India 17 times between 1001 and 1026, and created an empire that included Punjab and much of Persia. A great patron of the arts, he made Ghazna a remarkable cultural centre.

Maintenon, Françoise d'Aubigné, Marquise de (Marchioness of) (1635–1719) Second wife of Louis XIV of France, born in Niort, France. Orphaned, she married her guardian, the crippled poet Paul Scarron, in 1652, and on his death was reduced to poverty. In 1669 she discreetly took charge of the king's two sons by her

friend Mme de Montespan, and became the king's mistress. By 1674 the king had enabled her to purchase the estate of Maintenon, near Paris, which was converted to a marquisate. After the queen's death (1683), Louis married her secretly. She was accused of having great influence over him, especially over the persecution of Protestants. On his death in 1715 she retired to the educational institution for poor noblewomen which she had founded at St Cyr (1686).

Manasseh (no date) Biblical King of Judah, the eldest son of Joseph, who was adopted and blessed by Jacob. He was the eponymous ancestor of one of the 12 tribes of Israel, who later became the Jewish people.

Manasseh (7th-c BC) Biblical King of Judah (c.687–642 BC), the son of Hezekiah, whom he succeeded. He earned an evil name for idolatry and wickedness until he was taken captive by the Assyrians in Babylon, when he repented. *The Prayer of Manasseh* is apocryphal.

Manfredi (1232–66) Regent, and then King of Sicily, the natural son of Frederick II and Bianca Lancia. He was first regent of Sicily for Conrad IV, his stepbrother (1250–2), and then for his nephew Corradino (1254–8). At first he tried to have Corradino's claim recognized by the pope, but then spread the rumour of his death, and had himself crowned in Palermo (1258). He defeated the Guelphs at Montaperti (1260), but was defeated at Benevento

(1266) by Charles of Anjou, and died in battle.

Margaret of Angoulême, also known as **Margaret of Navarre** (1492–1549) Queen of Navarre, born in Angoulême, France. The sister of Francis I of France, she married first the **Duke of Alençon** (died 1525) and then, in 1527, **Henry d'Albret** (titular king of Navarre), but they were soon estranged. With a strong interest in Renaissance learning, she was much influenced by Erasmus and the religious reformers of the Meaux circle, who looked to her for patronage and protection. A woman of great intelligence, she encouraged agriculture, learning, and the arts, and her court was the most intellectual in Europe. The patron of men of letters, including the heretical poet Clément Marot, and François Rabelais, she was herself a prolific writer. Her works include tales and the *Histoires des Amans fortunés* whose first complete posthumous edition bore the name of *L'Heptaméron* (1558–9), a collection of stories on the theme of love in the manner of Boccaccio. Her best verse, including *Le Navire*, was not compiled until 1896 under the title *Les Dernières poésies*.

Margareta or **Margaret** (1353–1412) Queen of Denmark, Norway, and Sweden, born in Søborg, Denmark. She became Queen of Denmark in 1375, on the death of her father, Waldemar IV, without male heirs, but her infant son Olaf ruled in name until his death in 1387; by the death of her husband Haakon VI in 1380, she became ruler of Norway; and in 1388 she aided a rising of Swedish nobles against their king, Albert of Mecklenburg, and became Queen of Sweden. She had her infant cousin, Eric of Pomerania, crowned king of the three kingdoms at Kalmar in 1397, but remained the real ruler of Scandinavia until her death.

Margrethe II (1940–) Queen of Denmark (1972–), born in Copenhagen, the daughter of Frederick IX. She studied at Copenhagen, Cambridge, Århus, the Sorbonne, and London, and qualified as an archaeologist. Also an accomplished artist, she illustrated a 1977 edition of J. R. R. Tolkien's *The Lord of the Rings* using the pseudonym **Ingahild Grathmer**. In 1967 she married a French diplomat, **comte Henri de Laborde de Monpezat**, now **Prince Henrik** of Denmark. Their children are the heir apparent, **Prince Frederik André Henrik Christian** (1968–), and **Prince Joachim Holger Waldemar Christian** (1969–). Crown Prince Frederik married **Mary Elizabeth Donaldson**, an Australian businesswoman, in 2004; their son is **Prince Christian Valdemar Henri John** (2005–). Prince Joachim married **Alexandra Christina Manley** in 1995 (divorced 2005); their children are **Prince Nikolai William Alexander Frederik** (1999–) and **Prince Felix Henrik Valdemar Christian** (2002–). Queen Margrethe is one of Denmark's most popular monarchs. Her people can arrange to meet her to discuss an issue in the same way that a British MP holds a 'surgery' for constituents.

Margriet Francisca (1943–) Princess of The Netherlands, the third daughter of Queen Juliana and Prince Bernhardt of The Netherlands, born in Ottawa, Canada, during World War 2. She married Pieter van Vollenhoven, a lawyer, in 1967. There are four sons: **Maurits** (1968–), **Bernhard** (1969–), **Pieter** (1972–) and **Floris** (1975–), who follow their mother in line to the throne.

Maria Theresa (1717–80) Archduchess of Austria, and Queen of Hungary and Bohemia (1740–80), born in Vienna, the daughter of Emperor Charles VI (ruled 1711–40). In 1736 she married **Francis, Duke of Lorraine**, and in 1740 succeeded her father in the hereditary Habsburg lands. Her claim, however, led to the War of the Austrian Succession, during which she lost Silesia to Prussia. She received the Hungarian crown (1741), and in 1745 her husband was elected Holy Roman Emperor. Although her foreign minister, Kaunitz, tried to isolate Prussia by diplomatic means, military conflict was renewed in the Seven Years War, and by 1763 she was finally forced to recognize the status quo of 1756. In her later years she strove to maintain international peace, and reluctantly accepted the partition of Poland (1772). Of her 10 children who lived, the eldest son succeeded her as Joseph II.

Marie Antoinette (Josèphe Jeanne) (1755–93) Queen of France, born in Vienna, the daughter of Maria Theresa and Francis I. She was married to the Dauphin, afterwards Louis XVI (1770), to strengthen the Franco-Austrian alliance, and exerted a growing influence over him. Capricious and frivolous, she aroused criticism by her extravagance, disregard for conventions, devotion to the interests of Austria, and opposition to reform. From the outbreak of the French Revolution, she resisted the advice of constitutional monarchists (eg Mirabeau), and helped to alienate the monarchy from the people. However, the famous solution to the bread famine, 'let them eat cake', is unjustly attributed to her. In 1791 she and Louis tried to escape from the Tuileries to her native Austria, but were seized at Varennes and imprisoned in Paris. After the king's execution, she was arraigned before the Tribunal and guillotined.

Marie de Médicis, Italian **Maria de' Medici** (1573–1642) Queen consort of Henry IV of France, born in Florence, the daughter of Francesco de' Medici, Grand Duke of Tuscany. She married Henry in 1600, following his divorce from his first wife Margaret, and gave birth to a son (later Louis XIII) in 1601. After her husband's death (1610) she acted as regent, but her capricious behaviour and dependence on favourites led to her confinement in Blois when Louis assumed royal power in 1617. She continued to intrigue against Louis and her former protégé, Richelieu, who had become the king's adviser. She was banished to Compiègne, but escaped to Brussels (1631). Her last years were spent in poverty.

Marie Louise (1791–1847) Empress of

France, born in Vienna, Austria, the daughter of the Holy Roman Emperor, Francis II. She married Napoleon in 1810 (after his divorce from Joséphine), and in 1811 bore him a son, who was created King of Rome and who became Napoleon II. On Napoleon's abdication she returned to Austria. By the Treaty of Fontainebleau (1814) she was awarded the Duchies of Para, Piacenza, and Guastalla in Italy.

Matilde di Canossa (1046–1115) Ruler of Tuscany, and part of Lombardy and upper Lotharingia. The daughter of Boniface of Tuscany and Beatrix of Lorena, on the death of her brothers she inherited a number of territories. She supported the pope in the investiture contest with Henry IV, and gave hospitality to Gregory VII at her Canossa castle, where Henry IV went to make a public apology (1077). She left all her domains to the Church, an act which gave rise to more controversy between pope and emperor.

Matthias I, known as **Matthew Corvinus**, Hung. **Mátyás Corvin** (c.1443–90) King of Hungary (1458–90), born in Koloszvár, Hungary (now Cluj-Napoca, Romania), the second son of János Hunyady. He drove back the Turks, and made himself master of Bosnia (1462), Moldavia and Wallachia (1467), Moravia, Silesia, and Lusatia (1478), Vienna, and a large part of Austria proper (1485). His rule was arbitrary and his taxes heavy, but he greatly encouraged arts and letters, founded the Corvina library, promoted industry, and reformed finances and the system of justice.

Matthias, Kaiser (1557–1619) Holy Roman Emperor, born in Vienna, the son of Emperor Maximilian II of Austria. He was Statthalter of Austria and head of the House of Habsburg (1606). Commander-in-chief in the Turkish Wars (1594–5, 1598–1601), in 1601 he concluded a ceasefire agreement with the Turks and the rebellious Hungarians. The estates of Hungary, Austria, and Moravia allied themselves with him against his brother Emperor Rudolf II in 1608, and in 1611 Matthias gained the Bohemian crown. He became Holy Roman Emperor in 1612, but failed to achieve a compromise with the Bohemia Protestants and died the year after the outbreak of the Thirty Years War. He was succeeded by Ferdinand II.

Maurice, Prinz van Oranje, Graaf van Nassau (Prince of Orange, Count of Nassau) (1567–1625) Stadtholder of the United Provinces of The Netherlands, born in Dillenburg, Germany, the son of William the Silent. He was elected Stadtholder of Holland and Zeeland (1585) and later (1589) of Utrecht, Overijssel, and Gelderland, also becoming captain-general of the armies of the United Provinces during their War of Independence from Spain. He checked the Spanish advance, and by his steady offensive (1590–1606) liberated the northern provinces. He became Prince of Orange in 1618, on the death of his elder brother. In the renewed conflict with the Habsburgs, he commanded the new republic, seeking help from England and France (1624).

Maximilian I (1459–1519) Holy Roman Emperor (1493–1519), born as Archduke of Austria in Wiener Neustadt, Austria, the eldest son of Emperor Frederick III and Eleanor of Portugal. Elected King of the Romans (1486), he inherited the Habsburg territories and assumed the imperial title in 1493. He pursued an ambitious foreign policy, based on dynastic alliances, with far-reaching results for Habsburg power. His marriage to Mary of Burgundy brought his family the Burgundian inheritance, including Holland, followed by union with the Spanish kingdoms of Castile and Aragón when the Spanish crown passed to his grandson, Charles (1516). A double marriage treaty between the Habsburgs and the Jagiellons (1506) eventually brought the union of Austria–Bohemia–Hungary (1526). He was involved in conflict with the Flemish, the Swiss, the German princes, and especially with the Valois kings of France. Financial difficulties weakened his campaigns, and he was later forced to cede Milan (1504) to Louis XII. He incurred the hostility of the Venetians and, despite the League of Cambrai (1508), suffered defeat. He was succeeded by his grandson, as Charles V.

Maximilian I Joseph (1756–1825) King of Bavaria (from 1806), born in Mannheim, Germany. Due to his union with Napoleon I in 1801 he was made king, and acquired large territories in Franconia and Swabia. For the most part, he was able to secure these territories after changing sides to the Allies in 1813.

Maximilian, Ferdinand Joseph (1832–67) Emperor of Mexico (1864–7), born in Vienna, Austria, the younger brother of Emperor Francis Joseph, and an archduke of Austria. In 1863, he accepted the offer of the crown of Mexico, supported by France. When Napoleon III withdrew his troops, he refused to abdicate, and made a brave defence at Querétaro, but was betrayed and executed.

Menelik II, originally **Sahle Miriam**, also spelled **Sahlé Mariam** (1844–1913) Emperor of Ethiopia (1889–1909), born in Ankober, Shewa (Shoa), Ethiopia. As ruler of the Kingdom of Shoa, he conquered the Oromo people to the south, and annexed their land. When he succeeded as emperor, he united Shoa with the northern kingdoms of Tigray and Amhara, and signed the Treaty of Wichale with Italy. A disagreement over the interpretation of the treaty led to a war in which Menelik's forces defeated an Italian army at Adwa (1896). The European powers then recognized Ethiopian independence. During his reign he carried out a wide-ranging programme of modernization and founded the city of Addis Ababa.

Merneptah (13th-c BC) King of Egypt (1213–1204 BC), the son of Rameses II. He is famous principally for his great victory near Memphis over the Libyans and Sea Peoples (1209 BC).

Merovech or **Merovius** (5th-c)
Frankish ruler, the father of Childeric I
(who died c.481) and grandfather of
Clovis I. Little is known of his life
except that the Merovingian dynasty
is traditionally held to have taken its
name from him.

Michael VIII Palaeologus (c.1224–82)
Byzantine emperor (1261–82), born in
Nicaea into the Greek nobility. He
rose to be a successful general in the
empire of Nicaea. In 1258 he became a
regent for, and soon co-ruler with, the
eight-year-old emperor, John IV
Lascaris, whom he later had blinded
and imprisoned. In 1261 he became
emperor of Constantinople, incurring
the enmity of the papacy and Charles
of Anjou (1227–85) who aimed to re-
establish the Latin empire. The forced
reunion of the Orthodox Church with
Rome aroused great discontent
among his subjects but warded off
attacks until 1281. The hostile Pope
Martin IV (pontiff 1281–5) proclaimed
a crusade against him, but Michael
incited discontent in Sicily, which
was invaded by his allies the
Aragonese, thereby ending the
Angevin threat.

Michael (1921–) King of Romania
(1927–30, 1940–7), born in Sinaia,
Romania, the son of Carol II. He first
succeeded to the throne on the death
of his grandfather Ferdinand I, his
father having renounced his own
claims in 1925. In 1930 he was supplanted by his father (reigned
1930–40), but was again made king in
1940 when the Germans gained control of Romania. In 1944 he played a
considerable part in the overthrow of
the dictatorship of Antonescu. He
announced the acceptance of the
Allied peace terms, and declared war
on Germany. Forced in 1945 to accept
a Communist-dominated government, he was later compelled to abdicate (1947), and has since lived in exile
near Geneva.

Michael Romanov (1596–1645) Tsar of
Russia (1613–45), the great-nephew of
Ivan IV. He was the founder of the
Romanov dynasty that ruled Russia
until the revolution of 1917. Elected by
the boyars after a successful revolt
against the Poles, he brought an end
to the Time of Troubles that had
plagued Russia since the death of Boris
Godunov in 1605. He concluded peace

MEROVINGIANS

The Merovingians were the original Frankish royal family,
formerly chiefs of the Salians, named after the half-legendary
Merovech or Meroveus (the 'sea-fighter'). Clovis was the first
Merovingian king to control large parts of Gaul; the last to hold
significant power was Dagobert I (d.638), though the royal
dynasty survived until Childeric III's deposition in 751.

with Sweden (1617) and Poland (1618). He left the business of government largely in the hands of his father, the patriarch Filaret (Philaret) (**Fedor Nikitch Romanov**, c.1554/5–1633), who reorganized the army and industry with the help of experts from abroad, and consolidated the system of serfdom.

Mithridates VI (Eupator), also spelled **Mithradates**, known as **the Great** (?–63 BC) King of Pontus (c.115–63 BC), a Hellenized ruler of Iranian extraction in the Black Sea area, whose attempts to expand his empire over Cappadocia and Bithynia led to a series of wars (the Mithridatic Wars) with Rome (88–66 BC). Though worsted by Sulla (c.86 BC) and Lucullus (72–71 BC), he was not finally defeated until Pompey took over the Eastern command (66 BC). He avoided capture, but later took his own life.

Mohammed II or **Mehmet II**, known as **the Conqueror** (1432–81) Sultan of Turkey (1444–6, 1451–81), and founder of the Ottoman empire, born in Adrianople. He took Constantinople in 1453, renaming it Istanbul, thus extinguishing the Byzantine empire and giving the Turks their commanding position on the Bosphorus. Checked by Janos Hunyady at Belgrade in 1456, he nevertheless annexed most of Serbia, all of Greece, and most of the Aegean Is. He threatened Venetian territory, was repelled from Rhodes by the Knights of St John (1480), and took Otranto (1480). He died in a campaign against Persia.

Montespan, Françoise Athenaïs de Rochechouart, marquise de

MONARCHY

A monarchy is a political system in which a single person is the political ruler, whose position normally rests on the basis of divine authority, backed by tradition. The position is usually hereditary, passing through the male line. In Europe, the democratic revolutions of the 18th–20th centuries saw an end to what was until then the most widely known form of government. A number of countries, however, maintained the position of monarch, establishing *constitutional monarchies*, where the sovereign acts on the advice of government ministers who govern on his or her behalf. The monarchy's political power is thus largely formal and its role largely ceremonial, but its influence may increase in times of political crisis or when there is a vacuum in parliamentary politics.

(Marchioness of) (1641–1707) Mistress of Louis XIV, born in Tonnay-Charente, France, the daughter of the Duc de Mortemart. In 1663 she married the Marquis de Montespan, and joined the household of Queen Maria Theresa as lady-in-waiting. She became the king's mistress in c.1667, and after her marriage was annulled (1674), was given official recognition of her position. She bore the king seven children, who were legitimized (1673). Supplanted first by Mlle de Fontanges and later by Mme de Maintenon, she left court in 1687 and retired to the convent of Saint-Joseph in Paris, eventually becoming the superior.

Montezuma II (1466–1520) The last Aztec emperor (1502–20). A distinguished warrior and legislator, he died during the Spanish conquest of Hernán Cortés. One of his descendants was viceroy of Mexico (1697–1701).

Moshoeshoe II, originally **Constantine Bereng Seeiso** (1938–96) King of Lesotho (1966–90, 1994–6). He studied at Oxford, was installed as Paramount Chief of the Basotho people (1960), and proclaimed king when Lesotho became independent six years later. His desire for political involvement led to his being twice placed under house arrest, and in 1970 an eight-month exile in The Netherlands ended when Moshoeshoe agreed to take no further part in the country's politics. A military coup in 1986 replaced the government with a military council with the king as nominal executive head. When Moshoeshoe refused to sanction certain changes in 1990, he was forced to abdicate in favour of his son, **Letsie III**, but returned as king in 1994.

Murat, Joachim (1767–1815) French marshal and king of Naples (1808–15), born in La Bastide-Fortunière, France. He enlisted in the cavalry on the eve of the French Revolution (1787), and was promoted to general of division in the Egyptian campaign (1799). He married Napoleon's sister, Caroline, after helping him become First Consul. He failed to gain the Spanish crown (1808), and was proclaimed King of the Two Sicilies. After taking part in the Russian campaign, he won Dresden and fought at Leipzig, but concluded a treaty with the Austrians, hoping to save his kingdom. On Napoleon's return from Elba, he recommended war against Austria, but was twice defeated, and failed to recover Naples. He was captured and executed at Pizzo, Calabria.

Mutsuhito or **Meiji Tenno** (1852–1912) Emperor of Japan (1867–1912) who became the symbol of Japan's modernization, born in Kyoto, son of the titular Emperor, Komei, whom he succeeded. Within a year he had overthrown the last of the shoguns, who had exercised dictatorial authority in Japan for 700 years. His long reign saw the rapid political and military Westernization of Japan. The feudal system was abolished in 1871; most restrictions on foreign trade were removed; a constitution providing for an advisory cabinet and an imperial

Diet was promulgated in 1889; and a navy was created on the British model and an army on the German. Military success against China in 1894 and 1895 was followed by Japan's victories in the Russo-Japanese War (1904–5), and by the economic penetration of Korea and Manchuria.

Nadir Shah, Mohammed

(c.1880–1933) King of Afghanistan (1929–33). As commander-in-chief to Amanullah Khan, he played a prominent role in the 1919 Afghan War against Britain which secured the country's full independence in 1922. He subsequently fell into disfavour, and was forced to live in exile in France. In 1929, with British diplomatic support, he returned to Kabul and seized the throne, immediately embarking on a programme of economic and social modernization. These reforms, however, alienated the Muslim clergy, and in 1933 he was assassinated. He was succeeded by his son, Mohammed Zahir Shah.

Napoleon I, Fr. Napoléon Bonaparte, It. Napoleone Buonaparte

(1769–1821) French general, consul, and emperor (1804–15), a titanic figure in European history, born in Ajaccio, Corsica. He entered the military schools at Brienne (1779) and Paris (1784), commanded the artillery at the siege of Toulon (1793), and was promoted brigadier-general. In 1796 he married Joséphine, widow of the Vicomte de Beauharnais, and soon after left for Italy, where he skilfully defeated the Piedmontese and Austrians (at Lodi), and made several gains through the Treaty of Campo Formio (1797). Intending to break British trade by conquering Egypt, he captured Malta (1798), and entered Cairo, defeating the Turks; but after the French fleet was destroyed by Nelson at the Battle of the Nile in 1798 (also known as the Battle of Aboukir Bay), he returned to France (1799), having learned of French reverses in Europe. The *coup d'état* of 18th Brumaire followed (9 November 1799) in which Napoleon assumed power as First Consul, instituting a military dictatorship. He then routed the Austrians at Marengo (1800), made further gains at the Treaty of Luneville (1801), and consolidated French domination by the Concordat with Rome and the Peace of Amiens with England (1802).

Elected consul for life, he assumed the hereditary title of emperor in 1804. His administrative, military, educational, and legal reforms (notably the *Code Napoléon*) made a lasting impact on French society. War with England was renewed, and extended to Russia and Austria. Forced by England's naval supremacy at Trafalgar (1805) to abandon the notion of invasion, he attacked the Austrians and Russians, gaining victories at Ulm and Austerlitz (1805). Prussia was defeated at Jena and Auerstadt (1806), and Russia at Friedland (1807). After the Peace of Tilsit, he became the arbiter of Europe. He then tried to cripple England with the Continental System, ordering the

European states under his control to boycott British goods. He sent armies into Portugal and Spain, which resulted in the bitter and ultimately unsuccessful Peninsular War (1808–14).

In 1809, wanting an heir, he divorced Joséphine, who was childless by him, and married the Archduchess Marie Louise of Austria, a son being born in 1811. Believing that Russia was planning an alliance with England, he invaded (1812), defeating the Russians at Borodino, before entering Moscow, but he was forced to retreat, his army broken by hunger and the Russian winter. In 1813 his victories over the allied armies continued at Lützen, Bautzen, and Dresden, but he was routed at Leipzig, and France was invaded. Forced to abdicate, he was given the sovereignty of Elba (1814). The unpopularity which followed the return of the Bourbons motivated him to return to France in 1815. He regained power for a period known as the Hundred Days, but was defeated by the combination of Wellington's and Blücher's forces at Waterloo. He fled to Paris, abdicated, surrendered to the British, and was banished to St Helena, where he died.

Napoleon II, in full **François Charles Joseph Bonaparte** (1811–32) Son of Napoleon I by the Archduchess Marie Louise, born in Paris. He was styled King of Rome at his birth. After his father's abdication he was brought up in Austria, and in 1818 given the title of the Duke of Reichstadt, though allowed no active political role.

Napoleon III, until 1852 **Louis Napoleon**, originally **Charles Louis Napoleon Bonaparte** (1808–73) Third son of Louis Bonaparte, King of Holland (the brother of Napoleon I) and Hortense Beauharnais; the president of the Second French Republic (1848–52) and emperor of the French (1852–70), born in Paris. After the death of Napoleon II he became the head of the Napoleonic dynasty. He made two abortive attempts on the French throne (1836, 1840), for which he was imprisoned. He escaped to England (1846), but when the Bonapartist tide swept France after the 1848 revolution he was elected first to the Assembly and then to the presidency (1848). Engineering the dissolution of the constitution, he assumed the title of emperor, and in 1853 married **Eugénie de Montijo de Guzman** (1826–1920), a Spanish countess, who bore him a son, the Prince Imperial, **Eugène Louis Jean Joseph Napoleon** (1856). He actively encouraged economic expansion and the modernization of Paris, while externally the Second Empire coincided with the Crimean War (1854–6), expeditions to China (1857–60), the annexation (1860) of Savoy and Nice, and an ill-starred intervention in Mexico (1861–7). Encouraged by the empress, he unwisely declared war on Prussia in 1870, and suffered humiliating defeat, culminating in the Battle of Sedan. Confined at Wilhelmshohe until 1871, he went into exile in England.

Nebuchadnezzar II, also spelled **Nebuchadrezzar** (c.630–562 BC) King of Babylon (605–562 BC). He succeeded his father Nabopolassar, and during his 43-year reign recovered the long-lost provinces of the kingdom, once more making Babylon a supreme nation. He not only restored the empire and rebuilt Babylon, but almost every temple throughout the land underwent restoration at his hands. Every mound opened by explorers has contained bricks, cylinders, or tablets inscribed with his name. In 597 BC he captured Jerusalem, and in 586 BC destroyed the city, removing most of the inhabitants to Chaldea.

Nefertiti (14th-c BC) Egyptian queen, the consort of Akhenaton, by whom she had six children, and whose new religious cult of the Sun god Aton she supported. She is immortalized in the beautiful sculptured head found at Amarna in 1912, now in the Berlin Museum. Little is known of her background, but she is believed to have been an Asian princess from Mitanni.

Nero, in full **Nero Claudius Caesar**, originally **Lucius Domitius Ahenobarbus** (37–68) Emperor of Rome (54–68), the son of Gnaeus Domitius Ahenobarbus and the younger Agrippina, daughter of Germanicus. He owed his name and position to the driving ambition of his mother, who engineered his adoption by the Emperor Claudius, her fourth husband. Initially his reign was good, thanks to his three main advisers: his mother, the philosopher Seneca, and the Praetorian Prefect Burrus. But after her murder (59), and their fall from favour, Nero, more interested in sex, singing, acting, and chariot-racing than government, neglected affairs of state, and corruption set in. He was blamed for the Great Fire of Rome (64), despite assiduous attempts to make scapegoats of the Christians. A major plot to overthrow him (the Conspiracy of Piso) was formed (65) but detected, and Rome had to endure three more years of tyranny before he was toppled from power by the army, and forced to commit suicide.

Nerva, Marcus Cocceius (c.32–98) Emperor of Rome (96–98), elected by the Senate after the assassination of Domitianus. One of the 'five good emperors', he rejected terrorism and introduced liberal reforms, but lacked military support, and had to adopt Trajan as his successor.

Nicholas I (1796–1855) Tsar of Russia (1825–55), born in Tsarskoye Selo, near St Petersburg, the third son of Paul I. An absolute despot, he engaged in wars with Persia and Turkey, suppressed a rising in Poland, and attempted to Russianize all the inhabitants of the empire. He helped to quell the 1848 Hungarian insurrection, and drew closer the alliance with Prussia. The re-establishment of the French empire confirmed these alliances, and led him to think of absorbing Turkey, but the opposition of Britain and France brought on the Crimean War, during which he died.

Nicholas II (1868–1918) The last Tsar of Russia (1894–1917), born near St Petersburg, the son of Alexander III.

His reign was marked by the alliance with France (1894), an entente with Britain, a disastrous war with Japan (1904–5), and the establishment of the national assembly, or Duma (1906). When forced by the 1905 Revolution to accept a constitutional monarchy, he continued to believe that he was responsible only to God. He took command of the Russian armies against the Central Powers in 1915, leaving the government of the country to the Empress Alexandra and Rasputin. His mismanagement of the war and government chaos led to his abdication in 1917, and subsequent imprisonment. In July 1918 the Bolsheviks moved him and his family to Siberia, where they were executed at Ekaterinburg. The Russian Orthodox Church bestowed saint-hood on Nicholas, his wife and five children in 2000.

Numa Pompilius (c.700 BC) The second of Rome's early kings. According to tradition he ruled from 715 to 673 BC. He is described as a peaceful ruler, and was credited with organizing the religious life of the community.

leapt overboard and was never seen again.

Odoacer, also found as **Odovacar** (?–493) Germanic warrior who destroyed the Western Roman Empire, and became the first barbarian King of Italy (476–93). An able ruler, he was challenged and overthrown by the Ostrogothic King Theodoric (489–93) at the instigation of the Eastern Roman Emperor, Zeno.

Olaf I Tryggvason (c.965–c.1000) King of Norway (995–c.1000), the great-grandson of Harald I. He was the most spectacular Viking of his time and the subject of much legend. Brought up at the court of Prince Vladimir I of Russia, he was a Viking mercenary in the Baltic at the age of 18. He led the Viking army that defeated the Anglo-Saxons at the celebrated Battle of Maldon in Essex (991). He returned to harry England in a huge expedition led by the King of Denmark, Sweyn Forkbeard (994). Converted to Christianity, he seized the throne for himself (995) and attempted to convert Norway to Christianity by force. Overwhelmed by a combined Danish and Swedish · fleet at the Battle of Svold in 1000, he

Olaf II Haraldsson, also called **St Olaf** (c.995–1030) King of Norway (1015–28), the half-brother of Harald III (Hardrada). He became a Viking mercenary in the Baltic at the age of 12, going on to England, Frisia, and Spain. In England in 1010 he took part in a celebrated attack when London Bridge was torn down with grappling irons. He was converted to Christianity in Normandy in 1013, and returned to Norway in 1014, where he seized the throne and worked hard to complete the conversion of Norway begun by Olaf I Tryggvason and establish the Church. In 1028, faced by rebellion abetted from Denmark, he was forced to flee to Russia for safety. In 1030 he came back in an attempt to regain his crown, but was defeated and killed at the Battle of Stiklestad. Within 12 months he was regarded as a national hero and the patron saint of Norway. Feast day 29 July.

Olaf III Haraldsson (?–1093) King of Norway (1067–93), the son of Harald III (Hardrada). He was at the Battle of Stamford Bridge in Yorkshire in 1066 when his father was defeated and killed by Harold II of England, but was allowed to return to Norway with the survivors of the Norwegian invasion force, and assumed the throne of Norway the following year. His long reign was marked by unbroken peace and prosperity in Norway.

Olav V (1903–91) King of Norway (1957–91), born near Sandringham,

Norfolk, the son and successor of Haakon VII and Maud, daughter of Edward VII of Britain. He studied in Norway and at Oxford, and was an outstanding sportsman and Olympic yachtsman in his youth. He stayed in Norway when it was invaded by Germany in 1940, and was appointed head of the Norwegian armed forces. Later he escaped with his father to England, returning in 1945. In 1929 he married **Princess Martha of Sweden** (1901–54), and had two daughters and a son, **Harald** (1937–), who succeeded to the Norwegian throne as Harald V in 1991. His son, **Crown Prince Haakon**, married **Mette-Marit Tjessem Hoiby** in 2001 and they have a daughter, **Ingrid Alexandra** (2004–) who is second in line to the throne after her father. An amendment to the Norwegian constitution in 1990 means the succession goes to the first-born child of the ruling monarch, regardless of the child's sex.

Olympias (c.375–316 BC) Wife of Philip II of Macedon, mother of Alexander the Great, and daughter of Neoptolemus of Epirus. When Philip married Cleopatra, niece of Attalus, she left Macedon and ruled Epirus by herself, and is said to have murdered Cleopatra after Philip was assassinated (336 BC). Alexander died in 323 BC, and she returned to Macedon, where she secured the death of his half-brother and successor, and made Alexander's posthumous son, Alexander IV, king. Eventually Cassander besieged her in Pydna, and she was killed by relatives of those she had put to death.

Omri (9th-c BC) King of Israel (c.876–c.873 BC). An army commander, he was made king after Zimri assassinated Elah and seized the throne. He is the first Israelite monarch found to be mentioned in historical records other than the Bible. The Moabite Stone states that 'Omri, king of Israel, oppressed Moab many days and his sons after him'. Omri founded the city of Samaria on a hill and was buried there. He was succeeded by his son Ahab.

Orléans, Louis Philippe Joseph, duc d' (Duke of), known as **Philippe Egalité** ('equality') (1747–93) Bourbon prince, born in Saint-Cloud, France, the cousin of Louis XVI and father of Louis Philippe. He became the Duc de Chartres in 1752, and inherited his father's title in 1785. At the Revolution he proved a strong supporter of the Third Estate against the privileged orders, and in 1792 renounced his title of nobility for his popular name. At the Convention he voted for the king's death, but was himself arrested, after the defection of his eldest son to the Austrians (1793), and guillotined.

Otho, Marcus Salvius (32–69) Roman emperor for three months (69). Emperor Nero took Otho's wife for his mistress, and later married her. He was sent to govern Lusitania (58–68), and joined Galba in his revolt against Nero (68). When he was not proclaimed Galba's successor, he rose against the new emperor, who was slain. Otho was recognized as emperor everywhere except in Germany. Aulus Vitellius marched on Italy, defeated Otho's forces, and Otho committed suicide.

Otto I, known as **the Great** (912–73) King of the Germans (from 936) and Holy Roman Emperor (from 962). He subdued many turbulent tribes, maintained almost supreme power in Italy, and encouraged Christian missions to Scandinavian and Slavonic lands.

Otto II (955–83) Holy Roman Emperor, the son of Otto I the Great. He was crowned King of Germany (961) and co-emperor (967), and in 972 married Theophano, daughter of the Byzantine Emperor John Tzimiskes. He took over as sole ruler in 973, and was victorious against Henry the Quarrelsome of Bavaria (Heinrich II der Zänker) and the Danes. He acquired Lorraine for the German Reich (980), but was defeated by the Saracens in Lower Italy at Cotrone (982). The uprising by the Slavs and Danes in 983 led to the loss of nearly all the German territory acquired by his father east of the Elbe and Saale.

Otto II, Count of Gelre, nickname **the Lame** or **Horsefoot** (c.1200–71) Dutch ruler, the son of Gerard I and Margaret of Brabant. He set about expanding his influence and territory by various means. Firstly, he married Margaret, daughter of Count Dirk of Cleves, and later Philippa, daughter of the Count of Ponthieu. Secondly, he purchased Emmerik, Groenlo, Breevoort, and Zevenaar, judiciously granted privileges to towns, and acquired from William II, King of the

Romans, Nijmegen and the surrounding area. He was Regent of Holland during the minority of Floris V and conducted successful expeditions against Zeeland. With his brother Henry (prince-bishop elect of Liège) he supported the citizens of Cologne against Archbishop Engelbrecht II, and was rewarded with the title of 'protector of the city' for his successors.

Otto III (980–1002) Holy Roman Emperor, born in Reichswald bei Kleve, Germany, the son of Otto II. He was crowned King of Germany (983), but reigned under the guardianship of his mother Theophano until 991, and thereafter under that of his grandmother Adelheid until 994. He was called to Italy by Pope John XV to help him control the Roman aristocracy's power. At John's death he had his cousin elected pope as Gregory V, and was crowned emperor by him in 996. Another revolt by the aristocracy forced him to return to Rome in 998. He had his tutor, Gerbert d'Aurillac, elected pope as Sylvester II with the plan to re-establish a Christian Roman Empire (*Renovatio Imperii*), with Rome as the seat of a universal empire comprising Teutons (Germanen), Latins (Romanen), and Slavs under the common rule of emperor and pope. He was forced to flee from Rome following a revolt in 1001.

Otto IV of Brunswick (?–218) Holy Roman Emperor, the son of Henry of Bavaria and Mathilde of England. He was opposed to the Guelph Philip of Swabia, but became king in 1208, and was crowned emperor by Innocent III the next year. But his claim to the Sicilian throne had him excommunicated and deposed (1210), and Frederick of Swabia was elected King of the Romans in 1211.

P p

Pahlavi, Mohammad Reza (1919–80) Shah of Persia, born in Tehran, Iran, who succeeded on the abdication of his father, Reza Shah (1878–1944), in 1941. His reign was for many years marked by social reforms and a movement away from the old-fashioned despotic concept of the monarchy, but during the later 1970s the economic situation deteriorated, social inequalities worsened, and protest at Western-style 'decadence' grew among the religious fundamentalists. He introduced harsh measures of control, which failed to restore stability. He was forced to leave the country, and a revolutionary government was formed under Ayatollah Khomeini (1979). He was in the USA for medical treatment when the Iranian government seized the US embassy in Teheran (1979) and held many of its staff hostage for over a year, demanding his return to Iran. He made his final residence in Egypt at the invitation of President Sadat.

Paul I (1754–1801) Tsar of Russia (1796–1801), born in St Petersburg, the son of Catherine II and Peter III (though his paternity has been debated). His father's murder and his mother's neglect exerted a baneful influence on his character, and after succeeding his mother to the throne he soon revealed his violent temper and lack of capacity, and irritated his subjects by vexatious regulations. He suddenly declared for the Second Coalition Allies against France (1798), and sent an army of 56 000 into Italy. He sent a second army to co-operate with the Austrians, retired from the alliance, quarrelled with England, and entered into close alliance with Napoleon. After his convention with Sweden and Denmark, England sent a fleet into the Baltic under Nelson to dissolve the coalition (1801). His own officers conspired to compel him to abdicate, and in a scuffle he was strangled. Despite the deprivations of his childhood, he became a devoted husband to his second wife, Maria Feodorovna, and caring father of their 10 children. Among their children were two future tsars, Alexander I and Nicholas I, and two future queens, Catherine of Wurttemberg and Anna of The Netherlands.

Paul I (1901–64) King of the Hellenes (1947–64), born in Athens. In 1922 he served with the Greek navy against the Turks; but in 1924, when a Republic was proclaimed, went into exile, returning to Greece as crown prince in 1935. In World War 2 he served with the Greek general staff in the Albanian campaign, and was in exile in London (1941–6). His reign covered the latter half of the Greek Civil War (1946–9) and its difficult aftermath. During the early 1960s his personal role, and that of his wife Queen Frederika, became sources of bitter political controversy.

Pausanias (5th-c BC) Greek soldier, and regent of Sparta, the nephew of Leonidas. He commanded the Greek forces at Plataea (479 BC), where the Persians were routed. He then compelled the Thebans to give up the chiefs of the Persian party, and treated the Athenians and other Greeks haughtily. Capturing the Cyprian cities and Byzantium, he negotiated with Xerxes in the hope of becoming ruler under him of all Greece, and was twice recalled for treachery. He tried to stir up the helots, was betrayed, and fled to a temple of Athena on the Spartan acropolis, where he was walled up and taken out only when dying of hunger (c.470 BC).

Pedro I (1798–1834) Emperor of Brazil (1826–31), born in Lisbon, the second son of John VI of Portugal (reigned 1816–26). He fled to Brazil with his parents on Napoleon's invasion, and became prince-regent of Brazil on his father's return to Portugal (1821). A liberal in outlook, he declared for Brazilian independence in 1822, and was crowned as Emperor Pedro I in 1826. The new empire did not start smoothly, and in 1831 he abdicated and withdrew to Portugal, where he had succeeded his father as Pedro IV (1826), but abdicated that throne in favour of his daughter, Maria.

Pepin III, known as **Pepin the Short** (c.714–68) King of the Franks (751–68),

founder of the Frankish dynasty of the Carolingians, the father of Charlemagne. The son of Charles Martel, he was chosen king after the deposition of Childeric, the last of the Merovingians. He led an army into Italy (754), and defeated the Lombards. The rest of his life was spent in wars against the Saxons and Saracens.

Peter I, known as **the Great** (1672–1725) Tsar of Russia (1682–1721) and emperor (1721–5), born in Moscow, the son of Tsar Alexey and his second wife Natalia Naryshkin. He became accomplished in mechanics, with an abiding interest in military and naval technology. He was joint tsar with his mentally retarded half-brother, Ivan, under the regency of their sister, Sophia (1682–9). In 1697–8 he travelled to Germany, Holland, England, and Habsburg Vienna, his chief aim being to recruit foreign technicians and craftsmen. On Ivan's death (1696) he became sole tsar, and embarked on a series of sweeping military, fiscal, administrative, educational, cultural, and ecclesiastical reforms, many of them based on West European models. He brought the boyars under the authority of Church and throne; encouraged industry, trade, and education; modernized the state administration; and introduced Arabic numerals into the Russian alphabet. During his reign the first Russian-language newspaper was published and the Academy of Sciences was established. All classes of society suffered from the impact of the reforms and the brutality of their implementation; his own son, Alexis, died under torture (1718), suspected of leading a conspiracy against his father. Nevertheless, his efforts to modernize Russia turned it from a backward country into an imperial power to be feared. Peter fought major wars with the Ottoman empire, Persia, and in particular Sweden, which Russia defeated in the Great Northern War (1700–21). This victory established Russia as a major European power, and gained a maritime exit on the Baltic coast, where Peter founded his new capital, St Petersburg (1703). He failed to nominate a successor, and was succeeded by his wife, Catherine I.

Peter I (1844–1921) King of Serbia, born in Belgrade, Serbia and Montenegro (former Yugoslavia), the son of Prince Alexander Karadjordjević (reigned 1842–59). He fought in the French army in the Franco-Prussian war (1870–1), and was elected King of Serbia in 1903. In World War 1 he accompanied his army into exile in Greece in 1916. He returned to Belgrade in 1918, and was proclaimed titular king of the Serbs, Croats, and Slovenes until his death, although his second son, Alexander (later Alexander I), was regent.

Peter II, in full **Pyotr Alekseyevich** (1715–30) Tsar of Russia (1727–30), born in St Petersburg. The grandson of Peter I (the Great), he was named heir to the throne by Catherine I and was crowned at age 11. Catherine had named the Supreme Privy Council to act as regent for Peter under the guidance of Alexander D. Menshikov,

who arranged the betrothal of his own daughter to Peter. Peter objected and asked the Dolgoruky family for help. In 1727 they arrested and exiled Menshikov. A marriage between Peter and Princess Yekaterina Alekseyevna Dolgorukaya was arranged, but Peter died on his wedding day from smallpox.

Peter II (1923–70) King of Yugoslavia (1934–45), born in Serbia and Montenegro (former Yugoslavia), the son of Alexander I. He was at school in England when his father was assassinated in 1934. His uncle, Prince Paul Karadjordjević (1893–1976), a nephew of Peter I, was regent until 1941 when he was ousted by pro-Allied army officers, who declared King Peter of age and he assumed sovereignty. The subsequent German attack on Yugoslavia forced him to go into exile within three weeks. He set up a government-in-exile in London, but lost his throne when Yugoslavia became a communist dictatorship in 1945. King Peter never abdicated, and there was no referendum on the monarchy. From then on he lived in France, Italy, and briefly in the USA.

Philip II (382–336 BC) King of Macedon (359–336 BC), the father of Alexander the Great. He used his military and diplomatic skills first to create a powerful unified state at home (359–353 BC), then to make himself the master of the whole of independent Greece. His decisive victory at Chaeronea (338 BC) established Macedonian hegemony there for good. The planned Macedonian conquest of Persia, aborted following his assassination in 336 BC, was eventually carried out by his son.

Philip II, known as **Philip Augustus** (1165–1223) King of France (1179–1223), born in Paris, the son of Louis VII (reigned 1137–79). His reign formed a key period in the development of the mediaeval kingdom of France. He embarked on the Third Crusade in 1190, but returned the following year to concentrate on attacking the continental lands of the Angevin kings of England. By the time he died, Capetian power was firmly established over most of France.

Philip II (1527–98) King of Spain (1556–98) and Portugal (as Philip I, 1580–98), born in Valladolid, Spain, the only son of Emperor Charles V and Isabella of Portugal. Following the death of his first wife, **Maria of Portugal**, at the birth of their son, Don Carlos (1545), he married **Mary I** of England (1554), becoming joint sovereign of England. Before Mary's death (1558) he had inherited the Habsburg possessions in Italy, The Netherlands, Spain, and the New World. To seal the end of the Valois–Habsburg conflict he married **Elizabeth of France**, who bore him two daughters. His brief fourth marriage to his cousin **Anna of Austria** (1570) produced another son, the future Philip III. As the champion of the Counter-Reformation, he tried to destroy infidels and heretics alike. He sought to crush Protestantism, first in the Low Countries (from 1568), then in England and France. The destruc-

tion of the Armada (1588) and the continuing revolt of The Netherlands, along with domestic economic problems and internal unrest, suggest a reign marked by failure. However, among his political achievements were the curbing of Ottoman seapower after the Battle of Lepanto (1571) and the conquest of Portugal (1580).

Philip III (of Spain) (1578–1621) King of Spain, Naples, Sicily (1598–1621) and Portugal (as Philip II), born in Madrid, the son of Philip II of Spain and his fourth wife, Anna of Austria. Although exemplary in his private conduct, the new king was indifferent to the responsibilities of government and left that to his favourite, the Duke of Lerma. In 1599 he married his Habsburg cousin the Austrian archduchess Margaret, and their daughter, Anne of Austria, later married Louis XIII of France (1615). His reign saw a decline in Spain's economy, resulting partly from the expulsion (1609–14) of the Moriscos while the grandees accumulated huge estates and the Church prospered. He was succeeded by his son, Philip IV.

Philip V (1683–1746) First Bourbon King of Spain (1700–46), born in Versailles, France, the grandson of Louis XIV and Maria Theresa, and great-grandson of Philip IV of Spain. After a long struggle with the rival Habsburg candidate for the Spanish succession, Philip gained the throne at the Peace of Utrecht (1713), but lost the Spanish Netherlands and Italian lands. Twice married, he fell under the influence of his second wife,

Elizabeth Farnese of Parma, whose desire to secure Italian possessions for her sons brought Spain into conflict with Austria, Great Britain, France, and the United Provinces.

Philip VI (1293–1350) First Valois King of France (1328–50), the nephew of Philip IV, who became king on the death of Charles IV. His right was denied by Edward III of England, son of the daughter of Philip IV, who declared that females, though excluded from the succession by the Salic law, could transmit their right to their children. The Hundred Years War with England thus began (1337), and in 1346 Edward III landed in Normandy, defeating Philip at Crécy, just as the Black Death was about to spread through France.

Philip, known as **King Philip**, originally **Metacomet** (?1639–76) Wampanoag leader, born at Pawkunnakut in present-day Rhode Island, USA. Son of **Massasoit**, he became chief in 1661, and although he did not at first engage in open hostilities, he gradually came to resent the English colonists' increasing restrictions on the Indians' use of their own lands. In 1675 an Indian informer told the English he was planning a revolt; when the informer was killed, supposedly by three Wampanoag, the colonists executed them, and this led to immediate war by angry Wampanoags. Although this war came to be known as 'King Philip's War', there is some question as to whether he actually was the initial or major leader. In any case, it soon led to a major uprising of tribes from Rhode Island all the way to the Connecticut River in western Massachusetts; twelve colonial settlements were completely destroyed and thousands of settlers were killed, but the English gradually wore down the Indians. In the final battle (April 1676) near Mt Hope (now Bristol, RI), Philip was killed (by another Indian fighting for the colonists). The colonists' victory effectively broke up the tribal structures and ended Native American resistance in southern New England.

Philip, Duke of Burgundy, known as **the Good** (1396–1467) Duke of Burgundy from 1419, the son of John the Fearless. He acquired Namur, Brabant, and Limburg by inheritance through his uncle Antony, and Holland, Zeeland, and Hainault from Jacqueline of Bavaria. He tried to extend his power over Gelre and Friesland, and managed to have his candidates appointed to the bishoprics of Liège and Utrecht. He appointed a central Grand Council and a chancellor, and also stadtholders in the various provinces, and instituted a consultancy body, the States-General, in Brussels. This centralizing tendency was later carried much further by the Emperor Charles V, but Philip the Good is generally regarded as the founder of the unified Netherlands state. In 1430 he founded the Order of the Golden Fleece, and the same year had Joan of Arc, who had been captured by John of Luxemburg, handed over to the English.

Philip, Duke of Burgundy (Philip

IV), known as **the Fair** (1478–1506) Duke of Burgundy from 1482, the first Habsburg Duke of Burgundy and Archduke of Austria, the son of Mary of Burgundy and Maximilian I of Austria. He married Joanna ('Mad Joanna'), the daughter of Ferdinand and Isabella of Aragón and Castile. He inherited the dukedom in 1482 and in 1494 refused to honour the Great Privilege. On the death of his mother-in-law Isabella, he became King of Castile (1504), but never took over from Ferdinand, who continued ruling as her regent. His son was the future Emperor Charles V.

Philip William, Dutch **Filip Willem** (1554–1618) Dutch ruler, Prince of Orange, born in Buren, The Netherlands, the eldest son of William I of Orange and Anne of Buren. As a student in Louvain in 1568 he was abducted by Alva and taken to Spain as a hostage, and was further educated at the Spanish court. In 1596 he returned to the southern Netherlands with Archduke Albert's court. He was given his father's confiscated possessions by Philip II, took part in some skirmishes against France, but refused to take up arms against his brother Maurice. He married Eleonore Charlotte de Condé in 1606, but the marriage remained childless, and his titles and estates were inherited by Maurice.

Pisistratus, also spelled **Peisistratos** (c.600–527 BC) Tyrant of Athens (561–c.556 BC, 546–527 BC). A moderate and far-sighted ruler, he did much to improve the lot of the small farmer in Attica, and to boost Athenian trade abroad, especially in the Black Sea area. A patron of the arts, he invited the leading Greek poets of the day to settle in Athens, where he set about fostering a sense of national unity by instituting or expanding great religious and cultural festivals. He was succeeded by his sons Hippias and Hipparchus, the so-called *Pisistratidae*, but the dynasty was overthrown in 510 BC.

Porsenna, Lars (6th-c BC) Etruscan ruler of Clusium. According to Roman patriotic tradition he laid siege to Rome after the overthrow in 510 BC of Tarquinius Superbus, but was prevented from capturing the city by the heroism of Horatius Cocles defending the bridge across the Tiber. However, this tradition may conceal a temporary occupation of Rome by Porsenna.

Psamtik I (690–610 BC) King of Egypt (664–610 BC) who liberated Egypt from Assyrian control, and founded the XXVI dynasty.

Ptolemy I Soter ('Saviour') (c.366–c.283 BC) Macedonian general in the army of Alexander the Great, who became ruler of Egypt after Alexander's death (323 BC). In 305 BC he adopted the royal title, and thus founded the Ptolemaic dynasty. An able ruler, he secured control over Palestine, Cyprus, and parts of Asia Minor, and placed his regime everywhere on a sound military and financial basis. In 305 BC he defended the Rhodians against Demetrius, and received from them the title of *Soter*.

Abroad, the empire was maintained, and in Egypt, Alexandria (with its royally founded museum and library) became the chief centre for learning in the Mediterranean world. On his abdication in 283 BC, he was succeeded by his son as Ptolemy II Philadelphus.

Ptolemy II Philadelphus (308–246 BC) King of Egypt (285–246 BC), the son and successor of Ptolemy I Soter. Under him the power of Egypt attained its greatest height. He was generally successful in his external wars, founded the Museum and Library, purchased many valuable manuscripts of Greek literature, and attracted leading Greek intellectuals to his court. The Egyptian history of Manetho was dedicated to him, but the story that he commissioned the Greek translation of the Hebrew Scriptures (the Septuagint) is open to doubt.

Puyi, Pu Yi, or **P'u-i**, personal name of the **Xuantong** Emperor (1906–67) Last Emperor of China (1908–12) and the first of Manchukuo (1934–5), born in Beijing. Emperor at the age of two, after the 1912 revolution he was given a pension and a summer palace. Known in the West as **Henry Puyi**, in 1932 he was called from private life by the Japanese to be provincial dictator of Manchukuo, under the name of **Kangde**. Taken prisoner by the Russians in 1945, he was tried in China as a war criminal (1950), pardoned (1959), and became a private citizen. The story of his life was made into a successful film (*The Last Emperor*) in 1988.

Pyrrhus (c.318–272 BC) King of Epirus (modern Albania) (307–303 BC, 297–272 BC), an ambitious ruler whose aim was to revive the empire of his second cousin, Alexander the Great. Unsuccessful in this goal (283 BC), he turned to the West, where he became embroiled in Italian affairs and hence conflict with Rome. Though he won two battles (280–279 BC), his losses, particularly at Asculum (279 BC), were so great that they gave rise to the phrase *Pyrrhic victory*.

Qaboos bin Said (1940–) Sultan of Oman (1970–), born in Muscat, Oman, the son of Said bin Taimar, and the 14th descendant of the ruling dynasty of the Albusaid family. He studied in England and trained at Sandhurst Military Academy, from where his father recalled him and kept him prisoner for six years. In 1970 he overthrew his father in a bloodless coup and assumed the sultanship. He then headed the rapid and stable modernization of his country.

Qianlong, also spelled **Ch'ien-Lung** (1711–99) Seventh emperor of the Manchurian Qing (Ch'ing) dynasty, and the fourth to rule China. He succeeded at the age of 24. Wanting to be thought the greatest ruler in China's history, he ordered (1773) a great literary catalogue by 15 000 scribes (36 000 vols), studied painting and calligraphy, wrote 42 000 poems, published notes on his studies (1736) and a prose/verse collection (1737), patronized the arts and scholarship, and built a sumptuous summer palace. After three major campaigns (1755–9) he annexed eastern Turkestan (renamed Xinjiang, 'New Dominion'), conquered Burma (1769) and Nepal (1790–1), and suppressed revolt in Taiwan. This expensive foreign policy, allied to governmental corruption, provoked a rebellion which he was unable to suppress, and he abdicated in 1796.

Qin Shihuangdi, also spelled **Ch'in Shih Huang-ti** (259–210 BC) First true Emperor of China, who forcibly unified much of modern China following the decline of the Zhou dynasty. His achievements in unifying, centralizing, and bureaucratizing China may have been influenced by those of Darius I of Persia, and followed precepts laid out by the legalist philosopher Xunzi. Aided by his chief minister Li Si he consolidated northern defences into a Great Wall, and drove the Xiongnu (Huns) from south of the Yellow River. He conquered the south, built canals and roads, divided China into 36 military prefectures, destroyed feudalism, and disarmed nobles. He also standardized Chinese script, and harmonized axle lengths, weights, measures, and laws. His principal palace, accommodating 10 000, was connected to 270 others by a covered road network. He was buried in a starry mausoleum with 6000 life-size terracotta guards. The tomb has been excavated since 1974.

and went into a monastery, but soon ruled again at Aistulf's death in the same year until ousted by Desiderio.

Radbod (?–719) King of the Frisians, thought to have reigned over a large area across the whole of Friesland, extending to the Lower Rhine southwards and as far as the Weser eastwards. Defeated twice by the Franks, each time he had to allow Christian missionaries in. Legend has it that Willibrord tried to convert him. In 689 he was defeated by Pepin II at Dorestad, and as part of the peace settlement he lost the southern part of his country and married his daughter Theodeswinde to Pepin's son Grimoald. After Pepin's death he recovered territory down to Cologne, but was defeated again by Charles Martel in 714.

Rachis, also found as **Rachi** (?–c.757) King of the Lombards. Duke of Friuli, who became king in 744. As ruler he assimilated Rotari's code, maintained a good relationship with the papacy, but clashed with the Byzantines when he invaded the pentapolis. He abdicated in favour of his brother, Aistulf (756),

RAJAH or RAJA

Rajah is a title formerly used in India by a local prince or chief; the equivalent female title was **rani** or **ranee**, though this was also used for the wife of a rajah. **Maharaja(h)** and **maharani/ maharanee** were higher-ranking titles used in some areas. Other Indian princely titles include **nawab, nizam, rao** (**maharao**), and **rawal** (**maharawal**). Areas which used these titles include (*raja*) Cannanore, Cochin; (*maharaja*) Baroda, Bharatpur, Gwalior, Indore, Kolhapur, Lahore, Mysore; (*rana*) Mewar, Udaipur; (*nawab*) Bhopal, Tonk; (*rao*) Bundi, Cutch, Kotah; (*nizam*) Hyderabad; and (*rawal*) Jaisalmer. The princely system became less significant following the independence of India and Pakistan, and it ceased to be recognized after the Princely Derecognition Act of 1971. The title of *raja(h)* was also used in a few other areas, such as Perlis (Malaysia), and by the Brookes in Sarawak (1841–1946).

Rainier III, in full **Rainier Louis Henri Maxence Bertrand de Grimaldi** (1923–2005) Prince of Monaco (1949–2005), born in Monaco, a descendant of the Genoese House of Grimaldi. He attended school in Britain and Switzerland, and later studied at the French University of Montpellier and the Institut d'études politiques de Paris. He served in the First French Army and received the Croix de Guerre (1945) and the Legion of Honour (1947). In 1956 he married US film actress Grace Kelly. They had two daughters, **Princess Caroline Louise Marguerite** (1957–) and **Princess Stephanie Marie Elisabeth** (1965–), and a son, **Prince Albert Alexandre Louis Pierre** (1958–). Before 2002, the principality would have become part of France in the absence of a male heir but Rainier had the law changed so that, in the event of Albert remaining childless, Caroline and Stephanie and their children can succeed their brother, who acted as regent during his father's last days.

Rameses or **Ramses II**, known as **the Great** (13th-c BC) King of Egypt (1279–1213 BC), whose long and prosperous reign marks the last great peak of Egyptian power. Despite his doubtful victory over the Hittites at Kadesh in northern Syria (1274 BC), he managed to stabilize his frontier against them, making peace with them (1258 BC) and later marrying a Hittite princess. An enthusiastic builder, he has left innumerable monuments, among them the great sandstone temples at Abu Simbel.

Rameses or **Ramses III** (12th-c BC) King of Egypt (1187–1156 BC), famous primarily for his great victory over the Sea Peoples, invaders from Asia Minor and the Aegean Is. Tradition identifies him with the pharaoh who oppressed the Hebrews of the Exodus.

Ranjit Singh, known as **the Lion of the Punjab** (1780–1839) Sikh ruler, born in Budrukhan, Pakistan (formerly India). Succeeding his father as ruler of Lahore, he fought to unite all the Sikh provinces, and, with the help of a modernized army trained by Western soldiers, became the most powerful ruler in India. In 1813 he procured the Koh-i-noor diamond from an Afghan prince, as the price of assistance in war.

Raspe, Heinrich (c.1204–47) Landgraf of Thuringia and anti-king of the Holy Roman Empire from 1246 at the pope's instigation. He was banished from the court by his nephew Hermann II and his mother Elisabeth. He was nominated regent for the minor Konrad IV, whom he conquered at the battle of the Nidda on 5 August 1246.

René of Chalon (1518–44) Prince of Orange, the son of Henry III of Nassau and his second wife Claude of Chalon; he was previously **Renatus of Nassau**. In 1530 he inherited the principality of Orange and some French estates from his uncle Philibert of Chalon, and from his father in 1538 Dutch estates and the stadtholdership of Holland, Zeeland, Utrecht, and Franche-Comté. In 1540 he was made a Knight of the Golden Fleece. In 1543 he also became stadtholder of Gelre. His cousin William of Nassau (William the Silent) was his sole heir.

Rosamond or **Rosamund** (6th-c) Queen of the Lombards, the daughter of Cunimond (or Cunimund), King of the Gepidae. She was forced to marry Alboin, King of the Lombards, who had defeated her father. According to tradition, he forced her to drink from her father's skull; she plotted against him and had him poisoned by squire Elmichi. She escaped to Ravenna, but was in turn poisoned by Elmichi.

Rotari (?–652) King of the Lombards. Although Arian, he married his predecessor's Catholic widow, Gundeberga. He succeeded in strengthening central power, keeping the dukes in check, and expanded his domain to include Liguria (643) and part of Veneto. His reputation rests on the **Rotari edict** (643), the first written collection of Lombard laws. Although based mainly on Lombard tradition, the edict also incorporated elements of Roman law, and was reviewed and implemented by later Lombard kings.

Rudolf I (1218–91) German king (1273–91), the founder of the Habsburg sovereign and imperial dynasty, born in Schloss Limburg, Germany. He increased his possessions by inheritance and marriage until he was the most powerful prince in Swabia. Chosen king by the electors, he was recognized by the pope in 1274.

Rudolf II (1552–1612) King of Hungary (1572–1608) and Bohemia (1575–1611), and Holy Roman Emperor (1576–1612), born in Vienna, the son of Maximilian

ROMANOVS

Romanov is the name of the second (and last) Russian royal dynasty (1613–1917). It was adopted in the 16th century by a family of boyars that traced its origins back to the 14th century. The first Romanov tsar (Mikhail) was elected in 1613 after the Time of Troubles. The Romanovs ruled as absolute autocrats, allowing no constitutional or legal checks on their political power. The marriage of Nicholas II to Princess Alexandra of Hesse brought haemophilia into the family; their son, Alexey (1904–18), was afflicted with the disease. The dynasty ended with the abdication of Nicholas II in February 1917, and his execution and that of his immediate family by Bolshevik guards in July 1918. In 1998, under the orders of President Boris Yeltsin, their presumed remains were exhumed and laid to rest on an island in St Petersburg.

II. As a proponent of the Counter-Reformation he gave the Bohemian Stände his assurance of religious freedom in his *Majestätsbrief* of 1609. Due to mental illness he was forced to relinquish government in Austria, Hungary and Moravia (1608), and also in Bohemia (1611) to his brother Matthias.

Ruggero II (1095–1154) King of Sicily, the son of Ruggero I. He became count of Sicily in 1105 and began joining all the Norman territories in southern Italy under his rule. In 1127 he was made Duke of Puglia and Calabria, conquered Naples, Capua, and Bari, and in 1130 was crowned King of Sicily by antipope Anacleto II. After defeating a coalition comprising pope, emperor, Venice, Pisa, and the Byzantines, he was recognized king by Pope Innocent II. He expanded further, gaining Tripoli (1146) and Corfù (1147). He strengthened central government and promoted religious tolerance, making his court a haven for scientists, writers, and artists.

Saladin, in full **Salah al-Din Yussuf ibn Ayub** (1137–93) Sultan of Egypt and Syria, the leader of the Muslims against the crusaders in Palestine, born in Tekrit, Mesopotamia. He entered the service of Nur al-din, Emir of Syria, and on his death (1174) proclaimed himself sultan, asserted his authority over Mesopotamia, and received the homage of the Seljuk princes of Asia Minor. His remaining years were occupied in wars with the Christians, whom he defeated near Tiberias in 1187, recapturing almost all their fortified places in Syria. The Third Crusade, headed by the kings of France and England, captured Acre in 1191, and he was defeated.

Salote Tupou III (1900–65) Queen of Tonga, who succeeded her father, King George Tupou II, in 1918. She is remembered in Britain for her colourful and engaging presence during her visit for the coronation of Elizabeth II in 1953.

Samudragupta (?–c.380) North Indian emperor with a reputation as a warrior, poet, and musician. He epitomized the ideal king of the golden age of Hindu history.

Sancho IV, known as **Sancho the Brave** (c.1257–95) King of Castile and León (1284–95), the second son of Alfonso X. On the death (1275) of his elder brother, Ferdinand de la Cerda, Sancho was named as Alfonso's successor by a coalition of nobles, in place of the rightful heir, Ferdinand's son, Alfonso de la Cerda. Throughout his reign, Sancho had to defend his throne against Alfonso and his supporters, including Aragón, and finally removed the threat by arranging a marriage between his daughter, Isabel, and James II of Aragón. His wife, María de Molina, served as regent for their son, Ferdinand IV, who succeeded him.

Sardanapalus (7th-c BC) Legendary Assyrian king, notorious for his effeminacy and sensual lifestyle. He probably represents an amalgam of at least three Assyrian rulers, one of them being Assurbanipal.

Saul (11th-c BC) Biblical character, the first king to be elected by the Israelites. He conquered the Philistines, Ammonites, and Amalekites, became jealous of David, his son-in-law, and was ultimately engaged in a feud with the priestly class. Eventually, Samuel secretly anointed David king, and Saul fell in battle with the Philistines on Mt Gilboa.

Schwaben, Philipp von (c.1178–1208) Roman King (1198–1208), the youngest son of Frederick I Barbarossa, brother of the Emperor Henry VI. He made himself king in 1198 and fought a victory over the rival King Otto IV from the Guelphs, who was supported by Pope Innocent III. Shortly before concluding a peace treaty with the pope, Philipp was murdered by the Bavarian Pfalzgraf Otto VIII von Wittelsbach in Bamberg in 1208.

Seleucus I Nicator ('Conqueror') (c.358–281 BC) Macedonian general of Alexander the Great, and founder of the Seleucid dynasty. He rose from being satrap of Babylonia (321 BC) to being the ruler of an empire which stretched from Asia Minor to India. To hold his unwieldy empire together, he founded a new, more central capital at Antioch in northern Syria (300 BC).

Seleucus II, in full **Seleucus Callinicus** (?– 226 BC) Seleucid king of Syria (246–226 BC), the son and successor of Antiochus II and his first wife, Laodice. His succession was challenged by his stepmother Berenice (on behalf of her infant son), and Seleucus probably had them both murdered. In retaliation, Berenice's brother, Ptolemy III, arrived from Egypt and waged a long war against Seleucus. He was succeeded by his sons Seleucus III and Antiochus III (223 BC).

Semiramis (9th-c BC) Semi-legendary Queen of Assyria, the daughter of the goddess Derceto, and wife of Ninus, with whom she is supposed to have founded Babylon. The historical germ of the story seems to be the three-year regency of Sammu-ramat (811–808 BC),

widow of Shamshi-Adad V, but the details are legendary, derived from Ctesias and the Greek historians, with elements of the Astarte myth.

Sennacherib (8th–7th-c BC) King of Assyria (705–681 BC), the son of Sargon II and grandfather of Assurbanipal. He was an able ruler, whose fame rests mainly on his conquest of Babylon (689 BC) and his rebuilding of Nineveh. He figures prominently in the Bible, because of his attack on Jerusalem.

Sesostris, also known as **Senusrit** (20th–19th-c BC) According to Greek legend, an Egyptian monarch who invaded Libya, Arabia, Thrace, and Scythia, subdued Ethiopia, placed a fleet on the Red Sea, and extended his dominion to India. He was possibly Sesostris I (c.1980–1935 BC), II (c.1906–1887 BC), and III (c.1887–1849 BC) compounded into one heroic figure.

Severus, Lucius Septimius (c.146–211) Roman emperor (193–211), the founder of the Severan dynasty (193–235), and the first Roman emperor to be born in Africa (at Leptis Magna, of Romanized Punic stock). Declared emperor by the army in 193, he spent the early years of his reign securing his position against his rivals. Once established, he proved to be an able administrator, effecting many reforms, and showing a particularly close interest in the army and the law. His final years were spent in Britain, trying unsuccessfully to restore order in the north of the province.

Sforza, Ludovico, known as **the Moor** (1451–1508) Ruler of Milan, born in Vigevano, Italy. From 1476 he acted as regent for his nephew Gian Galeazzo Sforza (1469–94), but expelled him in 1481 and usurped the dukedom for himself. He made an alliance with Lorenzo de' Medici of Florence and, under his rule, Milan became the most glittering court in Europe. He was a patron of Leonardo da Vinci. He helped to defeat the attempts of Charles VIII of France to secure Naples, but in 1499 was expelled by Louis XII and imprisoned in France, where he died.

Shah Jahan (1592–1666) Mughal Emperor of India (1628–58), born in Lahore, Pakistan (formerly India). His reign saw two wars in the Deccan (1636, 1655), the subjugation of Bijapur and Golconda (1636), and attacks on the Uzbegs and Persians. A ruthless but able ruler, the magnificence of his court was unequalled. His buildings included the Taj Mahal (1632–54), the tomb of his beloved third wife, **Mumtaz Mahal** (1592–1631). From 1658 he was held prisoner by his son Aurangzeb.

Shaka (c.1788–1828) African ruler, born near Melmoth, KwaZulu Natal, South Africa. He was a highly successful military ruler, who intensified the centralization of Zulu power, adapted the weapons and tactics of local warfare, and set about the incorporation of neighbouring peoples. The rise of the Zulu kingdom under Shaka was associated with a series of wars and population move-

ments known as the *difagane*. He was killed by his half-brother Dingane. He remains an enigmatic and contentious figure, the subject of novels and films, and his career is a much debated issue in South African history.

Shapur or **Sapor I** (c.215–72) King of Persia (241–72), the son and successor of Ardashir I. A warrior king, he was defeated by the Roman emperor Gordian III (242), but concluded a peace with Gordian's successor, Philip, guaranteeing Shapur's power in Armenia and Mesopotamia. In 260 he triumphed by defeating Valerian at Edessa, a landmark in the decline of Rome. Shapur rebuilt the Persian economy, promoted a series of public works, and commissioned the translation of many Greek and Indian writings. He placed Mani, the founder of Manichaeism, under his protection.

Shapur or **Sapor II**, known as **the Great** (309–79) King of Persia (309–79). He was declared king at his birth by the Persian nobility, and ruled with the help of regents until the age of 16. Under him the Sassanian empire reached its zenith. He successfully challenged Roman control of the Middle East, forcing Jovian to cede five provinces to him (363), and establishing Persian control over Armenia.

Sheba, Queen of (c.10th-c BC) Monarch mentioned in the Bible (1 *Kings* 10 and 2 *Chron* 9), perhaps from south-west Arabia (modern Yemen), although placed by some in north Arabia. She is said to have journeyed to Jerusalem to test the wisdom of Solomon and to exchange gifts, though this may imply a trade pact. The story depicts the splendour of Solomon's court.

Shivaji (c.1627–80) Founder of the Maratha Empire in western India, born at Shivner, Pune (Poona). He campaigned against the Mughals, and was enthroned as an independent ruler in 1674. Renowned as a military leader, social reformer, and advocate of religious tolerance, his last years were made difficult by internal problems and pressure from outside enemies.

Shotoku Taishi (574–622) Japanese Yamato period ruler. A member of the Soga ruling clan, he was regent to Empress Suiko (c.592–628). Influenced by Chinese culture, he sent four embassies to the Sui court in China. His patronage of Buddhism, including importing Korean monks, and extensive temple building, aided its ascendancy from c.600.

Showa Tenno or (**'Emperor'**) **Hirohito** (1901–89) Emperor of Japan (1926–89), the 124th in direct lineage, born in Tokyo. His reign was marked by rapid militarization and aggressive wars against China (1931–2, 1937–45) and against the USA and Britain (1941–5), which ended with the two atomic bombs on Hiroshima and Nagasaki. Under US occupation, in 1946 Hirohito renounced his legendary divinity and most of his powers to become a democratic constitutional monarch.

Sigismund (1368–1437) Holy Roman Emperor (1410–37), probably born in Nuremberg, Germany, the son of Charles IV. He became King of Hungary (1387), Germany (1411), and Bohemia (1419). In 1396 he was defeated by the Ottoman Turks at Nicopolis, but later conquered Bosnia, Herzegovina, and Serbia. As emperor, he induced the pope to call the Council of Constance to end the Hussite schism (1414), but made no effort to uphold the safe conduct he had granted to John Huss to attend the Council, and permitted him to be burned. As a result, his succession in Bohemia was opposed by the Hussites.

Sihanouk, Prince Norodom (1922–) Cambodian leader, born in Phnom Penh, Cambodia. He was King of Cambodia (1941–55), chief of state (1960–70, and of the Khmer Republic 1975–6), prime minister on several occasions between 1952 and 1968, president of the government in exile (1970–5, 1982–91), president (1991–3), and once again king (1993–2004). He studied in Vietnam and Paris, was elected king in 1941, and negotiated the country's independence from France (1949–53). He abdicated in 1955 in favour of his father, in order to become an elected leader under the new constitution. As prime minister, and from 1960 head of state, he steered a neutralist course during the Vietnam War. In 1970 he was deposed in a right-wing military coup led by Lon Nol, fled to Beijing, and formed a joint resistance front with Pol Pot which successfully overthrew Lon Nol in 1975. Re-appointed head of state, he was ousted a year later by the Communist Khmer Rouge leadership. In 1982 he was elected president of the new government-in-exile. He returned to Cambodia in November 1991 as president of the Supreme National Council, after the signing of a peace treaty ended 13 years of civil war, and was crowned king under the new constitution in 1993. He abdicated in 2004 and was succeeded by his son, **Norodom Sihamoni** (1953–).

Silvia, originally **Silvia Renate Sommerlath** (1943–) Queen of Sweden (1976–), born in Heidelberg, Germany, the daughter of a West German businessman and his Brazilian wife. She studied at the Interpreters' School in Munich, graduating in 1969 as an interpreter in Spanish. In 1971 she was appointed chief hostess in the Organization Committee for the Olympic Games in Munich (1972), where she met Carl Gustaf, then heir to the Swedish throne. They were married in 1976.

Siraj-ud-Daula, originally **Mirza Muhammad** (c.1732–57) Ruler of Bengal under the nominal suzerainty of the Mughal empire. He came into conflict with the British over their fortification of Calcutta, and marched on the city in 1756. The British surrender led to the infamous Black Hole, for which he was held responsible. Following the recapture of Calcutta, the British under Clive joined forces with his general, Mir Jafar, and defeated him at Plassey in 1757. He fled to Murshidabad, but was captured and executed.

Solomon (10th-c BC) King of Israel, the second son of David and Bathsheba. His outwardly splendid reign (described in 1 *Kings* 1–11 and 2 *Chron* 1–10) saw the expansion of the kingdom and the building of the great Temple in Jerusalem. But high taxation and alliances with heathen courts bred discontent, which later brought the disruption of the kingdom under his son, Rehoboam. Solomon was credited with extraordinary wisdom, and became a legendary figure in Judaism, so that his name became attached to several biblical and extra-canonical writings.

Sophia (1630–1714) Electress of Hanover, born in The Hague, The Netherlands, the youngest daughter of Elizabeth Stuart (daughter of James I of England) and Frederick, Elector Palatine, also elected King of Bohemia (1618). In 1658 she married Ernest Augustus, Duke of Brunswick-Lüneburg, who became the first Elector of Hanover. Her son George, Elector of Hanover, became George I of Great Britain. Named in the Act of Settlement (1701) as the Protestant successor to the English crown after Anne, she died shortly before the queen.

Sophia (of The Netherlands), also known as **Sofia Frederika of Wurtemberg** (1818–77) Queen of The Netherlands, born in Stuttgart, Germany, the daughter of King William I of Wurtemburg and Catharina Pavlovna of Russia. She married the future King William III of The Netherlands in 1839. They had three children: Willem (1840–79), Maurits (1843–50) and Alexander (1851–84), all of whom died before their father.

Sophia Alexeyevna (1657–1704) Regent of Russia (1682–9), born in Moscow, the daughter of Tsar Alexey I Mihailovitch and his first wife, Maria Miloslavskaya. On the death of her brother, Tsar Fyodor Alexeyevich (1682), she opposed the accession of her half-brother, Peter (the future Peter the Great), and took advantage of a popular uprising in Moscow to press the candidature of her mentally deficient brother, Ivan. A compromise was reached whereby Ivan (V) and Peter were proclaimed joint tsars, with Sophia as regent. Supported by leading boyars, she became the *de facto* ruler of Russia. A faction of the nobility succeeded in removing her from power in 1689, and (apart from a failed attempt to regain power in 1698) she spent the rest of her life in a convent in Moscow.

Soraya, in full **Princess Soraya Esfandiari Bakhtiari** (1932–2001) Ex-queen of Persia, born in Isfahan, Iran, of Persian and German parents. She was educated at Isfahan, and later in England and Switzerland, and became Queen of Persia on her marriage to Muhammad Reza Shah Pahlavi (1951). The marriage was dissolved in 1958.

Stanisław I Leszczyński (1677–1766) King of Poland (1704–9, 1733–5), born in Lvov (Lwow), Ukraine (formerly Poland). After his election in 1704, he was driven out by Peter the Great, under the influence of Charles XII of Sweden. Re-elected in 1733, he lost the War of the Polish Succession, and formally abdicated in 1736, receiving the Duchies of Lorraine and Bar.

STADTHOLDER

In Dutch history, the stadtholder was originally the officer acting for or occupying the place of the ruler. Gradually, under the Burgundians, it developed into a permanent office as civil and military viceroy over one or more provinces. When the States renounced Philip II's sovereignty, they retained the office and functions of stadtholder, at the time held by William the Silent for Holland, Zeeland, and Utrecht. There was always, however, political tension between the interests of the stadtholders and those of the States, particularly the States of Holland, but the need for a single military commander repeatedly favoured the stadtholders in the argument.

Stanisław II Poniatowski (1732–98) Last King of Poland (1764–95), born in Wołczyn, Poland. He travelled to St Petersburg in 1757, and became a favourite of the future empress, Catherine II. Through her influence he was elected king, but was unable to stop the partitions of Poland (1772, 1793). Despite the rebellion of Kosciusko, the country was partitioned again in 1795, and he abdicated.

Stephen I, St (c.975–1038) The first king and spiritual patron of Hungary (997–1038). He formed Pannonia and Dacia into a regular kingdom, organized Christianity, and introduced many social and economic reforms. Married to a German princess, he encouraged German immigration. He received from Pope Sylvester II the title of 'Apostolic King' and, according to tradition, St Stephen's Crown, now a Hungarian national treasure. He was canonized in 1083. Feast day 16 August.

Sulaiman or **Suleyman I**, known as **the Magnificent** (1494–1566) Ottoman sultan (1520–66). He added to his dominions by conquest Belgrade, Budapest, Rhodes, Tabriz, Baghdad, Aden, and Algiers. His fleets dominated the Mediterranean, though he failed to capture Malta. His system of laws regulating land tenure earned him the name *Kanuni* ('lawgiver'), and he was a great patron of arts and architecture. He died during the siege of Szigeth in his war with Austria.

Sverrir Sigurdsson (c.1150–1202) King of Norway from 1184, born in the Faeroe Is. He claimed to be the illegitimate son of an ex-King of Norway (Sigurd Haraldsson, died 1155). He emerged from obscurity in 1179 to lay claim to the throne from Magnus V Erlingssonz (reigned 1162–84), whom he finally defeated and killed in 1184. One of Norway's greatest kings, he strengthened the crown against both Church and nobles with the support of the freeholding farmers. He commissioned one of the first Icelandic Sagas, a biography of himself, *Sverris saga* by Karl Jónsson.

Sweyn or **Svein II**, also known as **Sweyn Estridsen** (c.1020–74) King of Denmark from 1047, the son of Ulf, a regent of Denmark, and Estrid, sister of Canute the Great. He was appointed Regent of Denmark in 1045 by Magnus I Olafsson of Norway (reigned 1035–47), and acclaimed king himself when Magnus died in 1047. Harald III Sigurdsson (Hardrada), who became sole king of Norway, laid claim to Denmark as well, and now began a long and unrelenting war of attrition against Sweyn. Sweyn lost every battle, but never lost the war, and at the peace of 1064 Harald accepted his right to the throne of Denmark. In 1069, after the conquest of England by William I, Sweyn's army descended on northern England and captured York, but he made peace with William the following year and withdrew.

Taizong, also spelled **T'ai-tsung** (600–49) Second emperor of the Tang dynasty in China (627–49). As **Li Shimin** (Li Shih-min) he encouraged his father **Li Yuan** (566–635) to overthrow the Sui dynasty (618). He seized the crown after assassinating two brothers and their families, and forcing his father's abdication. His reign saw the zenith of Tang power. The government was restructured and Confucian ministers given prominence, the law was reformed, and new palaces, granaries, canals, and schools were built. Buddhism and Taoism were tolerated, and Xuanzang honoured. He suppressed frontier tribes, intervened in Nepal, invaded Korea (unsuccessfully), extended suzerainty over the Sassanids (Persia), defeated the eastern Turks (630), established protectorates over Annam, Manchuria, Mongolia, and the Tarim (Xinjiang), and united the royal houses of China and Tibet (649). Reputedly a great archer and horseman, he suffered from nightmares.

Taizu, also spelled **T'ai-tsu**, originally **Zhao Kuangyin** (928–76) First emperor of the Song (Sung) dynasty in China, born into a Beijing military family. He became a general, then reunified China after the post-Tang disintegration (after 907), having been put on the throne by the palace guard (960). Leaving the north under the Khitan Liao dynasty (907–1119) he defeated each southern state in succession, and reasserted control of Annam. He treated defeated warlords leniently, subdued military political influence, retired army commanders to country estates, and directed power into civilian administration.

Tarquinius Priscus, Lucius (c.7th–6th-c BC) Traditionally the fifth King of Rome (616–578 BC). Guardian to the sons of King Ancus Marcius, he assumed the throne on the king's death, but the sons eventually had him murdered. He is said to have started the building of the city wall, and to have instigated the Roman Games.

Tarquinius Superbus, Lucius (6th-c BC) Tyrannical King of Rome, possibly of Etruscan extraction, whose overthrow (510 BC) marked the end of monarchy at Rome, and the beginning of the Republic. Most of the details about his life are probably fictional.

Taufa'ahau Tupou IV (1918–) King of Tonga, the eldest son of Queen Salote Tupou III. He studied at Newington College and Sydney University. He served successively as minister for education and health, before becoming prime minister under his mother in 1949. On succeeding to the throne on his mother's death in 1965, he shared power with his brother, **Prince Fatafehi Tu'ipelehake**, who became prime minister.

Theodahad (?–536) Ostrogoth King of Italy (534–6). The nephew of King Theodoric, he was invited to share the throne with his cousin, Amalasuntha (543), on the death of her son Athalaric. He took the title of king, but Amalasuntha opposed the Ostrogoth nationalist faction and continued to rule as before. Theodahad had her exiled to an island in Lake Bolsena near Orvieto, where she was later strangled. Justinian responded by sending his general, Belisarius, to march on Rome (536). Theodahad was deposed and fled for Ravenna, but was captured and killed by a Goth.

Theodolinda (?–628) Queen of the Lombards, the daughter of a Bavarian duke. She married Autari in 589, and when he died she married Agilulf, Duke of Turin, who therefore became king in 591. She was a Christian, and helped Pope Gregory I in his efforts to convert the Lombards.

Theodore, called **King of Corsica**, also known as **Baron von Neuhoff** (1686–1756) Adventurer, born in Cologne, Germany. He served in the French army and the Swedish diplomatic service, became chargé d'affaires to Emperor Charles VI (ruled 1711–40) and, in 1736, led a Corsican rising against the Genoese, supported by the Turks and the Bey of Tunis. He was elected king, and left after a few months to procure foreign aid, but his attempts to return in 1738 and in 1743 were frustrated. He settled in London in 1749.

Theodore I Lascaris, also spelled **Laskaris** (1174–1221) First Emperor of Nicaea (1208–21), the son-in-law of Byzantine emperor Alexius III. He distinguished himself in the Fourth Crusade (1203–4) and formed a new Byzantine state after Constantinople was taken. In c.1214 he signed a treaty defining the frontiers between the new Greek empire of Nicaea and the now Latin empire of Constantinople. He strengthened his ties to the Latin empire by marrying Maria, daughter of Empress Yolande, and by proposing (1219) that Greek and Latin clergy meet to consider the reunion of the two churches. He also betrothed his daughter, Eudocia, to Robert of Courtenay, Yolande's son and successor as Latin emperor. Theodore was succeeded as emperor of Nicaea by his son-in-law, John III Vatatzes.

Theodoric or **Theoderic**, known as **the Great** (?–526) King of the Ostrogoths (471–526), who invaded Italy in 489, defeating the barbarian ruler, Odoacer. His long reign secured for Italy tranquillity and prosperity, the Goths and the Romans continuing as distinct nations, each with its own tribunals and laws. He established his capital at Ravenna.

Theodoric I (?–451) King of the Visigoths, the son of Alaric I, elected king in 418. Alternately an ally and an enemy of Rome, in 421 (or 422) he treacherously joined the Vandals and attacked the Roman troops from behind. In 435 he attacked the Romans in Gaul and besieged Narbonne. Forced to retreat to Toulouse, he there defeated a Roman army (439). On the invasion of Attila in 451, he joined the Romans, under Aëtius, and at Troyes commanded the right wing. He drove back the Huns under Attila, but was killed.

Theodoric II (?–466) King of the Visigoths. He rebelled against his brother and predecessor Thorismund, had him assassinated, and ascended the throne in 453. His policy at first was to spread Gothic dominion in Spain and Gaul through the Roman alliance. On the murder of the Emperor Petronius Maximus in 455, he supported Eparchius Avitus in his bid for the empire, and marched with him into Italy, where Eparchius was proclaimed emperor. On his abdication in 456, Theodoric broke the friendship with Rome and besieged Arles, but was forced by Emperor Majorian to make peace. In 462 he made another attempt in Gaul, but was defeated near Orléans (464). He was murdered in 466 by his brother Euric, who succeeded him.

Theodosius I, known as **the Great** (c.346–95) Roman emperor of the East (379–95). Made emperor because of his military abilities, he solved the long-standing Gothic problem by allowing the Goths to settle south of the Danube as allies of Rome. His title comes from his vigorous championship of orthodox Christianity.

Theodosius II (401–50) Roman emperor (408–50), the grandson of Theodosius I and, like him, a staunch champion of orthodox Christianity. He is chiefly remembered for his codification of the Roman law in 438.

Tiberius, in full **Tiberius Julius Caesar Augustus** (42 BC–AD 37) Roman emperor (AD 14–37), the son of Livia, and stepson and successor of the Emperor Augustus. Deeply conservative by nature, he was content to continue Augustus's policies and simply consolidate his achievements. Despite the soundness of his administration and foreign policy, politically his reign was a disaster. The suspicious death of his heir Germanicus (AD 19) was followed by the excesses of his chief henchman, the praetorian prefect Sejanus, and the reign of terror that followed Sejanus's downfall (d. AD 31) made him an object of universal loathing. Few mourned when he died on Capri, the island retreat that had been his home since AD 26.

Timur, known as **Timur Lenk** (Turkish 'Timur the Lame'), English **Tamerlane** or **Tamburlaine** (1336–1405) Tatar conqueror, born near Samarkand, Uzbekistan. In 1369 he ascended the throne of Samarkand, subdued nearly all Persia, Georgia, and the Tatar empire, and conquered all the states between the Indus and the lower Ganges (1398). He won Damascus and Syria from the Mameluke sovereigns of Egypt, then defeated the Turks at Angora (1402), taking Sultan Bayezit prisoner. His death, while taking an army of

200 000 to conquer Ming China, made possible the reopening of Chinese western trade routes, and a Persian trade mission to China (1409).

Tippoo Sultán, also known as **Tippoo Sahib** (1749–99) Sultan of Mysore (1782–99), born in Devanhalli, India, the son of Haidar Ali. He continued his father's policy of opposing British rule, and in 1789 invaded the British-protected state of Travancore. In the ensuing war (1790–2) he was defeated by Cornwallis, and had to cede half his kingdom. After recommencing hostilities in 1799, he was killed during the siege of Seringapatam.

Titus, in full **Titus Flavius Vespasianus** (39–81) Roman emperor (79–81), the elder son and successor of Vespasian. Popular with the Romans for his generosity, charm, and military prowess, he is execrated in Jewish tradition for his destruction of Jerusalem (70) and suppression of the Jewish Revolt. His brief reign was marred by many natural calamities, notably the eruption of Vesuvius (79). He completed the Colosseum, begun by his father.

Totila (?–552) King of the Ostrogoths (from 541). During the Gothic War he succeeded in winning back from the Byzantines large territories in central Italy. He defeated Belisarius and took first Rome in 546, and then Sicily. He was defeated at Senigallia and then at Gualdo Tadino by Narsete, and died while trying to escape.

Trajan, in full **Marcus Ulpius Trajanus** (c.53–117) Roman emperor (98–117), selected as successor by the aged Nerva for his military skills. He was the first emperor after Augustus to expand the Roman Empire significantly, adding Dacia and Arabia (106). The wealth from Dacia's gold mines enabled him to launch an ambitious building programme, especially in Rome, where he constructed a new forum, library, and aqueduct. A sensitive but firm ruler, he was one of Rome's most popular emperors.

Ulugh Beg (1394–1449) Ruler of the Timurid empire (1447–9). A grandson of Tamerlane, he made his name particularly as an astronomer. He founded an observatory at Samarkand, compiled astronomical tables, and corrected errors made by Ptolemy of Alexandria, whose figures were still in use. He also wrote poetry and history. After a brief reign, he was overthrown and slain by a rebellious son in 1449.

Umberto I (1844–1900) King of Italy (1878–1900), born in Turin. He fought in the war against Austria (1866), and as king brought Italy into the Triple Alliance with Germany and Austria (1882). He supported Italian colonialism in Africa, but his popularity declined after Italy's defeat by the Ethiopians at Adowa in 1896. A conservative with authoritarian leanings, he repressed popular risings with the help of right-wing prime ministers, and was assassinated at Monza by Gaetano Bresci.

Umberto II (1904–83) Last King of Italy (1946), born in Racconigi, Italy. He succeeded to the throne after the abdication of his father, Victor Emmanuel III, but himself abdicated a month later, after a national referendum had declared for a republic. He left Italy, and in 1947 he and his descendants were banished from the country. He then lived in Portugal.

Valentinian I, in full **Flavius Valentinianus** (321–375) Roman emperor (364–75), born in Pannonia (central Europe), the son of an army officer. He rose rapidly in rank under Constantius and Julian, and on the death of the Emperor Jovian was chosen as his successor (364). He resigned the East to his brother **Valens** (ruled 364–78), and himself governed the West, based in Paris, Trier, and other centres, successfully defending it against Germanic invasions.

Valentinian III, in full **Flavius Placidius Valentinianus** (419–55) Western Roman Emperor (425–55), born in Ravenna, Italy, the son of Flavius Constantius (r. as Constantius III in 421) and Galla Placidia. He was put on the throne by Theodosius II, Roman Emperor of the East, under the regency of his mother, who ruled the West in his name until 437. Weak and ineffective, it was General Flavius Aëtius who wielded the power. Africa was seized (429) by Gaiseric, King of the Vandals, and the Danubian provinces of Gaul and Italy were overrun (441) by Attila, King of the Huns.

Valentinian killed Aëtius in 454, but was himself murdered by two of the general's men.

Valerian, Publius Licinius (?–260) Roman emperor (253–60). He was proclaimed emperor by the legions in Rhaetia after the murder of Gallus (253), and appointed his eldest son Gallienus as co-ruler. Throughout his reign there were problems on every frontier of the empire. Marching against the Persians, he was completely defeated at Edessa (modern Urfa, Turkey, 260). He was seized by Shapur I (ruled 241–72), and died in captivity.

Vespasian, in full **Titus Flavius Vespasianus** (9–79) Roman emperor (69–79), born near Reate, Latium, the founder of the Flavian dynasty (69–96). Declared emperor by the troops in the East, where he was engaged in putting down the Jewish Revolt, he ended the civil wars that had been raging since Nero's overthrow, put the state on a sound financial footing, and restored discipline to the army. Among his many lavish building projects was the Colosseum. He was succeeded by his son, Titus.

Victor Emmanuel I (1759–1824) King of Sardinia, born in Turin, the second son of Vittorio Amedeo III. He became king in 1802 after the abdication of his brother, Carlo Emmanuel IV. He tried unsuccessfully to regain those territories taken by Napoleon and had to wait until the Congress of Vienna (1815). He spent the intervening years in Sardinia reorganizing the island's administration. He returned to Piedmont in 1814 and immediately re-established an absolutist regime. When faced with the 1821 revolutionary risings, he abdicated in favour of his brother Carlo Felice.

Victor Emmanuel II (1820–78) First King of Italy (1861–78), born in Turin. As King of Sardinia from 1849, he appointed Cavour as his chief minister (1852). He fought against Austria (1859), winning victories at Montebello, Magenta, and Solferino, and gaining Lombardy. In 1860 Modena, Parma, the Romagna, and Tuscany were peacefully annexed, Sicily and Naples were added by Garibaldi, and Savoy and Nice were ceded to France. Proclaimed King of Italy at Turin, he fought on the side of Prussia in the Austro–Prussian War (1866), and after the fall of the French empire (1870) he entered and annexed Rome.

Victor Emmanuel III (1869–1947) King of Italy (1900–46), born in Naples. He initially ruled as a constitutional monarch, but defied parliamentary majorities by bringing Italy into World War 1 on the side of the Allies in 1915, and in 1922 when he offered Mussolini the premiership. The Fascist government then reduced him to a figurehead. He played an important part in effecting Mussolini's fall (1943), but was irremediably tarnished by his association with Fascism. Having relinquished power to his son, he abdicated in 1946, and went into exile in Alexandria, Egypt.

Viktoria (1840–1901) Prussian Queen and German empress, born in London, the eldest daughter of the British Queen Victoria. In 1858 she married the Prussian Crown Prince Frederick Wilhelm who, as Frederick III, was German emperor for 99 days in 1888 before he died. The liberally educated Viktoria strongly criticized the authoritarian and anti-British politics of her son Wilhelm II. She died at Schloss Friedrichshof near Kronberg.

Visconti, Gian Galeazzo, known as **Count of Valour** (1351–1402) Milanese statesman, born in Milan. He succeeded his father, Galeazzo II, as joint ruler (1378–85) with his uncle Bernabò, whom he put to death in 1385. As duke, he made himself master of the northern half of Italy, bringing many independent cities into one state, and arranged marriage alliances with England, France, Austria, and Bavaria. He was also a great patron of the arts.

Visconti, Galeazzo II (c.1320–78) Ruler of Milan. He returned to Milan from the Holy Land in 1346, but was forced to leave by his uncle Luchino. In 1349, when Giovanni succeeded, he returned and conquered Bologna (1350) with the Visconti army, and was excommunicated by the pope. After Giovanni's death in 1354 he jointly ruled with brothers Matteo II and Bernabò. Galeazzo received the western territories, Milan and Genoa, but held court at Pavia and became a patron of the arts. Bianca di Savoia gave him a son, Gian Galeazzo.

Vitellius, Aulus (15–69) Roman emperor, a successor of Nero. Appointed by Galba to the command of the legions on the Lower Rhine (68), he was proclaimed emperor at Colonia Agrippinensis (Cologne) at the beginning of 69. His generals put an end to the reign of Otho by the victory of Bedriacum. Vitellius, during his brief reign, gave himself up to pleasure and debauchery. Many of his soldiers deserted when Vespasian was proclaimed emperor in Alexandria. Vitellius was defeated in two battles by his rival, dragged through the streets of Rome, and murdered.

Vittorio Amedeo II (1666–1732) Duke of Savoy, King of Sicily and of Sardinia, born in Turin, the son of Carlo Emanuele II. He formed alliances first with the French, then with Austria. The Treaty of Utrecht (1713), and then Rastatt (1714), gave him a number of territories, including Monferrato, and the Sicilian crown, which in 1720 he exchanged for the throne of Sardinia. He reorganized the state, limited the clergy's privileges, and promoted primary and higher education. In 1730 he abdicated in favour of his son, Carlo Emanuele III. He soon tried to resume power, but was arrested and confined to Rivoli.

Vladimir I, St, in full **Vladimis Svyatoslavich**, known as **the Great** (956–1015) First Christian sovereign of Russia (980–1015), the son of Svyatoslav, Grand Prince of Kiev (d.972). He became Prince of Novgorod in 970, and in 980 seized Kiev from his brother after his father's death. He consolidated the Russian realm from the Baltic to the Ukraine, extending its dominions into Lithuania, Galicia, and Livonia, with Kiev as his capital. He made a pact with Byzantine Emperor Basil II (c.987), accepting Christianity and marrying the emperor's sister. He then ordered the conversion to Christianity of his subjects, punishing those who resisted. Feast day 27 September.

Wendi, also spelled **Wen-ti** (ruled 179–157 BC) Han dynasty Chinese emperor and Confucian scholar, who consolidated his father Gaozu's achievements, including initiating the system of written civil service examinations (165 BC). Economic advance, administrative reform, and freedom from internal warfare laid the foundation for the later achievements of Wudi.

Wendi, also spelled **Wen-ti** (541–604) First emperor of the Chinese Sui dynasty. As **Yang Jian**, a northerner having close family ties both to the Han nobility and the northern Zhou dynasty (557–80), he slaughtered a king and 59 princes to seize the throne, ruling as Wendi ('cultured emperor', 589–604). His lands were around Changan (Xian), which he kept as the imperial capital. Conquering southern China with 518 000 men, he then secured Annam's submission (603). Anti-intellectual, he opposed Confucianism but favoured Buddhism. He simplified administration, demanded total obedience to severe laws, and stopped officials working in their home areas. He was murdered by his son and successor, Yang Guang (Yangdi).

Wilhelmina (Helena Pauline Maria) (1880–1962) Queen of The Netherlands (1890–1948), born in The Hague. She succeeded her father William III at the age of 10, her mother acting as regent until 1898. An upholder of constitutional monarchy, she especially won the admiration of her people during World War 2. Though compelled to seek refuge in Britain, she steadfastly encouraged Dutch resistance to the German occupation. In 1948, she abdicated in favour of her daughter Juliana, and assumed the title of Princess of The Netherlands.

William I (?–1222) Count of Holland (from 1203), the son of Floris II and Ada of Scotland. He married Aleida of Gelre in 1198, and in 1220 Maria of Brabant, widow of Emperor Otto IV. On his father's death he fought his elder brother Dirk VII for Holland, but after Dirk's death he managed to seize the county from his niece Ada. He joined the Anglo-Guelfs against the Franco-Hohenstaufens, was taken prisoner at Bouvines, and on gaining his freedom changed sides. He was excommunicated by Pope Innocent III for taking part in Louis VII's campaign against King John of England (1216), but made it up by crusading in Spain against the Moors and in Egypt, where he was present at the taking of Damietta. He encouraged the growth of towns, giving charters to Middelburg, Dordrecht,

Geertruidenberg, and probably also Leiden.

William I, known as **William the Silent** (1533–84) Dutch ruler, born in Dillenburg, Germany, the eldest son of William of Nassau. Brought up at Charles V's court, he was appointed stadtholder (governor) of Holland, Zeeland, and Utrecht by Philip II of Spain. He married (1) **Anne of Buren**, (2) **Anne of Saxony-Meissen**, (3) **Charlotte de Bourbon**, and (4) **Louise de Coligny**, and had three sons and eleven daughters. After the Treaty of Cateau Cambresis he was one of four hostages chosen by the French king to go to Paris. According to an apocryphal story Henry II of France told William of the secret plan, later carried out on St Bartholomew's night, to massacre all the leading Huguenots; William kept the secret to himself and so earned the soubriquet 'the Silent', but was always afterwards distrustful of France and Spain. He inherited the title of Prince of Orange from Réné de Chalon, and his first marriage in 1551 brought him extensive estates in The Netherlands, making him the most important aristocrat there. He committed himself to the revolt in The Netherlands, declared himself a Calvinist, and after being appointed Stadtholder of Holland, Zeeland, and Utrecht he took a leading part in achieving the Pacification of Ghent. He was assassinated in Delft by a Spanish agent.

William I (1772–1843) King of The Netherlands (1815–40), born in The Hague, the son of Stadtholder William V and Wilhelmina of Prussia. He married Frederica of Prussia in 1791. After leading the campaign against the French in 1793–4 he left for England, and from there joined the Prussian forces. His admiration for Napoleon led to an accommodation with him, gaining compensation from him for losses incurred by the House of Orange in Germany. He settled in Fulda, but lost this territory again by the Treaty of Tilsit. He then joined the alliance against Napoleon, serving in the Austrian army, and was again a refugee in England after Wagram. In 1813 he was invited back to The Netherlands as sovereign ruler. He ruled as an enlightened despot, restricting the States-General's control of finance and the freedom of the press. Dissatisfaction grew, particularly in the mainly Catholic south, resulting in the Belgian Revolution in 1830, partition of the kingdom, and the creation of Belgium. He abdicated in 1840, to be succeeded by his son as William II.

William I, Ger. **Wilhelm** (1797–1888) King of Prussia (1861–88) and first German emperor (1871–88), born in Berlin, Germany, the second son of Frederick William III. His use of force during the 1848 revolution made him unpopular, and he was forced to leave Prussia temporarily for London. As king he consolidated the throne and strengthened the army, placing Bismarck at the head of the ministry. He was victorious against Denmark (1864), Austria (1866), and France (1871), and was then proclaimed emperor. The rapid rise of Socialism in

Germany led to severe repressive measures, and he survived several attempts at assassination.

William II (1227–56) Count of Holland (from 1234), the son of Floris IV. In 1252 he married Elisabeth of Brunswick-Lüneburg. He started his rule as ward of his uncles, first issuing proclamations in his own name at the age of 13. He supported Innocent IV against Frederick II of Hohenstaufen, and in 1247, after being elected King of the Romans, took Aachen and was crowned there the next year. After refusing to pay homage to Margaret of Constantinople for Zeeland, he defeated her in 1253. He was invited to Rome to be crowned emperor, but wished to subdue the West Frisians before leaving; en route he fell through the ice and was killed by his enemies.

William II (1626–50) Prince of Orange, Count of Nassau, born in The Hague, the only son of Stadtholder Frederick Henry and Amalia of Solms. In 1641 he married Mary, the daughter of Charles I of England. He succeeded his father as stadtholder of the provinces of the northern Netherlands (except Friesland in 1647–50) and as captain-admiral-general of the Union in 1647. He was disappointed by the Treaty of Münster and fell out with the States of Holland, who wanted peace, while he wanted to recover the southern Netherlands from Spain, and restore the Stuarts in England. In 1650 he arrested six members of the States of Holland and imprisoned them in Loevestein, and set out to capture Amsterdam, but the city was anxious to protect its trade, and came to a settlement. He died suddenly of smallpox.

William II (1792–1849) King of The Netherlands (1840–9), born in The Hague, the son of William I. He served in the peninsula as Wellington's ADC, and commanded the Dutch troops in the Waterloo campaign. He was engaged in 1813 to Charlotte, daughter of the Prince Regent of England, but she broke it off, and in 1816 he married Anna Pavlovna of Russia. He was employed by William I as a negotiator with the rebels in the Belgian Revolution, but to the king's mind showed too much sympathy with them. In 1831 he successfully commanded against them in the Ten-Day Campaign until a French army, supported by the British, forced a truce. He succeeded to the throne in 1840 on the abdication of William I, but continued his father's repressive policies. In 1848, the year of revolutions, he suddenly declared his conversion from conservative to liberal, and appointed a commission to draft a new Constitution.

William II, Ger. **Wilhelm**, known as **Kaiser Wilhelm** (1859–1941) German emperor and King of Prussia (1888–1918), born in Potsdam, Germany, the eldest son of Frederick III (1831–88) and Viktoria (the daughter of Britain's Queen Victoria), and grandson of Emperor William I. He dismissed Bismarck (1890), and began a long period of personal rule, displaying a bellicose attitude in international affairs. He pledged full support to Austria–Hungary after the assassination of Archduke Francis Ferdinand at Sarajevo (1914), but then made apparent efforts to prevent the escalation of the resulting international crisis. During the war he became a mere figurehead, and when the German armies collapsed, and US President Wilson refused to negotiate while he remained in power, he abdicated and fled the country. He settled at Doorn, in The Netherlands, living as a country gentleman. He lived to see the resurgence of German military might in the Nazi period, dying in June 1941. Hitler admired him greatly (as much for his anti-Semitism as for his militarism), and had him buried with full military honours.

William III, known as **the Good** (1285–1337) Count of Holland (from 1304), and Count of Hainault (as William I), born in Valenciennes, France, the son of John II (Avesnes) and Philippina of Luxembury. He married Joanna, the daughter of Count Charles I of Valois, whose brother was the future King Philip IV of France. He was very active and influential politically, and married his daughters well. He was instrumental in replacing Edward II of England with Edward III, to whom he married his third daughter Philippa of Hainault. He gradually managed to separate Brabant from France, and when the Hundred Years War started he supported England, bringing with him Holland, Hainault, Flanders, and Brabant.

William III (1817–90) King of The Netherlands (1849–90), born in Brussels, the eldest son of William II. He married his cousin **Sophia of Wurtemberg**, by whom he had three sons, all of whom predeceased him. He disliked the 1848 Constitution and favoured personal rule, so that he was generally at odds with Thorbecke. He lived mostly at Het Loo, separated from his wife, and on her death in 1877 married **Emma of Waldeck-Pyrmont**, by whom he had one daughter, the future Queen Wilhelmina. He had the reputation of being tactless, autocratic, and unreasonable, constantly quarrelling with his ministers and with his own sons.

William IV, Dutch **Willem Karel Hendrik Friso** (1711–51) Prince of Orange-Nassau, Stadtholder of Friesland (from 1711), Groningen (1718), Drenthe and Gelderland (1722), Holland, Zeeland, Utrecht, and Overijssel (1747), born in Leeuwarden, The Netherlands. In 1734 he married **Anne of Hanover**, the daughter of George II of England. He was only appointed to the stadtholder's office in the southern provinces and made captain-general because of the poor progress of the war with France, but was not in fact able to improve the military situation. He had one son, the future William V, and four daughters.

William V (Batavus) (1748–1806) Dutch ruler, the son of William IV and Anne of Hanover. He married **Wilhelmina of Prussia** in 1767. He was under a regency until his majority in 1766, when he was installed as

Stadtholder of the United Provinces. He was an ineffective ruler, and after reverses in the fourth Anglo-Dutch War he was deprived of his military commands and retired to Het Loo; in the face of the revolutionary activities of the patriots he left it to his wife to get help from Prussia. When the French under Pichegru invaded, he fled to England, from where he complained about his eviction and raised a force of volunteers for the English invasion of Holland in 1799. In 1801 he moved to Nassau, and died in Brunswick.

Wu, Empress, in full **Wu Zhao** (?625–?706) Empress of China, the only woman ever to rule China in her own name. A concubine of Emperor Taizong, she married his son, **Emperor Gaozong**, whom she dominated after his stroke (660). After his death (683) she first ruled through her own sons, then following a reign of bloody terror she seized China in the title *emperor* in 690 with the dynastic name Zhou (Chou). To establish legitimacy, she claimed to be Maitreya, a supposed Buddhist 'messiah', ordered public prophecy of a female monarch 700 years after Buddha, and rewrote genealogies. Highly capable, she

expanded the bureaucracy and examination system, set up a personal secretariat, and dominated both Korea and Tibet. She was forced to abdicate in 705, and her family were assassinated in 710.

Wudi, also spelled **Wu-ti** (156–87 BC) Han dynasty Emperor of China (141–87 BC, his name means 'martial emperor'). He respected Confucian scholarship, and began selecting administrators by oral examination (setting questions himself). Appointing himself head of the bureaucracy, he established (124 BC) a Confucian university for scholar-administrators. He sequestered noble lands, extended crown possessions, annexed southern China, conquered Korea, Tonkin, and the south-west with large armies, and invaded the Hun territories. He sent a major expedition (138–125 BC) to Bactria to ensure western trade routes, and a second expedition (101 BC, 30 000 troops) conquered Ferghana (2200 miles from Wudi's capital). These expeditions ensured Chinese control over the Tarim (later Xinjiang), and set a precedent for later spectacular Han triumphs.

Xerxes I (c.519–465 BC) Achaemenid King of Persia (486–465 BC), the son of Darius I. He is remembered in the West mainly for the failure of his forces against the Greeks in the Second Persian War at Salamis, Plataea, and Mycale.

Xuanzong, also spelled **Hsüan-tsung** (685–761) Chinese Tang emperor (ruled 712–56). Of royal lineage, he eliminated the usurper Wei's family in 710, and seized the crown in 712. Known also as **Minghuang** ('brilliant emperor'), his reign displayed authentic imperial characteristics. He maintained a splendid court, reformed the coinage, initiated land registration, extended the Grand Canal, defeated the Tibetans (747), patronized leading painters and poets, and established the Academy of Letters (*Han Lin*) in 754, by which major scholars supervised all court documentation. His system lasted over 1000 years. After 745 he became obsessed with his concubine, Yang Guifei. Her protégé An Lushan rebelled in 755. Xuanzong fled, agreed to her execution, then abdicated in grief. Their love story inspired the poet Bo Juyi, and Ming period drama.

Yangdi, also spelled **Yang-ti** (569–618) Second Chinese Sui dynasty emperor (605–17). As Yang Guang he murdered his father, Wendi. To strengthen Chinese unification he married a southern princess. He received the first Japanese envoys, sent ambassadors to the Indies, India, and Turkestan, invaded Korea on four occasions with huge armies of over a million men (611–14), conquered Taiwan (610), and established colonies on the western trade routes. Retaining Changan (Xian) as a capital, he sumptuously rebuilt Luoyang as a second, and Yangzhou as a third. Six state granaries were constructed, the Great Wall fortified, and the Grand Canal built (610). The expense of his reign provoked insurrection in the north-west, and he was killed. The new Tang dynasty later propagandized him as a feckless womanizer.

Yongle or **Yung-lo**, originally **Zhu Di** (1360–1424) Third emperor (1402–24) of the Chinese Ming dynasty (1368–1644), known posthumously as Chengzu, born in Nanking, China. The fourth son of Hongwu, he seized the crown from his nephew after much bloodshed. He moved the capital to Beijing (1421) and reconstructed the Grand Canal, developed central and local government organs, and instituted the civil service examination format which lasted to the 20th century. He also patronized Confucianism, published the Buddhist Tripitaka, sponsored the Great Encyclopaedia (1408), and sent Admiral Zheng He to sea. He conquered the Mongols in five campaigns (dying on the fifth), annexed Annam, and enforced tribute from Borneo, Japan, Java, Korea, Siam, and SE India.

Z

Zahir Shah, King Mohammed
(1914–) King of Afghanistan (1933–73),
born in Kabul. He studied in Kabul
and Paris, and was assistant minister
for national defence and education
minister before succeeding to the
throne, after the assassination of his
father, Nadir Shah (c.1880–1933). His
reign was characterized by a concern
to preserve neutrality and promote
gradual modernization. He became a
constitutional monarch in 1964.
While in Italy receiving medical
treatment, he was overthrown in a
republican coup led by his cousin,
General Daud Khan, in the wake of a
three-year famine. He then lived in
exile in Rome, and became a popular
symbol of national unity for moderate
Afghan opposition groups. In the
aftermath of the war in Afghanistan
and the defeat of the Taliban (2001),
the former king called for a broad-
based government of national unity in
Kabul.

Zenobia (3rd-c) Queen of Palmyra (in
modern Syria), born there probably of
Arab descent. She became the wife of
the Bedouin Odenathus, lord of the
city, who in 264 was recognized by
Gallienus as Governor of the East. On
her husband's murder (c.267) she
embarked on a war of expansion,
conquered Egypt in 269, and in 270
overran nearly the whole of the eastern provinces in Asia Minor, and
declared her son the Eastern emperor.
When Aurelian became emperor he
marched against her and defeated her
at Antioch (now Antakya, Turkey).
She was led in triumphal procession at
Rome, and later married a Roman
senator.

Zog I, originally **Ahmed Bey Zogu**
(1895–1961) Albanian prime minister
(1922–4), president (1925–8), and king
(1928–39), born in Burgajet, Albania.
He studied in Istanbul, became leader
of the Nationalist Party, and formed a
republican government in 1922.
Forced into exile in 1924, he returned
with the assistance of Yugoslavia, and
became president, proclaiming himself king in 1928. After Albania was
overrun by the Italians (1939), he fled
to Britain, and later lived in Egypt and
France. He formally abdicated in 1946.

Ready Reference

This section includes a listing of royal rulers in the following 86 countries, territories, and empires, past and present:

Assyria 289
Austria 290
Babylon 290
Bahrain 291
Bangladesh 291
Belgium 292
Benin 292
Bhutan 292
Bosnia and
  Herzegovina 292
Brazil 292
Brunei 293
Bulgaria 293
Burgundy 293
Burundi 293
Byzantium 293
Cambodia 295
China 295
Croatia 298
Cyprus 298
Czech Republic 298
Denmark 299
Egypt 300
Ethiopia 301
France 301
Georgia 305
Germany 305
Ghana 308
Greece 309
Holy Roman Empire 310

Hungary 311
India/Indian States 312
Indonesia 319
Iran 319
Iraq 320
Israel 320
Italy 321
Japan 326
Jordan 328
Kazakhstan 328
Korea 328
Kuwait 329
Laos 329
Lebanon 329
Lesotho 330
Libya 330
Liechtenstein 330
Lithuania 330
Luxemburg 330
Madagascar 331
Malaysia 331
Maldives 333
Mexico 334
Monaco 334
Morocco 334
Nepal 335
Netherlands 336
Norway 336
Oman 337
Pakistan 337

Peru 337
Philippines 338
Poland 338
Portugal 339
Qatar 340
Romania 340
Rome 340
Russia 342
Rwanda 342
Saudi Arabia 343
Serbia and
  Montenegro 344
South Africa 345
Spain 345
Sri Lanka 346
Sudan 346
Swaziland 347
Sweden 347
Tanzania 348
Thailand 348
Tonga 348
Tunisia 348
Turkey 348
Ukraine 349
United Arab Emirates 350
Uzbekistan 351
Vietnam 351
Yemen 351

Royal Rulers

● **Assyria**
Monarch – Kingdom of Assyria

1813–1780 BC	Shamshi-Adad I
1780 BC–?	Ishme-Dagan I
	Mut-Ashkur
	Rimush
	Asinum
	Puzur-Sin
	Ashur-dugul
	Ashur-apla-idi
	Nasir-Sin
	Sin-namir
	Ipqi-Ishtar
	Adad-shalulu
	Adasi
1700–1690 BC	Belubani
1690–1673 BC	Libaia
1673–1661 BC	Sharma-Adad I
1661–1649 BC	Iptar-Sin
1649–1621 BC	Bazaia
1621–1615 BC	Lullaia
1615–1601 BC	Kidin-Ninua
1601–1598 BC	Sharma-Adad II
1598–1585 BC	Erishum
1585–1579 BC	Shamshi-Adad II
1579–1563 BC	Ishme-Dagan II
1563–1547 BC	Shamshi-Adad III
1547–1521 BC	Ashur-nirari I
1521–1497 BC	Puzur-Ashur
1497–1484 BC	Enlil-nasir I
1484–1472 BC	Nur-ili
1472 BC	Ashur-shaduni
1472–1452 BC	Ashur-rabi I
1452–1432 BC	Ashur-nadin-ahhe I
1432–1426 BC	Enlil-nasir II

1426–1419 BC	Ashur-nirari II
1419–1410 BC	Ashur-bel-nisheshu
1410–1402 BC	Ashur-rim-nisheshu
1402–1392 BC	Ashur-nadin-ahhe II
1392–1365 BC	Eriba-Adad I
1365–1329 BC	Ashur-uballit I
1329–1319 BC	Enlil-nirari
1319–1307 BC	Arik-den-ili
1307–1274 BC	Adad-nirari I
1274–1244 BC	Shulmanu-ashared (Shalmaneser) I
1244–1207 BC	Tukulti-Ninurta I
1207–1203 BC	Ashur-nadin-apli
1203–1197 BC	Ashur-nirari III
1197–1192 BC	Enlil-kudurri-usur
1192–1179 BC	Ninurta-apil-Ekur
1179 BC–?	Ashur-dan I
?	Ninurta-tukulti-Ashur
?–1133 BC	Mutakkil-Nusku
1133–1115 BC	Ashur-resha-ishi I
1115–1076 BC	Tukulti-apil-esharra (Tiglath-Pilesar) I
1076–1074 BC	Ashared-apil-Ekur
1074–1056 BC	Ashur-bel-kala
1056–1054 BC	Eriba-Adad II
1054–1050 BC	Shamshi-Adad IV
1050–1031 BC	Ashur-nasir-apli I
1031–1019 BC	Shulmanu-ashared II
1019–1013 BC	Ashur-nirari IV
1013–972 BC	Ashur-rabi II
972–967 BC	Ashur-resha-ishi II
967–935 BC	Tukulti-apil-esharra II
935–911 BC	Ashur-dan II
911–890 BC	Adad-nirari II

890–884 BC	Tukulti-Ninurta II
884–859 BC	Ashur-nasir-apli II
859–824 BC	Shulmanu-ashared III
824–811 BC	Shamshi-Adad V
811–782 BC	Adad-nirari III – Sammu-ramat (Semiramis) *Regent to 806 BC*
782–772 BC	Shulmanu-ashared IV
772–754 BC	Ashur-dan III
754–745 BC	Ashur-nirari V
745–727 BC	Tukulti-apil-esharra III Pulu
727–722 BC	Shulmanu-ashared V
722–705 BC	Sharrukin (Sargon) II
705–681 BC	Sin-ahhe-eriba (Sennacherib)
681–669 BC	Ashur-ahhe-iddina (Esarhaddon)
669–626 BC	Ashur-bani-apli (Ashur-banipal: Sardanapalus)
626–621 BC	Sin-shum-lishir
626–621 BC	Ashur-etil-ilani
621–612 BC	Sin-shar-ishkun
612–609 BC	Ashur-uballit II

● Austria
Margrave of Austria
House of Babenburg

976–94	Leopold I
994–1018	Heinrich I
1018–55	Adalbert
1055–75	Ernest
1075–96	Leopold II
1096–1136	Leopold III
1136–41	Leopold IV
1141–56	Heinrich II Jasomirgott

Duke of Austria
House of Babenberg

1156–77	Henry II Jasomirgott
1177–94	Leopold V
1194–8	Friedrich I
1198–1230	Leopold VI
1230–46	Friedrich II
1246–51	*No duke*
1251–76	Ottokar (II *of Bohemia*)

House of Habsburg

1276–91	Rudolf I
1282–1290	Rudolf II *Joint ruler*
1282–1298	Albrecht (Albert) *Joint ruler to 1290*
1298–1307	Rudolf III *Joint ruler*
1298–1330	Friedrich II *Joint ruler*
1298–1326	Leopold I *Joint ruler*
1298–1339	Otto *Joint ruler*
1298–1358	Albrecht II *Joint ruler to 1339*
1358–65	Rudolf IV
1365–79	Leopold III *Joint ruler*
1365–95	Albrecht III *Joint ruler to 1379*
1395–1404	Albrecht IV
1404–1439	Albrecht V
1439–57	Ladislas 'Posthumus'
1457–93	Friedrich V (Frederick III, *Holy Roman Emperor*)
1493–1804	*As Holy Roman Emperor*

Austrian Empire
Monarch – House of Habsburg

1804–1835	Franz I (Francis II, *Holy Roman Emperor*)
1835–1848	Ferdinand I
1848–67	Franz Josef (Francis Joseph) I

Austro-Hungarian Empire
Emperor – House of Habsburg

1867–1916	Franz Josef I
1916–18	Karl (Charles)

● Babylon
Monarch – Kingdom of Babylon

1156–1138 BC	Marduk-kabit-ahheshu
1138–1130 BC	Itti-Marduk-balatsu
1130–1124 BC	Ninurta-nadin-shumi
1124–1102 BC	Nabu-kudurri-usur (Nebuchadrezzar) I
1102–1098 BC	Enlil-nadin-apli
1098–1080 BC	Marduk-nadin-ahhe
1080–1067 BC	Marduk-shapik-zeri
1067–1045 BC	Adad-apla-Addina
1045–1044 BC	Marduk-ahhe-eriba
1044–1032 BC	Marduk-zer
1032–1024 BC	Nabu-shumu-libur
1024–1007 BC	Simbar-shikhu
1007–1006 BC	Ea-mukin-zeri
1006–1003 BC	Kashshu-nadin-akhi
1003–986 BC	E-ulmash-shakin-shumi
986–984 BC	Ninurta-kudurri-usur I
984–983 BC	Shirikti-shuqamuna

983–978 BC	Mar-biti-apla-usur
978–943 BC	Nabu-mukin-apli
943–942 BC	Ninurta-kudurri-usur II
942–941 BC	Mar-biti-ahhe-iddina
941–900 BC	Shamash-mudammiq
900–885 BC	Nabu-shum-ukin I
885–852 BC	Nabu-apla-iddina
852–851 BC	Marduk-bel-usate
851–827 BC	Marduk-zakir-shumi I
827–814 BC	Marduk-balatsu-iqbi
814–811 BC	Bau-ahhe-iddina
811–? BC	Adad-shuma-ibni
?	Marduk-bel-zeri
?–802 BC	Marduk-apla-usur
802–? BC	Eriba-Marduk
?–747 BC	Nabu-shum-ukin II
747–735 BC	Nabu-nasir
735–732 BC	Nabu-nadin-zeri
732 BC	Nabu-shum-ukin III
732–729 BC	Ukin-zer
729–722 BC	Assyrian rule
722–710 BC	Marduk-apla-iddina II (Merodach-Baladan)
710–703 BC	Assyrian rule
703 BC	Marduk-zakir-shumi II
703–702 BC	Marduk-apla-iddina II (*restored*)
702–700 BC	Bel-ibni
700–694 BC	Ashur-nadin-shumi
694–693 BC	Nergal-ushezib
693–689 BC	Mushezib-Marduk
689–669 BC	Assyrian rule
669–648 BC	Shamash-shuma-ukin
648–627 BC	Kandalanu

Neo-Babylonian Empire

626–605 BC	Nabu-apla-usur (Nabopolassar)
605–562 BC	Nabu-kudurri-usur II
562–559 BC	Awel-Marduk
559–556 BC	Nergal-shar-usur
556 BC	Labashi-Marduk
556–539 BC	Nabu-Na'id (Nabonidus)

● **Bahrain**
Emir (*King from 2002*)
al-Khalifa Dynasty

1783–96	Ahmad bin Khalifa
1796–1843	Abdulla
1796–1825	Salman I *Joint ruler*
1825–36	Khalifa *Joint ruler*
1834–68	Muhammad *Joint ruler to 1843*
1868–9	Ali
1869–1935	Isa I
1923–42	Hamad
1942–61	Salman II
1961–99	Isa II bin Salman al-Khalifa
1999–	Hamad II bin Isa al-Khalifa

● **Bangladesh**
Sultan of Bengal

1282–91	Nasir-ud-Din Bughra Khan
1291–8	Rukn-ud-Din Kai-Kaus
1298–1318	Shams-ud-Din Firuz Shah I
1318–30	Ghiyath-ud-Din Bhadur East Bengal *Joint ruler from 1324*
1324–39	Bahram Shah East Bengal *Joint ruler to 1330*
1339–49	Fakhr-ud-Din Mubarak Shah East Bengal
1349–52	Ikhtiyar-ud-Din Ghazi Shah East Bengal
1352–7	Shams-ud-Din Ilyas Shah East Bengal to 1345
1358–90	Sikandar Shah I
1390–1410	Ghiyath-ud-Din Azam Shah
1410–12	Saif-ud-Din Hamza Shah
1412–14	Shihab-ud-Din Bayazid Shah I
1414–15	Ala-ud-Din Firuz Shah II
1415–18	Raja Ganesh
1418–32	Jalal-ud-Din Muhammad Shah
1432–7	Shams-ud-Din Ahmad Shah
1437–60	Nasir-ud-Din Mahmud Shah I
1460–74	Rukn-ud-Din Barbak Shah I
1474–81	Shams-ud-Din Yusuf Shah
1481	Sikandar Shah II
1481–7	Jalal-ud-Din Fath Shah
1487–8	Sultan Shahzada Barbak Shah II
1488–90	Saif-ud-Din Firuz Shah III
1490–1	Nasir-ud-Din Mahmud Shah II

1491–4	Shams-ud-Din Muzaffar Shah
1494–1519	Ala-ud-Din Husain Shah
1519–32	Nasir-ud-Din Nusrat Shah
1532–3	Ala-ud-Din Firuz Shah IV
1533–9	Ghiyath-ud-Din Mahmud Shah III
1539–40	Shir Shah Sur
1540–5	Khidr Khan
1545–55	Muhammad Khan Sur
1555–61	Khidr Khan Bahadur Shah
1561–4	Ghiyath-ud-Din Jalal Shah
1564–72	Sulayman Kararani
1572	Bayazid Shah II
1572–6	Daud Shah
1576–1703	*Part of Moghul Empire*

Nawab of Bengal

1703–27	Murshid Quli Ja far Khan
1727–39	Shuja-ud-Din
1739–40	Safaraz Khan
1740–56	Alivardi Khan
1756–7	Siraj-ud-Dawlah (Suraja Dowlah)
1757–60	Mir Ja far
1760–3	Mir Qasim
1763–5	Mir Ja far (*restored*)
1765–6	Najm-ud-Dawlah
1766–70	Saif-ud-Dawlah
1770–1947	*British rule*
1947–71	*Part of Pakistan*

● Belgium
Monarch – Kingdom of Belgium

1831–65	Leopold I
1865–1909	Leopold II
1909–34	Albert I
1934–51	Leopold III
1951–93	Baudoin I
1993–	Albert II

● Benin
Monarch – Kingdom of Dahomey

c.1625–c.1650	Dakpodunu
c.1650–c.1680	Wegbaja
c.1680–c.1708	Akaba
c.1708–c.1730	Agaja

c.1730–1775	Tegbesu
1775–89	Kpengla
1789–97	Agonglo
1797–1818	Adandozan
1818–58	Gezo
1858–89	Glele
1889–94	Behanzin
1894–1960	*French rule*

● Bhutan
Monarch (Druk Gyalpo)

1907–26	Uggyen Wangchuk
1926–52	Jigme Wangchuk
1952–72	Jigme Dorji Wangchuk
1972–	Jigme Singye Wangchuk

● Bosnia and Herzegovina
Monarch – Kingdom of Bosnia

1376–91	Stephen Tvrtko I
1391–5	Stephen Dabisha
1395–8	Helena
1398–1404	Stephen Ostoja
1404–08	Stephen Tvrtko II
1408–18	Stephen Ostoja (*restored*)
1418–21	Stephen Ostojich
1421–43	Stephen Tvrtko II (*restored*)
1443–61	Stephen Thomas Ostojich
1461–3	Stephen Thomashevic
1463–1815	*Turkish rule*
1815–1918	*Austrian rule*
1918–92	*Part of Yugoslavia*

● Brazil
Emperor
House of Bragança

1822–31	Pedro I (IV *of Portugal*)
1831–89	Pedro II

● Brunei
Monarch (Sultan)

c.1405–c.1415	Muhammad
c.1415–?	Ahmad
?–c.1433	Sharif Ali Bilfakih
c.1433–?	Sulayman
	Abdul-Qahhar

	Bulkiah
c.1578–?	Saif al Rijal
	Shah Berunai
	Hasan
	Abdul-Jalil Akbar
	Abdul-Jalil Jabbar
?–c.1662	Muhammad Ali
c.1662–?	Abdul-Mubin
	Muhyi-ud-Din
	Nasr-ud-Din
	Kamal-ud-Din
	Ala-ud-Din
?–1780	Umar Ali Saif-ud-Din I
1780–92	Muhammad Taj-ud-Din
1792–3	Muhammad Jamal-ul-Alam I
1793–1806	Muhammad Taj-ud-Din (restored)
1806–22	Muhammad Khanz al Alam
1822	Muhammad Alam
1822–52	Umar Ali Saif-ud-Din II Jamal-ul-Alam
1852–85	Abdul Mu min
1885–1906	Hashim Jalil-ul-Alam Akam-ud-Din
1906–24	Muhammad Jamal-ul-Alam II
1924–50	Ahmad Taj-ud-Din
1950–67	Umar Ali Saif-ud-Din III
1967–	Muda Hassan al Bolkiah Mu'izz-Din-Waddaulah

● Bulgaria
Monarch – Kingdom of Bulgaria

1879–1886	Alexander of Battenburg Prince
1887–1918	Ferdinand I Prince until 1918
1918–43	Boris III
1943–6	Simeon II

● Burgundy
Dukedom of Burgundy
House of Valois

1363–1404	Philip 'the Bold'
1404–19	John 'the Fearless'
1419–67	Philip 'the Good'
1467–77	Charles 'the Bold'

1477–	United with Crown of Austria and later of Spain

● Burundi
Mwami (King)

c.1675–c.1705	Ntare I Rushatsi
c.1705–c.1735	Mwezi I
c.1735–c.1765	Mutaga I Seenyamwiiza
c.1765–c.1795	Mwambutsa I
c.1795–1852	Ntare II Rugaamba
1852–1908	Mwezi II Kisabo
1908–16	Mutaga II
1916–62	Mwambutsa II

Independence

1962–6	Mwambutsa II
1966	Ntare III Ndizeye

● Byzantium (Constantinople)
Emperors

323–37	Constantine I 'the Great'
337–61	Constantine II (Tiberius I)
361–3	Julian 'the Apostate'
363–4	Jovianos
364–78	Valens
379–95	Theodosius I 'the Great'
395–408	Arcadius
408–50	Theodosius II
450–7	Marcianus
457–74	Leo I
474	Leo II
474–91	Zeno
475–6	Basiliscus Joint emperor
491–518	Anastasius I
518–27	Justin I
527–65	Justinian I
565–78	Justin II
578–82	Tiberius II
582–602	Maurice
602–10	Phocas
610–41	Heraclius
641	Constantine III
641	Heracleonas Joint emperor
641–68	(Flavius Heraclius) Constans II
668–85	Constantine IV Pogonatus
685–95	Justinian II

695–8	Leontius
698–705	Tiberius III Apsimar
705–11	Justinian II (*restored*)
711–13	Philippicus
713–15	Anastasius II
715–17	Theodosius III
717–41	Leo III Isauricus
741–75	Constantine V Copronymus
775–80	Leo IV
780–97	Constantine VI
797–802	Irene
802–11	Nicephorus I
811	Stauracius
811–13	Michael I
813–20	Leo V 'the Armenian'
820–9	Michael II
829–42	Theophilus
842–67	Michael III
867–86	Basil I 'the Macedonian'
886–912	Leo VI
912–13	Alexander *Joint emperor*
912–59	Constantine VII Porphyrogenitus *Joint emperor to 913 and 920–44*
920–44	Romanus I Lecapenus *Regent and Joint emperor*
959–63	Romanus II
963–9	Nicephorus II Phocas
969–76	John I Tzimisces
976–1025	Basil II Bulgaroctonus *Joint emperor*
976–1028	Constantine VIII
1028–34	Romanus III Argyrus *Joint emperor*
1028–50	Zoë *Joint Empress*
1034–41	Michael IV 'the Paphlagonian' *Joint emperor*
1041–2	Michael V Calaphates *Joint emperor*
1042–56	Theodora *Joint Empress to 1055*
1042–55	Constantine IX Monomachus *Joint emperor*
1056–7	Michael VI Stratioticus
1057–9	Isaac I Comnenus
1059–67	Constantine X Ducas
1068–71	Romanus IV Diogenes
1071–8	Michael VII Ducas
1078–81	Nicephorus III Botaneiates

Comnenian Emperors

1081–1118	Alexius I Comnenus
1118–43	John II Comnenus
1143–80	Manuel I
1180–3	Alexius II
1183–5	Andronicus I Comnenus
1185–95	Isaac II Angelus
1195–1203	Alexius III
1203–4	Alexius IV *Joint emperor*
1203–4	Isaac II Angelus (*restored*)
1204	Alexius V Ducas

Latin Emperors

1204–5	Baldwin I
1205–16	Henry
1216–17	Peter of Courtenay
1217–19	Yolande
1219–28	Robert
1228–61	Baldwin II

Byzantine Emperors at Nicaea

1204–22	Theodore I Lascaris
1222–54	John III Varatzes
1254–8	Theodore II
1258–61	John IV *Joint emperor from 1259*
1259–61	Michael VIII Palaeologus *Regent and joint emperor*

Palaeologi Emperors at Byzantium

1261–82	Michael VIII Palaeologus
1282–1328	Andronicus II Palaeologus *Joint emperor 1295–1320*
1295–1320	Michael IX *Joint emperor*
1328–41	Andronicus III Palaeologus
1341–91	John V *Joint emperor 1347–54 and from 1376*
1347–54	John VI Cantacuzene *Regent and joint emperor*
1376–90	Andronicus IV *Joint emperor*
1390	John VII *Joint emperor*
1391–1425	Manuel II *Joint emperor 1399–1402*
1399–1402	John VII *Joint emperor*
1425–48	John VIII
1448–53	Constantine XI

● Cambodia

Monarch – Kingdom of Cambodia

Angkor Kings

802–50	Jayavarman II
850–77	Jayavarman III
877–89	Indravarman I
889–900	Yasovarman I
900–c.922	Harshavarman I
c.922–8	Isanavarman II
928–42	Jayavarman IV
942–4	Harshavarman II
944–68	Rajendravarman
968–1001	Jayavarman V
1001–2	Udayadityavarman I
1002	Jayaviravarman
1002–50	Suryavarman I
1050–66	Udayadityavarman II
1066–80	Harshavarman III
1080–1107	Jayavarman VI
1107–1113	Dharanindravarman I
1113–50	Suryavarman II
1150–60	Dharanindravarman II
1160–6	Yasovarman II
1166–81	Tribhuvanadityavarman
1181–1219	Jayavarman VII
c.1219–43	Indravarman II
1243–95	Jayavarman VIII
1295–1308	Indravarman III
1308–27	Indrajayavarman
1327–c.1353	Jayavarmadiparamesvara
c.1353–c.1362	*Period of instability*
c.1362–c.1371	Nirvanapada
c.1371–c.1377	Kalamegha
c.1377–c.1387	Kambudjadhiraja
c.1387–89	Dharmasokaraja
1389–1404	Paramarajadhiraja
1404–29	Narayana Ramadhipati
1429–44	Sodaiya
1444–86	Dharmarajadhiraja
1486–1512	Srey Sukonthor
1512–16	Nay Kan
1516–66	Ang Chan I
1566–76	Barom Reachea I
1576–94	Chettha I
1594–6	Reamea Chung Prei
1596–9	Barom Reachea II
1599–1600	Barom Reachea III
1600–03	Chao Ponhea Nhom
1603–18	Barom Reachea IV
1618–28	Chettha II
1628–30	Ponhea To
1630–40	Ponhea Nu
1640–2	Ang Non I
1642–59	Chan Rama Thupdey
1659–72	Batom Reachea
1672–3	Chettha III
1673–4	Ang Chei
1674–5	Obbarac Ang Non
1675–95	Chettha IV
1695	Outey I
1695–9	Chettha IV (*restored*)
1699–1701	Ang Em
1701–2	Chettha IV (*restored*)
1702–3	Thommo Reachea
1703–22	*Civil war*
1722–38	Satha Ang Chei
1738–47	Thommo Reachea (*restored*)
1747–9	Ang Ton
1749–55	Chettha V
1755–8	Ang Ton (*restored*)
1758–75	Prea Outey II
1775–9	Ang Non II
1779–96	Ang Eng
1796–1834	Ang Chan II
1834–41	Ang Mey
1841–60	Ang Duong
1860–1904	Norodom
1904–27	Sisovath
1927–41	Monivong
1941–55	Norodom Sihanouk II
1955–60	Norodom Suramarit
1960–70	Norodom Sihanouk II (*restored*)
1970–2004	*Republic*
2004–	Norodom Sihamoni

● China

The traditional dates for prehistoric dynasties are generally considered not to be accurate.

Emperor

Prehistoric Dynasties

1766–1122 BC	Shang (Yin) Dynasty *Probable actual dates c.1500–1027 BC*
1122–771 BC	Western Chou Dynasty

	Probable actual founding date
	1027 BC
770–249 BC	Eastern Chou Dynasty
249–221 BC	*Civil war*

Ch'in Dynasty

221–210 BC	Shih Huang Ti Cheng Wang
	of Ch'in from 246 BC
210–207 BC	Erh Shih Huang Ti
207–206 BC	Ch'in Wang

Western Han Dynasty

206–195 BC	Kao Tsu (Liu Pang)
195–188 BC	Hui Ti
188–179 BC	Kao Hou
179–157 BC	Wen Ti
157–141 BC	Ching Ti
141–87 BC	Wu Ti
87–74 BC	Chao Ti
74–48 BC	Hsuan Ti
48–33 BC	Yuan Ti
33–7 BC	Ch'eng Ti
7–1 BC	Ai Ti
1 BC–AD 6	P'ing Ti
6–8	Ju-Tzu Ying

Hsin Dynasty

9–23	Chia Huang Ti (Wang Mang)
23–5	*Civil war*

Eastern Han Dynasty

25–57	Kuang Wu Ti (Liu Hsiu)
57–75	Ming Ti
75–88	Chang Ti
88–106	Ho Ti
106	Shang Ti
106–25	An Ti
125	Shao Ti
125–44	Shun Ti
144–5	Ch'ung Ti
145–6	Chih Ti
146–68	Huan Ti
168–89	Ling Ti
189	Shao Ti
189–220	Hsien Ti
220–80	*Civil war*

Western Chin Dynasty

280–90	Wu Ti (Ssu-Ma Yen) *Ruler of Western Chin from 266*

290–307	Hui Ti
307–11	Huai Ti
311–13	*No emperor*
313–16	Min Ti

Eastern Chin Dynasty

317–23	Yuan Ti (Ssu-Ma Jui)
323–5	Ming Ti
325–42	Ch'eng Ti
342–4	K'ang Ti
344–61	Mu Ti
361–5	Ai Ti
365–72	Ti I (Hai Hsi Kung)
372	Chien Wen Ti
372–96	Hsaio Wu Ti
396–419	An Ti
419–20	Kung Ti

Earlier Sung Dynasty

420–2	Wu Ti (Liu Yu)
422–4	Shao Ti
424–53	We Ti
453–64	Hsaio Wu Ti
464–6	Ch'ien Fei Ti
466–72	Ming Ti
472–7	Hou Fei Ti
477–9	Shun Ti

Southern Ch'i Dynasty

479–82	Kao Ti (Hsaio Tao-Ch'eng)
482–93	Wu Ti
493–4	Yu-Lin Wang
494	Hai-Ling Wang
494–8	Ming Ti
498–501	Tung-Hun Hou
501–2	Ho Ti

Southern Liang Dynasty

502–49	Wu Ti (Hsiao Yen)
549–51	Chien Wen Ti
551–2	Yu-Chang Wang
552–5	Yuan Ti
555	Chen-Yang Hou
555–7	Ching Ti

Southern Ch'en Dynasty

557–9	Wu Ti (Ch'en Pa-Hsien)
559–66	Wen Ti
566–8	Fei Ti
568–82	Hsuan Ti
582–9	Hou Chu

Sui Dynasty

589–604	Wen Ti (Yang Chien)
605–17	Yang Ti
617–18	Gong Ti

T'ang Dynasty

618–26	Kao Tsu (Li Yuan)
627–49	T'ai Tsung (Li Shih-Min)
650–84	Kao Tsung
684–5	Chung Tsung
685–90	Jui Tsung
690–705	Wu Hou
705–10	Chung Tsung (*restored*)
710–12	Jui Tsung (*restored*)
712–56	Hsuan Tsung
756–62	Su Tsung
762–79	Tai Tsung
779–805	Te Tsung
805	Shun Tsung
805–20	Hsien Tsung
820–4	Mu Tsung
824–7	Ching Tsung
827–40	Wen Tsung
840–6	Wu Tsung
846–59	Hsuan Tsung
859–73	I Tsung
873–88	Hsi Tsung
888–904	Chao Tsung
904–7	Chao Hsuan Ti

Later Liang Dynasty

907–12	T'ai Tsu (Chu Wen)
912–13	Ying Wang
913–23	Mo Ti

Later T'ang Dynasty

923–6	Chuang Tsung (Li Ts'un-Hsu)
926–33	Ming Tsung
933–4	Min Ti
934–6	Mo Ti

Later Chin Dynasty

936–42	Kao Tsu (Shih Ching-T'ang)
942–7	Ch'u Ti

Later Han Dynasty

947–8	Kao Tsu (Liu Chih-Yuan)
948–51	Yin Ti

Later Chou Dynasty

951–4	T'ai Tsu (Kuo Wei)
954–9	Shih Tsung
959–60	Kung Ti

Northern Sung Dynasty

960–76	T'ai Tsu (Chao K'uang-Yin)
976–97	T'ai Tsung
997–1022	Chen Tsung
1022–63	Jen Tsung
1063–7	Ying Tsung
1067–85	Shen Tsung
1085–1100	Che Tsung
1100–26	Hui Tsung
1126–7	Ch'in Tsung

Southern Sung Dynasty

1127–62	Kao Tsung
1162–89	Hsaio Tsung
1189–94	Kuang Tsung
1194–1224	Ning Tsung
1224–64	Li Tsung
1264–74	Tu Tsung
1274–6	Kung Tsung
1276–8	Tuan Tsung
1278–9	Ti Ping

Yuan (Mongol) Dynasty

1206–27	T'ai Tsu (Genghis/Chingis Khan)
1227–9	Disputed succession
1229–41	T'ai Tsung (Ogodei Khan)
1241–6	Disputed succession
1246–8	Ting Tsung (Guyuk Khan)
1248–51	Disputed succession
1251–9	Hsien Tsung (Mengu Khan)
1260–94	Shih Tsu (Kublai/ Kubilai Khan) *Emperor of all China from 1279*
1294–1307	Ch'eng Tsung
1307–11	Wu Tsung
1311–20	Jen Tsung
1320–3	Ying Tsung
1323–8	T'ai Ting Ti
1328–9	Wen Tsung
1329	Ming Tsung
1329–32	Wen Tsung (*restored*)
1332	Ning Tsung
1332–68	Shun Ti

Ming Dynasty

1368–98	T'ai Tsu (Hung Wu; Chu Yuan-Chang)

1398–1402	Hui Ti (Chien Wen)
1402–24	Ch'eng Tsu (Yung Lo)
1424–5	Jen Tsung (Hung Hsi)
1425–35	Hsuan Tsung (Hsuan Te)
1435–49	Ying Tsung (Cheng T'ung)
1449–57	Tai Tsung (Ching T'ai)
1457–64	Ying Tsung (Cheng T'ung) (*restored*)
1464–87	Hsien Tsung (Ch'eng Hua)
1487–1505	Hsiao Tsung (Hung Chih)
1505–21	Wu Tsung (Cheng Te)
1521–67	Shih Tsung (Chia Ching)
1567–72	Mu Tsung (Lung Ch'ing)
1572–1620	Shen Tsung (Wan Li)
1620	Kuang Tsung (T'ai Ch'ing)
1620–7	Hsi Tsung (T'ien Ch'i)
1627–44	Chuang Lieh Ti (Ch'ung Chen)

Ch'ing (Manchu) Dynasty

1616–26	T'ai Tsu (T'ien Ming; Nurhachi)
1626–43	T'ai Tsung (T'ien Ts'ung/ Ch'ung Te)
1643–61	Shih Tsu (Shun Chih)
1661–1722	Sheng Tsu (K'ang Hsi)
1722–35	Shih Tsung (Yung Cheng)
1735–96	Kao Tsung (Ch'ien Lung)
1796–1820	Jen Tsung (Chia Ch'ing)
1820–50	Hsuan Tsung (Tao Kuang)
1850–61	Wen Tsung (Hsien Feng)
1861–75	Mu Tsung (T'ung Chih)
1875–1908	Te Tsung (Kuang-hsü)
1908–12	Mo Ti (Xuantong; Pu-yi)

● Croatia
Monarch – Kingdom of Croatia

924–30	Tomislav
930–69	Kresimir II
969–97	Stephen Drzhislav
997–c.1000	Svetolav
c.1000–30	Kresimir III
1030–58	Peter Kresimir
1058–76	Dimitar Zvonimir
1076–89	Stephen II
1091–5	Almos
1095–1918	*Part of Hungary*
1918–91	*Part of Yugoslavia*

● Cyprus
Monarch – Kingdom of Cyprus

Lusignan Dynasty

1192–4	Guy of Lusignan
1194–1205	Amalric
1205–18	Hugh I
1218–53	Henry I
1253–67	Hugh II
1267–84	Hugh III
1284–5	John I
1285–1324	Henry II
1324–59	Hugh IV
1359–69	Peter I
1369–82	Peter II
1382–98	James I
1398–1432	Janus
1432–58	John II
1458–64	Louis *Joint ruler*
1458–64	Charlotte *Joint ruler*
1460–73	James II *Rival king to 1464*
1473–4	James III
1473–89	Caterina Cornaro *Regent and joint ruler to 1474*
1489–1571	*Venetian rule*
1571–1914	*Turkish rule*
1914–60	*British rule*

● Czech Republic
Duke of Bohemia

House of Přemysl

873–95	Borzhivoi I
895–912	Spitihnev I *Joint ruler*
895–921	Vratislav I *Joint ruler to 912*
921–9	Vaclav I (St Wenceslas)
929–67	Boleslav I
967–99	Boleslav II
999–1002	Boleslav III
1002–3	Vladivoi
1003	Boleslav III (*restored*)
1003	Jaromir
1003–4	Boleslav IV
1004–12	Jaromir (*restored*)
1012–33	Udalrich
1033–4	Jaromir (*restored*)
1034–55	Bretislav I
1055–61	Spitihnev II
1061–92	Vratislav I *King from 1086*
1092	Conrad

1092–1100	Bretislav II
1100–7	Borzhivoi II
1107–9	Svatopluk
1109–17	Vladislav I
1117–20	Borzhivoi II (*restored*)
1120–5	Vladislav I (*restored*)
1125–40	Sobeslav I
1140–73	Vladislav II *King from 1158*
1173–9	Sobeslav II
1179–89	Frederick
1189–91	Conrad-Otto
1191–2	Václav II
1192–3	Přemysl Otakar I
1193–7	Bretislav-Henry
1197	Vladislav III
1197–98	Přemysl Otakar I (*restored*)

King of Bohemia
House of Přemysl

1198–1230	Přemysl Otakar I
1230–53	Václav I
1253–78	Přemysl Otakar II
1278–1305	Václav II
1305–6	Václav III

Later Kings

1306–7	Rudolf (III *of Austria*)
1307–10	Henry of Carinthia
1310–46	John 'the Blind' (*of Luxemburg*)
1346–78	Charles (IV, *Holy Roman Emperor*)
1378–1419	Vaclav IV (Wenceslas, *Holy Roman Emperor*)
1419–37	Sigismund (*Holy Roman Emperor*)
1437–40	Albert (*Holy Roman Emperor*)
1440–57	Ladislaus Posthumus (V *of Hungary*)
1457–71	George of Podebrady
1471–1516	Vladislav Jagiellon
1516–26	Louis (Lajos II *of Hungary*)

● Denmark
Monarch – Kingdom of Denmark
House of Gorm

c.900–c.940	Gorm 'the Old'
c.940–c.985	Harald I Gormsson 'Bluetooth'

c.985–1014	Svein I Haraldsson 'Forkbeard'
1014–19	Harald II
1019–35	Knut Sveinsson (Canute)
1035–42	Hardaknut Knutsson
1042–7	*As Norway*
1047–74	Svein II Estridsson
1074–80	Harald III Hen
1080–6	Knut IV 'the Holy'
1086–95	Olaf IV
1095–1103	Erik I Ejegod
1104–34	Niels
1134–7	Erik II Emune
1137–47	Erik III
1147–57	Knut V *Rival king*
1147–57	Svein III *Rival king*
1157–82	Valdemar I 'the Great'
1182–1202	Knut VI
1202–41	Valdemar II
1241–50	Erik IV
1250–2	Abel
1252–9	Kristofer I
1259–86	Erik V
1286–1320	Erik VI
1320–32	Kristofer II
1340–75	Valdemar III Atterdag
1375–87	Olaf V (Olaf IV *of Norway from 1380*)
1387–97	Margrethe I (Margareta, *Queen of Norway from 1387 and Sweden from 1389*)

Monarch – Kalmar Union
House of Gorm

1397–1412	Margrethe I (Margareta, *Queen of Norway and Sweden*)
1412–39	Erik VII (*of Pomerania*, Erik III *of Norway* and XIII *of Sweden*)
1439–48	Kristofer III (*of Bavaria*, Kristofer I *of Norway and Sweden*)

House of Oldenburg

1448–81	Kristian I (*King of Norway, King of Sweden 1457–64, 65–67 and 70–81*)
1481–1513	Hans (*King of Norway*; Johan II *of Sweden*)

1513–23	Kristian II (*King of Norway, King of Sweden to 1521*)

Monarch – Kingdom of Denmark and Norway
House of Oldenburg

1523–34	Frederik (Frederick) I
1534–59	Kristian III
1559–88	Frederik II
1588–1648	Kristian IV
1648–70	Frederik III
1670–99	Kristian V
1699–1730	Frederik IV
1730–46	Kristian VI
1746–66	Frederik V
1766–1808	Kristian VII
1808–14	Frederik VI

Monarch – Kingdom of Denmark
House of Oldenburg

1814–39	Frederik VI
1839–48	Kristian VIII
1848–63	Frederik VII
1863–1906	Kristian IX
1906–12	Frederik VIII
1912–47	Kristian X
1947–72	Frederik IX
1972–	Margrethe II

● **Egypt**
Dynasty – Old Kingdom

c.2925–c.2775 BC	I Dynasty
c.2775–c.2650 BC	II Dynasty
c.2650–c.2575 BC	III Dynasty
c.2575–c.2465 BC	IV Dynasty *including Khufu (Cheops) and Kha'fre' (Chephren)*
c.2465–c.2325 BC	V Dynasty
c.2325–c.2150 BC	VI Dynasty
c.2150–c.2130 BC	VII–VIII Dynasty
c.2130–c.2080 BC	IX Dynasty *Heracleopolis*
c.2080–c.1970 BC	X Dynasty *Hera*

Pharoah – Middle Kingdom
XI Dynasty (Thebes)

c.2081–c.2065 BC	Inyotef I *Joint ruler*
c.2081–c.2065 BC	Mentuhotpe I *Joint ruler*
c.2065–c.2016 BC	Inyotef II
c.2016–c.2008 BC	Inyotef III

c.2008–c.1957 BC	Mentuhotpe II
c.1957–c.1945 BC	Mentuhotpe III
c.1945–c.1938 BC	Mentuhotpe IV

XII Dynasty

c.1938–c.1908 BC	Amenemhet I
c.1918–c.1875 BC	Senwosret I *Joint ruler to 1908 BC*
c.1875–c.1842 BC	Amenemhet II
c.1844–c.1837 BC	Senwosret II *Joint ruler to 1842 BC*
c.1836–c.1818 BC	Senwosret III
c.1818–c.1770 BC	Amenemhet III
c.1770–c.1760 BC	Amenemhet IV
c.1760–c.1756 BC	Sebeknofru

Minor dynasties

c.1756–c.1630 BC	XIII Dynasty
c.1756–c.1577 BC	XIV Dynasty *Western Delta*
c.1630–c.1544 BC	XV (Great Hyskos) Dynasty
c.1630–c.1544 BC	XVI (Minor Hyskos) Dynasty
c.1630–c.1540 BC	XVII Dynasty *Upper Egypt*

Pharoah – New Kingdom
XVIII Dynasty

c.1539–c.1514 BC	Ahmose
c.1514–1493 BC	Amenhotpe I
1493–c.1482 BC	Thutmose (Tuthmosis) I
c.1482–1479 BC	Thutmose II
1479–1458 BC	Hashepsowe (Hatshepsut) Regent
1479–1424 BC	Thutmose III
1426–1400 BC	Amenhotpe (Amenhotep) II *Joint ruler to 1424 BC*
1400–1390 BC	Thutmose IV
1390–1353 BC	Amenhotpe (Amenhotep) III
1353–1336 BC	Amenhotpe IV (Akhenaton)
1335–1332 BC	Smenkhare
1332–1323 BC	Tutankhamun
1323–1319 BC	Ay
1319–c.1292 BC	Haremhab (Horemheb)

XIX Dynasty

c.1292–1290 BC	Ramesse (Rameses) I
1290–1279 BC	Seti I Merenptah

1279–1213 BC	Ramesse II Miamun ('the Great')
1213–1204 BC	Meryamun Merenptah
1204–1198 BC	Seti II Merenptah
1200–1194 BC	Amenmesse *Rival Pharoah*
1198–1193 BC	Merenptah Siptah
1193–1190 BC	Meryamun Tewosre

XX Dynasty

1190–1187 BC	Setnakhte
1187–1156 BC	Ramesse III
1156–1150 BC	Ramesse IV
1150–1145 BC	Ramesse V
1145–1137 BC	Ramesse VI
1137–1127 BC	Ramesse VII
1127–1126 BC	Ramesse VIII
1126–1108 BC	Ramesse IX
1108–1104 BC	Ramesse X
1104–c.1078 BC	Ramesse XI

Minor dynasties

c.1075–c.950 BC	XXI Dynasty *Tanis*
c.950–c.730 BC	XXII Dynasty *Bubastite*
c.832–c.730 BC	XXIII Dynasty *Tanite*
c.730–c.722 BC	*Invasion from Libya*
c.722–c.715 BC	XXIV Dynasty *Delta*
c.715–c.656 BC	XXV Dynasty *Napata*
c.656–525 BC	XXVI Dynasty
525–404 BC	XXVII Dynasty *Persian rule (see Iran)*
404–399 BC	XXVIII Dynasty
399–380 BC	XXIX Dynasty
380–343 BC	XXX Dynasty
343–332 BC	XXXI Dynasty *Persian rule (see Iran)*
332–305 BC	XXXII Dynasty *Macedonian rule (see Greece)* (Ptolemy Satrap 321–305BC)

Monarch – Kingdom of Egypt
Ptolemies – Lagid Dynasty

305–283 BC	Ptolemy I Soter
285–246 BC	Ptolemy II Philadelphus *(initially as co-ruler)*
246–222 BC	Ptolemy III Eurgetes
222–204 BC	Ptolemy IV Philopator
204–181 BC	Ptolemy V Epiphanes
181–145 BC	Ptolemy VI Philometor
145–116 BC	Ptolemy VII Euergetes
116–108 BC	Ptolemy VIII Sotor
108–88 BC	Ptolemy IX Alexander
88–80 BC	Ptolemy VIII Sotor (*restored*)
80 BC	Ptolemy X Alexander
80–58 BC	Ptolemy XI Auletes
58–55 BC	Berenice
55–51 BC	Ptolemy XI Auletes (*restored*)
51–47 BC	Ptolemy XII *Joint ruler*
51–30 BC	Cleopatra *Joint ruler*
47–44 BC	Ptolemy XIII *Joint ruler*
44–30 BC	Ptolemy XIV Caesarion *Joint ruler*
30 BC–AD 642	*Roman rule*
642–1250	*Various Arab dynasties and states*

Sultanate of Egypt – Mamluks
Bahri Sultans

1250–7	al-Muizz Izz-ud-Din Aibak
1257–9	al-Mansur Nur-ud-Din Ali
1259–60	al-Muzaffar Saif-ud-Din Qutuz
1260–77	az-Zahir Rukn-ud-Din Baibars I
1277–80	as-Said Nasir-ud-Din Baraka Khan
1280	al-Adil Badr-ud-Din Salamish
1280–90	al-Mansur Saif-ud-Din Qalaun
1290–4	al-Ashraf Salah-ud-Din Khalil
1294–5	an-Nasir Nasir-ud-Din Muhammad
1295–7	al-Adil Zain-ud-Din Kitbugha
1297–9	al-Mansur Husam-ud-Din Lajin
1299–1309	an-Nasir Nasir-ud-Din Muhammad (*restored*)
1309	al-Muzaffar Rukn-ud-Din Baibars II
1309–40	an-Nasir Nasir-ud-Din Muhammad (*restored*)
1340–1	al-Mansur Saif-ud-Din Abu-Bakr
1341–2	al-Ashraf Ala-ud-Din Kujuk

1342	an-Nasir Shihab-ud-Din Ahmad	1461	al-Muayyad Shihab-ud-Din Ahmad
1342–5	as-Salih Imad-ud-Din Ismail	1461–7	az-Zahir Saif-ud-Din Khushqadam
1345–6	al-Kamil Saif-ud-Din Shaban I	1467–8	az-Zahir Saif-ud-Din Bilbay
1346–7	al-Muzaffar Saif-ud-Din Hajji I	1468	az-Zahir Timurbugha
1347–51	an-Nasir Nasir-ud-Din Hasan	1468–96	al-Ashraf Saif-ud-Din Qait Bay
1351–4	as-Salih Salah-ud-Din Salih	1496–8	an-Nasir Muhammad
1354–61	an-Nasir Nasir-ud-Din Hasan (*restored*)	1498–1500	az-Zahir Qansuh
		1500–1	al-Ashraf Janbalat
1361–3	al-Mansur Salah-ud-Din Muhammad	1501	al-Adil Saif-ud-Din Tuman Bay
1363–76	al-Ashraf Nasir-ud-Din Shaban II	1501–17	al-Ashraf Qansuh al-Ghawri
1376–82	al-Mansur Ala-ud-Din Ali	1517	al-Ashraf Tuman Bay
1382	as-Salih Salah-ud-Din Hajji II	1517–1805	*Turkish rule*

Burji Sultans

1382–9	az-Zahir Saif-ud-Din Barquq

Bahri Sultans (*restored*)

1389–90	as-Salih Salah-ud-Din Hajji II (*restored*)

Burji Sultans (*restored*)

1390–9	az-Zahir Saif-ud-Din Barquq (*restored*)
1399–1405	an-Nasir Nasir-ud-Din Faraj
1405	al-Mansur Izz-ud-Din Abdul-Aziz
1405–12	an-Nasir Nasir-ud-Din Faraj (*restored*)
1412	al-Adil al-Mustain
1412–21	al-Muayyad Saif-ud-Din Tatar
1421	az-Zahir Saif-ud-Din Tatar
1421	al-Muzaffar Ahmad
1421–2	as-Salih Nasir-ud-Din Muhammad
1422–37	al-Ashraf Saif-ud-Din Barsbay
1437–8	al-Aziz Jamal-ud-Din Yusuf
1438–53	az-Zahir Saif-ud-Din Jaqmaq
1453	al-Mansur Fakhr-ud-Din Uthman
1453–61	al-Ashraf Saif-ud-Din Inal

Province of Egypt
Viceroy

1805–48	Mehemet Ali Pasha
1848	Ibrahim Pasha
1848–54	Abbas I
1854–63	Said Pasha
1863–66	Ismail Pasha

Khedive

1866–79	Ismail Pasha
1879–92	Mahmud Tawfiq (Tewfik Pasha)
1892–1914	Abbas II Helmi
1914–17	Hussein Kamel

Monarch – Sultanate of Egypt

1917	Hussein Kamel
1917–22	Ahmed Fouad

Monarch – Kingdom of Egypt

1922–36	Ahmed Fouad I
1936–7	Farouk *Trusteeship*
1937–52	Farouk
1952–3	Ahmed Fouad II

● **Ethiopia**
Monarch – Kingdom of Ethiopia
Zagwe Dynasty

1117–33	Marari
1133–72	Yemrehana Krestos
1172–1212	Gebra Maskal Lalibela
1212–60	Nakueto Laab
1260–8	Yetbarak

Solomonic Dynasty

1268–85	Yekuno Amlak
1285–94	Yagbea Seyon
1294–5	Senfa Ared
1295–6	Hezba Asgad
1296–7	Kedma Asgad
1297–8	Jin Asgad
1298–9	Saba Asgad
1299–1314	Wedem Ared
1314–44	Amda Seyon I
1344–72	Newaya Krestos
1372–82	Newaya Maryam
1382–1411	Dawit I
1411–14	Tewoderos I
1414–29	Yeshak
1429–30	Endreyas
1430–3	Takla Maryam
1433	Sarwe Iyasus
1433–4	Amda Iyasus
1434–68	Zara Yakob Constantine
1468–78	Baeda Maryam I
1478–94	Eskandar
1494	Amda Seyon II
1494–1508	Naod
1508–40	Lebna Dengel Dawit II
1540–59	Galawdewos
1559–63	Minas
1563–97	Sarsa Dengel
1597–1603	Yakob
1603–4	Za Dengel
1604–7	Yakob (*restored*)
1607–32	Susenyos
1632–67	Fasiladas
1667–82	Yohannes I
1682–1706	Iyasu I 'the Great'
1706–08	Takla Haymanot I
1708–11	Tewoflos
1711–16	Yostos
1716–21	Dawit III
1721–30	Asma Giyorgis
1730–55	Iyasu II
1755–69	Iyoas I
1769	Yohannes II
1769–77	Takla Haymanot II
1777–79	Salomon
1779–84	Takla Giyorgis I
1784–8	Iyasu III
1788–9	Takla Giyorgis I (*restored*)
1789–94	Hezekiyas

1794–5	Takla Giyorgis I (*restored*)
1795	Baeda Maryam II
1795–6	Takla Giyorgis I (*restored*)
1796–7	Walda Saloman
1797–8	Yonas
1798–1800	*Period of instability*
1800–1	Demetros
1801–18	Egwala Seyon
1818–21	Iyoas II
1821–6	Gigar
1826	Baeda Maryam III
1826–30	Gigar (*restored*)
1830–2	Iyasu IV
1832	Gabra Krestos
1832	Sahla Dengel
1832	Gabra Krestos (*restored*)
1832–40	Sahla Dengel (*restored*)
1840–1	Yohannes III
1841–50	Sahla Dengel (*restored*)
1850–1	Yohannes III (*restored*)
1851–5	Sahla Dengel (*restored*)
1855–68	Tewoderos II
1868–71	Takla Giyorgis II
1871–89	Yohannes IV
1889–1909	Menyelek II
1909–11	*Regency*
1911–16	Lej Iyasu (Joshua)
1916–28	Zawditu
1928–74	Haile Selassie *Emperor from 1930*

● **France**

Monarch – *Kingdom of the Franks*

House of Charlemagne

768–814	Charlemagne
814–40	Louis I 'the Pious'
840–3	*Civil war*

Monarch – *Kingdom of the West Franks*

House of Charlemagne

843–77	Charles I 'the Bald'
877–9	Louis II 'the Stammerer'
879–84	Carloman *Joint ruler to 882*
879–82	Louis III *Joint ruler*

Monarch – *Kingdom of France*

House of Charlemagne

884–7	Charles II 'the Fat'

House of Capet

888–98	Eudes

House of Charlemagne (restored)

893–922	Charles III 'the Simple' *Rival king to 898*

House of Capet (restored)

922–3	Robert I
923–36	Raoul

House of Charlemagne (restored)

936–54	Louis IV 'd'Outre-Mer'
954–86	Lothaire
986–7	Louis V 'le Fainéant'

House of Capet (restored)

987–96	Hugh Capet
996–1031	Robert II
1031–60	Henri I
1060–1108	Philippe I
1108–37	Louis VI 'the Fat'
1137–79	Louis VII
1179–1223	Philippe II (Philippe-Auguste)
1223–6	Louis VIII 'the Lion'
1226–70	Louis IX (St Louis)
1270–85	Philippe III 'the Bold'
1285–1314	Philippe IV 'the Fair'
1314–16	Louis X 'the Quarrelsome'
1316	Jean I
1316–22	Philippe V 'the Tall'
1322–8	Charles IV 'the Fair'

House of Valois

1328–50	Philippe VI
1350–64	Jean II 'the Good'
1364–80	Charles V 'the Wise'
1380–1422	Charles VI 'the Foolish'
1422–61	Charles VII
1461–83	Louis XI
1483–98	Charles VIII 'the Affable'

House of Valois/Orléans

1498–1515	Louis XII

House of Valois/Angoulême

1515–47	François I
1547–59	Henri II
1559–60	François II
1560–74	Charles IX
1574–89	Henri III

House of Bourbon

1589–1610	Henri IV (*of Navarre*)
1610–43	Louis XIII
1643–1715	Louis XIV
1715–74	Louis XV
1774–93	Louis XVI
1793–95	[Louis XVII *not crowned*]
1792–1804	*Revolutionary Government*

Monarch – French Empire

First Empire

1804–1814	Napoleon I
1815	Napoleon II [*not crowned*]

Monarch – Kingdom of France

House of Bourbon (restored)

1814–24	Louis XVIII
1824–30	Charles X

House of Orléans

1830–48	Louis-Philippe

Second Republic

1848–52	Charles Louis Napoleon Bonaparte

French Empire

Second Empire

1852–70	Napoleon III (Charles Louis Napoleon Bonaparte)

Duke of Lorraine

1697–1729	Leopold
1729–36	Francis III (I, *Holy Roman Emperor*)
1736–66	Stanisław Leszczyński

Duke of Normandy

911–32	Ganger-Hrolf (Rollo)
932–42	William I
942–96	Richard I
996–1027	Richard II
1027–8	Richard III
1028–35	Robert I
1035–87	William II (I *of England*) 'the Conqueror'
1087–1106	Robert Curthose
1106–35	*As England*
1135–44	*Civil war*
1144–50	Geoffrey of Anjou
1150–1204	*As England*
1204–	*Part of France*

● Georgia
Monarch – Kingdom of Georgia
Bagratid Dynasty

1008–14	Bagrat III
1014–27	Giorgi I
1027–72	Bagrat IV
1072–89	Giorgi II
1089–1125	David III
1125–55	Demetrius I
1155	David IV
1155–6	Demetrius I (restored)
1156–1184	Giorgi III *Joint ruler from 1179*
1179–1212	Thamar *Joint ruler to 1184*
1212–23	Giorgi IV
1223–45	Rusudan
1245–50	*No king*
1250–58	David V
1258–69	David VI
1269–73	*No king*
1273–89	Demetrius II
1289–92	Vakhtang II
1292–1301	David VII
1301–7	Vakhtang III
1307–14	Giorgi V
1314–46	Giorgi VI
1346–60	David VIII
1360–95	Bagrat V
1395–1405	Giorgi VII
1405–12	Constantine I
1412–42	Alexander I
1442–6	Vakhtang IV
1446–53	Demetrius III
1453–65	Giorgi VIII
1465–78	Bagrat VI *Rival king*
1465–90	Constantine II *Rival king to 1478*
1490–1810	*Divided into several small states*
1810–1991	*Russian rule*

● Germany
Elector of Brandenburg
House of Hohenzollern

1415–40	Friedrich I (*of Nuremberg*)
1440–71	Friedrich II
1471–86	Albrecht (Albert III) Achilles
1486–99	Johann Cicero
1499–1535	Joachim I
1535–71	Joachim II
1571–98	Johann Georg
1598–1608	Joachim Friedrich
1608–20	Johann Sigismund
1620–40	Georg Wilhelm
1640–88	Friedrich Wilhelm 'the Great Elector'
1688–1701	Friedrich III

King of Prussia
House of Hohenzollern

1701–13	Friedrich I (III *of Brandenburg*)
1713–40	Friedrich Wilhelm I
1740–86	Friedrich II 'the Great'
1786–97	Friedrich Wilhelm II
1797–1840	Friedrich Wilhelm III
1840–61	Friedrich Wilhelm IV
1861–71	Wilhelm I

Monarch (Kaiser) – German Empire
House of Hohenzollern

1871–88	Wilhelm I
1888–	Friedrich (III *of Prussia*)
1888–1918	Wilhelm II

Baden – Margrave of Baden
Baden – House of Zahringen

c.1100–30	Hermann I
1130–60	Hermann II
1160–90	Hermann III
1190–1243	Hermann IV
1243–50	Hermann V
1250–68	Friedrich I
1268–88	Rudolf I
1288–95	Rudolf II
1295–7	Hesso
1297–1332	Rudolf III
1332–5	Rudolf Hesso
1335–48	Rudolf IV
1348–53	Friedrich II
1353–72	Rudolf V
1372–91	Rudolf VI
1391–1431	Bernhard I
1431–53	Jakob I
1453–75	Karl I
1475–1527	Christoph

Baden-Baden – House of Zahringen

1527–36	Bernhardt II
1536–69	Philibert

1569–88	Philipp
1588–96	Eduard Fortunatus
1596–1622	*No margrave*
1622–77	Wilhelm
1677–1707	Ludwig-Wilhelm
1707–61	Ludwig-Georg
1761–71	August-Georg

Baden-Durlach – House of Zahringen

1527–53	Ernst
1553–77	Karl II
1577–90	Jakob II *Joint ruler*
1577–1604	Ernst-Friedrich *Joint ruler*
1577–1622	Georg-Friedrich *Joint ruler to 1604*
1622–59	Friedrich III
1659–77	Friedrich IV
1677–1709	Friedrich V
1709–38	Karl III
1738–1806	Karl-Friedrich *Margrave of Baden-Baden from 1771*

Grand-Duke of Baden
House of Zahringen

1806–11	Karl-Friedrich
1811–18	Karl
1818–30	Ludwig I
1830–52	Leopold
1852–8	Ludwig II
1858–1907	Friedrich I
1907–18	Friedrich II

Bavaria – Elector of Bavaria
House of Wittelsbach

1623–51	Maximilian I
1651–79	Ferdinand Maria
1679–1706	Maximilian II Emanuel
1706–14	*No elector*
1714–26	Maximilian II Emanuel (*restored*)
1726–45	Karl Albrecht (Karl VII, *Holy Roman Emperor*)
1745–77	Maximilian III Joseph
1777–99	Karl Theodor *Elector Palatine of the Rhine from 1742*
1799–1806	Maximilian IV Josef

King of Bavaria
House of Wittelsbach

1806–25	Maximilian I Josef
1825–48	Ludwig I

1848–64	Maximilian II
1864–86	Ludwig II
1886–1913	Otto
1913–18	Ludwig III

Brunswick – Duke of Brunswick
House of Welf

1735–80	Karl I
1780–1806	Karl II

House of Bonaparte

1807–13	Jérôme Bonaparte *King of Westphalia*

House of Welf

1813–15	Friedrich-Wilhelm
1815–30	Karl III
1830–84	Wilhelm

Hanover – Elector of Hanover
House of Welf

1692–8	Ernst-August
1698–1714	Georg (George I *of Great Britain*)
1714–1814	*As Great Britain*

King of Hanover
House of Welf

1814–37	*As Great Britain*
1837–51	Ernest Augustus
1851–66	Georg V

Hesse – Landgrave of Hesse-Darmstadt

1567–96	Georg I
1596–1626	Ludwig V
1626–61	Georg II
1661–78	Ludwig VI
1678	Ludwig VII
1678–1739	Ernst-Ludwig
1739–68	Ludwig VIII
1768–90	Ludwig IX
1790–1806	Ludwig X

Grand Duke of Hesse

1806–30	Ludwig I (X)
1830–48	Ludwig II
1848–77	Ludwig III
1877–92	Ludwig IV
1892–1918	Ernst-Ludwig

Mecklenburg – Duke of Mecklenburg
Mecklenburg-Strelitz

1611–58	Adolf-Friedrich I

1658–92	Christian-Ludwig I
1692–1713	Friedrich-Wilhelm
1713–47	Christian-Ludwig II
1747–56	Karl-Leopold
1756–85	Friedrich
1785–1815	Friedrich-Franz I

Mecklenburg-Schwerin

1701–8	Adolf-Friedrich II
1708–52	Adolf-Friedrich III
1752–94	Adolf-Friedrich IV
1794–1815	Karl

Grand Duke of Mecklenburg
Mecklenburg-Schwerin

1815–37	Friedrich-Franz I
1837–42	Paul
1842–83	Friedrich-Franz II
1883–97	Friedrich-Franz III
1897–1918	Friedrich-Franz IV

Mecklenburg-Strelitz

1815–16	Karl
1816–60	Georg
1860–1904	Friedrich-Wilhelm
1904–14	Adolf-Friedrich V
1914–18	Adolf-Friedrich VI

Oldenburg – Duke of Oldenburg

1777–85	Friedrich-August I
1785–1823	Wilhelm
1823–29	Peter I
1829–53	August
1853–1900	Peter II
1900–18	Friedrich-August II

Palatine – Count Palatine of the Rhine
House of Wittelsbach

1214–27	Ludwig I
1227–53	Otto
1253–5	Heinrich *Joint ruler*
1253–94	Ludwig II *Joint ruler to 1255*
1294–1317	Rudolf I *Joint ruler*
1294–1329	Ludwig III *Joint ruler to 1317*
1329–53	Rudolf II
1353–6	Rupprecht I

Elector Palatine of the Rhine
House of Wittelsbach

1356–90	Rupprecht I
1390–8	Rupprecht II
1398–1410	Rupprecht III

1410–36	Ludwig IV
1436–49	Ludwig V
1449–76	Friedrich I
1476–1508	Philipp
1508–44	Ludwig VI
1544–56	Friedrich II
1556–9	Otto Heinrich
1559–76	Friedrich III
1576–83	Ludwig VII
1583–1610	Friedrich IV
1610–23	Friedrich V, *King of Bohemia 1619–20*
1623–49	*Bavarian rule*
1649–80	Karl Ludwig
1680–5	Karl
1685–90	Philipp Wilhelm
1690–1716	Johann Wilhelm
1716–42	Karl Philipp
1742–99	Karl Theodor
1799–1918	*Part of Bavaria*

Saxony – Elector of Saxony
House of Wettin

1423–8	Friedrich I (*of Meissen*)
1428–64	Friedrich II
1464–85	Albrecht (V) *Joint ruler*
1464–86	Ernst *Joint ruler to 1485*
1486–1525	Friedrich III
1525–32	Johann
1532–47	Johann-Friedrich
1547–53	Moritz
1553–86	August
1586–91	Christian I
1591–1611	Christian II
1611–56	Johann-Georg I
1656–80	Johann-Georg II
1680–91	Johann-Georg III
1691–4	Johann-Georg IV
1694–1733	Friedrich-August I (Augustus II *of Poland*)
1733–63	Friedrich-August II
1763	Friedrich-Christian
1763–1806	Friedrich-August III

King of Saxony

1806–27	Friedrich-August I
1827–36	Anton
1836–54	Friedrich-August II
1854–73	Johann
1873–1902	Albrecht

1902–4	Georg
1904–18	Friedrich-August III

Württemberg – Count of Württemberg

1236–41	Eberhard
1241–65	Ulrich I
1265–79	Ulrich II
1279–1325	Eberhard I
1325–44	Ulrich III
1344–66	Ulrich IV *Joint ruler*
1344–92	Eberhard II *Joint ruler to 1366*
1392–1417	Eberhard III
1417–19	Eberhard IV
1419–50	Ludwig IV (Louis) I (Urach from 1441)
1450–80	Ulrich V (Stuttgart from 1441)
1450–7	Ludwig V (Louis) II (Urach)
1457–95	Eberhard V (Urach)
1480–95	Eberhard VI (Stuttgart)

Duke of Württemberg

1495–96	Eberhard VI *Joint ruler*
1495–1504	Eberhard VII *Joint ruler to 1496*
1504–19	Ulrich VI
1520–34	*No duke*
1534–50	Ulrich VI (*restored*)
1550–68	Christopher
1568–93	Ludwig VI
1593–1608	Friedrich I
1608–28	Johann-Friedrich
1628–74	Eberhard VIII
1674–7	Wilhelm-Ludwig
1677–1733	Eberhard-Ludwig
1733–7	Karl-Alexander
1737–93	Karl-Eugen
1793–5	Ludwig-Eugen
1795–7	Friedrich-Eugen
1797–1806	Friedrich I

King of Württemberg

1806–16	Friedrich I
1816–64	Wilhelm I
1864–91	Karl
1891–1918	Wilhelm II

● **Ghana**

King of Ashanti

c.1630–60	Oti Akenten
1660–97	Obiri Yeboa
1697–1731	Osei Tutu
1731–42	Opuku Ware
1742–52	Kwasi Obodum
1752–81	Osei Kojo
1781–97	Osei Kwamina
1797–1800	Opuku Fofie
1800–24	Osei Bonsu
1824–38	Osei Yaw
1838–67	Kwaku Dua I
1867–74	Kofi Karikari
1874–84	Mensa Bonsu
1884–8	Kwaku Dua II
1888–96	Kwaku Dua III Prempeh

King of Dagomba

c.1500	Nyagse
?	Zulande
?	Nagalogu
?	Datorli
?	Buruguyomda
?	Zoligu
?	Zonman
?	Ninmitoni
?	Dimani
?	Yanzo
?	Dariziegu
c.1660	Luro
?	Tutugri
?	Zagale
?	Zokuli
?	Gungobili
c.1700	Zangina
?	Andani Sigili
?	Ziblim Bunbiogo
c.1740	Gariba
?	Ziblim Na Saa
?	Ziblim Bandamda
?	Andani I
?	Mahama I
c.1820	Ziblim Kulunku
?	Sumani Zoli
c.1850	Yakubu I
?	Abudulai I
?–1899	Andani II
1899–1900	Darimani

1900–20	al-Hasan
1920–38	Abudulai II
1938–48	Mahama II
1948–53	Mahama III
1953–68	Abudulai III
1968–9	Andani III
1969–74	Muhammad Abudulai IV
1974–	Yakubu II

● Greece
Monarch – Kingdom of Greece

1832–62	Otho (Otto *of Wittelsbach*)
1863–1913	Georgios (George) I
1913–17	Konstantinos (Constantine) I
1917–20	Alexandros (Alexander)
1920–2	Konstantinos (Constantine) I (*restored*)
1922–4	Georgios (George) II

Monarch – Kingdom of Greece

1935	Georgios Kondylls *Regent*
1935–47	Georgios (George) II
1947–64	Pavlos (Paul) I
1964–7	Konstantinos (Constantine) II
1967–73	*Military junta*
1973	Georgios Papadopoulos *Regent*

King of Sparta

Sparta had a double kingship – there were two kings at any one time, usually one from each dynasty.

Agiad Dynasty

c.815–c.785 BC	Agesilaus I
c.785–c.760 BC	Archilaus
c.760–c.740 BC	Teleclus
c.740–c.700 BC	Alcmenes
c.700–c.665 BC	Polydorus
c.665–c.640 BC	Eurycrates
c.640–c.615 BC	Anaxander
c.615–c.590 BC	Eurycratides
c.590–c.560 BC	Leon
c.560–c.520 BC	Anaxandridas I
c.520–c.489 BC	Cleomenes I
c.489–480 BC	Leonidas I
480–c.458 BC	Pleistarchus

c.458–444 BC	Pleistoanax
444–394 BC	Pausanias
394–380 BC	Agesipolis I
380–371 BC	Cleombrotus I
371–369 BC	Agesipolis II
369–309 BC	Cleomenes II
309–264 BC	Areus I
264–c.262 BC	Acrotatus
c.262–254 BC	Areus II
254–242 BC	Leonidas II
242–241 BC	Cleombrotus II
241–235 BC	Leonidas II (*restored*)
235–221 BC	Cleomenes III
227–221 BC	Euclidas
219–215 BC	Agesipolis III

Eurypontid Dynasty

c.775–c.750 BC	Charillus
c.750–c.720 BC	Nicander
c.720–c.675 BC	Theopompus
c.675–c.645 BC	Anaxandridas I
c.645–c.625 BC	Zeuxidamus
c.625–c.600 BC	Anaxidamus
c.600–c.575 BC	Archidamus I
c.575–c.550 BC	Agasicles
c.550–c.515 BC	Ariston
c.515–c.491 BC	Demaratus
c.491–469 BC	Leotychidas
469–427 BC	Archidamus II
427–398 BC	Agis II
398–360 BC	Agesilaus II
360–338 BC	Archidamus III
338–331 BC	Agis III
331–c.300 BC	Eudamidas I
c.300–c.270 BC	Archidamus IV
c.270–c.245 BC	Eudamidas II
c.245–241 BC	Agis IV
241–228 BC	Eudamidas III
228–227 BC	Archidamus V
219–210 BC	Lycurgus
210–206 BC	Pelops
206–192 BC	Nabis

King of Macedonia
Argead Dynasty

c.650–c.630 BC	Perdiccas I
c.630–c.620 BC	Argaeus I
c.620–c.590 BC	Philip I
c.590–c.570 BC	Aeropus I
c.570–c.540 BC	Alcetas

c.540–c.495 BC	Amyntas I
c.495–c.452 BC	Alexander I
c.452–c.413 BC	Perdiccas II
c.413–c.399 BC	Archelaus
c.399–c.398 BC	Orestes
c.398–c.395 BC	Aeropus II
c.395–c.394 BC	Amyntas II
c.394–c.393 BC	Pausanias
c.393 BC	Amyntas III
c.393–c.392 BC	Argaeus II
c.392–369 BC	Amyntas III *(restored)*
369–368 BC	Alexander II
368–365 BC	Ptolemy I
365–359 BC	Perdiccas III
359–336 BC	Philip II
336–323 BC	Alexander III 'the Great'
323–317 BC	Philip III Arrhidaeus *Joint king* (Antipater *Regent to 319 BC*)
323–310 BC	Alexander IV *Joint king to 317 BC*
310–305 BC	*No king* (Cassander *Ruler of Macedonia*)

Antipatrid Dynasty

305–297 BC	Cassander
297 BC	Philip IV
297–294 BC	Antipater *(East)*; Alexander V *(West)*

Antigonid Dynasty

294–288 BC	Demetrius I Poliorcetes
288–285 BC	Pyrrhus *King of Epirus; rival king*
288–281 BC	Lysimachus
281–279 BC	Ptolemy II Ceraunus
279–276 BC	*Galatian invasion*
276–274 BC	Antigonus II Gonatas
274–272 BC	Pyrrhus *King of Epirus (restored)*
272–239 BC	Antigonus II Gonatas *(restored)*
239–229 BC	Demetrius II
229–221 BC	Antigonus III Doson
221–179 BC	Philip V
179–168 BC	Perseus

● **Holy Roman Empire**
Ruler
Many monarchs ruled as king before being crowned emperor, especially in the early period; dates given are of accession as king.

911–19	Conrad I (*of Franconia*)
919–36	Henry I 'the Fowler' (*of Saxony*)
936–73	Otto I 'the Great'
973–83	Otto II
983–1002	Otto III
1002–24	Henry II (*of Bavaria*)
1024–39	Conrad II (*of Franconia*)
1039–56	Henry III
1056–1106	Henry IV
1077–1080	Rudolf (*of Swabia*) *Rival*
1081–93	Hermann (*of Salm*) *Rival*
1093–1101	Conrad (*of Franconia*) *Rival*
1106–25	Henry V
1125–37	Lothair III (*of Supplinberg*)
1138–52	Conrad III (*of Hohenstauffen*) (*Duke of Franconia*)
1152–90	Frederick I Barbarossa (*Duke of Swabia*)
1191–7	Henry VI
1198–1208	Philip (*of Swabia*) *Rival*
1198–1218	Otto IV (*of Saxony*) *Rival*
1212–50	Frederick II 'the Wonder of the World' (*of Sicily*)
1246–7	Henry Raspe (*of Thuringia*) *Rival*
1247–56	William (II *of Holland*) *Rival*
1250–4	Conrad IV
1254–7	Conradin of Swabia
1257–73	Alfonso 'the Astronomer' (X *of Castile*) *Rival*
1257–72	Richard of Cornwall *Rival*
1273–91	Rudolf I (*of Habsburg*)
1292–8	Adolf (*of Nassau*)
1298–1308	Albert I (*of Austria*)
1308–13	Henry VII (IV *of Luxemburg*)
1314–30	Frederick (II *of Austria*) *Rival*
1314–47	Ludwig 'the Bavarian' (Louis IV *of Upper Bavaria*)
1349	Gunther (*of Schwarzburg*) *Rival*
1346–78	Charles IV (*of Luxemburg and Bohemia*)
1378–1410	Wenceslas (IV *of Bohemia*)

1400	Frederick (*of Brunswick-Luneburg*) *Rival*
1400–10	Ruprecht (III *of the Palatinate*) *Rival*
1410–11	Jobst (*of Moravia*) *Rival*
1410–37	Sigismund (*of Bohemia-Hungary*)
1437–9	Albert II (V *of Austria*)
1440–93	Frederick III (*of Styria*)
1493–1519	Maximilian I
1519–56	Charles V (I *of Spain*)
1556–64	Ferdinand I
1564–76	Maximilian II
1576–1612	Rudolf II
1612–19	Matthias
1619–37	Ferdinand II (*of Styria*)
1637–58	Ferdinand III
1658–1705	Leopold I
1705–11	Joseph I
1711–40	Charles VI
1740–2	*Interregnum*
1742–5	Charles VII (*of Bavaria*)
1745–65	Francis I (III *of Lorraine*)
1765–90	Joseph II
1790–2	Leopold II
1792–1806	Francis II *Emperor of Austria to 1835*

See also Austria

● **Hungary**
Monarch – Kingdom of Hungary
Arpad Dynasty

c.975–1038	István (St Stephen) I
1038–41	Peter Orseolo
1041–4	Samuel Aba
1044–6	Peter Orseolo (*restored*)
1046–60	András I
1060–3	Béla I
1063–74	Salomon
1074–7	Géza I
1077–95	Ladislas I
1095–1116	Kálmán
1116–31	István II
1131–41	Béla II
1141–62	Géza II
1161–72	István III

1162–3	Ladislas II *Rival king*
1163–5	István IV *Rival king*
1172–96	Béla III
1196–1204	Emeric
1204–5	Ladislas III
1205–35	András II
1235–70	Béla IV
1270–2	István V
1272–90	Ladislas IV
1290–1301	András III

Later Kings

1301–5	Vaclav (III *of Bohemia*)
1305–8	Otto (III *of Bavaria*)
1308–42	Charles Robert of Anjou
1342–82	Lajos I 'the Great' *King Louis of Poland from 1370*
1382–95	Mary *Joint ruler from 1387*
1387–1439	*As Holy Roman Emperor*
1440–44	Vladislav Jagiellon (VI *of Poland*)
1444–57	Ladislas V
1458–90	Mattias I Corvinus
1490–1526	*As Bohemia*
1526–1866	*Austrian rule*
1866–1916	Franz Josef (Francis Joseph) I *Dual monarchy*
1916–18	Károly IV (Charles)

● **India**
Early Emperors
Maurya Dynasty

c.320–c.300 BC	Chandragupta Maurya
c.300–c.273 BC	Bindusara
c.273–c.232 BC	Ashoka Vardhana
c.232–c.225 BC	Dasaratha *East*
c.232–c.225 BC	Kunala *West*
c.225 BC–?	Samprati
?	Salisuka
?	Devadharma
?–194 BC	Satamdhanu
c.194–c.187 BC	Brihadratha

Sunga Dynasty

c.187–c.151 BC	Pushyamitra Sunga
c.151–c.143 BC	Agnimitra
c.143–c.133 BC	Vasujyeshtha
c.133 BC–?	Vasumitra
?	Andhraka

?	Pulindaka
?	Ghosha
?	Vajramitra
c.100–c.85 BC	Bhagavata
c.85–c.75 BC	Devabhumi

Kanva Dynasty

c.75–c.66 BC	Vasudeva
c.66–c.52 BC	Bhumimitra
c.52–c.40 BC	Narayana
c.40–c.30 BC	Susarman

Sultan of Delhi

Slave Dynasty

1206–10	Qutb-ud-Din Aibak
1210–11	Aram Shah
1211–36	Shams-ud-Din Iltutmish
1236	Rukn-ud-Din Firuz Shah
1236–40	Jalalat-ud-Din Radiyya
1240–2	Muizz-ud-Din Bahram Shah
1242–6	Ala-ud-Din Masud Shah
1246–66	Nasir-ud-Din Mahmud Shah
1266–87	Ghiyath-ud-Din Balban
1287–90	Muizz-ud-Din Kayqubad
1290	Shams-ud-Din Kayumarth

Khalji Dynasty

1290–6	Jalal-ud-Din Firuz Shah
1296	Rukn-ud-Din Ibrahim Shah
1296–1316	Ala-ud-Din Muhammad Shah
1316	Shihab-ud-Din Umar Shah
1316–20	Qutb-ud-Din Mubarak Shah
1320	Nasir-ud-Din Khusraw Shah

Tughluq Dynasty

1320–5	Ghiyath-ud-Din Tughluq Shah I
1325–51	Ghiyath-ud-Din Muhammad Shah I
1351	Mahmud Shah
1351–88	Firuz Shah
1388–9	Ghiyath-ud-Din Tughluq Shah II
1389–90	Abu-Bakr Shah
1390–3	Nasir-ud-Din Muhammad Shah II
1393	Ala-ud-Din Sikandar Shah
1393–1413	Nasir-ud-Din Mahmud Shah
1413–14	Dawlat Khan Lodi

Lodi Dynasty

1414–21	Khidr Khan
1421–35	Muizz-ud-Din Mubarak Shah
1435–46	Muhammad Shah
1446–51	Ala-ud-Din Alam Shah

Sayyid Dynasty

1451–89	Bahlul Lodi
1489–1517	Nizam Shah Sikandar
1517–26	Ibrahim Lodi

Mughal Emperors

| 1526–30 | Zahir-ud-Din Babur |
| 1530–40 | Nasir-ud-Din Humayun |

Sultan of Delhi

Surrid Dynasty

1540–5	Shir Shah Sur
1545–54	Islam Shah
1554	Muhammad Adil Shah
1554–5	Ibrahim Shah
1555–6	Ahmad Khan Sikandar Shah

Mughal Emperors

1556	Nasir-ud-Din Humayun (*restored*)
1556–1605	Jalal-ud-Din Akbar I
1605–27	Nur-ud-Din Jahangir
1627–8	Dawar Bakhsh
1628–58	Shihab-ud-Din Shah Jahan I
1658–1707	Muhyi-ud-Din Aurangzib Alamgir I
1707	Azam Shah
1707–12	Shah Alam Bahadur Shah I
1712	Azim-ush-Shan
1712–13	Muizz-ud-Din Jahandar
1713–19	Farrukhsiyar
1719	Shams-ud-Din Rafi-ud-Darajat
1719	Rafi-ud-Dawlah Shah Jahan II
1719	Nikusiyar
1719–48	Nasir-ud-Din Muhammad
1748–54	Ahmad Shah Bahadur
1754–60	Aziz-ud-Din Alamgir II
1760	Shah Jahan III
1760–88	Jalal-ud-Din Ali Jauhar Shah Alam II
1788	Bidar Bakht

1788–1806	Jalal-ud-Din Ali Jauhar Shah Alam II (*restored*)
1806–37	Muin-ud-Din Akbar II
1837–58	Siraj-ud-Din Bahadur Shah II

● Indian States

Amber/Jaipur – Raja/Maharaja

c.1128–c.1136	Dulha Rao
c.1136–?	Kanka
?	Maidal
?	Hunadeva
?–c.1185	Kantal I
c.1185–?	Pujanadeva
?	Malesi
?	Byala
?	Rajadeva
?–1276	Kilhan
1276–?	Kantal II
?	Jansi
?	Udayakarna
?	Nara Singh
?	Banbir
?	Udha Rao
?–1502	Chandrasena
1502–34	Prithvi I
1534–?	Bhima
?–1547	Ratan
1547–?	Baharmalla
?–1589	Bhagwan Das
1589–1614	Man Singh I
1614	Jagat Singh I
1614–22	Bhao Singh
1622–67	Jaya Singh I
1667–88	Rama Singh I
1688–1700	Bishan Singh
1700–43	Sawai Jaya Singh II
1743–50	Ishwari Singh
1750–68	Madhu Singh I
1768–78	Prithvi Singh II
1778–1803	Pratap Singh
1803–18	Jagat Singh II
1818–35	Jaya Singh III
1835–81	Rama Singh II
1881–1922	Sawai Madhu Singh II
1922–49	Sawai Man Singh II

Baroda – Maharaja

1721–32	Pilaji Rao Geckwar
1732–68	Damaji Rao
1768–71	Govind Rao
1771–89	Sayaji Rao I
1789–93	Manaji Rao
1793–1800	Govind Rao (*restored*)
1800–18	Anand Rao
1818–47	Sayaji Rao II
1847–56	Ganpat Rao
1856–70	Khande Rao
1870–5	Malhar Rao
1875–1939	Sayaji Rao III
1939–49	Pratap Singh

Bharatpur – Maharaja

1722–56	Badan Singh
1756–63	Suraj Mal
1763–8	Jawahir Singh
1768–9	Ratan Singh
1769–76	Kesri Singh
1776–1805	Ranjit Singh
1805–23	Randhir Singh
1823–5	Baldeo Singh
1825–6	Durjan Sal
1826–53	Balwant Singh
1853–93	Jaswant Singh
1893–1900	Ram Singh
1900–29	Brijendra Sawai Kishan Singh
1929–48	Brijendra Singh

Bhopal – Nawab

1723–40	Dost Muhammad Khan
1740	Muhammad Khan
1740–54	Yar Muhammad Khan
1754–77	Faid Muhammad Khan
1777–1807	Hayat Muhammad Khan
1807–16	Wazir Muhammad Khan
1816–20	Nadhr Muhammad Khan
1820–44	Kudsiyya Begum
1844–68	Sikandar Begum
1868–1901	Shah Jahan Begum
1901–26	Sultan Jahan Begum
1926–48	Hamid-Allah Khan

Bikaner – Raja/Maharaja

1465–1504	Bika Rao
1504–5	Naro
1505–26	Lunkaran

1526–42	Jetsi
1542–71	Kalyan Singh
1571–1612	Raya Singh
1612–13	Dalpat Singh
1613–31	Sur Singh
1631–69	Karan Singh
1669–98	Anup Singh
1698–1700	Sarup Singh
1700–36	Sujan Singh
1736–45	Zorawar Singh
1745–87	Gaja Singh
1787	Raja Singh
1787	Pratap Singh
1787–1828	Surat Singh
1828–51	Ratan Singh
1851–72	Sardar Singh
1872–87	Dungar Singh
1887–1943	Ganga Singh
1943–9	Sadul Singh

Bundi – Rao/Maharao

c.1342–?	Devi Singh
?	Samar Singh
?	Napurji
?	Majirhi
?	Bar Singh
?–1503	Subhand Deva
1503–?	Narain Das
?–1531	Suraj Mal
1531–?	Surthan
?–1554	Arjun
1554–85	Surjan
1585–1607	Bhoja
1607–31	Ratan
1631–58	Chhatra Sal
1658–78	Bhao Singh
1678–1706	Aniruddha Singh
1706–29	Budh Singh
1729–48	Dalel Singh
1748–70	Ummed Singh
1770	Ajit Singh
1770–1821	Bishan Singh
1821–89	Ram Singh
1889–1927	Raghubir Singh
1927–45	Ishwari Singh
1945–9	Bahadur Singh

Cannanore – Raja

1545–91	Ali Adi-Raja I
1591–1607	Abu Bakr Adi-Raja I
1607–10	Abu Bakr Adi-Raja II
1610–47	Muhammad Ali Adi-Raja I
1647–55	Muhammad Ali Adi-Raja II
1655–6	Kamal Adi-Raja
1656–91	Muhammad Ali Adi-Raja III
1691–1704	Ali Adi-Raja II
1704–20	Kunhi Amsa Adi-Raja I
1720–8	Muhammad Ali Adi-Raja IV
1728–32	Harrabichi Kadavube Adi-Raja Bibi
1732–45	Junumabe Adi-Raja Bibi I
1745–77	Kunhi Amsa Adi-Raja II
1777–1819	Junumabe Adi-Raja Bibi II
1819–38	Mariambe Adi-Raja Bibi
1838–52	Hayashabe Adi-Raja Bibi
1852–70	Abdul-Rahman Ali Adi-Raja I
1870–99	Musa Ali Adi-Raja
1899–1907	Muhammad Ali Adi-Raja V
1907–11	Imbichi Adi-Raja Bibi
1911–21	Ahmad Ali Adi-Raja
1921–31	Ayisha Adi-Raja Bibi
1931–46	Abdul-Rahman Ali Adi-Raja II
1946–9	Mariyumma Adi-Raja Bibi

Cochin – Raja

1500–3	Unni Rama Koil I
1503–37	Unni Rama Koil II
1537–65	Vira Kerala Varma I
1565–1601	Kesara Rama Varma
1601–15	Vira Kerala Varma II
1615–24	Ravi Varma I
1624–37	Vira Kerala Varma III
1637–45	Goda Varma I
1645–6	Vira Rayira Varma
1646–50	Vira Kerala Varma IV
1650–6	Rama Varma I
1656–8	Gangadhara Lakshmi
1658–62	Rama Varma II
1662–3	Goda Varma II
1663–87	Vira Kerala Varma V
1687–93	Rama Varma III
1693–7	Ravi Varma II
1697–1701	Rama Varma IV
1701–21	Rama Varma V
1721–31	Ravi Varma III
1731–46	Rama Varma VI
1746–9	Kerala Varma I

1749–60	Rama Varma VII
1760–75	Kerala Varma II
1775–90	Rama Varma VIII
1790–1805	Rama Varna Saktan Tampuran
1805–9	Rama Varma IX
1809–28	Kerala Varma III
1828–37	Rama Varma X
1837–44	Rama Varma XI
1844–51	Rama Varma XII
1851–3	Kerala Varma IV
1853–64	Ravi Varma IV
1864–88	Rama Varma XIII
1888–95	Kerala Varma V
1895–1914	Rama Varma XIV
1914–32	Rama Varma XV
1932–41	Rama Varma XVI
1941–3	Kerala Varma VI
1943–6	Ravi Varma V
1946–8	Kerala Varma VII
1948–9	Rama Varma XVII

Cutch – Rao/Maharao

1548–85	Khengar I
1585–1631	Bharmal I
1631–45	Bhojaraja
1645–54	Khengar II
1654–62	Tamachi
1662–97	Rayadhan I
1697–1715	Pragmal I
1715–18	Godji I
1718–41	Desal I
1741–60	Lakha
1760–78	Godji II
1778–1814	Rayadhan II
1814–19	Bharmal II
1819–60	Desal II
1860–76	Pragmal II
1876–1942	Khengar III
1942–8	Vijayaraja
1948	Madan Singh

Gwalior – Maharaja

1726–45	Ranoji Sindhia
1745–55	Jayappa
1755–61	Jankoji I
1761–94	Madhava Rao I
1794–1827	Daulat Rao
1827–43	Jankoji Rao II
1843–86	Jayaji Rao
1886–1925	Madhava Rao II
1925–48	Jivaji Rao

Hyderab – Nizam

1724–48	Qamar-ud-Din Nizam-ul-Mulk Asaf Jah
1748–50	Muhammad Nasir Jang
1750–1	Muzaffar Jang
1751–62	Asaf-ud-Dawlah Salabat Jang
1762–1802	Nizam Ali
1802–29	Akbar Ali Khan Sikandar Jah
1829–57	Nasir-ud-Dawlah Farkhundah Ali
1857–69	Afzal-ud-Dawlah
1869–1911	Mahbub Ali Khan
1911–48	Uthman Ali Khan Bahadur Jang

Indore – Maharaja

1728–64	Malhar Rao I Holkar
1764–6	Malle Rao
1765–95	Ahalyu Bai
1795–8	Tukoji Holkar
1798–1811	Jaswant Rao I
1811–34	Malhar Rao II
1834–43	Hari Rao
1843–86	Tukoji Rao II
1886–1903	Shivaji Rao
1903–26	Tukoji Rao III
1926–48	Jaswant Rao II

Jaipur see Amber

Jaisalmer – Rawal/Maharawal

c.1180–?	Jaisal
?	Salivahan I
?	Baijal
?–c.1219	Kelan
c.1219–c.1250	Chachigdeva I
c.1250–c.1278	Karan Singh I
c.1278–c.1281	Lakhasena
c.1281	Punyapala
c.1281–c.1300	Jait Singh I
c.1300	Mulraja I
c.1300–c.1331	Duda
c.1331– c.1361	Ghar Singh
1361–?	Kehar
?–1436	Lakhmana
1436–c.1448	Bairi Singh
c.1448–67	Chachigdeva II

1467–96	Devidas
1496–1528	Jait Singh II
1528	Karan Singh II
1528–50	Lunkaran
1550–61	Malladeva
1561–77	Har Raja
1577–1613	Bhima
1613–50	Kalyandas
1650	Manohardas
1650–61	Sabal Singh
1661–1702	Amar Singh
1702–7	Jaswant Singh
1707–21	Budh Singh
1721–2	Tej Singh
1722	Sawai Singh
1722–62	Akhai Singh
1762–1819	Mulraja II
1819–46	Gaja Singh
1846–64	Ranjit Singh
1864–91	Bairi Sal
1891–1914	Salivahan II
1914–49	Jawahir Singh
1949	Girdhar Singh

Jodhpur see Marwar

Kashmir (I) – Sultan
Swati Dynasty

1339–49	Shams-ud-Din Shah Mirza Swati
1349–50	Jamshid
1350–9	Ala-ud-Din Ali Shir
1359–78	Shihab-ud-Din Shirashamak
1378–94	Qutb-ud-Din Hindal
1394–1416	Sikandar
1416–20	Ali Mirza Khan
1420–70	Zail-ul-Abidin Shahi Khan
1470–1	Haidar Shah Hajji Khan
1471–89	Hasan
1489–90	Muhammad
1490–8	Fath Shah
1498–9	Muhammad (restored)
1499–1500	Fath Shah (restored)
1500–26	Muhammad (restored)
1526–7	Ibrahim
1527–9	Nazuk
1529–33	Muhammad (restored)
1533–40	Shams-ud-Din II
1540	Nazuk (restored)
1540–51	Haidar Dughlat

1551–2	Nazuk (restored)
1552–5	Ibrahim (restored)
1555–7	Ismail
1557–61	Habib

Chak Dynasty

1561–3	Ghazi Khan Chak
1563–9	Nasr-ud-Din Husain
1569–79	Zahir-ud-Din Ali
1579–86	Nasr-ud-Din Yusuf
1586–9	Yaqub

Kashmir (II) – Maharaja

1846–57	Gulab Singh
1857–85	Rambir Singh
1885–1925	Partab Singh
1925–52	Hari Singh

Kolhapur – Maharaja

1700–12	Shivaji I
1712–60	Shambhuji
1760–1812	Shivaji II
1812–21	Shambhu
1821–37	Shahaji I
1837–66	Shivaji III
1866–70	Rajaram I
1870–83	Shivaji IV
1883–1922	Shahu
1922–1940	Rajaram II
1942–47	Shivaji V
1947–9	Shahaji II

Kotah – Rao/Maharao

1625–56	Madhu Singh
1656–7	Mokund Singh
1657–69	Jagat Singh
1669	Paim Singh
1669–85	Kishor Singh I
1685–1707	Ram Singh I
1707–19	Bhima Singh I
1719–23	Arjun Singh
1723–56	Durjan Sal
1756–9	Ajit Singh
1759–65	Chhatra Sal I
1765–70	Goman Singh
1770–1819	Ummed Singh I
1819–28	Kishor Singh II
1828–66	Ram Singh II
1866–89	Chhatra Sal II
1889–1941	Ummed Singh II

1941–9	Bhima Singh II

Lahore – Maharaja

1799–1839	Ranjit Singh
1839–40	Kharak Singh
1840	Nao Nehal Singh
1840–1	Chand Kaur
1841–3	Sher Singh
1843–9	Dalip Singh

Marwar/Jodhpur – Raja/Maharaja

1382–?	Chunda Rao
?	Kanha
?	Sata
?–1438	Ranamalla
1438–88	Jodha
1488–91	Satal
1491–1515	Suja
1515–32	Ganga
1532–84	Malladeva
1584–95	Udaya Singh Raja
1595–1620	Sura Singh
1620–38	Gaja Singh
1638–80	Jaswant Singh I
1680–1725	Ajit Singh
1725–50	Abhaya Singh
1750–1	Rama Singh
1751–2	Bakht Singh
1752	Vijaya Singh
1752–73	Rama Singh (restored)
1773–92	Vijaya Singh (restored)
1792–1803	Bhim Singh
1803–43	Man Singh
1843–73	Takht Singh
1873–95	Jaswant Singh II
1895–1911	Sardar Singh
1911–18	Sumer Singh
1918–47	Umaid Singh
1947–9	Hanwant Singh

Mewar/Udaipur – Rana/Maharana

730–c.753	Khommana I
753–?	Mattata
?	Bhartripatta I
?	Simha
?	Khommana II
?	Mahayaka
940–c.950	Khommana III
950–c.960	Bhartripatta II
960–c.971	Allata

971–c.977	Naravahana
977–?	Salivahana
?	Saktikumara
?	Ambaprasada
?	Suchivarman
?	Naravarman
?	Anantavarman
?	Kirtivarman
?	Yogaraja
?	Vairata
?	Hamsapala
?	Vairi Singh
1108	Vijaya Singh
?	Ari Singh I
?	Choda Singh
?–c.1168	Vikrama Singh
c.1168–?	Rana Singh
?–c.1171	Kshema Singh
c.1171–?	Samanta Singh
?	Kumara Singh
?	Mathana Singh
?–c.1213	Padma Singh
c.1213–c.1260	Jaitra Singh
c.1260–c.1273	Teja Singh
c.1273–c.1302	Samara Singh
c.1302–c.1303	Ratna Singh I
c.1303–c.1314	Lakhana Singh
c.1314–c.1378	Hammir I
c.1378–c.1405	Kshetra Singh
c.1405–c.1420	Laksha Singh
c.1420–c.1433	Mokala
c.1433–68	Kumbhakarna
1468–73	Udaya Karan
1473–1509	Rayamalla
1509–28	Sangrama Singh I
1528–32	Ratna Singh II
1532–5	Bikramajit
1535–7	Ranbir
1537–72	Udaya Singh
1572–97	Pratap Singh I
1597–1620	Amar Singh I
1620–8	Karan
1628–52	Jagat Singh I
1652–80	Raja Singh I
1680–99	Jaya Singh
1699–1711	Amar Singh II
1711–34	Sangrama Singh II
1734–52	Jagat Singh II
1752–4	Pratap Singh II

1754–61	Raja Singh II
1761–73	Ari Singh II
1773–8	Hammir II
1778–1828	Bhim Singh
1828–38	Jawan Singh
1838–42	Sardar Singh
1842–61	Sarup Singh
1861–74	Sambhu
1874–84	Sujjan Singh
1884–1930	Fateh Singh
1930–49	Bhopal Singh

Mysore – Maharaja

1399–1423	Yadu Raya
1423–59	Hiriya Bettada Chamaraja I
1459–78	Timmaraja I
1478–1513	Hiriya Chamarajasa II
1513–53	Hiriya Bettada Chamaraja III
1553–72	Timmaraja II
1572–6	Bola Chamaraja IV
1576–8	Bettada Devaraja
1578–1617	Raja Wadiyar
1617–37	Chamaraja V
1637–8	Immadi Raja
1638–59	Kanthirava Narasaraja I
1659–73	Kempa Devaraja
1673–1704	Chikkadevaraja
1704–14	Kanthirava Narasaraja II
1714–32	Krishnaraja I
1732–4	Chamaraja VI
1734–66	Krishnaraja II
1766–70	Nanjaraja
1770–6	Bettada Chamaraja VII
1776–96	Khasa Chamaraja VIII
1796–9	*Interregnum: Hyder Ali Khan and Tippoo Sultan joint rulers*
1799–1831	Krishnaraja III
1831–81	*No Maharaja*
1881–94	Chamaraja IX
1894–1940	Krishnaraja IV
1940–9	Jayachamarajendra Bahadur

Patiala – Maharaja

1762–5	Ala Singh
1765–81	Amar Singh
1781–1813	Sahib Singh
1813–45	Karam Singh
1845–62	Narindar Singh
1862–76	Mohindar Singh
1876–1900	Rajindar Singh

1900–38	Bhupindar Singh
1938–48	Yadavindar Singh

Sikkim – Maharaja

1642–70	Phuntsog Namgyal
1670–86	Tensung Namgyal
1686–1717	Chador Namgyal
1717–33	Gyurmed Namgyal
1733–80	Namgyal Phuntsog
1780–93	Tenzing Namgyal
1793–1863	Tsugphud Namgyal
1863–74	Sidkeong Namgyal I
1874–1914	Thutob Namgyal
1914	Sidkeong Namgyal II
1914–63	Tashi Namgyal
1963–75	Palden Thondup Namgyal

Tonk – Nawab

1798–1834	Amir Khan
1834–64	Wazir Muhammad Khan
1864–7	Muhammad Ali Khan
1867–1930	Hafiz Muhammad Ibrahim Ali Khan
1930–48	Hafiz Muhammad Sadat Ali Khan

Travancore – Maharaja

1729–58	Marthanda Varma
1758–98	Kartika Tirunal Rama Varma
1798–1810	Balarama Varma
1810–15	Gouri Lakshmi Bai
1815–29	Gouri Parvati Bai
1829–47	Swati Tirunal
1847–60	Utram Tirunal Marthandra Varma
1860–80	Ayilyam Tirunal
1880–5	Rama Varma Visakhan Tirunal
1885–1924	Sri Mulam Tirunal Rama Varma
1924–31	Setu Lakshmi Bai
1931–49	Sri Chitra Tirunal Balarama Varma

Udaipur *see* **Mewar**

● Indonesia
Sultan of Jogjakarta

1755–92	Abdul-Rahman Amangkubuwana I

1792–1810	Abdul-Rahman Amangkubuwana II
1810–14	Abdul-Rahman Amangkubuwana III
1814–22	Abdul-Rahman Amangkubuwana IV
1822–55	Abdul-Rahman Amangkubuwana V
1855–77	Abdul-Rahman Amangkubuwana VI
1877–1921	Abdul-Rahman Amangkubuwana VII
1921–39	Abdul-Rahman Amangkubuwana VIII
1939–49	Abdul-Rahman Amangkubuwana IX

Sultan of Maratam
1582–1601	Panembahan Senapati Ingalaga
1601–13	Mas Jolang Panembahan Krapyak
1613–45	Abdul-Rahman Agung
1645–77	Prabu Amangkurat I
1677–1703	Amangkurat II
1703–5	Amangkurat III
1705–19	Pakubuwana I
1719–25	Amangkurat IV
1725–49	Pakubuwana II
1749–55	Pakubuwana III

Susuhunan of Surakarta
1755–88	Pakubuwana (III *of Maratam*)
1788–1820	Pakubuwana IV
1820–3	Pakubuwana V
1823–30	Pakubuwana VI
1830–58	Pakubuwana VII
1858–61	Pakubuwana VIII
1861–93	Pakubuwana IX
1893–1939	Pakubuwana X
1939–44	Pakubuwana XI
1944–9	Pakubuwana XII

● Iran
Kingdom of Persia
House of Achaemenes
c.700–675 BC	Hakhamanish (Achaemenes)

c.675–640 BC	Chishpish (Teispes)
c.640–600 BC	Kurush (Cyrus) I
c.600–559 BC	Kambujiya (Cambyses) I
559–529 BC	Kurush II 'the Great'
529–522 BC	Kambujiya (Cambyses) II
522 BC	Badiya-Gaumata (Smerdis)
521–486 BC	Darayavahush (Darius) I 'the Great'
486–465 BC	Khshayarsha (Xerxes) I
465–424 BC	Artakhshassa (Artaxerxes) I Longimanus
424–423 BC	Khshayarsha II
423–404 BC	Darayavahush II Ochus
404–358 BC	Artakhshassa II Mnemon
358–338 BC	Artakhshassa III Ochus
338–336 BC	Arsha
336–330 BC	Darayavahush III Codomannus
330–329 BC	Artakhshassa IV (Bessus) *Satrap of Bactria*

Shah
Qajar Dynasty
1779–97	Agha Muhammad
1797–1834	Fath Ali
1834–48	Muhammad
1848–96	Nasir-ud-Din
1896–1907	Muzaffar-ud-Din
1907–9	Mohammed Ali
1909–25	Ahmad Mirza

Pahlavi Dynasty
1925–41	Reza Khan
1941–79	Mohammed Reza Pahlavi

● Iraq
Monarch – Kingdom of Iraq
1921–33	Faisal I
1933–9	Ghazi I
1939–58	Faisal II (Abdul Illah *Regent 1939–53*)

● Israel
Kings of Israel and Judah
c.1020–c.1000 BC	Saul
c.1000–c.961 BC	David
c.961–c.922 BC	Solomon

King of Israel

c.922–c.901 BC	Jeroboam I
c.901–c.900 BC	Nadab
c.900–c.877 BC	Baasha
c.877–c.876 BC	Elah
c.876 BC	Tibni
c.876 BC	Zimri
c.876–c.873 BC	Omri
c.873–c.852 BC	Ahab
c.852–c.849 BC	Ahaziah
c.849–c.842 BC	Jehoram
c.842–c.815 BC	Jehu
c.815–c.801 BC	Jehoahaz
c.801–c.786 BC	Jehoash
c.786–c.746 BC	Jeroboam II
c.746–c.745 BC	Zachariah
c.745 BC	Shallum
c.745–c.736 BC	Menahem
c.736–c.735 BC	Pekahiah
c.735–c.732BC	Pekah
c.732–c.724 BC	Hoshea

King of Judah
House of David

c.922–c.915 BC	Rehoboam
c.915–c.913 BC	Abijah
c.913–c.873 BC	Asa
c.873–c.849 BC	Jehoshaphat
c.849–c.842 BC	Jehoram
c.842 BC	Ahaziah
c.842–c.837 BC	Athaliah
c.837–c.800 BC	Joash
c.800–c.783 BC	Amaziah
c.783–c.742 BC	Uzziah
c.742–c.735 BC	Jotham
c.735–c.715 BC	Ahaz
c.715–c.687 BC	Hezekiah
c.687–c.642 BC	Manasseh
c.642–c.640 BC	Amon
c.640–609 BC	Josiah
609 BC	Jehoahaz
609–597 BC	Jehoiakim
597 BC	Jehoiachin
597–587 BC	Zedekiah

Kingdom of Syria
House of Seleucus

305–281 BC	Seleucus I Nicator *Rival king*
281–261 BC	Antiochus I Soter
261–246 BC	Antiochus II Theos
246–225 BC	Seleucus II Callinicus
225–223 BC	Seleucus III Soter
223–187 BC	Antiochus III 'the Great'
187–175 BC	Seleucus IV Philopator
175–163 BC	Antiochus IV Epiphanes
163–162 BC	Antiochus V Eupator
162–150 BC	Demetrius I Soter
150–145 BC	Alexander I Balas
145–142 BC	Antiochus VI Epiphanes *Joint king*
145–139 BC	Demetrius II Nicator *Joint king and regent to 142 BC*
139–129 BC	Antiochus VII Sidetes
129–125 BC	Demetrius II Nicator (*restored*)
125 BC	Seleucus V
125–123 BC	Alexander II Zabinas
125–96 BC	Antiochus VIII Gryphus *Rival king 125–123 and from 115 BC*
115–95 BC	Antiochus IX Cyzicenus *Rival king*
96–95 BC	Seleucus VI Epiphanes Nicator *Rival king*
95–88 BC	Demetrius III Eukairos Sotor *Rival king*
95–83 BC	Antiochus X Eusebes Philopator *Rival king*
92 BC	Antiochus XI Philadelphus *Rival king*
92–83 BC	Philip I Philadelphus *Rival king*
87–84 BC	Antiochus XII Dionysus *Rival king*
83–69 BC	Tigranes *King of Armenia*
69–4 BC	Antiochus XIII Asiaticus
65–4 BC	Philip II *Rival king*

Kingdom of Judaea
House of Maccabeus

166–161 BC	Jehudah Makkabi (Judas Maccabeus)
161–142 BC	Jonathan
142–134 BC	Simon
134–104 BC	John Hyrcanus I
104–103 BC	Aristobulus I
103–76 BC	Alexander Jannaeus
76–67 BC	Alexandra Salome
67–63 BC	Aristobulus II *Rival king*

67–40 BC	Hyrcanus II
40–37 BC	Antigonus

House of Herod

37–4 BC	Herod I 'the Great'
4 BC–AD 34	Philip *Tetrarch of Batanea*
4 BC–AD 6	Archelaus
4 BC–AD 39	Herod Antipas *Tetrarch of Galilee*
37–44	Herod Agrippa I *Tetrarch of Batanea, Galilee from 40 and Judaea from 41*
41–48	Herod II *Tetrarch of Chalcis*
50–100	Herod Agrippa II *Tetrarch of Chalcis, Batanea from 53*

Kingdom of Jerusalem

1099–1100	Godfrey of Bouillon
1100–18	Baldwin I
1118–31	Baldwin II 'of Bourcq'
1131–43	Fulk of Anjou
1143–62	Baldwin III
1162–74	Amalric I
1174–85	Baldwin IV
1185–6	Baldwin V
1186–90	Guy of Lusignan *King of Cyprus from 1192*
1190–2	Conrad of Montferrat
1192–7	Henry I (*of Champagne*)
1197–1205	Amalric II *King of Cyprus*
1205–10	Maria
1210–25	John of Brienne
1225–43	Frederick (II, *Holy Roman Emperor*)
1243–54	Conrad II (IV, *Holy Roman Emperor*)
1254–84	Conradin of Hohenstauffen
1284–91	*As Cyprus*

● Italy

Count of Savoy

1034–49	Umberto I
1049–56	Amedeo I
1056–7	Otto
1057–78	Pietro I
1078–80	Amedeo II
1080–1103	Umberto II
1103–49	Amedeo III
1149–89	Umberto III
1189–1233	Tommaso
1233–53	Amedeo IV
1253–63	Bonifacio
1263–8	Pietro II
1268–85	Filippo I
1285–1323	Amedeo V 'the Great'
1323–9	Edoardo
1329–43	Aimone 'the Peaceful'
1343–83	Amedeo VI 'the Green Count'
1383–91	Amedeo VII
1391–1416	Amedeo VIII 'the Red Count'

Duke of Savoy

1416–34	Amedeo VIII 'the Peaceful'
1434–65	Ludovico
1465–72	Amedeo IX
1472–82	Filiberto I
1482–90	Carlo I
1490–6	Carlo II
1496–7	Filippo II
1497–1504	Filiberto II
1504–53	Carlo III
1553–80	Emanuel-Filiberto
1580–1630	Carlo-Emanuele I
1630–7	Vittorio-Amedeo I
1637–8	Francesco-Giacinto
1638–75	Carlo-Emanuele II
1675–1720	Vittorio-Amedeo II *King of Sicily 1713–18*

Duke of Savoy and King of Sardinia

1720–30	Vittorio-Amedeo II
1730–73	Carlo-Emanuele III
1773–96	Vittorio-Amedeo III
1796–1802	Carlo-Emanuele IV
1802–21	Vittorio-Emanuele (Victor-Emmanuel) I
1821–31	Carlo-Felice
1831–49	Carlo-Alberto (Charles Albert)
1849–61	Vittorio-Emanuele II

Monarch – Kingdom of Italy

1861–78	Vittorio-Emanuele II
1878–1900	Umberto I
1900–46	Vittorio-Emanuele III
1946	Umberto II

Ferrara see Modena

Florence see Tuscany

Mantua – Captain General of Mantua
House of Gonzaga

1328–60	Luigi I
1360–9	Guido
1369–82	Luigi II
1382–1407	Francesco I
1407–33	Gian-Francesco

Marquis of Mantua
House of Gonzaga

1433–44	Gian-Francesco
1444–78	Luigi III
1478–84	Federigo I
1484–1519	Francesco II
1519–30	Federigo II

Duke of Mantua
House of Gonzaga

1530–40	Federigo II
1540–50	Francesco III
1550–87	Guglielmo
1587–1612	Vincenzo I
1612	Francesco IV
1612–26	Ferdinando
1626–7	Vincenzo II
1627–37	Carlo I
1637–65	Carlo II
1665–1707	Ferdinando-Carlo
1708–1861	*As Milan*

Milan – Count of Milan
House of Visconti

1310–22	Matteo I
1322–8	Galeazzo I
1328–39	Azzo
1339–49	Lucchino
1349–54	Giovanni
1354–78	Galeazzo II *Joint ruler*
1354–85	Bernabo *Joint ruler*
1354–5	Matteo II *Joint ruler*
1378–96	Gian Galeazzo (Visconti) *Joint ruler to 1385*

Duke of Milan
House of Visconti

1386–1402	Gian Galeazzo
1402–12	Giovanni Maria
1412–47	Filippo Maria

House of Sforza

1450–66	Francesco
1466–76	Galeazzo Maria
1476–94	Gian Galeazzo
1494–9	Ludovico Maria
1499–1500	*French rule*
1500	Ludovico Maria (*restored*)
1500–12	*French rule*
1512–15	Massimiliano
1515–21	*French rule*
1521–35	Francesco Maria
1535–1796	*Austrian rule*
1797–1815	*Part of Cisalpine Republic*
1815–59	*Austrian rule*
1859–61	*Part of Kingdom of Sardinia*

Modena – Lord of Ferrara
House of Este

1209–12	Azzo I
1212–15	Aldobrandino I
1215–64	Azzo II
1264–88	Obizzo I

Lord of Ferrara and Modena
House of Este

1288–93	Obizzo I
1293–1308	Azzo III
1308–10	*Disputed succession*
1310–17	*Papal rule*
1317–35	Rinaldo I *Joint ruler*
1317–44	Nicolÿ I *Joint ruler*
1317–52	Obizzo II *Joint ruler to 1344*
1352–61	Aldobrandino II
1361–88	Nicolÿ II
1388–93	Alberto
1393–1441	Nicolÿ III
1441–50	Lionello
1450–2	Borso

Duke of Modena
House of Este

1452–71	Borso

Duke of Ferrara and Modena
House of Este

1471	Borso
1471–1505	Ercole I
1505–34	Alfonso I
1534–59	Ercole II
1559–97	Alfonso II

Duke of Modena
House of Este
1597–1628	Cesare
1628–9	Alfonso III
1629–58	Francesco I
1658–62	Alfonso IV
1662–94	Francesco II
1694–1737	Rinaldo II
1737–80	Francesco III
1780–97	Ercole III
1797–1814	*French rule*

House of Habsburg
1814–46	Francesco IV
1846–59	Francesco V

Parma – Duke of Parma
House of Farnese
1545–7	Pier Luigi
1547–86	Ottavio
1586–92	Alessandro (Farnese)
1592–1622	Ranuccio I
1622–46	Oduardo
1646–94	Ranuccio II
1694–1727	Francesco
1727–31	Antonio

House of Bourbon–Parma
1731–5	*As Spain*
1735–48	*Habsburg Dukes of Parma*
1748–65	Philip
1765–99	Ferdinand
1799–1814	*French rule*
1814–47	Marie-Louise of Habsburg (*Duchess*)
1847–9	Charles II Louis
1849–54	Charles III Ferdinand
1854–9	Robert

Sicily – Count of Sicily
Norman rulers
1072–1101	Roger I of Hauteville
1101–5	Simon
1105–30	Roger II (Ruggero)

King of Naples and Sicily
Norman kings
1130–54	Roger II (Ruggero)
1154–66	William I
1166–89	William II
1189–94	Tancred

1194	William III

House of Hohenstauffen
1194–7	Henry (VI, *Holy Roman Emperor*)
1197–1250	Frederick (II, *Holy Roman Emperor*)
1250–4	Conrad (IV, *Holy Roman Emperor*)
1254–8	Conradin (*Holy Roman Emperor*)
1258–66	Manfred

House of Anjou
1266–82	Charles I of Anjou

King of Naples
House of Anjou
1282–5	Charles I of Anjou
1285–1309	Charles II
1309–43	Robert 'the Wise'
1343–81	Joanna (Giovanna) I (*Queen*)
1381–6	Charles III
1386–1414	Lancelot
1414–35	Joanna II

House of Aragón
1435–58	*As Aragón (see Spain)*
1458–94	Ferdinand I
1494–5	Alfonso II
1495–6	Ferdinand II
1496–1501	Frederick IV
1501–16	*As Aragón (see Spain)*

King of Sicily
House of Aragón
1282–5	Peter I (Pedro II *of Aragón*)
1285–95	James (Jaime II *of Aragón*)
1295–1337	Frederick II
1337–42	Peter II
1342–55	Louis
1355–77	Frederick III
1377–1402	Maria *Joint ruler from 1391*
1391–1409	Martin I *Joint ruler to 1402*
1409–1516	*As Aragón (see Spain)*

King of the Two Sicilies
House of Bourbon–Two Sicilies
1516–1700	*As Spain*
1700–13	*Disputed succession*
1713–18	*As Savoy*
1718–34	*Disputed succession*

1734–59	*As Spain*
1759–1825	Ferdinand I (Joseph Bonaparte, *King of Naples 1806–8*; Joachim Murat, *King of Naples 1808–15*)
1825–30	Francis I
1830–59	Ferdinand II
1859–60	Francis II

Tuscany – Lord of Florence
House of Medici

1434–64	Cosimo (Medici) 'Pater Patriae'
1464–9	Piero I (Medici) 'the Gouty'
1469–92	Lorenzo I (Medici) 'the Magnificent'
1492–4	Piero II (Medici) 'the Unfortunate'
1494–1512	*Republic*
1512–19	Lorenzo II
1519–23	Clement VII (Giulio de' Medici)
1523–7	Alessandro Medici (Silvio Passerini *Regent*)
1527–30	*Republic*
1530–1	Alessandro Medici (*restored*)

Duke of Florence
House of Medici

| 1531–7 | Alessandro (Medici) |
| 1537–69 | Cosimo I (Medici) 'the Great' |

Grand Duke of Tuscany
House of Medici

1569–74	Cosimo I (Medici) 'the Great'
1574–87	Francesco
1587–1609	Ferdinand I
1609–21	Cosimo II
1621–70	Ferdinand II
1670–1723	Cosimo III
1723–37	Gian Gastone

House of Habsburg-Lorraine

1737–65	Francis (I, *Holy Roman Emperor*)
1765–90	Leopold (II, *Holy Roman Emperor*)
1790–1801	Ferdinand III
1801–1814	*French rule*
1814–24	Ferdinand III (*restored*)
1824–59	Leopold II

Venice – Doge of Venice

697–717	Paolucci Anafest
717–726	Marcello Tegalliano
726–37	Orso
737–42	*Byzantine rule*
742–55	Diodata Orso
756–64	Domenico Monegario
764–87	Maurizio Galbaio I
787–804	Giovanni Galbaio
804–10	Obelerio Antenoreo
810–27	Angelo Parteciaco
827–9	Giustiniano Parteciaco
829–36	Giovanni Parteciaco I
836–64	Pietro Tradonico
864–81	Orso Parteciaco
881–7	Giovanni Parteciaco II
887	Pietro Candiano I
888–912	Pietro Tribuno
912–31	Orso Parteciaco
932–9	Pietro Candiano II
939–42	Pietro Parteciaco
942–59	Pietro Candiano III
959–76	Pietro Candiano IV
976–8	Pietro Orsolo I
978–9	Vitale Candiano
979–91	Tribune Menio
991–1008	Pietro Orsolo II
1008–26	Ottone Orsolo
1026–32	Pietro Centranico
1032–42	Domenico Fabiano
1043–70	Domenico Contarini
1070–84	Domenico Silvo
1084–96	Vitale Fahier
1096–1102	Vitale Michiel I
1102–18	Ordelaffe Fahier
1118–29	Domenico Michiel
1130–48	Pietro Polani
1148–56	Domenico Morosini
1156–72	Vitale Michiel II
1172–8	Sebastiano Ziani
1178–92	Orio Malipiero
1192–1205	Enrico Dandolo
1205–29	Pietro Ziani
1229–49	Iacopo Tiepolo
1249–53	Marino Morosini
1253–68	Ranieri Zen

1268–75	Lorenzo Tiepolo		1623–4	Francesco Contarini
1275–80	Iacopo Contarini		1625–9	Giovanni Corner I
1280–9	Giovanni Dandolo		1630–1	Nicolò Contarini
1289–1311	Pietro Gradenigo		1631–46	Francesco Erizzo
1311–12	Marino Zorzi		1646–55	Francesco da Molin
1312–28	Giovanni Soranzo		1655–6	Carlo Contarini
1329–39	Francesco Dandolo		1656	Francesco Corner
1339–42	Bartolomeo Gradenigo		1656–8	Bertucci Valier
1343–54	Andrea Dandolo		1658–9	Giovanni Pesaro
1354–5	Marin Faliero		1659–75	Domenico Contarini
1355–6	Giovanni Gradenigo		1675–6	Nicolò Sagredo
1356–61	Giovanni Dolfin		1676–84	Alvise Contarini
1361–5	Lorenzo Celsi		1684–8	M Antonio Giustinian
1365–8	Marco Corner		1688–94	Francesco Morosini
1368–82	Andrea Contarini		1694–1700	Silvestro Valier
1382	Michele Morosini		1700–9	Alvise Mocenigo II
1382–1400	Antonio Venier		1709–22	Giovanni Corner II
1400–13	Michele Steno		1722–32	Alvise Mocenigo III
1414–23	Tommaso Mocenigo		1732–5	Carlo Ruzzini
1423–57	Francesco Foscari		1735–41	Alvise Pisani
1457–62	Pasquale Malipiero		1741–52	Pietro Grimani
1462–66	Cristoforo Moro		1752–62	Francesco Loredan
1466–73	Nicolò Tron		1762–3	Marco Foscarini
1473–4	Nicolò Marcello		1763–78	Alvise Mocenigo IV
1474–6	Pietro Mocenigo		1779–89	Paolo Renier
1476–8	Andrea Vendramun		1789–97	Ludovico Manin
1478–85	Giovanni Mocenigo			
1485–6	Marco Barbarigo			
1486–1501	Agostino Barbarigo			
1501–21	Leonardo Loredan			
1521–3	Antonio Grimani			
1523–38	Andrea Gritti			

● Japan

The traditional dates for early reigns are not generally considered to be accurate.

Emperor

1539–45	Pietro Lando				*Traditional*
1545–53	Francesco Donà				*date*
1553–4	Marc'Antonio Trevisan				
1554–6	Francesco Venier		c.40–c.10 BC	Jimmu	660–581 BC
1556–9	Lorenzo Priuli		c.10 BC–c.AD 20	Suizei	581–549 BC
1559–67	Girolamo Priuli		c.20–c.50	Annei	549–510 BC
1567–70	Pietro Loredan		c.50–c.80	Itoku	510–475 BC
1570–7	Alvise Mocenigo I		c.80–c.110	Kosho	475–392 BC
1577–8	Sebastiano Venier		c.110–c.140	Koan	392–290 BC
1578–85	Nicolò da Ponte		c.140–c.170	Korei	290–214 BC
1585–95	Pasquale Cicogna		c.170–c.200	Kogen	214–157 BC
1595–1605	Marino Grimani		c.200–c.230	Kaika	157–97 BC
1606–12	Leonardo Donà		c.230–c.259	Sujin	97–29 BC
1612–15	Marc'Antonio Memmo		c.259–c.291	Suinin	29 BC–AD 71
1615–18	Giovanni Bembo		c.291–c.323	Keiko	71–131
1618	Nicolò Donà		c.323–c.356	Seimu	131–92
1618–23	Antonio Priuli		c.356–c.363	Chuai	192–201

c.363–c.380	Jingo (*Regent*)	201–70	Reizei
c.380–c.395	Ojin	270–313	Enyu
c.395–c.428	Nintoku	313–400	Kazan
c.428–c.433	Richu	400–6	Ichijo
c.433–c.438	Hanzei	406–12	Sanjo
c.438–c.455	Inkyo	412–54	Go-Ichijo
c.455–c.457	Anko	454–7	Go-Shujaku
c.457–c.490	Yuryaku	457–80	Go-Reizei
c.490–c.495	Seinei	480–5	Go-Sanjo
c.495–c.498	Kenso	485–8	Shirakawa
c.498–c.504	Ninken	488–99	Horikawa
c.504–c.510	Muretsu	499–507	Toba
c.510–34	Keitai	507–34	Sutoku
534–6	Ankan		Konoe
536–40	Senka	1142–56	Go-Shirakawa
540–71	Kimmei	1156–9	Nijo
572–86	Bidatsu	1159–66	Rokujo
586–8	Yomei	1166–9	Takakura
588–93	Sujun	1169–81	Antoku
593–629	Suiko	1181–4	Go-Toba
629–42	Jomei	1184–99	Tsuchi-Mikado
642–5	Kogyoku	1199–1211	Juntoku
645–55	Kotoku	1211–21	Chukyo
655–62	Saimei (Kogyoku *restored*)	1221–2	Go-Horikawa
662–72	Tenchi	1222–33	Shijo
672–3	Kobun	1233–43	Go-Saga
673–86	Temmu	1243–7	Go-Fukakusa
686–97	Jito	1247–60	Kameyama
697–708	Mommu	1260–75	Go-Uda
708–15	Gemmyo	1275–88	Fushima
715–24	Gensho	1288–99	Go-Fushima
724–49	Shomu	1299–1302	Go-Nijo
749–59	Koken	1302–8	Hanazono
759–65	Junnin	1308–19	Go-Daigo
765–70	Shotoku (Koken *restored*)	1319–31	Kogen
770–82	Konin	1331–3	Go-Daigo (*restored*) *South*
782–806	Kwammu		*only from 1336*
806–10	Heijo	1336–49	Komyo *North*
810–24	Saga	1339–68	Go-Murakami *South*
824–34	Junna	1349–52	Suko *North*
834–51	Nimmyo	1352–72	Go-Kogen *North*
851–9	Montoku	1368–73	Chokei *South*
859–77	Seiwa	1372–84	Go-Enyu *North*
877–85	Yozei	1373–92	Go-Kameyama *South*
885–9	Koko	1384–1413	Go Komatu *North only until*
889–98	Uda		*1392*
898–931	Daigo	1413–29	Shoko
931–47	Shujaku	1429–65	Go-Hanazono
947–68	Murakami	1465–1501	Go-Tsuchi-Mikado
968–70	Reizei		
970–85	Enyu		
985–7	Kazan		
987–1012	Ichijo		
1012–17	Sanjo		
1017–37	Go-Ichijo		
1037–47	Go-Shujaku		
1047–69	Go-Reizei		
1069–73	Go-Sanjo		
1073–87	Shirakawa		
1087–1108	Horikawa		
1108–24	Toba		
1124–42	Sutoku		

1501–27	Go-Kashiwabara
1527–58	Go-Nara
1558–87	Ogimachi
1587–1612	Go-Yozei
1612–30	Go-Mizu-no-o
1630–44	Myosho
1644–55	Go-Komyo
1655–63	Go-Saiin
1663–87	Reigen
1687–1710	Higashiyama
1710–36	Naka-no-Mikado
1736–48	Sakuramachi
1748–63	Momozono
1763–71	Go-Sakuramachi
1771–80	Go-Momozono
1780–1817	Kokaku
1817–47	Ninko
1847–67	Komei
1867–1912	Meiji (Mutsuhito)
1912–26	Taisho (Yoshihito)
1926–89	Showa (Hirohito)
1989–	Heisei (Akihito)

Shogun

Minamoto Shoguns

1192–9	Yoritomo Minamoto
1199–1203	Yori-ie Minamoto
1203–19	Sanemoto Minamoto

Fujiwara Shoguns

1220–44	Yoritsune Fujiwara
1244–51	Yoritsugu Fujiwara

Imperial Shoguns

1251–66	Munetaka
1266–89	Koreyasu
1289–1308	Hisakira
1308–33	Morikune

Ashikaga Shoguns

1338–58	Takuji Ashikaga
1358–67	Yoshiaki Ashikaga
1367–95	Yoshimitsu Ashikaga
1395–1423	Yoshimochi Ashikaga
1423–8	Yoshikazu Ashikaga
1428–41	Yoshinori Ashikaga
1441–3	Yoshikatsu Ashikaga
1443–74	Yoshimasa Ashikaga
1474–90	Yoshihisa Ashikaga
1490–3	Yoshitane Ashikaga
1493–1508	Yoshizume Ashikaga

1508–21	Yoshitane Ashikaga (*restored*)
1521–45	Yoshiharu Ashikaga
1545–65	Yoshiteru Ashikaga
1565–8	Yoshihide Ashikaga
1568–73	Yoshiaki Ashikaga

Tokugawa Shoguns

1603–5	Ieyasu Tokugawa
1605–23	Hidetada Tokugawa
1623–51	Iemitsu Tokugawa
1651–80	Ietsuna Tokugawa
1680–1709	Tsunayoshi Tokugawa
1709–13	Ienobu Tokugawa
1713–16	Ietsugu Tokugawa
1716–45	Yoshimune Tokugawa
1745–61	Ieshige Tokugawa
1761–87	Ieharu Tokugawa
1787–1838	Ienari Tokugawa
1838–53	Ieyoshi Tokugawa
1853–8	Iesada Tokugawa
1858–66	Iemochi Tokugawa
1866–7	Yoshinobu Tokugawa

● Jordan

Monarch – *Kingdom of Transjordan*

1921–46	Abdullah ibn Hussein

Kingdom of Jordan

1946–51	Abdullah ibn Hussein (Abdullah I)
1951–2	Talal I
1952–99	Hussein ibn Talal
1999–	Abdullah ibn Hussein (Abdullah II)

● Kazakhstan

Khans of the Golden Horde

1227–55	Batu
1255–6	Sartak
1256–7	Ulaghchi
1257–67	Berke
1267–80	Mengu Timur
1280–7	Tuda Mengu
1287–90	Tola Buqa
1290–1312	Toqtu
1312–41	Uzbeg
1341–2	Tinibeg

1342–57	Janibeg	1146–70	Ui-jong
1357–9	Berdibeg	1170–97	Myong-jong
1359–60	Qulpa	1197–1204	Sin-jong
1360–1	Nawruz Beg	1204–11	Hui-jong
1361–2	Khidr	1211–13	Kang-jong
1362	Timur Khoja	1213–59	Ko-jong
1362	Keldibeg	1259–74	Won-jong
1362–4	Murid	1274–1308	Ch'ung-yol
1364–7	Aziz Khan	1308–13	Ch'ung-son
1367–70	Abdullah	1313–30	Ch'ung-suk
1370–8	Muhammad Bulak	1330–2	Ch'ung-hye
1378–95	Tokhtamish	1332–9	Ch'ung-suk (*restored*)
1395–1400	Timur Qutlugh	1339–44	Ch'ung-hye (*restored*)
1400–7	Shadibeg	1344–9	Ch'ung-mok
1407–10	Pulad Timur	1349–51	Ch'ung-jong
1410–12	Timur Khan	1351–74	Kong-min
1412	Jalah-ud-Din	1374–88	Wi-ju
1412–14	Karim Berdi	1388–9	Ch'ang
1414–17	Kebek	1389–92	Kong-yang
1417–19	Jabbar Berdi		
1419–37	Ulugh Muhammad (*of Kazan*)	*Yi Dynasty*	
		1392–8	T'ae-jo
1437–65	Sayyid Ahmad I	1398–1400	Chong-jong
1465–81	Ahmad Khan	1400–18	T'ae-jong
1481–99	Murtada *Joint ruler*	1418–50	Se-jong
1481–1502	Sayyid Ahmad II *Joint ruler*	1450–2	Mun-jong
1481–1502	Shaikh Ahmad *Joint ruler*	1452–5	Tan-jong
		1455–68	Se-jo
		1468–9	Ye-jong
● **Korea**		1469–94	Song-jong
Monarch – Kingdom of Korea		1494–1506	Yon-san
Wang Dynasty		1506–44	Chung-jong
918–44	T'ae-jo	1544–5	In-jong
944–5	Hye-jong	1545–67	Myong-jong
945–9	Chong-jong	1567–1608	Son-jo
949–75	Kwang-jong	1608–23	Kwang-hae
975–81	Kyong-jong	1623–49	In-jo
981–97	Song-jong	1649–59	Hyo-jong
997–1009	Mok-chong	1659–74	Hyon-jong
1009–31	Hyon-jong	1674–1720	Suk-chong
1031–4	Tok-chong	1720–4	Kyong-jong
1034–46	Chong-jong	1724–76	Yong-jo
1046–83	Mun-jong	1776–1800	Chong-jo
1083	Sun-jong	1800–34	Sun-jo
1083–94	Son-jong	1834–49	Hon-jong
1094–5	Hon-jong	1849–64	Ch'ol-chong
1095–1105	Suk-chong	1864–1907	Ko-jong
1105–22	Ye-jong	1907–10	Sun-jong
1122–46	In-jong	1910–48	*Japanese rule*

● Kuwait

Emir

al-Sabah Dynasty

1756–62	Sabah I
1762–1812	Abdullah I
1812–59	Jaber I
1859–66	Sabah II
1866–92	Abdullah II
1892–96	Muhammad
1896–1915	Mubarak
1915–17	Jaber II
1917–21	Salim al-Mubarak
1921–50	Ahmad al-Jaber
1950–65	Abdullah III al-Salim
1965–77	Sabah III al-Salim
1977–2006	Jaber III al-Ahmad al-Jaber
2006	Saad al-Abdullah al-Salim al-Sabah
2006–	Sabah al-Ahmad al-Jaber al-Sabah

● Laos

Monarch – Lan Chang

1637–94	Souligna Vongsa
1694–1700	Tian T'ala
1700	Nan T'arat
1700–7	Sai Ong Hue

Monarch – Luang Prabang

1707–26	King Kitsarat
1726–7	Khamone Noi
1727–76	Int'a Som
1776–81	Sotika Koumane
1781–7	Tiao Vong
1787–91	*No king*
1791–1817	Anourout
1817–36	Mant'a T'ourat
1836–51	Souka Seum
1851–72	Tiantha
1872–87	Oun Kham
1887–94	*Siamese rule*
1894–1904	Zakarine
1904–47	Sisavang Vong

Monarch – Kingdom of Laos

1947–59	Sisavang Vong
1959–75	Sri Savang Vatthana

● Lebanon

Emirs

Ma'nid Emirs

1516–44	Fakhr-ud-Din I
1544–85	Qurqumaz
1590–1635	Fakhr-ud-Din II
1635–57	Mulhim
1657–97	Ahmad

Shihabid Emirs

1697–1707	Bashir I
1707–32	Haidar
1732–54	Mulhim
1754–70	Mansur
1770–88	Yusuf
1788–1840	Bashir II
1840–2	Bashir III
1842–1918	*Turkish rule*
1918–20	*Rule under negotiation*
1920–43	*French rule*

● Lesotho

Monarch – Basutoland

1823–70	Moshoeshoe I
1870–91	Letsie I
1891–1905	Lerotholi
1905–13	Letsie II
1913–39	Griffith
1939–40	Seeiso
1940–60	Mansebo *Regent*
1960–66	Moshoeshoe II

Monarch – Lesotho

1966–90	Moshoeshoe II
1990–4	Letsie III (*abdicated*)
1994–6	Moshoeshoe II
1996–	Letsie III (*restored*)

● Libya

Tripoli – Karamanli ruler

1711–45	Ahmad I
1745–54	Muhammad
1754–93	Ali I
1793–5	Ali Burghul
1795	Ahmad II
1795	Ali I (*restored*)
1795–1832	Yusuf
1832–5	Ali II

1835–1911	*Turkish rule*
1911–42	*Italian rule*

Libya – Sanusi leader

1837–59	Said Mohammed al-Senussi
1859–1902	Said al-Mahdi
1902–18	Said Ahmad ash-Sharif
1918–51	Said Mohammed Idris al-Mahdi al-Senussi

Monarch – Kingdom of Libya

1951–69	Said Mohammed Idris al-Mahdi al-Senussi

● **Liechtenstein**
Prince

1719–21	Anton-Florian
1721–32	Josef
1732–48	Johann-Karl
1748–72	Josef-Wenceslas-Lorenz
1772–81	Franz-Josef I
1781–1805	Alois I
1805–7	Johann I
1807–13	Karl
1813–36	Johann I (*restored*)
1836–58	Alois II
1858–1929	Johann II
1929–38	Franz von Paula
1938–89	Franz-Josef II
1989–	Hans Adam II

● **Lithuania**
Grand Duke

c.1235–63	Mindaugas
1263–4	Treniota
1264–7	Vaishvilkis
1267–70	Shvarnas
1270–83	Traidenis
1283–93	Pukuveras
1293–1316	Vitenis
1316–41	Gediminas
1341–5	Jaunutis
1345–77	Algirdas
1377–81	Jogaila
1381–2	Kestutis
1382–92	Jogaila (*restored*)
1392–1430	Vytautias
1430–2	Shvitrigaila

1432–40	Sigismund
1440–92	Casimir (IV *of Poland*)
1492–1506	Alexander *King of Poland from 1501*
1506–69	*As Poland*
1569–1918	*Part of Poland*

● **Luxemburg or Luxembourg**
Grand Duke of Luxemburg
House of Nassau-Weilberg

1816–39	William
1839–66	Adolf
1866–90	*No dukedom*

Duke of Nassau
House of Nassau

1890–1905	Adolf_
1905–12	William IV
1912–19	Marie-Adelaide
1919–64	Charlotte (*In exile 1940–4*)
1964–2000	Jean
2000–	Henri

● **Madagascar**
Monarch

1819–28	Radama I
1828–61	Ranavalona I
1861–3	Radama II
1863–8	Rasoaherina
1868–83	Ranavalona II
1883–96	Ranavalona III
1896–1960	*French rule*

● **Malaysia**
Head of State (Yang di-Pertuan Agong) – Malaya

1957–63	Abdul Rahman Negri Sembilan

Head of State (Yang di-Pertuan Agong) – Malaya

1963–5	Sayyid Harun Putra Jamal-ul-Lail Perlis
1965–70	Ismail Nasir-ud-Din Shah Trengganu
1970–5	Abdul-Halim Muazzam Shah Kedah

1975–9	Yahya Petra Kelantan
1979–84	Ahmad Shah al-Mustain Pahang
1984–9	Mahmud Iskandar Shah Johore
1989–94	Azlan Muhibbuddin Shah Perak
1994–9	Ja'afar ibn Abdul Rahman
1999–2002	Salehuddin Abdul Aziz Shah
2002–	Tuanku Syed Sirajuddin

Sultan – Kedah

c.1160–79	Muzaffar Shah I
1179–1201	Muazzam Shah
1201–36	Muhammad Shah
1236–80	Maazul Shah
1280–1320	Mahmud Shah I
1320–73	Ibrahim Shah
1373–1422	Sulayman Shah I
1422–72	Ata-illah Muhammad Shah I
1472–1506	Muhammad Jiwa Zain-ul-Abidin
1506–46	Mahmud Shah II
1546–1602	Muzaffar Shah II
1602–25	Sulayman Shah II
1625–51	Rijal-ud-Din Shah
1651–61	Muhyi-ud-Din Shah
1661–87	Zia-ud-Din Mukarram Shah
1687–98	Ata-illah Muhammad Shah II
1698–1706	Abdullah Muazzam Shah
1706–60	Muhammad Jiwa Zail-ul-Abidin Muazzam Shah
1760–98	Abdullah Mukarram Shah
1798–1803	Zia-ud-Din Muazzam Shah
1803–21	Ahmad Taj-ud-Din Halim Shah
1821–43	No sultan
1843	Ahmad Taj-ud-Din Halim Shah (restored)
1843–54	Zain-ul-Rashid Muazzam Shah I
1854–79	Ahmad Taj-ud-Din Mukarram Shah
1879–81	Zain-ul-Rashid Muazzam Shah II
1881–1943	Abdul-Hamid Halim Shah
1943–58	Badlishah
1958–	Abdul-Halim Muazzam Shah

Sultan – Kelantan

c.1790–c.1800	Long Yunus
c.1800–38	Muhammad Shah I
1838–86	Muhammad Shah II
1886–9	Ahmad Shah
1889–91	Muhammad Shah III
1891–9	Mansur Shah
1899–1919	Muhammad Shah IV
1919–46	Ismail Shah
1946–60	Ibrahim Shah
1960–79	Yahya Petra
1979–	Ismail Petra

Sultan of Malacca

c.1400–24	Megat Iskandar Shah
1424–44	Muhammad Shah
1444–6	Abu-Shahid Ibrahim Shah
1446–58	Muzaffar Shah
1458–77	Mansur Shah
1477–88	Ala-ud-Din Riayat Shah
1488–1511	Mahmud Shah

Sultan of Johore

1511–29	Mahmud Shah I (of Malacca)
1529–64	Ala-ud-Din Riayat Shah I
1564–80	Muzaffar Shah
1580	Abdul-Jalil Shah I
1580–97	Abdul-Jalil Riayat Shah I
1597–1613	Ala-ud-Din Riayat Shah II
1613–23	Abdullah Maayat Shah
1623–77	Abdul-Jalil Shah II
1677–85	Ibrahim Shah
1685–99	Mahmud Shah II
1699–1717	Abdul-Jalil Riayat Shah II
1717–22	Abdul-Jalil Rahmat Shah
1722–60	Sulayman Badr-ul-Alam Shah
1760–1	Abdul-Jalil Muazzam Shah
1761	Ahmad Riayat Shah
1761–1812	Mahmud Riayat Shah
1812–19	Abdul-Rahman Muazzam Shah
1819–25	Abdul-Rahman
1825–62	Ibrahim
1862–95	Abu-Bakr
1895–1959	Ibrahim Shah
1959–81	Isma il Shah

1981–	Mahmood Iskandar Shah

Head of State (Yang Di-Pertuan Besar) – Negri Sembilan

1773–95	Raja Melawar
1795–1808	Raja Hitam
1808–24	Raja Lenggang
1824–6	Raja Kerjan
1826–30	Raja Laboh
1830–61	Raja Radin
1861–9	Raja Ulin
1869–72	*Regent*
1872–88	Tengku Antah
1888–1933	Muhammad
1933–60	Abdul-Rahman
1960–7	Munawir
1967–	Jafar

Sultan – Pahang

1884–1914	Ahmad Muazzam Shah
1914–17	Mahmud Shah II
1917–32	Abdullah Muktasim Billah Shah
1932–74	Abu-Bakr Riyat-ud-Din Muazzam Shah
1974–	Ahmad Shah III al-Mustain

Sultan – Perak

1529–49	Muzaffar Shah I
1549–77	Mansur Shah I
?1577–?	Ahmad Taj-ud-Din Shah
?	Taj-ul-Arifin Shah
?–1603	Ala-ud-Din Shah
1603–19	Muqadam Shah
1619	Mansur Shah II
1619–30	Mahmud Shah I
1630–5	Salah-ud-Din Shah
1635–54	Muzaffar Shah II
1654–c.1720	Muhammad Iskandar Shah
c.1720–c.1728	Ala-ud-Din Riayat Shah
c.1728–c.1750	Muhammad Shah
c.1728–c.1754	Muzaffar Shah III
c.1754–65	Iskandar Dhu'l-Qarnain Shah
1765–c.1773	Mahmud Shah II
c.1773–?	Ala-ud-Din Mansur Iskandar Shah
?–1806	Ahmadin Shah
1806–25	Abdul-Malik Mansur Shah
1825–31	Abdullah Muazzam Shah
1831–51	Shihab-ud-Din Riayat Shah
1851–7	Abdullah Muazzam Shah I
1857–65	Ja far Muazzam Shah
1865–71	Ali al-Kamil Riayat Shah
1871–4	Isma il Muabidin Shah
1874–7	Abdullah Muazzam Shah II
1877–87	Yusuf Sharif-ud-Din Mufzal Shah
1887–1916	Idris Murshid-ul-Azam Shah
1916–18	Abdul-Jalil Shah
1918–38	Iskandar Shah
1938–48	Abdul-Aziz Shah
1948–63	Yusuf Izz-ud-Din Shah
1963–85	Idris al-Mutawakkil Shah
1985–	Azlan Muhibbuddin Shah

Raja – Perlis

1843–73	Sayyid Husain Jamal-ul-Lail
1873–97	Sayyid Ahmad Jamal-ul-Lail
1897–1905	Sayyid Safi Jamal-ul-Lail
1905–43	Sayyid Alwi Jamal-ul-Lail
1945–2000	Sayyid Harun Putra Jamal-ul-Lail
2000–	Syed Sirajuddin Jamal-ul-Lail

Sultan – Selangor

1756–78	Salah-ud-Din Shah
1778–1826	Ibrahim Shah
1826–57	Muhammad Shah
1857–9	*Interregnum*
1859–98	Abdul-Samad Shah
1898–1938	Ala-ud-Din Sulayman Shah
1938–42	Hisam-ud-Din Alam Shah
1942–5	Musa Ghiyath-ud-Din Riayat Shah
1945–60	Hisam-ud-Din Alam Shah (*restored*)
1960–2001	Salah-ud-Din Abdul-Aziz Shah
2001–	Sharafuddin Idris Shah

Sultan – Terengganu

1725–33	Zain-ul-Abidin Shah I
1733–93	Mansur Shah I
1793–1808	Zain-ul-Abidin Shah II
1808–27	Ahmad Shah
1827–31	Abdul-Rahman Shah
1831	Daud Shah
1831–6	Mansur Shah II

1836–9	Muhammad Shah I
1839–76	Umar Shah
1876–81	Ahmad Muazzam Shah
1881–1918	Zain-ul-Abidin Muazzam Shah
1918–20	Muhammad Shah II
1920–45	Sulayman Badr-ul-Alam Shah
1945–79	Isma il Nasir-ud-Din Shah
1979–98	Mahmud al-Muktafi Billah Shah
1998–	Mizan Zainal Abidin

Rajah – Sarawak

1841–68	James Brooke
1868–1917	Charles Brooke
1917–46	Charles Vyner Brooke
1946–57	*British rule*

● **Maldives**
Monarch (Sultan)

1573–84	Muhammad Tukrufan al-Alam
1584–1609	Ibrahim ibn Muhammad
1609–20	Husain Famuderi
1620–48	Imad-ud-Din Muhammad I
1648–87	Ibrahim Iskandar I
1687–91	Muhammad ibn Ibrahim
1691–2	Muhi-ud-Din Muhammad
1692	Shams-ud-Din Muhammad al-Hamawi
1692–1700	Muhammad ibn Hajji Ali
1700–1	Ali
1701	Hasan ibn Ali
1701–5	Muzhir-ud-Din Ibrahim
1705–21	Imad-ud-Din Muhammad II
1721–50	Ibrahim Iskandar II
1750–4	Imad-ud-Din Muhammad Mukarram
1754–60	As Cannanore (*see* Indian States, p. 313)
1760–6	Izz-ud-Din Hasan Ghazi
1766–73	Ghiyath-ud-Din Muhammad
1773–4	Shams-ud-Din Muhammad
1774–8	Mu izz-ud-Din Muhammad
1778–98	Nur-du-Din Hajji Hasan
1798–1834	Mu in-ud-Din Muhammad I
1834–82	Imad-ud-Din Muhammad III
1882–86	Nur-ud-Din Ibrahim
1886–8	Mu in-ud-Din Muhammad II
1888–92	Nur-ud-Din Ibrahim (*restored*)
1892–3	Imad-ud-Din Muhammad IV
1893	Shams-ud-Din Muhammad Iskandar
1893–1903	Imad-ud-Din Muhammad V
1903–35	Shams-ud-Din Muhammad Iskandar (*restored*)
1935–45	Nur-ud-Din Hasan Iskandar
1945–52	Abdul-Majid Didi
1952–4	*Republic*
1954–68	Muhammad Farid Didi

● **Mexico**
Aztec Kings of Tenochtitlan

1372–91	Acamapichtli
1391–1415	Huitzilihuitl
1415–26	Chimalpopoca
1426–40	Itzcoatl
1440–68	Moctezuma I Ilhuicamina
1468–81	Axayacatl
1481–6	Tizoc
1486–1502	Ahuitzotl
1502–20	Moctezuma II Xocoyotzin
1520	Cuitlahuac
1520–1	Cuauhtemoc
1521–1821	*Spanish rule*

Aztec Rulers of Texcoco

c.1300–c.1357	Quinatzin
c.1357–c.1409	Techotlala
c.1409–18	Ixlilxochitl
1418–26	Tezozomoc
1426–8	Maxtla
1428–72	Nezahualcoyotl
1472–1515	Nezahualpilli
1515–20	Cacma
1520–1	Coanacochtzin
1521–1821	*Spanish rule*

Emperor

1822–3	Agustín de Itúrbide

● **Monaco**
Lord of Monaco
House of Grimaldi

1297–1314	Rainier I
1314–57	Charles I
1357–1407	Rainier II
1407–27	Antoine Ambroise and Jean I
	Joint lords
1427–54	Jean I
1454–7	Catalan
1457–8	Claudine
1458–94	Lambert of Antibes
1494–1505	Jean II
1505–23	Lucien
1523–32	Augustin
1532–81	Honoré I
1581–9	Charles II
1589–1604	Hercule
1604–12	Honoré II

Prince of Monaco

1612–62	Honoré II
1662–1701	Louis I
1701–31	Antoine
1731	Louise-Hyppolyte (*Princess*)
1731–33	Jacques of Torrigny
1733–93	Honoré III
1793–1814	*French rule*
1814–19	Honoré IV
1819–41	Honoré V
1841–56	Florestan
1856–89	Charles III
1889–1922	Albert
1922–49	Louis II
1949–2005	Rainier III
2005–	Albert II

● **Morocco**
Sultan
Filawi Dynasty (Fez and Morocco)

1631–5	Muhammad I ash-Sharif
1635–64	Muhammad II
1664–72	ar-Rashid
1672–1727	Isma il as-Samin
1727–9	Ahmad Adh-Dhahabi
1729–35	Abdullah
1735–7	Ali ibn Isma il
1737–8	Abdullah (*restored*)
1738–40	al-Mustadi ibn Isma il
1740–5	Abdullah (*restored*)
1745	Zain-ul-Abidin
1745–57	Abdullah (*restored*)
1757–90	Muhammad III
1790–2	Yazid
1792–3	Hisham
1793–1822	Sulayman
1822–59	Abdul-Rahman
1859–73	Muhammad IV
1873–94	Hasan I
1894–1907	Abdul-Aziz
1907–12	Abdul-Hafiz
1912–27	Yusuf
1927–53	Muhammad V
1953–5	Muhammad VI
1955–57	Muhammad V (*restored*)

Monarch – Kingdom of Morocco

1957–61	Muhammad V
1961–99	Hasan (Hassan) II
1999–	Mohammad VI

● **Nepal**
Monarch – Kingdom of Nepal
Raghavadeva Dynasty

c.879	Raghavadeva
?	Jayadeva
?	Vikramadeva
?	Narendradeva I
?	Gunakamadeva I
?	Udayadeva
c.1008	Rudradeva
c.1008	Nirbhayadeva
c.1015	Lakshmikamadeva I
c.1015	Bhoja
c.1039–46	Jayakamadeva

Thakuri Dynasty

1046–59	Bhaskaradeva
1059–64	Baladeva
1064–?	Pradyumnakamadeva
?–1068	Nagarjunadeva
1068–80	Shankaradeva
1080–90	Vamadeva
1090–1118	Harshadeva
1118–28	Sivadeva
1128–?	Indradeva
?	Manadeva

?–1146	Narendradeva II
1146–?	Anandadeva
?–1176	Rudradeva
1176–?	Amritadeva
?	Ratnadeva
?–1187	Somesvaradeva
1187–93	Gunakamadeva II
1193–6	Lakshmikamadeva II
1196–1201	Vijayakamadeva

Malla Dynasty

c.1201–c.1216	Arimalladeva
c.1216	Ranasura
c.1216–c.1235	Abhayamalla
c.1235–c.1258	Jayadevamalla
c.1258–c.1271	Jayabhimadeva
c.1271–c.1274	Jayasimhamalla
c.1274–c.1310	Anantamalla
c.1310–c.1347	Jayanandadeva *Joint ruler*
c.1320–c.1344	Jayarimalla *Joint ruler*
c.1320–c.1326	Jayarudramalla *Joint ruler*
c.1347–c.1361	Jayarajadeva
c.1361–c.1382	Jayajunamalla
c.1382–c.1395	Jayasthitimalla
c.1395–c.1428	Jayajyotimalla *Joint ruler to 1408*
c.1395–c.1403	Jayakitimalla *Joint ruler*
c.1395–c.1408	Jayadharmamalla *Joint ruler*
c.1428–c.1482	Jayayakshmamalla

Monarch – Kingdom of Katmandu
Malla Dynasty

c.1482–c.1520	Ratnamalla
c.1520–c.1530	Suryamalla
c.1530–c.1538	Amaramalla
c.1538–c.1560	Narendramalla
c.1560–c.1574	Mahenramalla
c.1574–c.1583	Sadasivamalla
c.1583–c.1620	Sivasimhamalla
c.1620–c.1641	Lakshminarasim-hamal-la
c.1641–c.1674	Pratapamalla
c.1674–c.1680	Jayanripendramalla
c.1680–c.1687	Parthivendramalla
c.1687–c.1700	Bhupendramalla
c.1700–c.1714	Bhaskaramalla
c.1714–1722	Mahendrasim-hamalla
1722–36	Jagajjayamalla
1736–68	Jayaprakasamalla

Monarch – Kingdom of Bhatgaon
Malla Dynasty

c.1482–c.1519	Rayamalla
c.1519–c.1547	Pranamalla
c.1547–c.1560	Vishvamalla
c.1560–c.1613	Trailokyamallamalla
c.1613–c.1637	Jagatjotimalla
c.1637–c.1644	Naresamalla
c.1644–c.1673	Jagatprakasamalla
c.1673–c.1696	Jitamitramalla
c.1696–1722	Bhupatindramalla
1722–69	Ranjitamalla

Monarch – Kingdom of Nepal
Gurkha Kings

1768–75	Prithvi Narayan Shah
1775–8	Pratap Singh Shah
1778–99	Rana Bahadur Shah
1799–1816	Girvana Judha Bikram Shah
1816–47	Rajendra Bir Bikram Shah
1847–81	Surendra Bir Bikram Shah
1881–1911	Prithvi Bir Bikram Shah
1911–55	Tribhuvana Bir Bikram Shah
1956–72	Mahendra Bir Bikram Shah
1972–2001	Birendra Bir Bikram Shah
2001–	Gyanendra Bir Bikram Shah

● **Netherlands, The**
Stadtholder of the Netherlands
House of Orange

1572–84	Willem (William) I 'the Silent' of Nassau
1585–1625	Maurice
1625–47	Frederik Henrik
1647–50	Willem II
1650–72	*No stadtholder* (Jan de Witt, Grand Pensionary 1653–72)
1672–1702	Willem III *King of England and Scotland from 1689*
1702–47	*No stadtholder*
1747–51	Willem IV (Charles Henry Friso)
1751–66	*Regency*
1766–95	Willem V
1795–1806	*Batavian Republic*

Monarch – Kingdom of Holland
House of Bonaparte

1806–10	Lodewijk I (Louis Bonaparte)
1810–13	*French rule*

Monarch – Kingdom of the Netherlands
House of Orange (*restored*)

1813–40	Willem I
1840–49	Willem II
1849–90	Willem III
1890–1948	Wilhelmina (*Queen Emma Regent to 1898*)
1948–80	Juliana
1980–	Beatrix

● **Norway**
Monarch
Yngling Dynasty

c.870–c.940	Harald I Halfdanarson 'Fine/ Fairhair'
c.940–c.945	Erik Haraldsson 'Bloodaxe'
c.945–c.960	Haakon I Haraldsson 'the Good'
c.960–c.970	Harald II Eriksson 'Greycloak'
c.970–c.995	Haakon, Jarl of Lade
c.995–1000	Olaf I Tryggvason
1000–15	Erik, Jarl of Lade
1015–28	Olaf II Haraldsson (St Olaf)
1028–35	Knut 'the Great' (Cnut) *Joint ruler from 1030*
1030–35	Svein Knutsson *Joint ruler*
1035–47	Magnus I Olafsson 'the Good'

House of Ulfing

1047–66	Harald III Sigurdsson 'Hardrada' ('the Ruthless')
1066–9	Magnus II *Joint ruler*
1067–93	Olaf III Haraldsson 'the Peaceful' *Joint ruler to 1069*
1093–1103	Magnus III Olafsson 'Barelegs'
1103–22	Eystein I Magnusson *Joint ruler*
1103–15	Olaf Magnusson *Joint ruler*
1103–30	Sigurd I Magnusson 'the Crusader' *Joint ruler to 1122*

1130–6	Harald IV Gille *Joint ruler to 1135*
1130–5	Magnus IV 'the Blind' *Joint ruler*
1136–55	Sigurd II *Joint ruler*
1136–61	Inge I *Joint ruler to 1157*
1142–57	Eystein II *Joint ruler*
1161–2	Haakon II
1162–84	Magnus V Erlingsson
1184–1202	Sverrir Sigurdsson
1202–4	Haakon III
1204	Gutorm Sigurdsson
1204–17	Inge II Baardsson
1217–63	Haakon IV Haakonsson 'the Old'
1263–80	Magnus VI Haakonsson 'the Law-Reformer'
1280–99	Erik II
1299–1319	Haakon V
1319–43	*As Sweden*
1343–80	Haakon VI

Danish kings

1380–87	Olaf IV (V *of Denmark*)
1387–97	Margrethe I (Margareta)
1397–1814	*As Denmark*
1814–1905	*As Sweden*

House of Oldenburg

1905–57	Haakon VII
1957–91	Olaf V
1991–	Harald V

● **Oman**
Sultan – Oman and Zanzibar
Ya'rubid Dynasty

1625–49	Nasir ibn Murshid
1649–69	Sultan I
1669–1711	Abdu l-Arab
1711	Saif I
1711–19	Sultan II
1719	Saif II
1719–22	Muhanna
1722–3	Yarub
1723–5	Saif I (*restored*)
1725–8	Muhammad ibn Nasir
1728–41	Saif II (*restored*)
1739–41	Sultan ibn Murshid *Joint*

Al-Bu-Sa'id Dynasty

1741–83	Ahmad ibn Said
1783–86	Said I
1786–92	Hamid
1792–1806	Sultan
1806	Salim I
1806–56	Said II

Sultan – Oman
Al-Bu-Sa'id Dynasty

1856–66	Thuwaini
1866–8	Salim II
1868–70	Azan ibn Qais
1870–88	Turki
1888–1913	Faisal ibn Turki
1913–32	Taimur ibn Faisal
1932–70	Said III ibn Taimur
1970–	Qaboos ibn Said (Qaboos bin Said)

● Pakistan
Nawab of Bahawalpur
Daudputra Dynasty

1739–46	Sadiq Muhammad Khan I
1746–9	Muhammad Bahawal Khan I
1749–72	Mubarak Khan
1772–1809	Muhammad Bahawal Khan II
1809–25	Saadiq Muhammad Khan II
1825–52	Muhammad Bahawal Khan III
1852–3	Sadiq Muhammad Khan III
1853–8	Fateh Muhammad Khan
1858–66	Muhammad Bahawal Khan IV
1866–99	Sadiq Muhammad Khan IV
1899–1907	Muhammad Bahawal Khan V
1907–55	Sadiq Muhammad Khan V

Khan of Kalat

?–1666	Mir Hasan Khan Mirwari
1666–95	Sardar Mir Ahmad Khan
1695	Mir Mehrab Khan I
1695–1714	Mir Samandar Khan
1714–34	Mir Abdullah Khan
1734–49	Mir Mohabat Khan
1749–1817	Mir Nasir Khan I
1817–31	Mir Mahmud Khan I
1831–40	Mir Mehrab Khan II
1840–57	Mir Nasir Khan II
1857–93	Mir Khudadad Khan
1893–1931	Mir Mahmud Khan II
1931–3	Mir Azam Khan
1933–48	Mir Ahmad Yar Khan

● Peru
Inca

c.1100–?	Manco Capac
?–c.1200	Mayta Capac
c.1200–?	Capac Yupanqui
?	Sinchi Roca
?	Lloque Yupanqui
?	Inca Roca
?	Inca Yupanqui (Yahuar Huacac)
?–1438	Viracocha
1438	Inca Urco
1438–71	Pachacuti
1471–93	Tupac Yupanqui
1493–1526	Huayna Capac
1526–32	Tupac Cusi Hualpa (Huascar)
1530–3	Atahualpa, *North only to 1532*
1533–1821	*Spanish rule*

● Philippines
Sultan of Sulu

c.1450–c.1480	Sharif-ul-Hashim
c.1480–?	Kamal-ud-Din
?	Ala-ud-Din
?	Amir-ul-Umara
?	Muizz-ul-Mutawadi in
?	Nasir-ud-Din I
?–c.1596	Muhammad al-Halim
c.1596–c.1610	Batarah Shah Tengah
c.1610–c.1650	Muwallit Wasit
c.1645–c.1648	Nasir-ud-Din II *Rival*
c.1650–c.1680	Salah-ud-Din Bakhtiyar
c.1680–?	Ali Shah Nur-ul-Azam Sultanah
?–c.1685	al-Haqunu
c.1685–c.1710	Shihab-ud-Din
c.1710–c.1718	Mustafa Shafi-ud-Din
c.1718–1732	Badr-ud-Din I
1732–5	Nasr-ud-Din III

1735–48	Azim-ud-Din I
1748–64	Muizz-ud-Din
1764–74	Azim-ud-Din I (restored)
1774–8	Muhammad Isra il
1778–91	Azim-ud-Din II
1791–1808	Sharaf-ud-Din
1808	Azim-ud-Din III
1808–21	Ali-ud-Din
1821–3	Shakirullah
1823–42	Jamal-ul-Kiram I
1842–62	Muhammad Fadl
1862–81	Jamal-ul-Azam
1881–6	Badr-ud-Din II
1886–94	Harun ar-Rashid
1894–1915	Jamal-ul-Kiram II
1915–35	US rule

Sultan of Maguindanao

c.1645–c.1671	Qudarat Nasir-ud-Din
c.1671–c.1678	Dundang Tidulay Saif-ud-Din
c.1678–c.1699	Abdul-Rahman
c.1699–c.1702	Qahhar-ud-Din Kuda
c.1702–c.1736	Bayan-ul-Anwar
c.1710–c.1733	Jafar Sadiq Manamir (rival)
c.1733–c.1736	Tahir-ud-Din (rival)
c.1733–c.1755	Khair-ud-Din (rival)
c.1755–c.1780	Pahar-ud-Din
c.1780–c.1805	Kibad Sahriyal
c.1805–c.1830	Kawasa Anwar-ud-Din
c.1830–1854	Iskandar Qudratullah Muhammad
1854–84	Muhammad Makakwa
1884–88	Muhammad Jalal-ud-Din Pablu
1888–98	Spanish rule
1898–1935	US rule

● Poland
Monarch – Prince of all Poland
House of Piast

c.960–992	Mieszko I
992–1025	Bolesław I 'the Brave' King 1024–5
1025–31	Mieszko II Lambert
1031–2	Bezprim
1032–4	Mieszko II (restored)
1034–58	Casimir I 'the Restorer'

1058–79	Bolesław II 'the Bold' King 1076–9
1079–1102	Władysław I Herman
1102–38	Bolesław III 'the Wry-Mouthed'

Monarch – Prince of Little Poland and Krakow
House of Piast

1138–46	Władysław II 'the Exile' (of Silesia)
1146–73	Bolesław IV 'the Curly' Prince of Mazovia from 1138
1173–7	Mieszko III 'the Old' Prince of Great Poland from 1138
1173–86	Leszek I Mazovia Rival
1177–94	Casimir II 'the Just'
1194–8	Leszek II 'the White' Prince of Mazovia to 1202
1198–1202	Mieszko III 'the Old' (restored)
1202–6	Władysław III Prince of Great Poland to 1231
1206–27	Leszek II 'the White' (restored)
1227–79	Bolesław V
1279–88	Leszek III Prince of Kujavia from 1267
1288–90	Henry Prince of Silesia
1290–1	Przemisław Prince of Great Poland 1270–96
1291–1306	As Bohemia (see Czech Republic)
1306–20	Władysław IV 'the Short' Prince of Kujavia from 1267 and of Great Poland from 1314

Monarch – King of Poland
House of Piast

1320–33	Władysław IV 'the Short'
1333–70	Casimir III 'the Great'

House of Anjou

1370–82	Louis of Anjou (Lajos I of Hungary)
1382–95	Jadwiga

House of Jagieo

1386–1434	Władysław V Jagiello (Grand Duke Jogaila of Lithuania)

1434–44	Władysław VI *King of Hungary from 1440*
1444–7	*No king*
1447–92	Casimir IV *Grand Duke of Lithuania from 1440*
1492–1501	John I Albert
1501–6	*As Lithuania*
1506–48	Sigismund I 'the Old'
1548–72	Sigismund II Augustus

Elected kings

1573–5	Henry (Henri III *of France*)
1575–86	Stefan (Stephen) Bathory
1587–1632	Sigismund III Vasa
1632–48	Władysław VII (Ladislas IV)
1648–68	John II Casimir
1669–73	Michael Wisniowecki
1674–96	John III Sobieski
1697–1706	(Frederick-)Augustus II 'the Strong' (*of Saxony*)
1706–9	Stanisław I (Stanislas) Leszczynski
1709–33	(Frederick-)Augustus II 'the Strong' (*restored*)
1733–63	(Frederick-)Augustus III (*of Saxony*)
1764–95	Stanisław II (Stanislas Augustus) Poniatowski

● Portugal
Monarch – Kingdom of Portugal
House of Burgundy

1095–1112	Henrique (*of Burgundy*) *Count of Portugal*
1112–85	Afonso (Alfonso) I Henriques *King from 1139*
1185–1211	Sancho I
1211–23	Afonso II
1223–45	Sancho II
1245–79	Afonso III
1279–1325	Diniz (Denis)
1325–57	Afonso IV
1357–67	Pedro I
1367–83	Fernando (Ferdinand)
1383–5	*Disputed succession*

House of Aviz

1385–1433	João I
1433–8	Duarte

1438–81	Afonso (Alfonso) V 'el Africano' ('the African')
1481–95	João II
1495–1521	Manuel I
1521–57	João III
1557–78	Sebastião (Sebastian)
1578–80	Henrique
1580–1640	*Spanish rule*

House of Bragança

1640–56	João (John) IV
1656–83	Afonso VI
1683–1706	Pedro II
1706–50	João V
1750–77	José
1777–86	Pedro III *Joint ruler*
1777–1816	Maria I *Joint ruler to 1786*
1816–26	João VI
1826	Pedro IV (I *of Brazil*)
1826–8	Maria II
1828–34	Miguel
1834–53	Maria II (*restored*)
1853–61	Pedro V
1861–89	Luis
1889–1908	Carlos
1908–10	Manuel II

● Qatar
Emir
al-Thani Dynasty

1868–76	Muhammad bin Thani
1876–1905	Ahmad I
1905–13	Qasim
1913–49	Abdullah
1949–60	Ali
1960–72	Ahmad II ibn Ali
1972–95	Khalifah ibn Hamad
1995–	Hamad bin Khalifa

● Romania
Monarch – Kingdom of Romania

1859–66	Alexandru Ioan Cuza *Prince*
1866–1914	Carol I
1914–27	Ferdinand I
1927–30	Mihai (Michael)
1930–40	Carol II
1940–47	Mihai (*restored*)

● Rome

753–715 BC	Romulus	
715–673 BC	Numa Pompilius	
673–640 BC	Tullus Hostilius	
640–616 BC	Ancus Marcius	
616–578 BC	Lucius Tarquinius Priscus	
578–534 BC	Servius Tullius	
534–510 BC	Lucius Tarquinius Superbus	
510–27 BC	*Republic ruled by joint consuls*	

Emperor

27 BC– AD 14	Augustus (Gaius Julius Caesar Octavianus)
14–37	Tiberius (Tiberius Julius Caesar Augustus)
37–41	Caligula (Gaius Julius Caesar Germanicus)
41–54	Claudius I (Tiberius Claudius Nero Germanicus)
54–68	Nero (Lucius Domitius Ahenobarbus)
68–9	(Servius Sulcipius) Galba
69	(Marcus Salvius) Otho
69	(Aulus) Vitellius
69–79	Vespasian (Titus Flavius Vespasianus)
79–81	Titus (Flavius Sabinus Vespasianus)
81–96	Domitian (Titus Flavius Domitianus)
96–98	(Marcus Cocceius) Nerva
98–117	Trajan (Marcus Ulpius Trajanus)
117–38	Hadrian (Publius Aelius Hadrianus)
138–61	(Titus Aurelius Fulvus) Antoninus Pius
161–9	(Lucius Aurelius) Verus *Joint emperor*
161–80	Aurelius (Marcus Aurelius Verus)
180–92	(Marcus Aurelius Antoninus) Commodus
193	(Publius Helvius) Pertinax
193	(Marcus) Didius Julianus
193–4	Gaius Pescennius Niger *Rival emperor*

193–7	Decimus Clodius Albinus *Rival emperor*
	(Lucius Septimius) Severus
211–12	Publius Septimius Antoninus Geta *Joint emperor*
211–17	(Marcus Aurelius Antoninus) Caracalla
217–18	(Marcus Opellius) Macrinus
218–22	Heliogabalus (Varius Avitus Bassianus)
222–35	(Marcus Aurelius) Alexander Severus
235–8	(Gaius Julius) Maximinus
238	Gordian I (Marcus Antonius Gordianus)
238	Gordian II (Marcus Antonius Gordianus) *Joint emperor*
238	(Marcus Clodius) Pupienus
238	(Decimus Caelius) Balbinus
238–44	Gordian III (Marcus Antonius Gordianus Pius)
244–9	Philip the Arab (Marcus Julius Philippus Arabs)
249–51	(Gaius Messius Quintus Trajanus) Decius
251–3	(Gaius Vibius Trebonianus) Gallus *Joint emperor*
251–3	(Gaius Vibius) Volusianus *Joint emperor*
253	(Marcus Aemilius) Aemilianus
253–60	Valerian (Publius Licinius Valerianus) *Joint emperor*
253–68	(Publius Licinius) Gallienus *Joint emperor*
260–1	Titus Fulvius Quietus *Rival emperor*
260–1	(Titus Fulvius) Macrianus *Rival emperor*
260–9	(Marcus Latinius) Postumus *Emperor in Gaul*
268–70	(Marcus Aurelius) Claudius II Gothicus
269–70	(Marcus Piavonius) Victorinus *Emperor in Gaul*
269	Marcus Aurelius Marius *Emperor in Gaul*

269	Lucius Aelianus, *Emperor in Gaul*
270	(Marcus Aurelius) Quintillus
270–4	(Gaius Pius) Tetricus I *Emperor in Gaul*
270–5	Aurelian (Lucius Domitius Aurelianus)
274	(Gaius Pius) Tetricus II *Emperor in Gaul*
275–6	(Marcus Claudius) Tacitus
276	(Marcus Annius) Florianus
276–82	(Marcus Aurelius) Probus
282–3	(Marcus Aurelius) Carus
283–4	(Marcus Aurelius) Numerianus *Joint emperor*
283–5	(Marcus Aurelius) Carinus *Joint emperor to 284*
284–305	Diocletian (Gaius Aurelius Diocletianus) *Joint emperor (East)*
286–93	(Marcus Aurelius) Carausius *Emperor in Britain*
286–305	Maximian (Marcus Aurelius Maximianus) *Joint emperor (West)*
293–96	Allectus *Emperor in Britain*
305–11	(Gaius) Galerius (Valerius Maximianus) *Joint emperor (East)*
305–06	(Marcus Flavius) Constantius Chlorus *Joint emperor (West)*
306–37	Constantine I 'the Great' (Flavius Valerius Aurelius Constantinus) *Joint emperor (West) to 324*
306–12	(Marcus Aurelius) Maxentius *Rival emperor (West)*
306–08	Maximian (Marcus Aurelius Maximianus) *(restored as rival emperor – West)*
307–24	(Gaius Flavius Valerius) Licinius *Joint emperor (East)*
308–13	(Galerius Valerius) Maximinus Daia *Joint emperor (East)*
337–61	(Flavius Valerius Julius) Constantius II *Joint emperor (East) to 350 and from 360*
337–50	(Flavius Valerius Julius) Constans I *Joint emperor (West)*
337–40	Constantine II (Flavius Valerius Claudius Constantinus) *Joint emperor (Flavius Magnus)*
350–3	Magnentius *Rival emperor*
360–3	Julian 'the Apostate' (Flavius Claudius Julianus) *Joint emperor to 361*
363–4	Jovian (Flavius Claudius Jovianus)
364–78	(Flavius) Valens, *Joint emperor (East)*
364–75	Valentinian I (Flavius Valentinianus) *Joint emperor (West)*
367–83	Gratian (Augustus Gratianus) *Joint emperor (West)*
375–92	Valentinian II (Flavius Valentinianus) *Joint emperor (West)*
379–95	(Flavius) Theodosius I 'the Great' *Joint emperor (East)*
383–8	Magnus (Clemens) Maximus *Joint emperor (West)*
392–4	Eugenius *Joint emperor (West)*

Western Empire

395–423	(Flavius) Honorius
407–11	Constantine III (Flavius Claudius Constantinus) *Joint emperor*
421	(Flavius) Constantius III *Joint emperor*
423–5	Johannes
425–55	Valentinian III (Flavius Placidius Valentinianus)
455	(Flavius Ancius) Petronius Maximus
455–6	(Flavius Maecilius Eparchius) Avitus
457–61	(Julius Valerius) Majorianus

461–5	(Libius Severianus) Severus
467–72	(Procopius) Anthemius
472	(Anicius) Olybrius
473–4	(Flavius) Glycerius
474–5	Julius Nepos
475–6	(Flavius Momyllus)
	Romulus Augustulus

● **Russia**
Grand Duke of Moscow
House of Riurik

1283–1303	Daniel
1303–25	Yuri
1325–41	Ivan I Kalita
1341–53	Semeon
1353–9	Ivan II
1359–89	Dmitri I Donskoy
1389–1425	Vasily I
1425–62	Vasily II
1462–1472	Ivan III 'the Great'

Ruler of all Russia
House of Riurik

1472–1505	Ivan III 'the Great'
1505–33	Vasily III
1533–47	Ivan IV 'the Terrible'

Russian Empire – Tsar of Russia
House of Riurik

1547–84	Ivan IV 'the Terrible'
1584–98	Fedor I
1598–1605	Boris Godunov
1605	Fedor II
1605–6	Dmitri II (the 'false Dmitri')
1606–10	Vasily IV Shuisky
1610–13	*Civil war*

House of Romanov

1613–45	Mikhail (Michael Romanov)
1645–76	Alexey I Mihailovitch
1676–82	Fedor III
1682–96	Ivan V *Joint ruler*
1682–1725	Peter I 'the Great' *Joint ruler*
	to 1696
1725–7	Catherine I
1727–30	Peter II
1730–40	Anna Ivanovna
1740–1	Ivan VI
1741–62	Elizabeth Petrovna

1762	Peter III
1762–96	Catherine II 'the Great'
1796–1801	Paul
1801–25	Alexander I
1825–55	Nicholas I
1855–81	Alexander II 'the Liberator'
1881–94	Alexander III
1894–1917	Nicholas II

● **Rwanda**
Monarch – Mwami (King)

c.1350–c.1386	Ndahiro I Ruyange
c.1386–c.1410	Ndoba
c.1410–c.1434	Samembe
c.1434–c.1458	Nsoro Samukondo
c.1458–c.1482	Ruganza I Bwimba
c.1482–c.1506	Cyilima I Rugwe
c.1506–c.1528	Kigeri I Mukobanya
c.1528–c.1552	Mibambwe I Mutabaazi
c.1552–c.1576	Yuhi I Gahima
c.1576–c.1600	Ndahiro II Cyaamatare
c.1600–c.1624	Ruganza II Ndoori
c.1624–c.1648	Mutara I Seemugeshi
c.1648–c.1672	Kigeri II Nyamuheshera
c.1672–c.1696	Mibambwe II Gisanura
c.1696–c.1720	Yuhi II Mazimpaka
c.1720–c.1744	Karemeera Rwaaka
c.1744–c.1768	Cyilima II Rujugira
c.1768–c.1792	Kigeri III Ndabarasa
c.1792–c.1797	Mibambwe III Seentaabyo
c.1797–c.1830	Yuhi III Gahindro
c.1830–53	Mutara II Rwoogera
1853–95	Kigeri IV Rwabugiri
1895–96	Mibambwe IV Rutulindwa
1896–1931	Yuhi IV Musinga
1931–59	Mutara III Rudahigwa
1959–61	Kigeri V Ndahundirwa

● **Saudi Arabia**
Includes several periods of overlapping rule.

Sharif of Mecca

967–80	Abu-Muhammad Jafar ibn
	Muhammad
980–94	Isa ibn Jafar
994–1010	Abul-Futuh Hasan

1010–12	Abul-Tayyib Daud	1684–8	Ahmad ibn Zaid
1012–39	Abul-Futuh Hasan (*restored*)	1688–90	Ahmad ibn Ghalib
1039–61	Muhammad Shukr ibn Hasan	1690–1	Muhsin ibn Husain
		1691–2	Said ibn Said
1061–9	Hamza ibn Wahhas	1692–4	Said ibn Zaid (*restored*)
1069–94	Abu-Hashim Muhammad ibn Jafar	1694–5	Abdullah ibn Hashim
		1695–1702	Said ibn Zaid (*restored*)
1094–1123	Abu-Fulaita al-Qasim	1702–4	Said ibn Said (*restored*)
1123–33	Fulaita ibn al-Qasim	1704–12	Abdul-Karim ibn
1133–54	Hashim ibn Fulaita		Muhammad
1154–61	al-Qasim ibn Hashim	1712–16	Said ibn Said (*restored*)
1161–74	Isa ibn Fulaita	1716–18	Abdullah ibn Said
1174–5	Daud ibn Isa	1718–20	Yahya ibn Barakat
1175–6	Mukaththir ibn Isa	1720–22	Mubarak ibn Ahmad
1176–89	Daud ibn Isa (*restored*)	1722–30	*Civil war*
1189–94	Mukaththir ibn Isa (*restored*)	1730–2	Muhammad ibn Abdullah
1194–1201	al-Mansur ibn Daud	1732–3	Masud ibn Said
1201–20	Abu-Aziz Qatada ibn Idris	1733–4	Muhammad ibn Abdullah
1220–32	Hasan ibn Qatada		(*restored*)
1232–41	Rajih ibn Qatada	1734–52	Masud ibn Said (*restored*)
1241–54	Abu-Said Ali ibn Qatada	1752–70	Masaid ibn Said
1254–1301	Abu-Numay Muhammad ibn Ali	1770–3	Ahmad ibn Said
		1773–88	Surur ibn Masaid
1254–70	Idris ibn Qatada	1788–1813	Ghalib ibn Masaid
1301–46	Rumaitha ibn Abi-Numay	1813–27	Yahya ibn Surur
1303–18	Humaida ibn Abi-Numay	1827–51	Muhammad ibn Abdul-Muin
1346–75	Ajlan ibn Rumaitha		
1361–86	Shihab-ud-Din Ahmad ibn Ajlan	1851–6	Abdul-Muttalib ibn Ghalib
		1856–8	Muhammad ibn Abdul-Muin (*restored*)
1386–7	Inan ibn Mughamis		
1387–95	Ali ibn Ajlan	1858–77	Abdullah ibn Muhammad
1392–6	Muhammad ibn Ajlan	1877–80	Husain ibn Muhammad
1396–1426	Hasan ibn Ajlan	1880–2	Abdul-Muttalib ibn Ghalib
1407–55	Barakat ibn Hasan		(*restored*)
1455–97	Muhammad ibn Barakat	1882–1905	Aun ar-Rafiq ibn
1497–1525	Barakat ibn Muhammad		Muhammad
1504–12	Qait Bay ibn Muhammad	1905–8	Abi ibn Abdullah
1512–66	Abu-Numay Muhammad ibn Barakat	1908–16	Husain (Hussein) ibn Ali
1539–54	Ahmad ibn Muhammad		
1554–1602	Hasan ibn Muhammad	***Amir of Najd***	
1603–29	Muhsin ibn Husain	*al-Saud Dynasty*	
1603–24	Idris ibn Hasan	c.1720–6	Saud I
1629–30	Masud ibn Idris	1726–65	Muhammad
1630–1	Abdullah ibn Hasan	1765–1803	Abdulaziz I
1631–66	Zaid ibn Muhsin	1803–14	Saud II
1666–72	Said ibn Zaid	1814–18	Abdullah I
1672–82	Barakat ibn Muhammad	1818–23	*Egyptian rule*
1682–4	Said ibn Barakat	1823–34	Turki
		1834–7	Faisal I

1837–41	Khalid I
1841–3	Abdullah II
1843–65	Faisal I (*restored*)
1865–71	Abdullah III
1871	Saud III
1871–3	Abdullah III (*restored*)
1873–6	Saud III (*restored*)
1876–89	Abdullah III (*restored*)
1889–1901	Abdul-Rahman
1901–27	Abdulaziz ibn Abdur-Rahman ibn Saud

Monarch – Kingdom of the Hijaz
Sharifs of Mecca

1916–24	Husain (Hussein) ibn Ali *Sharif of Mecca from 1908*
1924–5	Ali ibn Husain

al-Saud Dynasty

1925–32	Abdulaziz ibn Abdur-Rahman ibn Saud

Head of state (Monarch)
al-Saud Dynasty

1932–53	Abdul Aziz ibn Abdur-Rahman ibn Saud
1953–64	Saud IV ibn Abdulaziz
1964–75	Faisal II ibn Abdulaziz
1975–82	Khalid (II) ibn Abdulaziz
1982–96	Fahd ibn Abdulaziz
1996	Abdullah ibn Abdulaziz (*acting*)
1996–	Fahd ibn Abdulaziz

● **Serbia and Montenegro**
Grand Zhupan of Serbia

1168–96	Stephen Nemanja
1196–1217	Stephen Nemanjich

Monarch – Prince of Serbia

1217–27	Stephen Nemanjich
1227–34	Stephen Radoslav
1234–43	Stephen Vladislav
1243–76	Stephen Urosh I
1276–82	Stephen Dragutin
1282–1321	Stephen Urosh II Miliutin
1321–31	Stephen Urosh III
1331–45	Stephen Urosh IV Dushan

Monarch – Emperor of Serbia

1345–55	Stephen Urosh IV Dushan
1355–71	Stephen Urosh V

Monarch – Prince of Serbia

1371–89	Lazar I Hrebeljanovich
1389–1427	Stephen
1427–56	George Brankovich
1456–8	Lazar II
1458–9	Stephen Tomashevich
1459–1815	Turkish rule (*Kara George Petrovich Hospodar of Serbia 1804–13*)

Karageorgevich and Obrenovich Dynasties

1815–39	Milosh Obrenovich
1839	Milan I
1839–42	Michael
1842–58	Aleksandar I
1858–60	Milosh Obrenovich (*restored*)
1860–8	Michael (*restored*)
1868–82	Milan II

Monarch – Kingdom of Serbia
Karageorgevich Dynasty

1882–9	Milan II
1889–1903	Aleksandar II
1903–1918	Petar (Peter) I

Monarch – King of the Serbs, Croats and Slovenes

1918–21	Petar I (*Prince Aleksandar Regent*)
1921–29	Aleksandar (Alexander) I

Monarch – Kingdom of Yugoslavia

1929–34	Aleksandar (Alexander) I
1934–45	Petar II (*Prince Paul Regent 1934–41, King Petar in exile from 1941*)

Montenegro – Vladika of Montenegro
Petrovich Dynasty

1696–1735	Danilo I
1735–81	Sava *Co-ruler 1750–66*
1750–66	Vasil *Co-ruler*
1782–1830	Petar I
1830–51	Petar II

Prince of Montenegro
Petrovich Dynasty
1851–60   Danilo II
1860–1910   Nicholas

Monarch – Kingdom of Montenegro
Petrovich Dynasty
1910–18   Nicholas

● South Africa
King of the Zulu
c.1781–1816   Senzangakhona
1816–28   Shaka
1828–40   Dingane (Dingaan)
1840–72   Mpande
1872–9   Cetewayo

● Spain
Monarch – Kingdom of Navarre
c.810–c.851   Iñigo Arista
c.851–c.880   Garcia Iñiguez
c.880–905   Fortun Garces
905–26   Sancho I
926–70   Garcia II
970–94   Sancho II
994–1000   Garcia III
1000–35   Sancho III 'the Great'

Monarch – Kingdom of Castile-Leon
1035–65   Fernando (Ferdinand) I *King of Castile; King of Leon from 1037*
1065–1109   Alfonso VI *King of Leon; King of Castile from 1072*
1065–72   Sancho II *King of Castile*
1109–26   Urraca
1126–57   Alfonso VII
1157–8   Sancho III *King of Castile*
1157–88   Fernando II *King of Leon*
1158–1214   Alfonso VIII *King of Castile*
1188–1230   Alfonso IX *King of Leon*
1214–17   Enrique I *King of Castile*
1217–52   Fernando III *King of Castile; King of Leon from 1230*
1252–84   Alfonso X 'the Astronomer' *Holy Roman Emperor from 1257*
1284–95   Sancho IV

1295–1312   Fernando IV
1312–50   Alfonso XI
1350–66   Pedro 'the Cruel'
1366–7   Enrique II (of Trestamara)
1367–9   Pedro 'the Cruel' (*restored*)
1369–79   Enrique II (of Trestamara) (*restored*)
1379–90   Juan I
1390–1406   Enrique III
1406–54   Juan II
1454–74   Enrique IV
1474–1504   Isabel (Isabella) I of Castile
1504–06   Felipe (Philip) I 'the Handsome' *Joint ruler*
1504–16   Juana 'the Mad' (*King Fernando II of Aragón Regent*)

Monarch – Kingdom of Aragón
1035–63   Ramiro I
1063–94   Sancho
1094–1104   Pedro I
1104–34   Alfonso I 'the Battler'
1134–7   Ramiro II
1137–62   Petronila
1162–96   Alfonso II
1196–1213   Pedro II
1213–76   Jaime I 'the Conqueror'
1276–85   Pedro III *King of Sicily from 1282*
1285–91   Alfonso III
1291–1327   Jaime II *King of Sicily from 1285*
1327–36   Alfonso IV
1336–87   Pedro IV
1387–95   Juan I
1395–1410   Martín I *King of Sicily from 1409*
1410–12   *Disputed succession*
1412–16   Fernando I
1416–58   Alfonso V 'the Magnanimous'
1458–79   Juan II
1479–1516   Fernando II 'the Catholic' *Fernando V of Castile from 1506*

Monarch – Kingdom of Spain
House of Habsburg
1516–56   Carlos I (Charles V, *Holy Roman Emperor*)

1556–98	Felipe II
1598–1621	Felipe III
1621–65	Felipe IV
1665–1700	Carlos II

House of Bourbon

1700–24	Felipe V
1724	Luis
1724–46	Felipe V (*restored*)
1746–59	Fernando VI
1759–88	Carlos III
1788–1808	Carlos IV
1808	Fernando VII

House of Bonaparte

1808–13	José (Joseph Bonaparte)

House of Bourbon (restored)

1813–33	Fernando VII (*restored*)
1833–68	Isabel II (*Queen Maria Christina Regent*)

First Republic

1868–70	Antonio Cánovas del Castillo

Monarch – Kingdom of Spain
House of Savoy

1870–73	Amadeo I

House of Bourbon (restored)

1874–85	Alfonso XII
1886–1931	Alfonso XIII

Monarch – Kingdom of Spain
House of Bourbon (restored)

1975–	Juan Carlos I

● **Sri Lanka**
King of Kandy

1591–1604	Vimala Dharma Surya I
1604–35	Senarat
1635–87	Rajasinha
1687–1707	Vimala Dharma Surya II
1707–39	Narendra Sinha
1739–47	Sri Vijaya Rajasinha
1747–82	Kirti Sri Rajasinha
1782–98	Rajadhi Rajasinha
1798–1815	Sri Vikrama Rajasinha

● **Sudan**
Darfur
Kayra Dynasty

c.1640–c.1670	Sulayman Solong
c.1670–82	Musa
1682–1722	Ahmad Bakr
1722–32	Muhammad I Dawra
1732–9	Umar Lele
1739–56	Abul-Qasim
1756–87	Muhammad II Tairab
1787–1801	Abdul-Rahman ar-Rashid
1801–39	Muhammad III al-Fadl
1839–73	Muhammad IV Husain
1873–1874	Ibrahim
1874–98	Conquered by Mohammad Ahmed and his successor
1898–1916	Ali Dinar ibn Zakariyya

● **Swaziland**
Head of State (Monarch)

c.1820–39	Sobhuza I
1839–68	Mswazi (Mswati) II
1868–74	Ludvonga
1874–89	Mbandzeni
1889–99	Bhunu (Ngwane)
1899–1982	Sobhuza II (*Chief from 1921*)
1983	Dzeliwe *Queen Regent*
1983–6	Ntombi *Queen Regent*
1986–	Mswati (III)

● **Sweden**
Monarch – Kingdom of Sweden
Early Kings

c.970–c.995	Erik VIII
c.995–c.1022	Olaf Skotkunung
c.1022–c.1050	Anund Jakob
c.1050–c.1060	Emund
c.1060–c.1066	Stenkil Ragnvaldsson
c.1066–c.1070	Halsten *Joint king*
c.1066–c.1112	Inge I *Joint king to c.1070*
c.1081–c.1083	Blot-Sven *Rival king*
c.1112–c.1118	Filip *Joint king*
c.1112–c.1130	Inge II *Joint king to c.1118*
c.1130–c.1156	Sverker I *Rival king from c.1150*
c.1150–60	Erik IX Jedvarsson 'the Saint' *Rival king to 1156*

1160–1	Magnus II
1161–7	Karl VII Sverkersson
1167–96	Knut I Eriksson
1196–1208	Sverker II Karlsson
1208–16	Erik X Knutsson
1216–22	Johan I Sverkersson
1222–9	Erik XI Eriksson
1229–34	Knut II Holmgersson
1234–50	Erik XI (restored)

Folkung Dynasty

1250–75	Valdemar I Birgerson (Birger Jarl co-ruler to 1266)
1275–90	Magnus III Birgerson
1290–1319	Birger Magnusson
1319–65	Magnus IV Eriksson Joint king 1356–9
1356–9	Erik XII Joint king
1365–89	Albert of Mecklenburg
1389–97	Margrethe I (Margareta) of Denmark

Monarch – Kalmar Union

1397–1448	As Denmark
1448–57	Karl VIII
1457–64	As Denmark
1464–5	Karl VIII (restored)
1465–67	Civil war
1467–70	Karl VIII (restored)
1470–97	As Denmark (Sten Sture the Elder Regent)
1497–1501	As Denmark
1501–3	As Denmark (Sten Sture the Elder Regent)
1504–12	As Denmark (Svante Nilsson Sture Regent)
1512–23	As Denmark (Sten Sture the Younger Regent to 1520)

Monarch – Kingdom of Sweden
House of Vasa

1523–60	Gustav I Vasa (Gustav Eriksson)
1560–8	Erik XIV
1568–92	Johan III
1592–1604	As Poland
1604–11	Karl IX Regent from 1599
1611–32	Gustav II Adolf (Gustavus Adolphus)
1632–54	Kristina (Christina)

Palatinate Kings

1654–60	Karl X Gustav
1660–97	Karl XI
1697–1718	Karl XII
1719–20	Ulrika Eleonora
1720–51	Fredrik I

House of Holstein-Gottorp

1751–71	Adolf Fredrik
1771–92	Gustav III
1792–1809	Gustav IV Adolf
1809–18	Karl XIII

House of Bernadotte

1818–44	Karl XIV Johan (Jean-Baptiste Jules Bernadotte)
1844–59	Oskar I
1859–72	Karl XV
1872–1907	Oskar II
1907–50	Gustav V
1950–73	Gustav VI Adolf
1973–	Carl XVI Gustaf

● **Tanzania**
Sultan of Zanzibar
Oman Dynasty

1806–56	Said ibn Sultan (of Oman)
1856–70	Majid ibn Said
1870–88	Barghash ibn Said
1888–90	Khalifa ibn Barghash
1890–3	Ali ibn Said
1893–6	Hamid ibn Thuwaini
1896–1902	Hammud ibn Muhammad
1902–11	Ali ibn Hammud
1911–60	Khalifa ibn Harub
1960–3	Abdullah ibn Khalifa
1963–4	Jamshid ibn Abdullah

● **Thailand**
Monarch – Kingdom of Siam

1767–82	P'ya Taksin
1782–1809	P'ra P'utt'a Yot Fa Chulalok (Rama I)
1809–24	Phendin-Klang (Rama II)
1824–51	P'ra Nang Klao (Rama III)
1851–68	Maha Mongkut (Rama IV)
1868–1910	Chulalongkorn Phra Paramindr Maha (Rama V)

1910–25	Maha Vajiravudh (Rama VI)
1925–35	Prajadhipok (Rama VII)
1935–46	Ananda Mahidol (Rama VIII) (*Nai Pridi Phanomyong Regent 1939–46*)

Monarch – Kingdom of Thailand

| 1946– | Bhumibol Adulyadej (Rama IX) (*Rangsit of Chainat Regent 1946–50*) |

● **Tonga**
Monarch

1845–93	George Tupou I
1893–1918	George Tupou II
1918–65	Salote Tupou III
1965–	Taufa'ahau Tupou IV

● **Tunisia**
Bey of Tunis
House of Murad

1628–31	Murad I
1631–62	Muhammad I
1662–75	Murad II
1675	Muhammad II
1675	Ali
1675	Muhammad III
1675–6	Muhammad II (*restored*)
1676–88	Ali (*restored*)
1688–95	Muhammad II (*restored*)
1695–8	Ramadan
1698–1702	Murad III
1702–5	Ibrahim ash-Sharif

House of Husain

1705–35	Husain I
1735–56	Ali I
1756–9	Muhammad I
1759–82	Ali II
1782–1814	Hammuda
1814	Uthman
1814–24	Mahmud
1824–35	Husain II
1835–7	Mustafa
1837–55	Ahmad I
1855–9	Muhammad II
1859–82	Muhammad III as-Sadiq
1882–1902	Ali Muddat

1902–6	Muhammad IV al-Hadi
1906–22	Muhammad V an-Nadir
1922–9	Muhammad VI al-Habib
1929–42	Ahmad II
1942–3	Muhammad VII al-Munsif
1943–57	Muhammad VIII al-Amin

● **Turkey**
King of Hatti (Hittites)

c.1800 BC	Pitkhana
?	Anitta
?	Tudkhaliash I
c.1700 BC	Pu-Sharruma
?	Labarnash
c.1650 BC	Khattushilish I
?	Murshilish I
?	Khantilish I
?	Zidantash I
c.1550 BC	Ammunash
?	Khuzziyash I
?	Telepinush
c.1500 BC	Alluwamnash
?	Khantilish II
?	Zidantash II
c.1450 BC	Khuzziyash II
?	Tudkhaliash II
?	Arnuwandash I
c.1400–1390 BC	Khattushilish II
c.1390–c.1380 BC	Tudkhaliash III
c.1380–c.1346 BC	Shuppiluliumash I
c.1346–c.1345 BC	Arnuwandash II
c.1345–c.1320 BC	Murshilish II
c.1320–c.1294 BC	Muwatallish
c.1294–c.1286 BC	Murshilish III (Urkhi-Teshub)
c.1286–c.1265 BC	Khattushilish III
c.1265–c.1220 BC	Tudkhaliash IV
c.1220–c.1200 BC	Arnuwandash III
c.1200 BC	Shuppiluliumash II

Sultan of the Ottoman Empire

1299–1326	Osman I
1326–59	Orkhan
1359–89	Murad I
1389–1403	Bayezit I
1403–10	Süleyman I *Rival sultan*
1403–21	Mehmet I *Rival sultan to 1413*
1410–13	Musa *Rival sultan*

1421–44	Murad II
1444–6	Mehmet II 'the Conqueror'
1446–51	Murad II (*restored*)
1451–81	Mehmet II 'the Conqueror' (*restored*)
1481–1512	Bayezit II
1512–20	Selim I 'the Grim'
1520–66	Süleyman II 'the Magnificent'
1566–74	Selim II
1574–95	Murad III
1595–1603	Mehmet III
1603–17	Ahmet I
1617–18	Mustafa I
1618–22	Osman II
1622–3	Mustafa I (*restored*)
1623–40	Murad IV
1640–8	Ibrahim
1648–87	Mehmet IV
1687–91	Süleyman III
1691–5	Ahmet II
1695–1703	Mustafa II
1703–30	Ahmet III
1730–54	Mahmut I
1754–7	Osman III
1757–74	Mustafa III
1774–89	Abd-ul-Hamid I
1789–1807	Selim III
1807–8	Mustafa IV
1808–39	Mahmut II
1839–61	Abd-ul-Medjid
1861–76	Abdul-Aziz
1876	Murad V
1876–1909	Abd-ul-Hamid II
1909–18	Mehmet V Resat
1918–22	Mehmet VI Vahideddin

● Ukraine
Prince of Kiev

c.880–c.912	Oleg
c.912–45	Igor I
945–64	St Olga
964–72	Sviatoslav I
972–8	Yaropolk I
978–1015	St Vladimir I 'the Great'
1015–19	Sviatopolk I
1019–54	Yaroslav I 'the Wise'
1054–68	Iziaslav I

1068–9	Vseslav
1069–73	Iziaslav I (*restored*)
1073–6	Sviatoslav II
1076–8	Iziaslav I (*restored*)
1078–93	Vsevolod I
1093–1113	Sviatopolk II
1113–25	Vladimir II Monomachus
1125–32	Mstislav I Harald
1132–9	Yaropolk II
1139	Viacheslav
1139–46	Vsevolod II
1146	Igor II
1146–9	Iziaslav II
1149–50	Yuri Dolgoruky
1150–4	*Period of instability*
1154–5	Rostislav I
1155–7	Yuri Dolgoruky (*restored*)
1157–9	Iziaslav III
1159–67	*Period of instability*
1167–9	Mstislav II
1169–71	Gleb
1171–2	Roman
1172–3	Vsevolod III
1173–4	Riurik
1174–5	Yaroslav II
1175–6	Roman (*restored*)
1176–80	Sviatoslav III
1180–1200	*Period of instability*
1200–3	Ingvar
1203–4	Riurik (*restored*)
1204–5	Rostislav II
1205–6	Riurik (*restored*)
1206–12	Vsevolod IV
1212–23	Mstislav III
1223–36	Vladimir III
1236–8	Yaroslav III
1238–40	Michael
1240	Daniel

● United Arab Emirates
Abu Dhabi – Shaikh
al-Nahayan Dynasty

c.1761–93	Dhiyab I bin Isa
1793–1816	Shakhbout I
1816–18	Mohammed
1818–33	Tahnoun I
1833–45	Khalifa
1845	Isa bin Khaled

1845	Dhiyab II bin Isa
1845–55	Sayed
1855–1909	Zayed I
1909–12	Tahnoun II
1912–22	Hamdan
1922–6	Sultan
1926–8	Saqr
1928–66	Shakhbout II
1966–	Zayed II bin Sultan al-Nahayan

Ajman – Shaikh
al-Nuaimi Dynasty

c.1820–38	Rashid I bin Humaid
1838–41	Humaid I
1841–8	Abd-el-Aziz I
1848–73	Humaid I (*restored*)
1873–91	Rashid II
1891–1900	Humaid II
1900–10	Abd-el-Aziz II
1910–28	Humaid III
1928–81	Rashid III
1981–	Humaid IV

Dubai – Shaikh
al-Maktoum Dynasty

1833–52	Maktoum I bin Butti
1852–9	Said I
1859–86	Hashar
1886–94	Rashid I
1894–1906	Maktoum II
1906–12	Butti bin Suhail
1912–58	Said II
1958–90	Rashid II
1990–2006	Maktoum III
2006–	Mohammed bin Rashid al-Maktoum

Fujairah – Shaikh
al-Sharqi Dynasty

1952–75	Mohammed bin Hamad
1975–	Hamad

Ras al-Khaimah – Shaikh
al-Qassimi Dynasty

1869–1900	Humaid bin Abdullah
1900–21	*Incorporated into Sharjah*
1921–48	Sultan
1948–	Saqr bin Muhammed

Sharjah – Shaikh
al-Qasimi Dynasty

c.1727–77	Rashid bin Matar
1777–1803	Saqr I
1803–66	Sultan I
1866–8	Khaled I
1868–83	Salim
1883–1914	Saqr II
1914–24	Khaled II bin Ahmed
1924–51	Sultan II
1951–65	Saqr III
1965–72	Khaled III bin Mohammed
1972–87	Sultan III
1987	Abd-el-Aziz
1987–	Sultan IV

Umm al-Qaiwain – Shaikh
al-Mualla Dynasty

c.1775–?	Majid
c.1776–1816	Rashid I
1816–53	Abdullah I
1853–73	Ali
1873–1904	Ahmad I
1904–22	Rashid II
1922–3	Abdullah II
1923–9	Hamad bin Ibrahim
1929–81	Ahmad II
1981–	Rashid III

● Uzbekistan
Khan of Bokhara
Haidarid Dynasty

1785–1800	Mir Masum Shah Murad
1800–26	Haidar Tora
1826	Husain
1826–7	Umar
1827–60	Nasr-Allah
1860–85	Muzaffar-ud-Din
1885–1910	Abdul-Ahad
1910–20	Abdul Said Mir Alim
1920–91	*Part of Soviet Union*

Khan of Khokand
Shah-Rukhid Dynasty

1694–?	Rustam Haji
?	Ashur Qul
1710–21	Shah Rukh I
1721–36	Abd ar-Rahman
1736–46	Abd al-Karim

1746–70	Irdana Bi Erdeni
1770	Shah Rukh II
1770	Sulayman
1770–1800	Narbuta
1800–9	Alim Khan
1809–22	Muhammad Umar
1822–40	Muhammad Ali
1840–5	Shir Ali
1845	Murad
1845–57	Khudayar
1857–9	Muhammad Mala
1859–61	Shah Murad
1861–4	Khudayar (*restored*)
1864–71	Muhammad Sultan
1871–5	Khudayar (*restored*)
1875–6	Nasir-ud-Din
1876–1991	*Part of Russia*
1917–91	*Part of Soviet Union*

● Vietnam
Emperor
Tay-Son Dynasty

1788–92	Nguyen Van-Hue (Quang-Trung)
1792–1802	Nguyen Quang-Toan (Cahn-Thinh)

Nguyen Dynasty

1802–20	Gia-Long (Nguyen Anh)
1820–41	Minh-Mang
1841–8	Thieu-Tri
1848–83	Tu-Duc
1883	Nguyen Duc-Duc
1883–4	Nguyen Hiep-Hoa
1884–5	Kien-Phuc
1885–6	Ham-Nghi
1886–9	Dong-Khanh
1889–1907	Thanh-Thai
1907–16	Duy-Tan
1916–25	Khai-Dinh
1925–55	Bao Dai *President from 1949*

● Yemen
Imam of Sana

1891–1904	Mohammed bin Yahya Hamaddin

Monarch – Kingdom of Yemen

1904–48	Yahya Mohammed bin Mohammed
1948–62	Saif-al-Islam Ahmed bin Yahya
1962–70	Mohammed al-Badr bin Ahmed

Sultan of Lahej
Abdali Dynasty

1728–42	Fadl I
1742–53	Abdul-Karim I
1753–77	Abdul-Hadi
1777–92	Fadl II
1792–1827	Ahmad I
1827–47	Muhsin
1847–9	Ahmad II
1849–63	Ali I
1863	Fadl III
1863–74	Fadl IV
1874–98	Fadl III (*restored*)
1898–1914	Ahmad III
1914–15	Ali II
1915–47	Abdul-Karim II
1947–52	Fadl V
1952–8	Ali al-Karim
1958–67	Fadl VI ibn Ali ibn Ahmad

Sultan of Shihr and Mukalla
Kuwaiti Dynasty

1866–1909	Awadh I ibn Umar
1909–22	Ghalib I
1922–36	Umar
1936–56	Salih
1956–66	Awadh II
1966–67	Ghalib II

PENGUIN POCKET REFERENCE

THE PENGUIN POCKET DICTIONARY OF QUOTATIONS
EDITED BY DAVID CRYSTAL

The Penguin Pocket Dictionary of Quotations is essential reading for
anyone searching for the perfect quotation – whether you need a
snappy one-liner for a speech or a remark of brilliant insight for your
written work. With this pithy and provocative selection of wit and
wisdom, you will never be lost for words again.

– Includes quotations from a vast range of people, from film stars to
  politicians

– Arranged alphabetically by name of person quoted, with the original
  source for each quotation given

– Provides a full index of key words to help you find each quotation
  quickly and easily

PENGUIN POCKET REFERENCE

THE PENGUIN POCKET DICTIONARY OF BABIES' NAMES
DAVID PICKERING

The Penguin Pocket Dictionary of Babies' Names is essential reading for all expectant parents wishing to choose the perfect name for their child. It gives the meanings and stories behind thousands of names from all parts of the world – ranging from the most well-known choices to more unusual names.

– Gives variations and shortened forms for each name

– Highlights names popularized by books, films and celebrities

– Lists the most popular girls' and boys' names from 1700 to the present

– Shows how tastes for names have changed in the twenty-first century

PENGUIN POCKET REFERENCE

THE PENGUIN POCKET BOOK OF FACTS
EDITED BY DAVID CRYSTAL

The Penguin Pocket Book of Facts is a goldmine of information, figures and statistics on every conceivable subject – from the world's highest mountains and longest rivers to the gods of mythology, and from time zones to Nobel Prize winners. The ultimate one-stop factfinder, this is the essential book for browsers, crossword and trivia addicts, and for anyone who needs to check facts at home or at work.

– Up-to-date information about everything from astronomy to zoology

– Easy to use

– Illustrated throughout with maps and diagrams

www.penguin.com

PENGUIN POCKET REFERENCE

THE PENGUIN POCKET ENGLISH DICTIONARY

This pocket edition of the bestselling *Penguin English Dictionary* is the perfect reference book for everyday use. Compiled by Britain's foremost lexicographers, up to date and easy to use, it is the ideal portable companion for quick reference.

- Includes a wealth of words, phrases and clear definitions, with more information than other comparable dictionaries

- Covers standard and formal English, as well as specialist terms, slang and jargon

- Provides invaluable guidance on correct usage, commonly confused words and grammar and spelling

He just wanted a decent book to read ...

Not too much to ask, is it? It was in 1935 when Allen Lane, Managing Director of Bodley Head Publishers, stood on a platform at Exeter railway station looking for something good to read on his journey back to London. His choice was limited to popular magazines and poor-quality paperbacks – the same choice faced every day by the vast majority of readers, few of whom could afford hardbacks. Lane's disappointment and subsequent anger at the range of books generally available led him to found a company – and change the world.

'We believed in the existence in this country of a vast reading public for intelligent books at a low price, and staked everything on it'
Sir Allen Lane, 1902–1970, founder of Penguin Books

The quality paperback had arrived – and not just in bookshops. Lane was adamant that his Penguins should appear in chain stores and tobacconists, and should cost no more than a packet of cigarettes.

Reading habits (and cigarette prices) have changed since 1935, but Penguin still believes in publishing the best books for everybody to enjoy. We still believe that good design costs no more than bad design, and we still believe that quality books published passionately and responsibly make the world a better place.

So wherever you see the little bird – whether it's on a piece of prize-winning literary fiction or a celebrity autobiography, political tour de force or historical masterpiece, a serial-killer thriller, reference book, world classic or a piece of pure escapism – you can bet that it represents the very best that the genre has to offer.

Whatever you like to read – trust Penguin.